INTRODUCTION TO REFERENCE WORK

VOLUME I   *Basic Information Sources*

McGRAW-HILL SERIES IN LIBRARY EDUCATION
Jean Key Gates, Consulting Editor
University of South Florida

Boll INTRODUCTION TO CATALOGING, VOL. I:
DESCRIPTIVE CATALOGING
Boll INTRODUCTION TO CATALOGING, VOL. II:
ENTRY HEADINGS
Chan CATALOGING AND CLASSIFICATION:
AN INTRODUCTION
Gardner LIBRARY COLLECTIONS:
THEIR ORIGIN, SELECTION, AND DEVELOPMENT
Gates INTRODUCTION TO LIBRARIANSHIP
Jackson LIBRARIES AND LIBRARIANSHIP IN THE WEST:
A BRIEF HISTORY
Katz INTRODUCTION TO REFERENCE WORK, VOL. I:
BASIC INFORMATION SOURCES
Katz INTRODUCTION TO REFERENCE WORK, VOL. II:
REFERENCE SERVICES AND REFERENCE PROCESSES

INTRODUCTION

TO REFERENCE WORK

Volume I **Basic Information Sources**

Fourth Edition

William A. Katz

Professor, School of Library and Information Science
State University of New York at Albany

McGraw-Hill Book Company

New York   St. Louis   San Francisco   Auckland   Bogotá
Hamburg   Johannesburg   London   Madrid   Mexico
Montreal   New Delhi   Panama   Paris   São Paulo
Singapore   Sydney   Tokyo   Toronto

INTRODUCTION TO REFERENCE WORK, Volume I
Basic Information Sources

Copyright © 1982, 1978, 1974, 1969 by McGraw-Hill, Inc. All
rights reserved. Printed in the United States of America. Except
as permitted under the United States Copyright Act of 1976, no
part of this publication may be reproduced or distributed in any
form or by any means, or stored in a data base or retrieval
system, without the prior written permission of the publisher.

4 5 6 7 8 9 0   D O D O   8 9 8 7 6 5 4

ISBN 0-07-033333-5

This book was set in Baskerville by Black Dot, Inc. (ECU).
The editors were Marian D. Provenzano and Scott Amerman;
the production supervisor was Dominick Petrellese.
R. R. Donnelley & Sons Company was printer and binder.

Library of Congress Cataloging in Publication Data

Katz, William A., date
    Introduction to reference work.

    (McGraw-Hill series in library education)
    Includes bibliographies and index.
    Contents: v. 1. Basic information sources —
v. 2. Reference services and reference processes.
    1. Reference services (Libraries)   2. Reference
books.   I. Title.   II. Series.
Z711.K32   1982   025.5'2   81-12432
ISBN 0-07-033333-5 (v.1)   AACR2
ISBN 0-07-033334-3 (v. 2)

For Frances Neel Cheney

CONTENTS

PREFACE

The purpose of this text is to acquaint librarians, students, and library users with various information sources. Although written with the reference librarian in mind, the chapters introduce basic sources which will help the student and the layperson to use the library effectively.

Basic Information Sources is the first volume in the two-volume set, *Introduction to Reference Work.* In this fourth edition, revision is extensive and all material is updated. The organizational pattern remains the same as in the third edition. A section has been added to provide a brief, nontechnical description of computer-assisted reference services. For a more thorough overview, the reader should turn to the second volume. Throughout the text, basic reference sources now available in machine-readable form are indicated.

Only foundation, or basic, reference works are considered here. The vast and growing area of subject specialization and bibliography is left to other texts and other courses. Notes of some major subject forms are primarily illustrative and not intended to be exhaustive.

After a brief introduction to reference work, information sources, and the computer in the library, the text is divided into chapters on traditional forms, such as bibliographies, indexes, and encyclopedias. Each chapter considers various common aspects of one of the forms and how they relate to answering questions. It is pointless for students to memorize details about specific reference sources, but they should grasp the essential areas of agreement and difference among the various forms. To this end, every effort is made to compare rather than to detail. Not all so-called basic titles are included or annotated, because (1) there is no consensus on what constitutes "basic"; (2) more important, the objective of this text is to discuss various forms, and the titles used are those which best illustrate those forms; and finally, (3) the annotations for a specific title are duplicated over and over again in Sheehy's *Guide to Reference Books* and Walford's *Guide to Reference Materials*, which list the numerous subject bibliographies.

Suggested readings are found at the end of each chapter and in the footnotes. When a publication is cited in a footnote, the reference is rarely duplicated in the "Suggested Reading." For the most part, the readings are limited to publications issued since 1979; thus the citations in the third edition have been updated, and it is easier for the student to find the readings. A number of the suggested reading items will be found in the author's *Library Lit: The Best of . . .* and in *Reference and Information Sources, A Reader*, 2d ed. Both are published by Scarecrow Press: the former from 1970 to date (annual), the latter in 1982.

A critic wisely points out that the readings need not be current, that many older articles and books are as useful today as they were when first published. This is beyond argument. Still, thanks to many teachers' retaining earlier editions of this text and the aforementioned Scarecrow titles, it is possible to have a bibliography of previous readings. Also, some readings are retained from edition to edition—particularly in the footnotes.

Prices are noted for most of the major basic titles, as has been done since the first edition. This seems particularly useful today, when the librarian must look more and more to budgetary considerations when selecting reference titles. If a particular work is available online, the gross hourly rate as charged by Lockheed or other vendors is given for its use. Both this rate and the book prices are as of early 1981 and are useful in determining relative costs, though increases may occur to quickly outdate what is given here.

Bibliographic data are based on publishers' catalogs, *Books in Print*, and examination of the titles. The information is applicable as of mid-1981 and, like prices, is subject to change.

I am grateful to many teachers of reference and bibliography for their advice and help. My thanks also go to the students who so kindly made suggestions. I am particularly grateful to Prof. Kay Murray, who carefully read and corrected the manuscript. Her efforts have gone a long way to ensure an improved edition. Also, my thanks to Prof. Harold E. Holland, who not only made corrections but had some good-humored suggestions. Praise for McGraw-Hill editor Marian D. Provenzano, who managed to survive the ordeal of assisting the author in need.

William A. Katz

INTRODUCTION TO REFERENCE WORK

VOLUME I *Basic Information Sources*

INTRODUCTION

CHAPTER ONE

The Reference Process

WHAT IS REFERENCE SERVICE? At its most fundamental it may be defined as answering questions. An individual has a query about a topic and approaches the reference desk expecting the librarian to provide an answer or indicate where or how an answer may be found.

Answers take as many forms as questions. The librarian may point to the stairs (Where is the periodical room?); look up data to answer a question about the population of California; or search diligently for books, articles, and other documents to help answer a query on the benefits and dangers of nuclear power.

The librarian knows enough about people and about sources of probable answers to usually arrive at a satisfactory solution to the individual's problem. Depending on the type of question, one may imagine reference service as a tremendous bore or a source of considerable intellectual pleasure. In most libraries, reference librarians face both situations. After they have told the 101st person where the telephone is located or how to use the card catalog, after they have decided reference service is more pain than pleasure, along comes someone with a challenging query which requires effort, imagination, and knowledge of possible sources of answers. Some days are up, some days are down, but on the average it is a fascinating and exciting profession.

There is much more to reference service than answering questions, but for the moment consider that everyone is involved with queries, and, therefore with at least some aspect of reference. On a day-to-day level, reference entertains and enlightens millions of magazine and newspaper readers. "Is it true that drinking milk after eating lobster will poison us?" a nervous reader asks. "The Doctor Answers," a daily newspaper column, asserts, "There's no truth in that old wheeze." On another page of the paper, "Dear Abby," everyone's friendly reference librarian, copes with problems of mind, heart, and state. The Sunday newspaper supplement "Parade" features a page given over to answering queries and *Games* magazine (July/August 1981, pp. 54–55) features a trivia question and answer contest. A twist of the radio or television dial brings local or national quiz and talk shows based on the question-answer syndrome. In 1981 the American Library Association supplied *The Tonight Show* and other media with library questions and answers such as whose picture is on the $100,000 bill? The answer: Woodrow Wilson. Mention of these resources is not to suggest that the library should become a substitute for the popular media, but only that the average man or woman who takes an interest in finding answers to questions has a need, if not always an understanding, of the basic reference process.

The reverse side of this popular information approach is represented by the specialists concerned with theoretical (some would say more practical) aspects of knowledge and communications. Involved in what is sometimes called the foundation or theory of information science are people trying to puzzle out methods of distinguishing false from true information or finding data or documents for individual needs. The latter, in turn, requires a much better understanding than we have about how people ask questions.

INFORMATION AND THE LIBRARY

The father of the American reference process, Samuel Green, instituted the first formal reference service at the Worcester Public Library in Massachusetts in 1876. He emphasized the importance of personal aid to people requesting information. Until Green made his policy statement, the tendency of librarians was to look upon themselves as keepers of archives rather than as active providers of information for the public.[1] The library as a storehouse had to be kept in nice order, and Justin Winsor advocated employment of women in

[1]The standard history of American reference service is Samuel Rothstein, *The Development of Reference Service Through Academic Traditions, Public Library Practice and Special Librarianship* (Chicago: American Library Association, 1955) (ACRL Monograph no. 14).

1877 because "their familiarity with housekeeping chores would make them excellent library workers."[2]

The attitude that the library is a kind of rest home for less-than-qualified people has hampered reference service. The reference section often is seen as a convenient place to get an answer for a crossword puzzle or have someone look up an address. In many communities it is not visualized as a major information source. Fortunately, because of the renewed respect for information, this attitude seems to be changing, if only gradually.

A foreign observer stresses the power that information now commands in developing countries. Noting that many nations send students to America to master library science, the writer says, "It is the hope of their countries that they will come back and transform the weak and often backward national library system into powerful knowledge banks needed for the modernization and development of their societies in science, culture, technology and economy."[3]

Information is essential to government, to business, to research, to almost anyone. The degree and type of information required will depend on the individual. Professional people, from technologists and teachers to scientists and attorneys, need more data than do the average laypeople, although in the solution of day-to-day problems no line should be drawn in terms of what group's needs are more important. All needs are important.

Government could not function without current information; thus, billions of dollars are spent to gather data on business, weather, taxation, agriculture, medicine, and other interests. Congress spends an enormous amount of time and money in gathering information. As one critic puts it: "The smartest opinion changers on Capitol Hill today are the ones who know the facts of an issue, and how it will affect a Congressman's own district. Information is power, and it has become far more efficient to change a member's outlook than twist his arm."[4]

An example of the value of reference services is illustrated by the military success of the Prussians in the late nineteenth century. They used an information system which was later adopted by the Americans. The approach is equally applicable to reference service. It consists of four steps which are cyclical because the essential elements

[2]Eldred Smith in review of *Changing Times* in *Journal of Academic Librarianship,* January 1979, p. 453.

[3]Bjorn V. Tell, "The Changing Role of Library and Information Centre Specialists," *International Forum on Information and Documentation,* vol. 4, no. 1, 1979, p. 32.

[4]Steven Roberts, "Mass Protest Has Simply Gone Out of Style," *The New York Times,* March 18, 1979, p. E5.

are continually modified—as a battle plan—as the objectives and tasks of the users are modified.

1. Develop the *essential elements of information*.
2. Collect the information.
3. Record, sort, evaluate, and interpret the information.
4. Disseminate the processed information to the user.[5]

REFERENCE SERVICE GUIDELINES

The Reference and Adult Services Division of the American Library Association offers reference librarians a set of guidelines which help both to define their work and to chart, if only in a tentative way, a philosophy of service. The guidelines are called "A Commitment to Information Services."[6] Directed "to all those who have any responsibility for providing reference and information services," the guidelines' most valuable contribution is a succinct description of a reference librarian's duties. Defined by function, reference services can be divided into two categories: direct and indirect.

1. The direct category includes:
   a. *Reference or information services.* This is the "personal assistance provided to users in pursuit of information." The depth and character of such service vary with the type of library and the kinds of users it is designed to serve.
   This service may range from answering an apparently simple query to supplying information based on a bibliographical search combining the librarian/information specialist's competence in information-handling techniques with competence in the subject of inquiry.
   b. *Formal and informal instruction in the use of the library or information center and its resources.* This direct service may consist of various activities ranging from helping the user to understand the card catalog to "interpretative tours

---

[5]Jack King, "Put a Prussian Spy in Your Library," *RQ,* Fall 1978, p. 30.

[6]"A Commitment to Information Services: Developmental Guidelines," *RQ,* Spring 1979, pp. 275–278. First adopted in 1976, and a section "Ethics of Service" adopted in 1979. Quotations which follow are from the guidelines. For a perceptive discussion of the guidelines see Anne Roberts, "Prescriptive, Descriptive, or Proscriptive . . ." *RQ,* Spring 1978, pp. 223–225. Another approach is suggested by Bernard Vavrek, "Reference Evaluation—What the Guidelines Don't Indicate," *RQ,* Summer 1979, pp. 335–340.

and lectures" on how to use the library. In most libraries, "instruction" is interpreted as showing the user how to find an article, book, or other item by "interpreting" the mysteries of an index, reference work, and so on.

2. Indirect services may be summarized thus:

Indirect services reflect user access to a wide range of informational sources (e.g., bibliographies, indexes, information databases), and may be the extension of the library's information-service potential through cooperation with other library or information centers. This type of service recognizes the key role of interlibrary and interagency cooperation to provide adequate information service to users.

The average reference librarian is likely to perform many indirect services:

Selection of Materials   This service requires the recognition of the various types of materials needed for adequate reference service —not only books, but periodicals, manuscripts, newspapers, and anything else which can conceivably assist the librarian in giving direct service. Another aspect of selection is the weeding of book collections and files.

Reference Administration   The organization and administration of reference services will not involve everyone, but will be a major consideration for small-to-medium libraries with only one or two librarians.

Interlibrary Loan   With the increasing emphasis on networks and the recognition that the whole world of information should be literally at the command of the user, interlibrary loan may be categorized as an access activity. In recent years, it has become a major element in reference service. Administratively, some libraries now divorce it from reference and maintain it as a separate division; others consider it a function of the circulation section.

Evaluation of Reference Section   How well is the reference section serving the public? What has been done and what can be done to improve service? This analysis presupposes a method of evaluating not only the collection, but the organization of the reference section and the library as a whole.

Miscellaneous Tasks   There are a variety of "housekeeping" duties, including assisting with photocopying, filing, checking in materials, keeping a wary eye on reading rooms, maintaining records, plus all the chores that are the responsibility of any library department—from budgeting to preparing reports and publicity releases. Other services may include creating reference sources, local indexes, and information and referral sources. The extent of this kind of activity depends to a great degree on the size of the library and the philosophy and the financial support of the reference section.

REFERENCE SERVICE AND THE LIBRARY

The reference librarian does not function alone in a library but is part of a larger unit. Briefly, how do reference services fit into the library?

The specific purpose of any library is to obtain, preserve, and make available the recorded knowledge of human beings. The system for doing so can be as intricate and involved as the table of organization for the Library of Congress or General Motors or as simple as that used in the one-man small-town library or the corner barbershop.

Regardless of organizational patterns or complexities, the parts of the system are interrelated and common to all sizes and types of libraries. They consist of administrative work, technical services (acquisition and cataloging), and reader's services (circulation and reference). These broad categories cover multiple subsections. They are not independent units but parts of larger units; all are closely related. They form a unity essential for library service in general and reference in particular. Let one fail and the whole system will suffer.

Administrative work

The administration is concerned with library organization and communication. The better the administration functions, the less obvious it appears—at least to the user. The reference librarian must be aware of, and often participate in, administrative decisions ranging from budget to automation. Precisely how administration functions effectively is the subject of countless texts and coffee conversations. It is not the topic of this text, although specific administration of reference sections and departments is discussed later.

Technical services: Acquisitions

The selection and acquisition of materials are governed by the type of library and its users. Policies vary, of course, but the rallying cry of the nineteenth-century activist librarians, "The right book for the right reader at the right time," is still applicable to any library. It presents many challenges. For the general collection, it presupposes a knowledge of the clientele as well as of the material acquired and its applicability to the reader. The librarian must cope with publishers, sources, and reviews and must cooperate with other libraries. The unparalleled production of library materials over the past 50 years makes the process of selection and acquisition a primary intellectual responsibility.

Reference librarians are responsible for the reference collection, but their responsibility extends to the development of the library's entire collection—a collection which may serve to help them answer questions.

Technical services: Cataloging

Once a piece of information is acquired, the primary problem is how to retrieve it from the hundreds, thousands, or millions of bits of information in the library. There are a number of avenues open, from oral communication to abstracts; but for dealing with larger information units such as books, recordings, films, periodicals, or reports, the normal finding device is the card catalog. The catalog is the library's main bibliographical instrument. When properly used, it (1) enables persons to find books for which they have the author, the title, or the subject area; (2) shows what the library has by any given author, on a given subject, and in a given kind of literature; (3) assists in the choice of a book by its form (e.g., handbook, literature, or text) or edition; (4) assists in finding other materials, from government documents to films; and, often most important, (5) specifically locates the item in the library. It is a primary resource for reference librarians, and it is essential they understand not only the general aspects of the card catalog but also its many peculiarities.

Reader's services: Circulation

Circulation is one of the two primary public service points in the library. The other is reference.

After the book has been acquired and prepared for easy access, the circulation department is concerned with (1) charging out the material to the reader, (2) receiving it on return, and (3) returning it to its proper location. Other activities of the circulation department include registering prospective borrowers, keeping records of the number of books and patrons, and maintaining other statistics pertinent to charting the operation of the library. In small libraries, more than 50 percent of the reference work may be centered at the circulation desk. Such a library normally has one or two professionals who must pinch-hit in almost every capacity from administering to cataloging. Also, there may be no space for a separate reference desk, and the circulation point is a logical center where people come not only to check out books but also to ask questions.

Adult services: Reference[7]

An important aspect of reference service in the 1980s is adult services, often used as a synonym for "adult education." This is a specialized area, although in daily work the average reference librarian will be involved in a range of adult services such as giving assistance with job and occupational information to providing service for the handicapped.

REFERENCE QUESTIONS[8]

There are various methods of categorizing reference questions. By way of an introduction to a complex situation, queries may be divided into two general types:

1. *The user asks for a known item.* The request is usually for a specific document, book, article, film, or other item, which can be identified by citing certain features such as an author, title, or source. The librarian only has to locate the needed item through the card catalog, an index, a bibliography, or a similar source.

2. *The user asks for information without any knowledge of a specific source.* Such a query triggers the usual reference interview. Most reference questions are of this type, particularly in

[7]Most of the Spring 1979 issue of *RQ* is devoted to reference and adult services. A definition of the term is the subject of Joyce Wente, "What Are Adult Services?" pp. 231–234.

[8]There are numerous sources of reference questions, but a useful collection, divided by form (encyclopedias, yearbooks, directories, and so on), is Thomas P. Slavens, *Informational Interviews and Questions* (Metuchen, New Jersey: Scarecrow Press, 1978). Each section begins with a typical reference interview, followed by equally typical questions. Answers are not given. Slavens is also the compiler of a monograph, "Computer Assisted Instruction in the Education of Reference Librarians," *Information Reports and Bibliographies,* no. 4–5, 1979. His coauthor is Carl F. Orgren.

school and public libraries where the average user has little or no knowledge of the reference services available.

Handling the two broad types of questions may not be as easy as it seems. For example, the person who asks for a specific book by author may (1) have the wrong author, (2) actually want a book by that author other than the one requested, (3) discover the wanted book is not the one required (for either information or pleasure), or (4) ask the librarian to obtain the book on interlibrary loan and then fail to appear when the book is received. All of this leads most experienced reference librarians to qualify the "known-item" type of question. The assumption, which is usually correct, is that the user really needs more information or help than indicated. Therefore, librarians tend to ask enough questions to bring out the real needs of the user as opposed to what may be only a weak signal for help. There are other variables which may turn the first type of question into the second type.

A more finely drawn categorization of reference questions is the division into four types:[9]

(1) *Direction.* "Where is the card catalog?" "Where are the indexes?" "Where is the telephone?" The general information or directional question is of the information booth variety, and the answer rarely requires more than a geographical knowledge of key locations. The time required to answer such questions is negligible, but directional queries may account for 30 to 50 percent or more of the questions put to a librarian in any day. (It should be stressed that the percentages—here and in what follows—are relative and may vary from library to library.)

(2) *Ready reference.* "What is the name of the governor of

[9] There are many methods of analyzing types of reference questions. This is only one. For others, see John P. Wilkinson and William Miller, "The Step Approach to Reference Service," *RQ,* Summer 1978, pp. 293–300, where the authors expand on an idea that "reference questions can be defined in terms of the number of steps involved in finding their solutions, that is, as one-step, two-step and multiple-step questions" (p. 296). Particular attention is given to details of several studies in this important area. Mary Seng, "Reference Service Upgraded," *Special Libraries,* January 1978, pp. 21–28, where the author breaks down questions as directional, information (which concerns information sources in the library) and general (which requires use of information sources). Percentages given for types of questions and relative time it takes to answer are drawn from numerous sources, such as Miller and Seng above and Robert Balay "Use of the Reference Service in a Large Academic Library," *College and Research Libraries,* January 1975, pp. 21 +. Figures are only relative and vary not only from library to library but from season to season and year to year. Still, they give the beginner at least a notion of what to expect.

Alaska?" "How long is the Amazon River?" "Who is the world's tallest person?" Here is the typical ready-reference or data query which requires only a single, usually uncomplicated, answer. The requested information is normally found without difficulty in standard reference works, ranging from encyclopedias to almanacs and indexes. The time to answer this type of question is usually no more than a minute or two. The catch is that while 90 percent of such queries are simple to answer, another 5 to 10 percent may take hours of research because no standard reference source in the library will yield the necessary data. Apparently simple questions are sometimes complicated; such as, "What are the dates of National Cat Week?" (Answer: Flexible, but usually in early November.) "When was Russian roulette first played?" (Answer: Cambridge University in 1801. Lord Byron describes the incident in his memoirs.) Difficult questions of this type are often printed in a regular column in *RQ,* the official journal of reference librarians.[10]

The percentage of ready-reference questions will differ from library to library, although they constitute a large proportion (30 to 40 percent) of all queries other than directional questions in public libraries. In one study it was found that about 60 percent of the questions asked in a public library were of the ready-reference type. Requests for background information make up the other 40 to 60 percent or so of the queries.[11] Public libraries, which have a well-developed phone service for reference questions as well as a high percentage of adult users, tend to attract the ready-reference question.[12] In academic, school, and special libraries, search questions may account for 30 to 60 percent of the total.

(3) *Specific search.* "Where can I find information on sexism in business?" "What is the difference between the conservative and the liberal view on inflation and unemployment?" "Do you have anything on the history of atomic energy?" "I have to write a paper on penguins for my science class. What do you have?" The essential difference between the specific search and the ready-reference ques-

---

[10]The column, called "The Exchange," has various editors. It is devoted to "tricky questions, notes on unusual information sources, general comments concerning reference problems . . ." The two questions above, with answers, appeared in *RQ* in Spring 1979, p. 284 and Summer 1978, p. 339.

[11]Maurice Walsh, "Reference Librarians; Do They Play Their Hunches or Go by the Book?" *LLA Bulletin,* Winter 1977, p. 105.

[12]Wilkinson and Miller, op. cit., p. 298, 299. In a college science library it was found that 31 percent of the queries were ready reference; in a general college library, 60 percent. The percentages increase as the reference library becomes more general and serves a public with diverse interests.

tions is twofold. Ready-reference queries usually can be answered with data, normally short answers from reference books. Specific search answers almost always take the form of giving the user a document, e.g., a list of citations, a book, or a report.

More information is required if the user is writing a school paper, is preparing a speech, or is simply interested in learning as much about a subject as necessary for his or her needs. This query often is called a "bibliographic inquiry," because the questioner is referred to a bibliographic aid such as the card catalog, an index, or a bibliography. The user than scans what seems available and determines how much and what type of materials are needed.

One can hardly suggest that all specific search questions involve bibliographies. At a less-sophisticated level, the librarian may merely direct the user to an encyclopedia article, a given section of the book collection, or a newspaper index. If directional queries are discounted, specific search questions constitute the greatest proportion of reference questions in school and academic libraries as well as in many special libraries.

The time taken to answer the question depends not only on what is available in the library (or through interlibrary loan) but also on the attitude of the librarian. If the librarian offers a considerable amount of help, the search may take from 10 minutes to an hour or more. Conversely, the librarian may turn the question into a directional one by simply pointing the user in the direction of the card catalog.

Some types of specific search questions are treated by librarians as reader advisory problems. These are the types of questions that, in essence, ask, "What is the best source of information for my needs?" Some questioners are seeking everything from fiction and poetry to hobby magazines. Depending on the size and the organizational pattern of the library, their queries may be handled by subject or reader advisory librarians or by reference librarians.

(4) *Research.* Almost any of the types of questions described in the "Specific Search" section may be turned into research questions. A research query is usually identified as coming from an adult specialist who is seeking detailed information to assist in specific work. The request may be from a professor, a business executive, a scientist, or anyone else who wishes data for a decision or for additional information about a problem. With the exception of some academic and special libraries, this type of inquiry is a negligible part of the total reference pattern.

Ready-reference and specific search queries presuppose specific answers and specific sources, which, with practice, the librarian usually is able to locate quickly. Research questions differ in that most involve trial-and-error searching or browsing, primarily because (1) the average researcher may have a vague notion of the question but usually cannot be specific and (2) the answer to the yet-to-be-completely-formulated question depends on what the researcher is able to find (or not find). The researcher recognizes a problem, identifies the area that is likely to cover the problem, and then attempts to find what has been written about the problem.

The complete library, as well as resources outside the library, may be used to assist the researcher. There is no way of measuring the difficulty or the average amount of time spent on such questions. Research queries are usually more interesting for the reference librarian because of the intellectual challenge they present, and they certainly enable the librarian to be more than a directional signal. Fortunately, reference work of the future seems to be turning toward research-oriented situations.

The reader will note another useful method of distinguishing types of queries. The first two types of queries (directional and ready-reference) may be classified as *data retrieval,* i.e., individuals have specific questions and expect answers in the form of data. The specific search and research questions might be classified as *document retrieval* in that the users want information, not just simple answers, and the information is usually in the form of some type of document, i.e., book, report, article, and so on.[13]

Questions can rarely be so easily classified into the four types in terms of effort, sources employed, or ease of determining search strategies. A directional query may become a ready-reference question or a specific search problem. And under some circumstances it may even change to a research question. The point is worth stressing that categorization of queries is no more certain than the type of question likely to be asked at this or that library at any given moment.

Looking at questions from another viewpoint, several studies report that in public libraries the queries related to school work account for 30 to as high as 50 or 60 percent of the total, with about one-third being average. Another 25 to 30 percent are business-related, and 35 to 50 percent are queries relating to personal interest or research; e.g., "how-to-do-it," what is the best book or article on a subject, or how to solve a problem from curing bad skin to selecting an automobile. School and academic libraries, of course, have a

[13]For a detailed discussion of the differences between document and data retrieval see M. E. Maron, "Theory and Foundation of Information Retrieval: Some Introductory Remarks," *Drexel Library Quarterly,* April 1978, pp. 3–5. The entire issue is on the subject of information retrieval.

heavier emphasis on educational and research questions, although hidden under some of them are very personal queries.

In an analysis of questions at the Urbana (Indiana) public library, it was found that 48 percent were asked in person and 52 percent by telephone. The librarians judged that 86 percent of the questions had been answered fully and 14 percent unanswered or only partially answered.[14]

Who is to answer?

The fascinating result of analyses of types of questions is that (1) the majority of queries are directional or ready-reference pure and simple; (2) generally, the queries and sources used are basic and easy to understand; (3) most questions, therefore, could be answered by a well-trained person with a bachelor's degree.[15]

There are many who advocate using nonprofessionals at the reference or information desk, backed up by trained librarians. The latter would be free to provide in-depth service at the specific search or research level. Actually, where there is a computer in the library, this is already happening, i.e., a professional librarian is involved with questions that require an increasing amount of knowledge and sophistication.

Not everyone agrees that the trained nonprofessional can or should replace the professional librarian for the purpose of answering directional and ready-reference queries. As indicated, oftentimes the simple questions develop into complex ones requiring professional aid; for, as one critic points out, "Even though reference questions statistics show that a large percentage of reference questions do not require a bibliographical/instructional background, it is difficult for paraprofessionals (and sometimes even professionals) to define the depth and extent of an initial inquiry."[16] There is also the practical consideration of employment opportunities. With fewer professional

[14]Herbert Goldhor, "The Patrons' Side of Public Library Reference Questions," *Public Library Quarterly,* Spring 1979, pp. 36, 37.

[15]Jeffrey St. Clair and Rao Aluri, "Staffing the Reference Desk: Professionals or Nonprofessionals?" *The Journal of Academic Librarianship,* no. 3, 1977, pp. 149–153. "The authors conclude that carefully trained nonprofessionals at the reference desk can completely answer 80 percent of the questions." For another approach, this time suggesting catalogers and reference librarians take turns at each other's jobs, see David Peele's "Staffing the Reference Desk," *Library Journal,* September 1, 1980, pp. 1708–1711.

[16]Maureen Pastine, "A Response," *Journal of Academic Librarianship,* July 1977, p. 152. The "response" is to the just cited St. Clair and Aluri article.

library positions it is questionable that many librarians (this side of administrators) will be pushing to replace themselves, even if there is real promise of doing more fulfilling reference work at a higher level.

Reference interview

The most common complaint heard among reference librarians about their work is that few people know how to ask reference questions. There are numerous reasons for the public's failure to appreciate the need for clarity at the reference desk, and these are considered throughout this text. Suffice it to say here that the dialogue between the user and the librarian is called the reference interview and has several objectives. The first is to find out what is required and how much data is needed. This is simplicity itself—except that most people do not know how to frame questions. The child looking for horses may be interested in pictures, an encyclopedia article, or possibly a book on riding. No matter what the scope of the query, it probably will come out as "Do you have anything on horses?"

Searching for answers

Once the actual needs of the library patron are understood, the next step is to formulate a search strategy of possible sources. This requires translating the terms of the question into the language of the reference system. If a basic book on gardening is required, the librarian will find it readily enough in the card catalog under a suitable subject heading. At the other specific extreme, the question may involve searching indexes, such as the *Biological & Agricultural Index,* to find the latest information on elm blight or perhaps checking out various bibliographies, such as *Subject Guide to Books in Print* or a union catalog, to find what may be available on elm blight in general and in other libraries. Once the information is found, it has to be evaluated. That is, the librarian must determine whether it is really the kind and at the level that the patron wants. Is it too technical or too simple? Is it applicable in this geographic area?

INFORMATION SOURCES

In day-to-day activities in most reference libraries, the librarian relies on reference books which are carefully marked and segregated in a special section of the library. The reference book is well known to most people, and the dictionary and the encyclopedia are found in many homes.

A question of interest for reference librarians concerns how many titles the new librarian should be familiar with when taking over a reference position. Some would argue that specific knowledge of specific titles is not very important; but that debate aside, several studies at least indicate the degree of disagreement about how many and which titles every reference librarian should know.

Larsen polled 31 library schools and found only seven titles were listed by all: *New Encyclopaedia Britannica, World Book, Current Biography, Dictionary of American Biography, The New York Times Index, The Readers' Guide to Periodical Literature,* and the *World Almanac.* The lack of agreement among schools is striking but not unusual. How many librarians, for example, would agree with the Chicago Public Library "top 10" where number 1 was the system of files produced by the staff? *World Book* and *World Almanac* were numbers 2 and 3. Number 4 was a staff-produced desk folder; and rounding out the top 10 were *Haines Criss Cross Directories, The Legislative Directory, Who's Who in America, Chase's Calendar of Annual Events, Random House College Dictionary,* and the Chicago phone directory.[17]

There are no end of select lists, which indicate some consensus but do not dictate "basic" reference collections. Much the same is true when one turns to lists of other reference forms, from data bases to video. Ultimately the working, basic collection is the one which is best for the individual librarian and the audience served—and determining this type of list is one of the joys of active reference service.

Information chain

If the ideal reference service, to paraphrase André Malraux, is "reference service without walls," the nature of information does impose certain limitations on that service. Aside from asking experts in the community for "firsthand" information, the library generally must rely on published data—data which, by the nature of publishing,

---

[17]John C. Larsen, "Information Sources Currently Studied in General Reference Courses," *RQ,* Summer 1979, pp. 341–348. The author makes reference to an earlier study of the same type of lists by Wallace Bonk. The Chicago Public Library list, which includes the 100 "most-used tools" at the reference desk will be found in *Multitype Library Cooperative News,* March 1979, but a copy of the list is available from the library, 425 N. Michigan Ave., Chicago, IL 60611. For a select list for school libraries see Kenneth F. Kister, "Recommended Reference Sources of School Media Centers," *School Library Journal,* December 1980, pp. 17–22.

may be weeks, months, or even years out of date. A rough way of measuring the usual timeliness of materials is to classify them as primary, secondary, or tertiary.

(1) *Primary Sources* These are original materials which have not been filtered through interpretation, condensation, or, often, even evaluation by a second party. The materials tend to be the most current in the library, normally taking the form of a journal article, monograph, report, patent, dissertation, or reprint of an article. Some primary sources for information are not published, as, for example, the offering of firsthand information ("I was there," or "I discovered," or "I interpreted. . . .") orally by one person to one or more others at a meeting or seminar, or in a letter which may be destroyed. Where primary sources are available in a library, the controls to call them up for reference work are usually secondary sources, such as indexes, abstracts, and bibliographies.

(2) *Secondary Sources* If an index is used to locate primary sources, the index itself is a secondary source. A secondary source is information about primary or original information which usually has been modified, selected, or rearranged for a purpose or an audience. The neat distinction between primary and secondary sources is not always apparent. For example, a person at a meeting may not be stating original views, but may simply be repeating what he or she has read or heard from someone else. A journal article is usually a primary source if it represents original thinking or a report on a discovery; but the same journal may include secondary materials which are reports or summaries of the findings of others.

(3) *Tertiary Sources* These consist of information which is a distillation and collection of primary and secondary sources. Twice removed from the original, they include almost all the source types of reference, works such as encyclopedias, reviews, biographical sources, fact books, and almanacs.

The definitions of primary, secondary, and tertiary sources are useful only in that they indicate (1) relative currency (primary sources tend to be more current than secondary sources) and (2) relative accuracy of materials (primary sources will generally be more accurate than secondary sources, only because they represent unfiltered, original ideas; conversely, a secondary source may correct errors in the primary source).

Whenever a reference source has become part of our experience, it requires little thought to match a question with a probable answer form. Those forms may be divided into two large categories: the control-access-directional type and the source type.

The control-access-directional type of source

The first broad class or form of reference sources is the bibliography. This form is variously defined, but in its most general sense it is a systematically produced descriptive list of records.

Control   The bibliography serves as a control device—a kind of checklist. It inventories what is produced from day to day and year to year in such a way as to enable both the compiler and the user to feel they have a control, through organization, of the steady flow of knowledge. The bibliography is prepared through research (finding the specific source), identification, description, and classification.

Access   Once the items are controlled, the individual items are organized for easy access to facilitate intellectual work. All the access types of reference works can be broadly defined as bibliographies; but they may be subdivided as follows:

1. Bibliographies of reference sources and the literature of a field, if either a general or a subject nature. Example: Sheehy's *Guide to Reference Books* or *The Information Sources of Political Science*. Another type of bibliography includes the bibliography of bibliographies and the index to bibliographies.
2. The library card catalog or the catalogs of numerous libraries arranged for eacy access through a union list. Technically, these are not bibliographies but are often used in the same manner.
3. General systematic enumerative bibliography which includes various forms of bibliography. Example: *The National Union Catalog.*
4. Indexes and abstracts, which are usually treated separately from bibliographies, but are considered a bibliographical aid. They are systematic listings which help to identify and trace materials. Indexes to the contents of magazines and newspapers are the most frequently used types in the reference situation. Examples: *The Readers' Guide to Periodical Literature* and *The New York Times Index.*

Direction   Bibliographies themselves normally do not give definitive answers, but serve to direct users to the sources of answers. For their effective use, the items listed must be either in the library or available from another library system.

Source type

Works of the source type usually suffice in themselves to give the answers. Unlike the access type of reference work, they are synoptic.

Encyclopedias   The most-used single source are encyclopedias; they may be defined as works containing informational articles on subjects in every field of knowledge, usually arranged in alphabetical order. They are used to answer specific questions about X topic or Y person or general queries which may begin with "I want something about Z." Examples: *Encyclopaedia Britannica; World Book Encyclopedia.*

Fact Sources   Yearbooks, almanacs, handbooks, manuals, and directories are included in this category. All the types have different qualities, but they share one common element: They are used to look up factual material for quick reference. Together, they cover many facets of human knowledge. Examples: *World Almanac; Statesman's Year-Book.*

Dictionaries   Sources which deal primarily with all aspects of words, from proper definitions to spelling, are classified as dictionaries. Examples: *Webster's Third New International Dictionary; Dictionary of American Slang.*

Biographical Sources   The self-evident sources of information on people distinguished in some particular field of interest are known as biographical sources. Examples: *Who's Who; Current Biography.*

Geographical Sources   The best-known forms are the atlases, which not only show given countries but may illustrate themes such as historical development, social development, and scientific centers. Geographical sources also include gazetteers, dictionaries of place names, and guidebooks. Example: *The Times Atlas of the World.*

Government documents

Government documents are official publications ordered and normally published by the federal, state, and local governments. Since they may include directional and source works, their separation into a particular unit is more one of convenience and organization than of different reference use. Examples: *Monthly Catalog of United States Government Publications* (access type); *United States Government Manual* (source type).

The neat categorization of reference types by access and by source is not always so distinct in an actual situation. A bibliography may be the only source required if the question is merely one of verification or of trying to complete a bibliographical citation. Conversely, the bibliography at the end of an encyclopedia article or a statement in that article may direct the patron to another source. In general, the two main categories—access and source—serve to differentiate between the principal types of reference works.

Unconventional reference sources

A term frequently seen in connection with reference service at the public library level is "information and referral," or simply "I&R." There are other terms used to describe this service, such as "community information center." Essentially, the purpose of this special reference service is to offer the users access to resources that will help them with health, rent, consumer, legal, and similar problems. The economic situation has caused many people to look for jobs if they are laid off. The libraries often provide free information on sources of employment. While I&R is discussed in the second volume of this text, the beginner should realize that in even the most traditional library, it is now common to (1) call individual experts, including anyone from a local professor to a leader in a local special-interest group, for assistance; (2) provide files, pamphlets, booklists, and so on, which give users information on topics ranging from occupations to local housing regulations; and (3) provide a place which active groups in the community may identify as an information clearinghouse for their needs.

EVALUATING REFERENCE SOURCES

A thorough understanding of the day-to-day sources of answers requires some evaluation of those sources. How does the librarian know whether a reference source is good, bad, or indifferent? A detailed answer will be found throughout each of the chapters in this volume. However, in rather simplistic terms, a good reference source is one that answers questions, and a poor reference source is one that fails to answer questions. Constant and practical use will quickly place any source (whether a book or a database) in one of these two categories.

What follows is primarily concerned with traditional reference books, but much of it is applicable to other reference forms, including machine-readable records. Evaluation of data bases is considered in the second volume of this text.

Because of the expense of most reference sources, the typical practice is to read one or more book reviews before deciding whether or not to buy. Large libraries usually request or automatically receive examination copies before purchase. Smaller libraries may have no choice but to accept the word of the reviewer and order or not order. Ideally, the reference source should be examined by a trained reference librarian before it is incorporated into the collection. No review or review medium is infallible.

The librarian must ask at least four basic questions about a reference work: What is its purpose? Its authority? Its scope? Its proposed audience? Finally, the format of the work must be considered.

(1) *Purpose* The purpose of a reference work should be evident from the title or form. The evaluative question Has the author or compiler fulfilled the purpose? must be posed. An encyclopedia of dance, for example, has the purpose of capturing essential information about dance in encyclopedic form. But immediately the librarian must ask such questions as What kind of dance and for what period? For what age group or experience or sophistication in dance? For what countries? Is the emphasis on history, biography, practical application, or some other element?

The clues to purpose are found in the (a) table of contents; (b) introduction or preface, which should give details of what the author or compiler expects this work to accomplish; and (c) index, the sampling of which will tell what subjects are covered. A reference book without an index is usually of little or no value. Exceptions are dictionaries, indexes, directories, and other titles where the index is built into an alphabetical arrangement. This system is suitable for the data type of reference work, but not for running prose; then an index is absolutely essential.

Other hints of the purpose of a specific work are often given in the publisher's catalog, in advance notices received in the mails, and in the copy on the jacket of the book. Such descriptions may help to indicate purpose and even relative usefulness, but are understandably less than objective.

(2) *Authority* The question of purpose brings us close to a whole series of questions which relate to the author:

(a) What are the author's qualifications for the fulfillment of his or her purpose? If the writer is a known scholar, there is no problem with authority. Where the difficulty arises is with the other 95 percent of reference works that are prepared by experts but not those who make the best-seller list. Here the librarian must rely on (1) the qualifications of the author given in the book; (2) the librarian's own understanding and depth of knowledge of the subject; and (3) a check of the author in standard biographical works such as *Who's Who* or *American Men and Women of Science.*

(b) What were the sources of the author's knowledge? This question, properly answered, may also serve to answer the query about the author's qualifications. Did he or she go to primary source material—or rely on secondary material? If new sources were explored, were they well chosen and sufficient? Answers to these questions may be found by looking for footnotes, citations to sources, and bibliographies. Many reference works are secondary material (encyclopedias, almanacs, yearbooks, and so on) but draw heavily on primary sources. A book based on derivative material is often useful, but the authority is highly suspect if the primary sources are not cited. In collective works, such as encyclopedias and many handbooks, the articles should be signed or some indication given of who is responsible for the work.

(c) The imprint of the publisher may indicate the relative worth of a book. Some publishers have excellent reputations for issuing reference works; others are known for their fair-to-untrustworthy titles. In a few cases, for example, encyclopedias and dictionaries, the cost of publishing is so high that the field is narrowed down to three or four firms. Even at best, publishers are generally less interested in the progress of learning than in making money; a given group of publishers may have a well-deserved reputation for excellent reference books, but they, too, can slip. A reputable publisher may issue a half-dozen fine reference works, but the seventh may be a "bomb," possibly initiated for commercial purposes; or even if written by a knowledgeable author and fairly informative, it may be superfluous.

Authority, then, is a matter of the author and the publishers. But neither is infallible; the best sometimes miss. For example, in 1978 it was found that one of the world's leading contributors to educational psychology had manufactured most of his data for major articles and books on intelligence. The lopsided argument had been widely accepted and the author knighted for his contributions before his death in 1971.[18]

[18]Boyce Rensberger, "Data on Race Role In I.Q. Called False," *The New York Times,* November 8, 1978. The psychologist was Cyril Burt. "According to the September 29, 1978, issue of *Science,* new findings show beyond any reasonable doubt that Dr. Burt fabricated the data he presented as having been scientifically derived."

Authority can be measured, finally, only by careful scrutiny of the book by the knowledgeable librarian.

(d) Although writing style is not usually a major consideration in reference works, there is no excuse for poor writing. In fact, a poor presentation is often indicative of middled thinking or, even worse, lack of impartiality. No writer, not even the statistician, can be completely objective. Still, reference works, more than other books, should reflect independence of mind. They should state both sides of controversial issues, giving a just picture of the relevance and comparative merit of various viewpoints. Readers then should be able to draw their own conclusions. When a reference work is dealing with any controversial subject, bias may be detected not only in the style of presentation, but also in the relative length of articles, the selection of facts, and the sources cited.

(3) *Scope* The first question of major importance in selecting a reference work is, Will this book be a real addition to our collection, and if so, what exactly will it add? The publisher usually will state the scope of the book in the publicity blurb or in the preface, but the librarian should be cautious. The author may or may not have achieved the scope claimed. For example, the publisher may claim that a historical atlas covers all nations and all periods. The librarian may check the scope of the new historical atlas by comparing it against standard works. Does the new work actually include *all* nations and *all* periods, or does it exclude material found in the standard works? If an index claims to cover all major articles in X and Y periodicals, a simple check of the periodicals' articles against the index will reveal the actual scope of the index.

(a) What has the author contributed that cannot be found in other bibliographies, indexes, handbooks, almanacs, atlases, dictionaries, and so on? If the work is comprehensive within a narrow subject field, one may easily check it against other sources. For example, a who's who of education which limits itself to educators in the major colleges and universities in the Northeast may easily be checked for scope by comparing the current college catalog of P & Q University against the new who's who. If a number of faculty members are missing from the new work, one may safely conclude the scope is not what is claimed.

Most reference works are selective, and in this case the publisher and author should clearly state what is and is not included. What methods were employed for selection or rejection? And does the selection plan fit the audience claimed by the reference work. An encyclopedia of detection, for example, may or may not include fictional detectives, but if it claims to list the masterminds of detection from novels, are they *all* included? Are the detectives included in keeping with the purpose and the audience of the work?

Other general questions involving scope are almost as numerous as are reference works. One might ask the national or political scope of a work; the scope of the bibliographies in terms of numbers, length, language, timeliness, and so on; the inclusion or lack of guides, indexes, illustrations, and so on; the number of this or that actually covered or considered, for example, the number of entries in a dictionary. Beyond these important general considerations are others a bit easier to pinpoint.

(b) Currency is one of the most important features of any reference work, particularly one used for ready reference. Data change so quickly that last year's almanac may be historically important but of little value in answering current queries.

Except for current indexes, such as *Facts on File* and *The Readers' Guide to Periodical Literature,* most published reference works are dated before they are even off the presses. The time between the publisher's receipt of a manuscript and its publication may vary from six months to two years. Thus, in determining the recency of a work, some consideration must be given to the problems of production. Normally, a timely reference book will be one that contains information dating from six months to a year prior to the copyright date.

The copyright date in itself may be only a relative indication of timeliness. Is this a new work, or is it based on a previous publication? In these days of reprints, this is a particularly important question. A standard reference work may be reissued with the date of publication shown on the title page as, say, 1980, but on the verso of the same title page, the original copyright date may be 1976. If the work has been revised and updated, the copyright date will usually correspond to the date on the title page. A marked discrepancy should be sufficient warning that content must be carefully checked for currency.

Few reference works, unless entirely new, will not contain some dated information. The best method of ascertaining whether the dated material is of value and checking the recency factor is to sample the work. This is a matter of looking for names currently in the news, population figures, geographical boundaries, records of achievement, new events, and almost any other recent fact which is consistent with the purpose and scope of the work. Needless to add, no reference work should be accepted or rejected on a sampling of one or two items.

If the work purports to be a new edition, the extent of claimed revisions should be carefully noted. This can easily be done by checking it against the earlier edition or by noting any great discrepancy between the dates of the cited materials and the date of publication. For example, when an encyclopedia purports to be up to date but has no bibliographies dated within two or three years of the date on the title page, something a bit odd is certainly indicated.

(c) Within the work itself, the scope should be consistent for comparable entries. For example, in a biographical dictionary the reader should be certain to find the same general type of information for each entry: birth date, place of birth, address, achievements, and so on.

(d) Can the reference work be used alone, or must it be supplemented by another work? For example, the scope of *Contemporary Authors* is considerably greater than that of *World Authors*. The emphasis on many little-known authors in the former work makes it a valuable finding aid, but the latter is much more useful for detailed biographical sketches. Where a choice must be made, the librarian will have to consider carefully the potential users.

(4) *Audience* With the exception of juvenile encyclopedias, most reference works are prepared for adults. When considering the question of audience, the librarian must ask one major question: Is this for the scholar or student of the subject, or is it for the layperson with little or no knowledge? For example, in the field of organic chemistry, Beilstein's *Handbuch der Organischen Chemie* is as well known to chemists as the "top 10" tunes are to music fans. It is decidedly for the student with some basic knowledge of chemistry. Often the distinction in terms of audience is not so clear-cut, however.

A useful method of checking the reading level of a given reference work is for the librarian to examine a subject well known to him or her and then turn to one that is not so well understood. If both are comprehended, if the language is equally free of jargon and technical terminology, if the style is informative yet provocative, the librarian can be reasonably certain the work is for the layperson. Of course, if the total book is beyond the subject competency of the librarian, advice should be sought from a subject expert. Still, this is an unlikely situation, e.g., reference librarians tend to be experts in fields within which they operate.

(5) *Format* The questions which have been discussed are essential, but one of the most meaningful questions of all concerns arrangement, treated here as part of the format. Arrangement is of major importance. There must be a handy form of access to the material.

There are some general rules for arrangement which are significant guides to the relative worth of a particular work as a tool in answering questions. Briefly:

(a) Wherever possible, information should be arranged alphabetically in dictionary form. The advantage is that there is no need to learn a scheme of organization.

(b) Where alphabetical arrangement is not used, there should be an author, subject, and title index or an index covering aspects of content. Even with alphabetical order, it is usually advisable to have an index, particularly where bits of information must be extracted from long articles.

(c) Where needed (in either the text, the index, or both), there should be sufficient cross-references that lead to other material and not merely to blind entries. For example, a book which refers readers to "archives" when they look up "manuscripts" should have an entry for "archives." This is a simple rule; but too frequently, in the process of editing and revising, the entry for the cross-reference is deleted.

(d) In some works another method must be employed, particularly in scientific sources. The classification should be as simple as possible; certainly it should be consistent and logical throughtout. If it is difficult to comprehend, this may be a warning about the merits of the work as a whole.

The arrangement can be either hindered or helped by the physical format. Even the best-arranged work can be a nuisance if bound so that the pages do not lie flat, or if there is no clear distinction between headings on a page and subheads within the page. The apparatuses of abbreviation, typography, symbols, and indication of cross-references must be clear and in keeping with what the user is likely to recognize. The use of offset printing from computerized materials has resulted in some disturbing complexities of format. For example, it may be impossible to tell West Virginia, when abbreviated, from western Virginia. Uniform lower-case letters will be equally confusing. Lack of spacing between lines, poor paper, little or no margins, and other hindrances to reading are all too evident in even some standard reference works.

A word regarding illustrations: When photographs, charts, tables, and diagrams are used, they should be current, clear, and related to the text. They should be adjacent to the material under discussion or at least clearly identified.

The last word on the subject may sound as cynical or as simplistic as the reader cares to interpret it, but it is this: Trust no one. The reviewer, the publisher, and the author do make mistakes, sometimes of horrendous proportions. The librarian who evaluates reference sources with the constant suspicion of the worst is less likely to be the victim of those mistakes.

THE REFERENCE LIBRARIAN

By now it is obvious that information and reference service is something more than the stereotyped little old soul in tennis shoes stumbling around the library looking for last year's almanac. Today's librarian must know reference sources and, for that matter, any of the sources in or outside the library likely to yield answers, which, in turn, requires a basic familiarity with methods of acquiring and organizing information sources, from books to microform to computer data bases.

On these assets depends what is referred to as collection development. The librarian must be able to separate out the worthwhile from the worthless in terms of probable information value. It is one thing to locate 5 or 50 articles on women painters, quite another to be able to tell which of the 5 or 50 are likely to be of use to the person with the question. To avoid an information failure, the librarian must be able to translate a question into terms which can be met by the information sources. If someone, for example, asks for information on nuclear waste, the librarian must know, at a rudimentary level, the subject headings under which articles, reports, and books about nuclear waste are listed. And the librarian must be able to search for answers quickly and efficiently.

Every librarian should try to develop the following skills: (1) The ability to organize data and information for people to use; (2) awareness of the totality of information resources and the probabilities of success of strategies for searching for information in any specific situation; (3) awareness of and ability to use the range of information technologies, from print to sound and image to computing; (4) sensitivity to use, uses, and users of information, and a strong tradition of service, which demands attention to client satisfaction.[19]

Reference librarians are analyzed, psychoanalyzed, and quantified. Usually some additional, more personalized, traits are suggested for the perfect librarian. They include *imagination,* which helps the librarian interpret the question and find precisely the right data or documents to answer it; *perseverence,* which keeps the librarian going when the logical source yields nothing; *judgment* to know when to ask for more information from the user, when to stop, and when to go

---

[19]Robert S. Taylor, "Reminiscing about the Future," *Library Journal,* September 15, 1979, p. 1873.

on; and *accuracy, thoroughness,* and *orderliness,* which are necessary particularly when the librarian is being counted on for the correct answer. Unfortunately, many studies and surveys indicate that too many librarians often give wrong or no answers to questions.[20]

Librarian as evaluator

A familiar, even hackneyed phrase in library work is the "information explosion." This refers to the ever-increasing amount of information produced at almost every level. Typical statistics quoted to show the size of the explosion: (1) There are now about 100,000 scientific and technical periodicals, which publish over 2 million articles each year. (2) Book titles in America have increased from about 4000 in 1960 to over 40,000 in the early 1980s. (3) There are about 300 billion pieces of information reported to the federal government by states, local government, individuals, and corporations each year. It costs about $125 billion a year or $500 per person to collect, review, and store that information. (4) Academic library holdings have increased over 100 percent in the past decade or so.[21]

All these distant figures may be reduced to the reader's practical world by simply consulting the index of this text, where can be found only a few of the 10,000-plus reference titles suggested as "basic" for larger libraries—too many for any single person to use, much less remember. Yet some 1500 to 2000 reference works (or new editions) are published in America each year. This compares with almost the total annual production of *all* books a few decades ago.

Given the vast amount of material, the average individual is much in the same position as the person looking for the needle in the haystack. The librarian can help by using an educated magnet and by limiting the size of the haystack (i.e., the size of the collection of materials) to some size relevant for the users.[22] The obvious questions: What retrieval devices are best for locating the needed information? What processes should be employed to separate out the good from

---

[20]David E. House, "Reference Efficiency or Reference Deficiency," *Library Association Record,* November 1974, pp. 223–224. This is one such study where the majority of librarians did not give false information but simply could not even answer the question.

[21]The figures vary, depending on a dozen or so statistical articles and reports. For example, see Don Avedon, "Micropublishing: Why, What and Who," *IMC Journal,* 2d quarter, 1979, p. 32.

[22]The librarian, of course, will not remember all the reference works but will have the tremendous advantage of knowing where to go to find them listed—or, as in many cases, will have a vague memory of a tall, red volume in the third stack of shelves which might help. Not all locating of information is objective.

the worthless in the acquisition of materials? These, by the way, lead to scores of other queries which take up a good deal of time of so-called information scientists, who are as much concerned with the future implications of the growth of information as with the daily activities of the library. The different formats of information add to the confusion.

As each year goes by, it becomes increasingly evident that the librarian is more than someone who acquires and processes materials and delivers them to storage. The librarian must be a guide, a gatekeeper between the mass of undifferentiated information and the specific needs of the individual.

For example, in the average medium-to-large library there may be twenty, thirty, or several hundred different indexes and abstracting services. Which one should the reader use who knows little or nothing about the library or (more likely) uses the library often but has never needed an index in a particular subject area? This individual should ask the librarian who, as gatekeeper, will advise which indexes are best for the particular service. Going a step further, the librarian will go on to explain the use of the service, or help the individual find articles and other materials. Beyond that, the librarian may, again in the role of gatekeeper, advise which periodicals are likely to be best for the user's need; actively help the user find the periodicals; and, where necessary, suggest substitutes.

This approach represents the *liberal* philosophy of reference service, in which the librarian is convinced it is a professional duty to be an active gatekeeper and to produce information as needed. Not all librarians, by any means, agree with this philosophy. At the other extreme is the *conservative,* who believes the individual should not depend on the librarian for active assistance. The conservative thinks it is enough to acquire and process materials, and perhaps show someone how to find or use an index, but certainly not help that person decide which article to use or where to find the article. Between the two is the *moderate* who sometimes gives total service, other times points rather than assists.

In this text the emphasis is on the liberal attitude, that is, that the librarian should give the greatest amount of help to people. The primary function of a reference librarian is to answer questions, and that, essentially, is what the liberal gatekeeper is about.[23]

The fulfillment of this role as gatekeeper is not always possible

---

[23]See the second volume of this text for a summary of the three arguments of reference service. A useful, brief analysis of the viewpoints is offered by Harold N. Boyer, "Academic Reference Service: Conservative or Liberal Application?" *Southeastern Librarian,* Fall 1979, pp. 155–157.

or even desirable. Some people, after all, want to search through the information to find what they need without any help from anyone. Still, the role of the librarian as gatekeeper or interpreter of available data is a valuable, increasingly important one.

During the atomic plant near-disaster at Three Mile Island, for example, it was not lack of information which caused so much difficulty. It was lack of the *proper* information, lack of someone not only to find what was needed but to filter out what could be used. As one expert put it, the accident "was primarily an information failure. Signals showed erroneous information about critical gauges. . . . The people running the plant did not have accurate information."[24]

Few daily reference situations are that critical, although in the mind of the person asking the question, the need for accurate information is often as personally pressing. The trained, professional librarian should be there with the accurate answer.

COMPUTER-ASSISTED REFERENCE SERVICE

Note: This section is covered in great detail in the second volume of this text. It may be read now, or there may be a reason to defer discussion of the subject until the conclusion of the text. Either approach is satisfactory.

When approaching such terms as "data bases," "online," "machine-readable records," and "CRT," the reference librarian may imagine what it was like when the fifteenth-century librarian first was confronted with printing.[25] It took time for the Renaissance librarian to recognize that while the form had changed, the message was the same. It became easier to find more and more information because it was possible to produce more and more books at less cost. Essentially, printing was a labor-saving device, releasing the calligrapher and the others involved with the laborious efforts of preparing hand-copied books for other pursuits, including, of course, printing.

[24]Paul Zurkowski, "Information and the Economy," *Library Journal*, September 15, 1979, p. 1804. Nuclear power and safety is a major concern, and where there is concern publishers are not far behind; e.g., in early 1980 *The New York Times Information Bank* offered (at $99) an annotated bibliography on the subject taken from a search of their machine-readable files.

[25]Jeff Pemberton, "The Inverted File," *Online*, April 1980, pp. 6–7. Here the editor considers the proper spelling, meaning, and usage of basic terms employed, e.g., vendor (vender), database, CRT, search analyst. He suggests much more descriptive terms than commonly used. However, the commonly employed terms are used in this text.

Modern technology has produced a similar result. Potentially, the information (although not the knowledge and common sense) of the world may be viewed on a television screen in the library or the home. Given a terminal and an acoustic coupler, hundreds of indexes and abstracts are at the service of the librarian. It does require certain new skills to find citations and abstracts in a system where they are stored away on a disk or a magnetic tape rather than on a printed page, but the end result may be similar to scanning a printed volume.

Although the results are basically the same, in many ways procedures are different. It is the purpose of this section to point up the differences as much as the similarities.

Terminology

There are several terms commonly used in speaking of computer-aided reference service in the library.

Online (sometimes hyphenated as "on-line") simply means that the librarian is directly in communication with the computer, just as one would be when talking to someone on the telephone. One may talk directly to the computer, put questions, ask for answers, make corrections, and so on.

An *offline* search is somewhat analogous to talking to a telephone answering service, rather than directly to the person. It means that the material needed is printed offline, usually outside the library. The offline printout is often preferable because, until recently, it has always been less expensive. High-speed terminals can be expected to make online printing more convenient and cheaper in the near future. Another phrase connected with offline printouts is batch mode. In this mode, "individual search requests are accumulated as they come into the computer center. Then on some regular schedule, all the searches in the batch are queued and processed simultaneously in a single pass through the computer."[26]

Data base (sometimes spelled "database") is the machine-readable record on which is stored the index, abstract, or card catalog which the computer searches for the librarian. Actually, it is no more than another medium for storing printed material. When a librarian says a data base is being searched, it is equivalent to saying a card catalog is being searched or the librarian is looking for an author, title, or subject in an index or abstracting service.

Data storage may be quite simple, in that is consists of no more

---

[26]Pauline Atherton and Roger W. Christian, *Librarians and Online Service*, White Plains, New York: Knowledge Industry Publications, 1977, p. 3.

than a tape cassette which can be "played" through the system or even a magnetic card (which can hold from 50 to 100 lines of text and is often used in word-processing systems). Most library data storage is on magnetic tape, magnetic disks, or floppy disks. Video disks will become increasingly more important. Microchips and other new forms, from holographic memory to bubble memory, are now accepted.

Types of data bases

Of the several types of data bases, this text is primarily concerned with the bibliographic data base, and more particularly that one devoted to indexing and abstracting services.

A second type of bibliographic data base (discussed in the section on networks in the second volume of the text) is concerned with information on books, serials, and other library materials. Here, in effect, is the national or trade bibliography online and in machine-readable form. Students will see frequent references to this type of database: MARC is an acronymn for machine-readable cataloging, primarily in reference to the Library of Congress catalog. The catalog is made available on tape and is then sent to individual libraries, but more likely to bibliographic utilities such as OCLC, the first of several such utilities which now supply libraries with basic cataloging information online. In addition, OCLC and other such networks provide access to serials and other forms. Possibly more important, the utilities offer a method of eventually bringing reference databases and other services into the library and the individual home.

Advantages of the online search

Practical experience with computer-aided searches indicates certain basic advantages over the manual search as well as some disadvantages. The only absolute certainty in this discussion is that there are times when one type of search is better than the other, but there is no situation in which one type is always better than the other.

Among the most often cited reasons for using the computer in a search are:

(1) *Speed of searching.* A computer-aided search may take only a fraction of the time needed for a manual search, particularly when it is retrospective and requires searching several years of material. Various studies indicate that in general a computer search may be performed in 5 to 10 percent of the time required for a manual search. A considerable amount of time and effort is saved just in not

having to look up the same term in each volume of the printed service. Another reduction in time is made possible by the printing out of the citations, which sidesteps the need to photocopy or laboriously write out the citations.

The combination of convenience and time saved is the greatest benefit for the user. In one study, users were asked to rank the advantages of a computer search. Time saved was ranked highest by 82 percent. The next benefit, introduction to new areas, was ranked highest by only 47 percent of the users.

(2) *Convenience*. A terminal is all that is needed, and one need not go from reference work to reference work, volume to volume, on different floors and in different places in the library. More important, the terminal opens up the resources of countless indexes and abstracting services heretofore too costly for all but the largest of research libraries. Terminals may be located almost anywhere and searchers are not limited to the indexes or abstracts they may find in the library.

One may turn from one index or abstracting service to another by the push of a key. The key (a code number or initials for the desired base) puts 150 to 175 services at the disposal of the librarian who sits before the terminal.

(3) *In-depth searching*. The primary benefit for the librarian is the qualitative advantage of enhanced information-delivery capability. There is a higher level of subject specificity than is possible with most printed indexes. This is so because the user is not limited to assigned subject categories which are often too broad or narrow. Through Boolean connectors and free text searches the online user may considerably narrow or broaden the search as necessary for a given set of documents. And there are other approaches, because almost the whole of a citation online becomes a searchable element. One may search by author, by address, by words in the title, by journal title, by type of article, and by words in the abstract. Also, a document can be retrieved through searches on many different category "tags" in logical combinations, rather than on just one. For example, one may search by such tags as date, language, publication type, and so on. Each tag either expands or limits what may be retrieved.

A related benefit is that new areas (often new subjects and authors) are turned up. Also, the online search is particularly useful for finding difficult bits of information when only minor clues are available. For example, someone may want an article by Smith in the midwestern United States. The user does not know the initials of Smith but does remember that the term "archways" appears in a book or article about sparrows that he wrote. Given one or all of these clues, the search analyst may be able to locate the item by employing multiple coordinates in the search.

(4) *Currency.* Because the printed volumes are usually produced from a modified machine-readable database, the actual database may be ready for delivery weeks or months before the printed version. The elapsed time between indexing and the published index is a constant problem, which can be overcome with the database. For example, *The New York Times Index,* which in printed form is two to three months behind, may be updated daily and weekly online. However, some databases are still quite late compared to their printed counterparts. The actual speed of the printed or the online form depends on the individual publisher and the technology employed, as well as how material is compiled, indexed, and so on.

(5) There are numerous other advantages of online searches which are discussed in the second volume of this text.

Who uses the service?

No one is certain how many librarians are active in computer-assisted reference service, but by the early 1980s a fair estimate would be that from 600 to 700 of the more than 2000 university and college libraries offer such service. This contrasts with probably no more than 100 computer terminals in public libraries. There is no accurate data on school libraries, but the number of online terminals is probably less than in public libraries. At the same time the computer has become a basic reference aid in from 4000 to 5000 government, law, business, industry, and other kinds of special libraries.

Most academic and special library users are (1) specialists in private and public universities and research centers, often faculty; (2) specialists in government agencies and departments; (3) technologists and business people in the private sector; or (4) students, normally at the university graduate level.

Who uses the available public library services?[27] Business people dominate, followed by students, teachers, university administrators, and local government agencies and individuals. A three-year study of computer-search use in four northern California libraries revealed that from 33 to 43 percent was for job- or education-related matters.

[27]James M. Kusack, "On Line Reference Service in Public Libraries," *RQ,* Summer 1979, pp. 331–334. The results of a 1978 survey of 31 large public library systems indicated that only 41.9 percent offered one or more online reference services.

As Kusack observes, "The use of online reference services by public employees can be a public relations bonanza for libraries willing and able to develop this clientele. A constructive image can be built or reinforced with the members of the public that most influence the future of the library.[28]

It is likely that public demand, lower costs, and librarian acceptance will result in much greater use of computer searches in public libraries as well as in academic, school, and special libraries in the next 4 to 5 years.

Few now question the prevailing and spectacular development of online services in libraries. Developments have become so rapid that within the next 5 to 10 years the services will be a regular feature of all reference service. There are numerous questions and problems to be answered and solved, not the least of which include: (1) Who is to pay for the service, particularly when library budgets are being cut? (2) Will the library maintain free services, or charge for those services? (3) Will the library be squeezed out by private information services?

Anita Schiller sums it up: "As the new technology is applied . . . new tensions in the information economy may emerge."[29] It is with those tensions that every reference librarian will be concerned.

SUGGESTED READING

Childers, Thomas, "The Future of Reference and Information Service in the Public Library," *The Library Quarterly*, October 1978, pp. 463–475. An expert on public libraries believes that future patterns will be shaped more by local than national guidelines and that while there are dreams of superior service, reference work is likely to pretty much maintain its present, possibly disastrous, course.

Davinson, Donald, *Reference Services*. London: Clive Bingley, 1980. While written for an English audience, the author's overview of current problems and activities in reference service is one of the best now available. The fine style is matched by the objective, wide net. It serves as a realistic introduction to the profession and is highly recommended for both beginners and teachers.

Garfield, Eugene, "Online and Print Information Services are Not Always Equivalent for All Users," *Database*, September 1980, pp. 4–6. The publisher of several citation indexes makes a clear case for times when the printed version is better than the online version of a service.

Hinckley, Ann T., "The Reference Librarian," *College and Research Libraries News*, March 1980. The head of the reference department at the University of

---

[28]Kusack, op. cit. p. 333.

[29]Anita Schiller, "Shifting Boundaries in Information," *Library Journal*, April 1, 1981, p. 709.

California, Los Angeles, spells out what is required to be a reference librarian in practice, not in theory. One of the best introductions to the profession for the beginner.

"Information in America," *Library Journal,* September 15, 1979. The entire issue is devoted to the subject and offers a good overview of what to expect in the 1980s. See, too, *The Reference Librarian,* No. 1, 1981 for another version of what the 1980s hold for reference librarians, and *An Information Agenda for the 1980s* (Chicago: American Library Association, 1981).

Josey, E. J. (ed.), *The Information Society: Issues and Answers.* Phoenix: Oryx Press, 1978. A collection of papers on various social issues which are now confronting libraries, particularly in terms of computer technology.

Mancall, Jacqueline, and M. C. Drott, "Materials Used by High School Students in Preparing Independent Study Projects: A Bibliometric Approach." *Library Research,* vol. 1, 1979, pp. 223–236. A look at the needs expressed by high school students when confronting a question. Useful indication of the types of materials they are inclined to request.

McInnis, Raymond, *New Perspectives for Reference Service in Academic Libraries.* Westport, Connecticut: Greenwood Press, 1978. A discussion of how the reference librarian may best educate the public in the use of the library, primarily in the social sciences. Along the way the author offers insight into daily reference work and reference sources.

"1985: New Technology for Libraries," *Library Journal,* July 1980, pp. 1473–1478. A half-dozen information company executives guess at what technologic al innovations will change libraries over the next few years. Most focus on the development of online reference services.

Oklahoma Librarian, January 1980. Almost the entire issue is given over to what some outstanding people see as the future of the library and, of course, reference and information services.

Rettig, James, "A Theoretical Model and Definition of the Reference Process," *RQ,* Fall 1978, pp. 19–29. A well-written, easy-to-understand summary of reference theory today and the need for such a theory. Rettig gives excellent daily examples.

Rosenblum, Joseph, "Reference Service in Academia—Quo Vadis?" *Journal of Academic Librarianship,* no. 3, 1980, pp. 151–153. An attack on the theory that reference service is communication. The author calls for a return to basics.

Wagers, Robert, "Reference and Information Service: The Inner Game," *Wilson Library Bulletin,* May 1980, pp. 561–567. A practical, clear analysis of what goes on at the reference desk and the use of consciousness-altering techniques to help the librarian. See also the author's "American Reference Theory and the Information Dogma," *The Journal of Library History,* Summer 1978, pp. 265–281. A summary of the history of reference theory with some fine suggestions on how to give substance to current discussions of what reference work is about.

Webber, N. A. "Testing the Specialist Reference Work: A Case Study," *Library Review,* Winter 1980, pp. 265–270. A careful evaluation of a reference source (*Jane's All the World's Aircraft*) and (a) the need to question standard reviews which tend to gloss over errors and (b) the need for individual study of reference works in depth by reference librarians.

INFORMATION: CONTROL AND ACCESS

CHAPTER TWO

Bibliographies: Introduction and Selection of Reference Works

BIBLIOGRAPHY is one of the most common terms used by reference librarians. As a listing of data and documents, a bibliography is the primary tool in the three-step service of the reference librarian. Given a good bibliography the librarian is able to (1) identify what someone requests by title, by author, or by subject (common questions answered this way: What do you have by Kurt Vonnegut? Do you have the novel *Eyes and Nose Together*? Where can I find a book on small rockets?); (2) locate the items either in the library or in another library by using the card catalog or a catalog which shows the holdings of other libraries; (3) deliver the items to the user.

In a broader sense, the bibliography brings order out of chaos. The frightening thing about many libraries is that there appears to be too much of everything. How can one person even imagine the contents of a small portion of this mass of information, delight, and frustration? A partial answer to the query, as well as a method of at least controlling the fear of abundance, is the bibliography.

There are numerous definitions of bibliography, but no single definition is suitable for all situations. For most people, it is a list of books, but for experts it has a different meaning—the critical and historical study of printed books. In France, particularly during the late eighteenth century, the term emerged as a form of library science, i.e., the knowledge and the theory of book lists. The Americans and English now tend to divide it into critical, analytical, and historical, as differentiated from a simple listing. The central problem of definition is not likely to be solved, but for most purposes it is enough to say that when Americans are talking about bibliography they are concerned with the study of books, and lists of books or other materials.

Often the list of items is arranged by author, title, and subject— or a combination of all three.

The best-known bibliography in a library is the card catalog. It fits the definition of a bibliography in that it is a list of holdings of the library arranged by author, title, and subject. This particular type of bibliography helps to identify and locate books. On a broader scale the same thing is done by *Books in Print,* which identifies what is available from American publishers.

A bibliography is a complex structure of lists which extends from the local library to the region, nation, and world. A bibliography records not only what is available but what has been available in the past and what will be available in the immediate future.

Estimates of the number of bibliographies vary (particularly if indexes and abstracts are included). A rough estimate of a working collection of bibliographies might be about 10,000 titles, at least in a large university or research collection.[1] Most follow definite patterns of organization, scope, and structure, although it is simplistic to think that bibliographies can be reduced to a series of basic patterns. Their coverage is too wide, particularly when one embarks upon certain subject fields and strives for a unifying principle. Still, general types of bibliographies can at least be indicated, and that is what is attempted in this and the following chapter.

SYSTEMATIC ENUMERATIVE BIBLIOGRAPHY

The average librarian, when speaking of bibliography, is probably referring to systematic enumerative bibliography, i.e., a list of books, films, or recordings. If a bibliography is adequately to meet the need for control and access, several elements are required.

Completeness Through either a single bibliography or a combination of bibliographies, the librarian should have access to the

---

[1]Don Swanson, "Libraries and the Growth of Knowledge," *The Library Quarterly,* January 1979, p. 17. Swanson uses the figure 10,000, although other estimates place the figure at from 20,000 to 55,000.

complete records of all areas of interest; not only what is now available but also what has been published in the past and what is being published today or is proposed for publication tomorrow. Also, the net should be broad enough to include the world, not only one nation's works.

Access to a Part Normally the librarian is apt to think of bibliographies in terms of the whole unit—book, periodical, manuscript, or the like; but an ideal bibliography should also be analytical, allowing the librarian to approach the specific unit in terms of the smallest part of a work.

Various Forms Books are considered the main element of most bibliographies, but a comprehensive bibliographical tool will include all forms of published communication from reports and documents to phonograph records and databases.

These three elements are usually referred to as parts of bibliographical control or organization, that is, of effective access to sources of information. No bibliography or set of bibliographies has yet met all these needs. At best, a bibliography is a compromise between completeness, access to parts, and various forms.

With the bibliography ready at hand, how does the librarian use it on a day-to-day basis? Regardless of form, a bibliography is used primarily for three basic purposes: (1) to identify and verify, (2) to locate, and (3) to select.

Identification and Verification The usual bibliography gives standard information similar to that found on most catalog cards: author, title, edition (if other than a first edition), place of publication, publisher, date of publication, a collation (i.e., number of pages, illustrations, size), and price. Another element added to many bibliographies is the International Standard Book Number, abbreviated as ISBN or simply SBN, which is employed by publishers to distinguish one title from another. The ISBN number usually is on the verso of the title page. A similar system, the International Standard Serial Number (ISSN) is employed to identify serials. In seeking to identify or verify any of these elements, a librarian will turn to the proper bibliography, usually beginning with the general, such as *Books in Print* or *The National Union Catalog,* and moving to the particular, such as a bibliography in a narrow subject area.

Location Location may be in terms of where the book is published, where it can be found in a library, or where it can be purchased. However, from the point of view of the patron's needs, the location is more apt to be in terms of subject. What is available in this subject area, in a book, periodical, article, report, or some other form of communication?

Selection The primary aim of a library is to build a useful collection to serve users. This objective presupposes selection from a vast number of possibilities. In order to assist the librarian, certain bibliographies indicate what is available in a given subject area, by a given author, in a given form, or for certain groups of readers. A bibliography may give an estimate of the value of the particular work for a certain type of reader.

Forms of systematic enumerative bibliography: Universal bibliography

A true universal bibliography would include everything published, issued, or pressed in the field of communications from the beginning through the present to the future. Such universality is now an impossible dream. In practice, the term is employed in a narrower sense. It generally means a bibliography that is not necessarily limited by time, territory, language, subject, or form. National library catalogs, some book dealers' catalogs, and auction catalogs are the nearest thing to a universal bibliography now available.

Forms of systematic enumerative bibliography: National and trade bibliographies[2]

These kinds of works are limited to materials published within a given country. They may be limited in scope to a section of the country, a city, or even a hamlet. For ease of use and convenience, national bibliographies normally are divided into even finer parts.

Time This is a matter of listing works previously published, works being published, or works to be published. Such bibliographies are normally labeled as either retrospective or current.

Form This classification may be in terms of bibliographical form: collections of works, monographs, components (e.g., essays,

[2]The term "trade" bibliography is often used as synonymous with "national." Trade bibliography refers to a bibliography issued for and usually by the booksellers and publishers of a particular nation. The emphasis of a trade bibliography is on basic purchasing data. A national bibliography includes basic data plus much other information used primarily by bibliographers.

periodical articles, poems); physical form: books, recordings, pamphlets, microfilm; or published and unpublished works (manuscripts, dissertations).

A typical national bibliography will set itself limits of time; form; and, obviously, origin. For example, *Books in Print* is limited to books available for purchase (time); it includes only printed books, both hardbound and paperback, and some monographs and series (form); and it is a trade bibliography, i.e., issued by a commercial organization (origin).

There is no limit to the possible subdivisions of national bibliography. For example, within the overall area appear bibliographies (works by and about a given author) and anonym and pseudonym listings. Other sieves continue to be devised as needed.

Subject bibliography

The universal and the national bibliographies are the base for any subject bibliography. While the two major forms tend to be used almost exclusively by generalists such as the book dealer, the librarian, and the publisher, the subject bibliography is intended for the research worker and for others in special areas.

Once a subject is chosen, the sieves common to national bibliographies may be employed—time, form, origin, and others. However, unlike most national bibliographies, a subject work may use all the sieves. For example, a definitive bibliography on railroad engines may be retrospective, current (at least at date of publishing), inclusive of all forms from individual monographs to government publications, and reflective of various sources or origins.

Guides to reference materials

Theoretically, lists which include the "best" works for a given situation or audience are not bibliographies in the accepted definition of the term. In practice, however, they are normally so considered. They include guides to reference books, special reading lists issued by a library, and books devoted to the "best" works for children, adults, students, business people, and others.

Bibliography of bibliographies

There are a few of this type of bibliography, but they guide the user to other helpful bibliographies, normally by subject, by place, or by individual.

This description of five types of bibliography does not exhaust the innumerable possibilities for methods of organizing and describing bibliographies. It barely touches on the various combinations. There is no universally accepted method of even approaching parts and divisions of a bibliography. The problem is to bring order out of this chaotic, primarily free-wheeling approach to listing materials.

Analytical and textual bibliography

Analytical bibliography is concerned with the physical description of the book. Textual bibliography goes a step further and highlights certain textual variations between a manuscript and the printed book or between various editions. Often the two are combined into one scientific or art form. This type of research is designed to discover everything possible about the author's ultimate intentions. The goal is to recover the exact words that the author intended to constitute his or her work. In driving toward this goal, one group of bibliographers may be experts, for example, in nineteenth-century printing practices and bookbinding, another group in paper watermarks or title pages.

There are differences between analytical and textual bibliographies—the most basic being that analytical bibliography is more concerned with the physical aspects of the book, and textual bibliography with the author's words, i.e., the exact text as the author meant it to appear in printed form.[3]

Daily use

Returning to the standard enumerative bibliography, how is this form used in a library? Normally it directs the individual to an item, and it is employed primarily to find X book or Y article. There are two basic approaches for looking in the bibliography for X or for Y.

Most people (as high as 70 percent in some surveys) look up X or Y by its title or by the author's name. If, for example, Tom Smith wants a book on automobiles, he is likely to approach the card catalog, a periodical index, or a librarian with the name or the title of the book.

About 50 percent of the searches of bibliographies in a library is by subject. Here, Mr. Smith does not know the author or the title but turns to a subject heading to help him find what is needed.

The more sophisticated, the more knowledgeable a person is in

[3]G. Thomas Tanselle, "The State of Bibliography Today," *The Papers of the Bibliographical Society of America*, no. 3, 1979, pp. 289–304. After a brief description of published bibliographies, the author launches into a discussion, an explanation and a justification of analytical bibliography.

any field (whether it be automobiles or psychology), the more likely the individual is to try to search a bibliography by author or by title.[4] This is not only more precise but much easier, because one does not have to guess the subject headings in the bibliography. For example, is automobile under automobiles or cars or transportation or (you fill in your own guess)? The most complex search is a subject search.

GUIDES TO REFERENCE BOOKS

The basic purpose of a bibliographical guide to reference material is to introduce the user to (1) general reference sources which will be of assistance in research in all fields and (2) specific reference sources which will help in research in particular fields. These guides take a number of forms, but primarily are either (1) annotated lists of titles with brief introductory remarks before each section or chapter or (2) handbooks which not only list and annotate basic sources, but also introduce the user to tools of investigative study by a discursive, almost textbooklike, approach. There are numerous subclassifications and types of guides.

Another type of guide is more didactic and is usually limited to a broad or even a narrow subject or area, e.g., *The Literature of Political Science* (broad) or *How to Find Out in Iron and Steel* (narrow). Like the general guides, these guides give an overview of the subject, but they go a step further and consider the core of highly specialized publications which probably are not listed in the more familiar general guides. In addition, they may list textbooks, journals, newspapers, societies, libraries, subject experts, recordings, films—in fact, just about anything which is applicable to an understanding of research and reference in the given field.

The singular contribution of the better subject guides is not so much a rote listing of materials as a discursive discussion of (1) the field as a whole; (2) peculiarities of research (and reference) in the discipline; (3) the place of the subject in the mainstream of knowledge; and (4) various forms which are especially applicable for work in the field, i.e., everything from specialized abstract services to patent guides to sources of unpublished research reports.

There are several publications that can be extremely helpful in the selection and use of reference books. The most valuable are the following:

[4]Ruth Hafter, "Types of Search by Type of Library," *Information Processing and Management*, no. 5, 1979, pp. 261–264. The author is drawing on numerous user studies, which she lists in her article.

Sheehy, Eugene P. *Guide to Reference Books,* 9th ed. Chicago: American Library Association, 1976, 1050 pp., $30. *Supplement,* 1980, 315 pp., $15.

Walford, Albert John. *Guide to Reference Materials,* 4th ed. London: The Library Association, 1980—in progress. 3 vols. $55 each. (Distributed in the United States by American Library Association, Chicago.)

Wynar, Bohdan. *American Reference Books Annual.* Littleton, Colorado: Libraries Unlimited, Inc., 1970 to date, annual. $45.

Ryder, Dorothy E. *Canadian Reference Sources: A Selective Guide.* Ottawa: Canadian Library Association, 1973; 185 pp. *Supplement,* 1975, 121 pp. $10; paper $7.

The two basic guides which tell a reference librarian what reference books are basic in all fields are those by Sheehy and Walford. Most librarians refer to them as "Sheehy" and "Walford." (Prior to Sheehy's ninth edition of *Guide to Reference Books,* the work was compiled by Constance Winchell. Many librarians still refer to the guide as "Winchell.")

The guides list and annotate the major titles used in reference service. Sheehy includes some 10,000 entries, Walford about 14,000. Complete bibliographical information is given for each entry, and most of the entries are annotated.

Numbers are an ambiguous criterion of evaluation. For example, Walford points out in the first volume of his 4th edition that there are "about 5,000 items, of which over 1,000 are subsumed," i.e., are part of one of the 4,000 major entries. Here, the count is of no major importance, but when counting words in a dictionary, the use of major and subsumed words as separate entries can run up the count considerably. Their arrangements differ. Sheehy has five main sections in a single volume. Walford, using the Universal Decimal Classification System, divides his work into three separate volumes: science and technology; social sciences; and generalities, languages, the arts, and literature.

Both works begin with a large subject and then subdivide by smaller subjects and by forms. For example, Sheehy has a section on economics under the social sciences. This is subdivided by forms: guides, bibliographies, periodicals, dissertations, indexes and abstract journals, dictionaries and encyclopedias, atlases, handbooks, and so on. The economics section is later broken down into smaller subjects and often, within the subject, a further division is made by country, as, for example, in political science. Walford subdivides economics by bibliographies, thesauruses, encyclopedias and dictionaries, dissertations, and so on, generally following the Sheehy pattern. In practice, the arrangement is not really important. Each volume has an excellent title, author, and subject index.

Sheehy concentrates on American, Canadian, and English titles, and Walford is stronger on English and European titles. In the second volume of Walford, about 13 percent of the listings are from American publishers, 31 percent from Great Britain, and over 50 percent from European and Commonwealth nations.

The problem with Sheehy is currency. The ninth edition, issued in late 1976, includes titles published only until the end of 1973, with a small number of 1974 entries. The guide was almost three years in arrears when published. Supplements are issued about every four years but also have a history of being behind; e.g., the 1980 supplement "focuses on works published between Fall 1974 and Fall 1978 . . . with items added in some sections as late as December 1978, but October of last year represents a more realistic cutoff date." Walford is much more current, and usually no more than 12 to 18 months separates a new edition from current titles. The complete three-volume revision is carried out over six years, and then begins again.[5]

A partial answer to the time-lapse problems of Sheehy and Walford is offered by the *American Reference Books Annual* (usually cited as *ARBA*). It differs from both Sheehy and Walford in three important respects: (1) It is limited to reference titles published or distributed in the United States; (2) it is comprehensive for a given year and makes no effort to be selective; (3) the annotations are written by more than 350 subject experts and are both more critical and more expository than those found in Sheehy or Walford. Depending on the extent of American publishing, the annual volume usually available in March or April of the year following the year covered in text analyzes some 1600 to 1800 separate reference titles. (Since its inception, the service has examined 18,813 reference sources.) The work is well-organized and indexed. A useful feature is that references are made to reviews published in periodicals such as *Library Journal, Choice,* and *Wilson Library Bulletin.* The librarian may easily compare the opinion of the subject expert found in *ARBA* with that of a reviewer elsewhere.

Every five years the publisher issues a cumulative index to the set; e.g., *Index to American Reference Books Annual, 1975–1979* was issued in mid-1979. This provides access to reviews of close to 8400

---

[5]Of some limited help in the updating of *Guide to Reference Books* is the biannual listing by Eugene P. Sheehy in *College and Research Libraries,* i.e., "Selected Reference Books of 1981–1982." The annotated listings usually appear in the July and January issues.

titles and is of considerable help in locating a work not to be found in Sheehy or Walford. Conversely, *ARBA* suffers from a limitation—it reviews only what is sent by publishers. If the publisher does not send the reference work, there usually is no review. This is particularly true of some expensive sets—the sets most librarians would welcome additional commentary about.

Data bases are not considered in *ARBA* either, but this is hardly exceptional. While the *Supplement* to Sheehy does have a section on the subject by Martha Williams, it is too limited (only six pages) to be of real value. True, there are separate guides to data bases (and they are considered in the second volume of this text), but the time has come when the data base should no longer be omitted from selection guides.

Guides for smaller libraries

There are scores of listings, guides, and catalogs of reference works which are either smaller, larger, or more specialized than Sheehy or Walford. But two are the most often used in smaller libraries:

> *Reference Books for Small and Medium-Sized Libraries.* 3d ed. Chicago: American Library Association, 1979, 214 pp. This is compiled by an American Library Association committee and lists and annotates, by broad subject areas, 1046 titles. There is a good title and author index with a detailed table of contents for subjects. The annotations are well-written, and the selection of titles represents a careful judgment of what is most useful for the small or medium library. Before each section the compilers add a few words of explanation and description of the subject.
> *Reference Books: A Brief Guide.* 8th ed. Baltimore: Enoch Pratt Free Library, 1978, 180 pp. While this lists and annotates about one-half the number of titles found in the ALA guide, it remains one of the oldest, most reliable sources for information on basic reference titles for small to medium-sized collections. It has been published for a great number of years and has established itself as *the* guide in the field. It is under $3, and the fine, descriptive annotations give it a certain intellectual touch.

CURRENT SELECTION AIDS

Librarians who want to build collections in given subjects need only consult their preferred guides for basic titles. Beyond that, they run into the problem of currency. The ninth edition of *Guide to Reference Books Supplement* has a cutoff date of late 1978, and the *American*

Reference Books Annual is of limited help for a title issued between publication of the annual volumes. The reference librarian with an interest in current titles must study reviews in periodicals. Most of the periodicals to be discussed review books ranging from fiction to technical publications.

The selection of reference sources is a highly individualized process. The character and the distribution of the elements which constitute the needs of users differ from library to library. Consequently, the first and most important rule when considering the selection of reference materials, or anything else for the library, is to recognize the needs, both known and anticipated, of the users.

How is a satisfactory selection policy arrived at? First and foremost, there must be a librarian who has some subject competence; that is, one who knows the basic literature of a field, or several fields, including not only the reference works but also the philosophy, jargon, ideas, ideals, and problems that make up that field. There is no substitute for substantive knowledge. Second, the librarian must be aware in some depth of the type of writing and publishing done in that special field. Where is there likely to be the best review? Who are the outstanding authors, publishers, and editors in this field? What can and cannot be answered readily?

Selection is charted, rather than dictated, by the following:

1. Knowing as much as possible about the needs of those who use the reference collection.
2. Calling upon expert advice. In a school situation the expert may be the teacher who is knowledgeable in a certain area. In a public library it may be the layperson, skilled practitioner, or subject specialist who uses the library. Most people are flattered by a request that draws upon their experience and knowledge, and one of the best resources for wise selection of reference materials is the informed user.
3. Keeping a record of questions. This is done to determine not only what materials the library has but what it does not have. Most important, a record of *unanswered* queries will often be the basis for an evaluation of the reference collection.
4. Knowing what other libraries have, and what resources are available. For example, the small library contemplating the purchase of an expensive run of periodicals or a bibliography would certainly first check to see whether the same materials may be readily available in a nearby library.

These four points only begin to suggest the complexity of selection. Many libraries have detailed selection policy statements which consider the necessary administrative steps only hinted at here.

Once a title has been determined for purchase, the material is normally ordered through the regular channels. In large libraries, the process consists of turning over the order with full bibliographical citation to the acquisitions department. In smaller libraries, the reference librarian (who also may be the head librarian and the only professional on the staff) may go through the whole ordering process singlehandedly.

Reference book reviews

Library Journal. New York: R. R. Bowker Company, 1876 to date, semimonthly. $27.

Choice. Chicago: American Library Association, 1964 to date, monthly. $40.

RQ. Chicago: American Library Association, 1960 to date, quarterly. $15.

The Booklist. Chicago: American Library Association, 1905 to date, semimonthly. $32.

Wilson Library Bulletin. New York: The H. W. Wilson Company, 1914 to date, monthly. $17.

Reference Services Review. Ann Arbor, Michigan: Pierian Press, 1972 to date, quarterly. $25.

The most exhaustive essay-reviews appear in *The Booklist* in "Reference and Subscription Books Reviews," a separate section at the back of each issue of *The Booklist*.[6] Prepared by a committee of librarians and teachers, the reviews are detailed and highly critical, primarily of subscription reference works—in this case encyclopedias, dictionaries, atlases, and major bibliographies and guides.

The editor briefly explains the scope of the reviews: "We give first consideration to general encyclopedias, other information tools of wide scope . . . and bibliographical tools of wide scope."[7]

There are usually two to four long reviews followed by a dozen

---

[6]The reviews are now compiled annually (previously they were compiled every two years) and published in a separate paperback by the American Library Association. As the reviews are extensively used in evaluating expensive encyclopedias, atlases, etc., they should be purchased in the compilation form for the permanent reference collection. (Although "Reference and Subscription Books Reviews" is a physical part of *The Booklist*, it is a separate entity administratively. Formerly two separate magazines, they were combined in 1956. *The Booklist* is a general review medium for all types of books and has nothing to do with the reference reviews.)

[7]Robert M. Pierson, "Letter to Our Readers," *The Booklist*, September 15, 1979, p. 58. (See also a one-page profile of the group by Pierson in *American Libraries*, January 1980, p. 32.) This is a good short summary of the philosophy which governs the "Reference and Subscription Books Reviews."

or more shorter notices. (In a year, i.e., September 1 to July 15, there will be an average of 100 long reviews and about 250 shorter ones.) The lengthy criticism is reserved for multivolume sets, controversial works, or those of exceptionally high cost. The shorter reviews are for more conventional, less expensive titles from almanacs to handbooks and directories. Selection is based on the widest possible use of a book by school and public libraries. Titles of interest only to college and university or special libraries rarely are reviewed.

The editor makes another important point applicable to most types of review. Just because a title is not reviewed does not mean it is not worthy of consideration. Lack of a review is not to be taken as a minus sign. "Our decision to evaluate or not evaluate a particular work does not imply our opinion as to its merit."[8] Still, certain choices are questionable as are nonchoices—a situation applicable to almost all review services.

The primary criticism of the "Reference and Subscription Books Reviews" is the lack of currency. It is not unusual to have a review appear 10 months to even 3 years after the title was published. Almost all reviews in other media are late, but the average time lapse between date of publication of a book and the review is normally no more than a few weeks or months.

The "Reference and Subscription Books Reviews" are now the best available, but there are others equally reliable although not as detailed.

Other current sources are:[9]

1. *Choice.* While specifically geared to college libraries, the professional journal evaluates a number of reference titles of value to all libraries. The reference books lead off the main section of general reviews. Also, from time to time bibliographical essays in the front of the magazine highlight reference titles. There are approximately 6000 reviews a year, of which about 500 are of reference books. The reviews

---

[8]Ibid.

[9]There are too few studies of reference books reviews. One of the most thorough, although dated, is Alma A. Covey, *Reviewing of Reference Books* (Metuchen, New Jersey: Scarecrow Press, 1972). A more recent survey, along with a method of evaluating reviews is suggested by Daniel Ream, "An Evaluation of Four Book Review Journals" *RQ,* Winter 1979, pp. 149–158. I am grateful to a former student, Edward Wirth, for a check of the Covey findings in an unpublished paper he completed for a seminar in December 1978. Much of the data in this section is drawn from Mr. Wirth's paper, "An Evaluation of Reference Book Reviews." See also the detailed and controversial annotations of not only the reviews but the magazines in which they appear in the *Serials Review.* no. 3, 1979, pp. 4–49. This includes many other library periodicals which carry reference reviews.

are usually 120 to 500 words in length and are not signed. Almost all reviewers make an effort to compare the title under review with previously published titles in the same subject area, a feature which is particularly useful but rarely found in the other reviews. When budgets are tight, when choices must be made, it is of considerable importance that comparisons are available. Apparently this has not been brought to the attention of most review editors.

2. *Library Journal.* Again, the general book review section leads off with "Reference." (To be more precise, it follows "The Contemporary Scene" section.) There are about 450 reference reviews each year. These are 100 to 150 words long, usually written by librarians or teachers, and all are signed. Approximately the same number of reviews appear annually in *Library Journal*(LJ) as in *Choice.* Also, *School Library Journal* includes reviews of reference titles.

3. *RQ.* The last section of this quarterly is given over entirely to the review of reference books. A few other related titles are considered, but, unlike *Library Journal* and *Choice, RQ* makes no effort to review general books. About 140 to 150 reference titles are considered each year. Reviews average about 200 words each.

4. *Wilson Library Bulletin.* One section is devoted to "Current Reference Books," and all the reviews are written by the section editor, Charles Bunge. (In mid-1981 a new editor was appointed who may or may not continue to write all the reviews.) Some 20 to 30 titles are noted in each issue. The reviews are usually about 75 to 100 words long. Many consider these some of the best reviews available, because they are consistent; timely; and, possibly more important, the work of an individual with considerable experience in the field.

5. *Reference Services Review.* This quarterly, edited by Nancy Jean Melin, offers a discursive study of reference books in particular and subject areas in general. Numbers vary, but about 300 titles are considered each year. The columns, bibliographies, and news notes are written by experts, most of whom have writing styles as good as their knowledge of their fields. Coverage includes government documents, indexes, reference serials, data bases, "landmarks of reference," etc. The service is particularly valuable on two counts: (1) Each issue features "comparative reviews" where similar reference works are critically compared, and (2) there are also several

subject categories which include both current and retrospective titles.

The limited number of reviews in the five services just considered explains the high percentage of favorable comments in the journals. As the editor and reviewer are forced to limit the number of books considered, the very process eliminates questionable titles. It is not that the reviewers look kindly on all reference books, but that the really bad ones have been eliminated before the reviewer sits down to consider an evaluation. Favorable reviews range from 66 percent (*RQ*) to 74 percent ("Reference and Subscription Book Reviews"). Put another way, and discounting the so-called mixed reviews which fail to take a stand, *Library Journal* had the highest percentage of "unfavorable" recommendations (10 percent) as compared with an average of 6 to 8 percent for the other services.

> *There is no single tool, nor a combination of tools in existence today, that enables the conscientious reference librarian systematically and efficiently to select the best reference books for her or his particular library. . . . In view of the continuing importance of reference books, there should be further and periodic study of the media that review them.*[10]

Covey's assumption is based on the magazines mentioned here (plus the *School Library Journal*), and she may be right. Calling for further study seems relatively pointless, however. The fact remains that there is no single, totally satisfactory source of reference book reviews any more than there is a single satisfactory source of trade book reviews. And this condition will continue until all librarians begin to act and think alike. There is, certainly, a variety of review media, and if they do not cover all reference titles, perhaps it is just as well that a few be lost. If not all the reviews are as scholarly or as critical as they might be, consider that the reviewers are librarians and teachers, not omniscient statisticians. Finally, in any evaluation of the review, the choice must be made by the librarian, not a reviewer.

INDEXES TO REVIEWS[11]

Reference Sources. Ann Arbor, Michigan: Pierian Press, 1977 to date, annual. $65.

[10]Covey, op. cit., pp. 129, 130.

[11]Floria W. Wood, "Reviewing Book Review Indexes," *Reference Services Review,* April/June 1980, pp. 47–52. This is a careful analysis of the basic indexes. The conclusion is that each of the services is really quite different.

Book Review Digest. New York: The H. W. Wilson Company, 1905 to date, monthly, service. *Author/Title Index, 1905–1974,* 4 vols. $270.

Book Review Index. Detroit: Gale Research Company, 1965 to date, bimonthly. $72. (Annual cumulations, $72; 10-year cumulation, 1969–1979, 6 vols., 1980–1981, $450.)

Current Book Review Citations. New York: The H. W. Wilson Company, 1976 to date, monthly (except August). $75.

The one index which is limited solely to listing reviews of reference books is *Reference Sources.* Drawing from about 300 periodicals, the editors arrange the reviews with full bibliographic information for each book. For most of the 4000 or so titles listed, one will find subject tracings and a few words of description, brief entries from the review, or both. The 1980 volume, issued in 1981, dropped the annotations, and adopted an LC subject arrangement. As well as indexing published reviews, the editors' list titles received by the index but not reviewed in any of the analyzed periodicals. This index is useful but has the drawback of appearing only once a year.

For reference questions involving reviews not only of reference titles, but of general trade books, the answer can usually be found in any of the H. W. Wilson indexes, where reviews are listed separately. (For a discussion of these indexes see Chapter 4.)

The *Magazine Index* offers a handy book review listing, differing from those in other indexes in that with each review is a grade from A to F. This began in 1978, and, although limited to opinions in about 370 magazines, it is useful in many ways.

All the titles considered here are considered specialized because their sole purpose is to list reviews. They are used by students and others seeking background material on a given work as well as by the reference librarian on the lookout for notices about specific reference books.

The major indexes in this field—*The Book Review Digest, Book Review Index,* and *Current Book Review Citations*—rely on author or title entries. In addition, the librarian must know the approximate date that the book was published. The fastest method is simply to search *The Book Review Digest Author/Title Index, 1905–1974.* For reviews published after 1974, one needs to go to the annual index volumes or other services. If the date cannot be found in these indexes, the librarian should turn to the card catalog where the title may be entered, or to one of the national or trade bibliographies such as *Books in Print.*

Another approach is to use the *Book Review Index* 10-year cumulation. This covers 960,000 entries from 1969 through 1979. About 455,000 books are cited.

Book Review Index (BRI) and *Current Book Review Citations (CBRC)* are competitive; they frequently index the same periodicals and therefore include references to the same reviews; i.e., both analyze the major sources of reference reviews, including *Library Journal, Choice,* and *The Booklist.*

They differ in that (a) *BRI* analyzes nearly 385 widely read periodicals and *CBRC* analyzes more than 1200 periodicals which are indexed in the various H. W. Wilson indexes. Also, *CBRC* includes reviews from major book-reviewing periodicals not usually indexed by Wilson, for example, *The Booklist, Choice, Kirkus, The New York Times, Library Journal,* and *School Library Journal.* (b) *BRI* has the distinct advantage of ease of use in that it is cumulated three times during the year and annually. *CBRC* has only an annual cumulation, which means each issue must be searched—a nuisance. With the publication of a 10-year cumulation in 1980–1981, *BRI* has an added advantage in ease of use. The six-volume set contrasts with the only-annual cumulations and the consequent volume-by-volume search, of the *CBRC.* (c) *BRI's* second advantage is currency: review citations frequently appear here faster than in *CBRC.* (d) *CBRC* has the edge of indexing more titles, and listing names of reviewers, a feature not found in *BRI.*

The Book Review Digest (BRD) lists about 6000 titles a year. It is not only an index of book reviews, but has the added feature of including two or three excerpts from reviews for each book as well as a short descriptive note. Hence the user often does not have to consult the reviews but can make judgments about a title by merely reading *BRD.* Found in almost every library, the *BRD,* going back to 1905, often serves the scholar as an invaluable key to contemporary reviews.

The catch is in the limitations exercised by the *BRD.* It analyzes only 83 periodicals, and even more unfortunately, it includes reviews of nonfiction only when there have been a minimum of two reviews and of fiction only when four or more reviews have appeared. The result is that the BRD is a bastion of conservatism and is about the last place anyone might hope to find a review of a book by a beginning author. Therefore, for most purposes it is best first to check out the *Book Review Index* or the *Current Book Review Citations.*

Book Review Index lists approximately 95,000 reviews for 48,500 titles each year. *Current Book Review Citations* covers about the same number of titles but lists almost twice as many reviews.

WEEDING

Weeding is the process of eliminating certain materials from the reference collection. It is a delicate process. Conceivably any book, pamphlet, magazine, newspaper, or other written material can have reference value, particularly for the historian or anyone else concerned with social mores and records of the past. To discard such a work is little short of destroying the past. For example, one of the most difficult research problems is to locate materials in local newspapers of the nineteenth century.

Anyone who has sought contemporary opinion or a biography of a little-known figure or statistical data knows that there is no limit to the material that may be found in older reference works, certainly in books from both the general and the specific reference collections. Many, such as the early editions of the *Encyclopaedia Britannica*, are now classics, invaluable sources of material found nowhere else.

Given these warnings, there is a need for judicious weeding. Libraries are always short of space, and this is particularly true in the reference section. Weeding clears the shelves of little-used, or sometimes never-used, materials. Actually, few works are discarded in larger libraries. They are sent off to storage. Smaller libraries cannot afford this luxury, and the material normally is systematically removed.

Guidelines for discarding

Each library must establish its own general and specific guidelines for discarding materials. As with acquisitions, each library has its own peculiar needs, its own type of users, which makes it important to weed materials to meet the needs of those users, not the standards established in a text or at another library.

With that word of caution, some general criteria may be suggested.

Currency   Most of the reference books that are used for ready reference have to be up to date. Older ones may be helpful historically, but are of little value for current material.

Reliability   Data and viewpoints change, and the changes must be reflected in the reference collection. Yesterday's reliable explanation of a given event or phenomenon may no longer be applicable.

Use   Needs change from generation to generation, and yesterday's valued reference work may no longer be used by today's reference librarian or the public.

Physical Condition   Some books wear out and must be either discarded or replaced with new editions.

Later Editions   Most popular reference works go into several editions, and it normally is pointless to maintain earlier editions of a standard work. Another linked consideration: duplication of materials. Perhaps a title four or five years ago was unique, but today there are more recent, even better titles in the field. In that case the older title may be discarded.

Language   Sometimes a foreign language work may be discarded because no one is using it. It was purchased at a time when the particular language was important to the library.

To select discards wisely requires:

Thorough Knowledge of the Collection   The librarian should know how it is used and by whom. Should X work be totally eliminated, or should a new edition be purchased, or should a similar work be considered? These are all questions that vary from situation to situation and can be answered only by the librarian working closely with the collection and the public.

Knowledge of Other Resources   An understanding of the collections of regional and national libraries is needed. Is at least one copy of what you propose to discard in a local or national collection for use at some later date? Obviously a much-used work, such as a 10-year-old copy of the *World Almanac,* need not be checked. But any material that is purely local (particularly pamphlets and ephemera) or anything more than 50 years old or any items about which there is any question at all regarding use or value, should first be cleared with the larger libraries in the region. Such an item may appear shabby and of little use, but may prove to be a unique copy.

Older Works Worth Keeping   One should appreciate that age does not necessarily dictate discarding. No worthwhile reference collection lacks, for example, the dated *Encyclopedia of the Social Sciences* or the mass of bibliographies and other guides that were published a number of years ago and are still basic works.

Some general guidelines for reference works may be suggested, but specific rules for discarding depend on use, not on any arbitrary set of rules.

Encyclopedias   Maintain as many older editions as possible, *but* a new edition is needed at least very five years, and preferably every year.

Almanacs, Yearbooks, Manuals   These are usually superseded by the next edition or the succeeding volume. Nevertheless, as the information in each is rarely duplicated exactly (new material is added, old material deleted), it is wise to keep old editions for at least 5 years, preferably 10.

Dictionaries   In a sense, these are never dated and should never be discarded unless replaced by the same editions. An exception might be the abridged desk-type dictionaries. The unabridged works and those devoted to special areas are of constant value.

Biographical Sources   Again, the more of these and the more retrospective the sources, the better. Only in a few select cases should any be discarded.

Directories   Like yearbooks, almanacs, and other such works, these are frequently updated, and the older ones (5 to 10 years) can generally be discarded safely.

Geographical Sources   Inexpensive atlases may be safely discarded after 5 to 10 years. More expansive, expensive works are invaluable. In fact, many gain in both research and monetary value over the years.

Government Documents   Never discard these if they are part of a permanent collection. Discards should be considered where material is used only peripherally for pamphlet files. However, be particularly careful to check local and state materials before discarding.

In the subject areas, it is relatively safe to assume that except for botany and natural history, science books are generally dated within five years. The recurrent yearbooks, manuals, and encyclopedias may be discarded as new editions are obtained. In the humanities, discarding should rarely take place unless the material is quite obviously totally dated and of no historical or research value. In the social sciences, timely or topical materials may be considered for discard after 10 to 15 years.[12]

---

[12]Joseph P. Segal, *Evaluating and Weeding Collections* (Chicago: American Library Association, 1980). A 25-page offset guide for small and medium-sized libraries, the suggestions are applicable for other situations, too.

SUGGESTED READINGS

Blum, Rudolf, *Bibliographia: An Inquiry into its Definition and Designations.* London: Dawson Publishing, 1980. First published in 1969, this is a translation of a basic work in the never-ending history and effort for definition of bibliography.

Brenni, Vito, *The Bibliographic Control of American Literature 1920–1975.* Metuchen, New Jersey: Scarecrow Press, 1979. A survey of national and regional bibliographic control with a focus on literature. Most of the points are as applicable to other forms of bibliography. About half of its 200-plus pages consist of notes.

Colaianne, A. J., "The Aims and Methods of Annotated Bibliography," *Scholarly Publishing,* July 1980, pp. 321–331. An effort to set down the principles of annotated bibliography, from form of citation to organization of entries and useful tips on writing an annotation.

Kister, Kenneth and Sanford Berman, "Right Here in River City: ALA Censorship, and Alternatives," *CALL,* January–February, 1978, pp. 3–5. Two well-known experts in the field of reference charge that the otherwise excellent Reference and Subscription Books Review Committee have been not only critics but censors of competing and alternative commentaries on reference service. See, too, Kister's article "Wanted: More Professionalism in Reference Book Reviewing," *RQ,* Winter 1979, pp. 144–148 for both a general comment on reviewing and specific charges against the References and Subscription Book Reviews Committee. See, too, replies to Kister's argument in the letters section of *RQ,* Summer 1980, pp. 407–410.

Macleod, Beth, "Library Journal and Choice: A Review of Reviews," *The Journal of Academic Librarianship,* March 1981, pp. 23–28. A statistical analysis of both the number of works reviewed and the types of comments and evaluations to be found. While the author is concerned with all types of reviews, much of the data is applicable to the reference book review. Note, too, that the evaluation methods might be applied to other review media.

Walford, A. J., "Compiling the Guide to Reference Material," *Journal of Librarianship,* April 1978, pp. 88–96. The compiler describes the difficulties of and some of the solutions to compiling a major bibliographic guide. A useful article to read in conjunction with a similar look at the problems of the *Guide to Reference Books,* e.g., Art Plotnik, "They Have Created the Ultimate Reference Guide . . ." *American Libraries,* March 1977, pp. 129–132.

CHAPTER THREE

Bibliographies:
National Library Catalogs
and Trade Bibliographies

A FAIRLY COMMON PROBLEM concerns the person who wants to know just how much is available on a given subject, such as eighteenth-century gardens or nuclear-waste dumping facilities. One searches the library and may even tap other resources by computer, the telephone, or reference works, but even the most refined search inevitably ends with the question: Yes, but is that all? Furthermore, is what was found the best available information for the query? We would not have these puzzling questions if we knew everything available had been considered; but this simply is not possible—at least today.

There is no single place a reader can go to find what materials are available from all parts of the world or from the United States or another country. The lack of a universal finding tool, called "universal bibliography," has frustrated librarians for centuries, and while the computer and its ability to store massive amounts of information suggests the technological possibility of listing everything in one gigantic bibliography, the numerous problems associated with the dream of universal control have yet to be solved. Still, the effort continues to fascinate, and inevitably the time will come when UBC (universal bibliographic control) is realized.[1]

[1]This is a recurrent theme of scores of meetings; e.g., the International Federation of Library Associations (IFLA) is deeply involved in the problem, and there are numerous articles on the subject; e.g., J. M. Elrod, "Universal Availability of Bibliographic Records," *IFLA Journal*, no. 4, 1978, pp. 347–350.

Meanwhile, there is a type of coordination—some would say fitting together of different pieces of a puzzle—which allows at least a fairly good overview of what is available from many parts of the world. The procedure is to consult various national library catalogs. This does not work well for bits of information (say in periodicals or reports) or for different forms (from recordings to films), but it is quite sophisticated for specific books. For example, if the reader wants to locate a copy of a 1934 autobiography, *I Remember,* by J. Henry Harper, the search is facilitated by the use of one of a number of national catalogs. One simply turns to the catalog, looks up Harper, Henry, and locates the book as well as a full bibliographical description and probably where it may be found in a number of libraries. The same procedure might be exercised in London, Paris, or communities in any of the numerous Western countries which have national catalogs.

As a national library catalog is not limited by time, territory, language, subject, or forms of communication, it does come close to the ideal universal bibliography. And although none of the national library catalogs claims to be universal in scope, collectively they do offer a relatively comprehensive record of international publishing. The Library of Congress, for example, catalogs materials from around the world, and a good proportion of its holdings are books, magazines, music, and the like from international publishers. Numerically, an idea of the scope of the Library of Congress holdings may be gathered from the fact that the Library contains more than 80 million discrete items and, on the average, adds from 1 to 1.5 million new items each year. More than 5 million authors are represented among the 23 million cards in the Library's complete catalogue. Comparatively speaking, the average number of books published in America each year hovers around 40,000 titles, a small part of the overall annual acquisitions of the Library's net, which sweeps in titles of books as well as other published items from around the world. Quite similar figures apply to the British Library.

UNION CATALOGS

A term associated with national catalogs is "union catalog," for example, the Library of Congress's *National Union Catalog* and *Union List of Serials.* Interlibrary cooperation on local, regional, and international scale makes a union list of particular importance. In fact, wherever two or more libraries band together, there is apt to be a by-product of that cooperation—a union list. The use of the union list and bibliography is considered in Chapter 3, "Interview and Search" in the second volume of this text; but because the term appears through this volume, it is well to define it clearly, if only briefly, at this point.

A union catalog indicates who has what. A fuller, often repeated definition is: an inventory common to several libraries and listing some or all of their publications maintained in one or more orders of arrangement. The user turns to a union list to locate a given book, periodical, or newspaper in another library, which may be in the same city or thousands of miles away. Given the location and the operation of an interlibrary loan or copying process, the user can then have the particular book or item borrowed from the holding library.

When each library in the bibliographical network or bibliographic center knows what fellow members have purchased, a union list can be helpful in acquisitions. Expensive and little-used items, for example, need be purchased by only one or two of the cooperating libraries, because those items are always on call for members.

Some, although not all, of the union lists will give pertinent bibliographical information to help the library trace and identify a given item. When the sole purpose of the union catalog is location, the descriptive entry is normally kept to a minimum, e.g., *New Serial Titles*. However, when it serves numerous other purposes as well (e.g., *The National Union Catalog*), the description will be relatively complete. In most cases, arrangement is alphabetical by title or author.

National library catalogs

U.S. Library of Congress. *The National Union Catalog: A Cumulative Author List*. Washington: Library of Congress, Card Division, 1956 to date. Nine monthly issues and three quarterly cumulations. $1275.
Cumulations, at various prices, from 1956:[2]

1. 1956–1967 Totowa, New Jersey: Rowman & Littlefield, 125 vols.
2. 1968–1972 Ann Arbor, Michigan: Edwards Brothers, Inc., 128 vols.
3. 1973–1977 Totowa, New Jersey. Rowman & Littlefield, approximately 150 vols.

[2]The four quinquenniums, as well as the annual cumulations, are available on microfiche from Advanced Library Systems of Andover, Massachusetts.

4. 1978 to date. Washington: Library of Congress, annual cumulations.

The National Union Catalog: Pre-1956 Imprints. London: Mansell, 1968–1980, 685 vols.; plus 70-vol. supplement, 1980–1982, $35,000. (Note: In mid-1981 Mansell was purchased by the H. W. Wilson Company, who now market the set.)

U.S. Library of Congress. *Library of Congress Catalogs: Subject Catalog* (formerly: *Library of Congress Catalog. Books: Subjects*). Washington: Library of Congress, Card Division, 1950 to date. Three quarterly issues with annual cumulations, $800. Quinquennial cumulations from 1950: 1950–1954, 1955–1959, 1960–1964, 1965–1969, 1970–1974, 1975–1980.

The two ongoing book catalogs of the Library of Congress are essentially no different from the familiar card catalog found in the local library. This is important to recognize. Sometimes the imposing sets which run to many hundreds of volumes confuse the novice.

First, what is the scope of *The National Union Catalog*? One will note that each page photographically reproduces catalog cards—the same familiar cards found in most libraries. Each card represents an item cataloged by the Library of Congress or by one of more than 1100 libraries in the United States and Canada. This feature makes it a union catalog in that it shows the holdings of more than one library.

What is cataloged? Almost every communication medium. In this case, the entries are primarily for books; maps; atlases; pamphlets; and serials, including periodicals. The magazines are listed by title, and only those cataloged by the Library of Congress are included. The various forms are in separate sets; i.e., books in one set, music and recordings in another set, and so on. See the foreword to any issue of *The National Union Catalog* for an explanation of the parts.[3] The following discussion is limited to the basic book sets.

[3]Some parts are discussed in this text. Of primary interest is the fact that there is a separate catalog for music and another for films. The former is *Music, Books on Music and Sound Recording* (1953 to date, semiannual). Until 1973 this represented holdings only of the Library of Congress. Beginning in 1973 it became a union catalog in that several other universities and colleges now report to the system—but nowhere near the number involved in the basic *NUC. Films and Other Materials for Projections* (1953 to date, quarterly) includes films, filmstrips, slides, transparencies, and some video recordings. Both titles have limited subject approaches. Other parts of the *NUC* include: *Monographic Series* (1974 to date, quarterly), *New Serial Titles* (1950 to date, monthly), *The National Register of Microform Masters* (1965 to date, frequency varies), *National Union Catalog of Manuscript Collections* (1959 to date, frequency varies), and *Newspapers in Microform* (1973 to date, frequency varies, but now annual).

How is it arranged and what information is given? The volumes are arranged alphabetically by author or main entry. Generally, the heading of a main entry is an author's name, but lacking such information, it may be a title. It is never both author and title.[4] There is no subject approach in the main *National Union Catalog* and cross-references are minimal. (A subject approach is offered but in another set to be discussed.)

The reproduced card varies in quantity and type of information given, but in almost all cases it includes the typical bibliographical description in this order: full name of author, dates of birth and death; full title; place, publisher, and date; collation (e.g., paging, illustrations, maps); series; edition; notes on contents, history; tracing for subject headings and added entries; the Library of Congress and, usually, the Dewey classifications; and The International Standard Book Numbers.

How is *The National Union Catalog* used in reference work?

1. Since this is a union catalog, showing not only the holdings of the Library of Congress but also titles in over 1100 other libraries, it allows the reference librarian to locate a given title quickly. Hence users who need a work not in their library may find the nearest location in *The National Union Catalog*. For example, the first edition of *I Remember,* by J. Henry Harper, is identified as being in eight other libraries. Location symbols for the eight are: OOxM, TxU, OCU, OCL, MnU, NIC, ViBibV, and WU. The initials stand for libraries in various parts of the country and are explained in the front of cumulative volumes. Depending on the policy of the holding library, the librarian may or may not be able to borrow the title on interlibrary loan. Failing a loan, it may be possible to get sections copied.

2. *The National Union Catalog* amounts to virtually a basic, full author bibliography. Anyone wanting to know everything

---

[4]Search by title may be done by computer online searches of MARC tapes and through other systems such as OCLC—to be discussed later. Also, there is *The Cumulative Title Index to the Classified Collections of the Library of Congress* (Arlington, Virginia: Carrollton Press, 1978, in progress). To be completed in 1982, the 132-volume set is a single-alphabet title approach to the NUC. There will be about 6.5 million titles listed. The author and LC class number and LC card order number is given, so the user may go from the title to the author to the main set or may search the MARC files. Cost of the set, about $12,000. Known as REMARC, it also will be available in machine-readable form and will serve to pick up, in an abbreviated fashion, earlier material not entered in MARC. See pp. 70–71.

(magazine articles and other such items aside) that author X has published has only to consult the author's name under the full *National Union Catalog* set.

3. The full cataloging not only gives details on a book (e.g., when it was published, by whom, and where), but helps the reference librarian to verify that it exists—an important matter when there is a question on whether X actually did publish this or that. Verification, however, is even more important when the reference librarian is attempting to straighten out the misspelling of a title or an author's name. In other words, *The National Union Catalog* sets the record straight when there is doubt about the validity of a given bit of information.

4. In terms of acquisitions, particularly of expensive or rare items, *The National Union Catalog* permits a library to concentrate in subject areas with the assurance that the less-developed areas may be augmented by interlibrary loan from other libraries.

5. In terms of cataloging (which is basic to reference service), *The National Union Catalog* offers a number of advantages (and headaches). The primary asset is central cataloging, which should limit the amount of original cataloging necessary.

6. The sixth advantage of *The National Union Catalog* is as much psychological as real. Its very existence gives the librarian (and more-involved users) a sense of order and control which would otherwise be lacking in a world that cries for some type of order.

The National Union Catalog is primarily an approach by author. What does one do when one wants to find books in a given subject area? The user turns to the *Library of Congress Catalogs: Subject Catalog*. Here *The National Union Catalog* entries are rearranged by subject.[5]

---

[5]Another avenue to subject headings is offered by the *Library of Congress Shelflist Card Catalog*, available on microform. LC class numbers can be looked up in LC class order in the shelflist. The LC class numbers may be found in several sources, although the most exhaustive approach is to use the *Cumulative Subject Index to the MARC Data Base 1968–1978* (Arlington, Virginia: Carrollton Press, 1979 to date, quarterly). This lists subjects, and under each LC subject are countless subdivisions. Both the main heading and the subdivisions include LC class numbers, which may be used against the shelflist. And there are other uses of the set which are beyond the scope of this text.

There is one important catch. The subject approach can be used only for material published since 1945. (The set begins in 1950, but cataloging goes back to books published in 1945.) Prior to that date, there is no subject avenue to *The National Union Catalog* titles.

The subject catalog includes all works cataloged by the Library of Congress, but not necessarily by libraries who contribute location data to *The National Union Catalog*. Hence it is not a complete *National Union Catalog*. When there is doubt and the author's name is known, *The National Union Catalog* should be double-checked. Also, some, but not all, *National Union Catalog* location symbols are given; again, the main *National Union Catalog* set must be checked for location.

So far, the discussion has concerned only ongoing issues of *The National Union Catalog*, i.e., those published monthly and cumulated annually. But how does one locate a title published, say, in 1950 or, for that matter, any one of 10 million retrospective entries not in the current *National Union Catalog?* The answer requires a brief historical sketch of *The National Union Catalog*.

The National Union Catalog in card form began in 1901. By 1926, the *NUC* had over 2 million cards, physically located in the Library of Congress. Anyone who wanted to consult the *NUC* had to query the Library of Congress or go there in person. The problem was solved, or so it was thought, by sending duplicate cards of the *NUC* to key research libraries throughout the United States. This procedure proved as costly as it was inefficient. Therefore, beginning in the early 1940s, work started on the printed book catalog; the individual cards were reproduced in the familiar *NUC* book form instead of being sent to libraries card by card. However, it was not until January 1, 1956, that it was decided that the book catalogs should be expanded to include not only Library of Congress holdings but also the imprints of other libraries.

So, since July 1956, the book catalog has borne the new name: *The National Union Catalog*. This means that most large libraries have several sets of book catalogs from the Library of Congress, but the catalogs issued before 1956 represent books cataloged only by the Library of Congress, not the entire *National Union Catalog*. What was to be done with *The National Union Catalog* prior to 1956, that is, with the card catalog in the Library of Congress which was not in book form? The answer came in 1968 when *The National Union Catalog: Pre-1956 Imprints* began to be published.

The *Pre-1956 Imprints*, which is well over 700 volumes, is a cumulative *National Union Catalog* up to 1956. The several million entries represent the *NUC* holdings prior to 1956 and take the place of other sets.[6] Now the librarian has only to go here instead of to the multiple earlier-published sets.

Completed in 1980, the basic work consists of 685 volumes, but at least 70 supplemental volumes are to be added. This is to pick up material lost in the initial set or badly in need of revision. It should be noted that volumes 53 to 56 were not published until 1980. The reason: these are the listings of the Bible and took 15 years to prepare. Such is the importance of these four volumes that they are issued as separate publications, with a fifth added, by the publisher.

When looking for material after 1956, one turns to the regular *NUC* series. And even here there are more cumulations planned, e.g., *The NUC Author List Master Cumulation 1956–1977* (Costa Mesa, California: Knowledge Resources, Inc. 1980 to date. 300 vols. estimated. $12,900). To be published over a five-year period, the set will also be available in 2500 fiche cards.

The same publisher will issue a title index (to be updated by annuals) to the Pre-1956 Imprints as well as to the ongoing *NUC*.

NUC online

In many libraries it is now possible to search *The National Union Catalog* at a computer terminal. This is MARC (an acronym for Machine-Readable Cataloging) and is usually accessed through a national bibliographic networking system such as OCLC. MARC records go back only to 1968, and only about 1 million of the Library of Congress's vast records are in this form. Some 5 million records in LC's classified collections, including much foreign material, are not in MARC. In an effort to include this and retrospective material, an abbreviated form (REMARC) is in the process of picking up earlier imprints.

---

[6]If the librarian does not have *Pre-1956 Imprints,* one of the four following series of catalogs (now replaced by the *Pre-1956 Imprints*)—may be consulted: (1) 1898–1942. *A Catalog of Books Represented by Library of Congress Printed Cards Issued to July 31, 1942.* Ann Arbor, Michigan: Edwards Brothers, Incorporated, 1942–1946, 167 vols. This series consists of printed catalog cards produced only by the Library of Congress from 1898 to 1942, and *not* by member libraries. Therefore, it is not properly a union catalog, although some of the cards printed at the Library of Congress do represent scattered holdings of member libraries. (2) 1942–1947. *A Catalog of Books Represented by Library of Congress Printed Cards: Supplement: Cards Issued August 1, 1942–December 31, 1947.* Ann Arbor, Michigan: Edwards Brothers, Incorporated, 1948, 42 vols. (3) 1948–1952. *Library of Congress Author Catalog: A Cumulative List of Works Represented by Library of Congress Printed Cards, 1948–1952.* Ann Arbor, Michigan: Edwards Brothers, Incorporated, 1953, 24 vols. (4) 1953–1957. *National Union Catalog . . . , 1953–1957.* Ann Arbor, Michigan: Edwards Brothers, Incorporated, 1958, 28 vols.

One enters the name of the author or title, and the desired bibliographic information appears on a screen or as a printout. Another shortcut is COM (computer output microform) which can be read on a reader. Most national catalogs are *not* available in this form, although private companies have produced, for example, the MARC records of the Library of Congress on fiche.[7]

Which library has X collection?[8]

A major use of *The National Union Catalog* is to discover which library has what title. But how does the reference librarian answer such a question as, What library has the best *collection* of books—or perhaps manuscripts—on waffle irons or the history of science? Experts know where primary collections are to be found without consulting librarians. Still, it is useful to realize there are several guides to collections.

The best is Lee Ash, *Subject Collections,* 5th ed. (New York: R. R. Bowker Company, 1978, 1184 pp.). Arranged under Library of Congress subject headings, data is given for collections in some 15,000 libraries in the United States (including Puerto Rico) and Canada. For each entry, there is the name of the collection and its location; the name of the librarian; the number of volumes, including nonprint materials; and the annual budget. If a catalog has been published concerning the collection, it is cited. Within each subject area the libraries are arranged alphabetically by state. A companion volume with much the same purpose and arrangement is *Subject Collections in European Libraries,* 2d ed. (New York: R. R. Bowker Company, 1978, 900 pp.).

Printed book catalogs

The printed book or library catalog (usually three columns of seven cards each per page) is a form employed by several large research libraries. The publisher often is the G. K. Hall Company of Boston. The most ambitious is the: *Dictionary Catalogue of the Research Libraries of The New York Public Library, 1911–1971.* Eventually this will be an 800-volume set with some 10 million catalog cards arranged by author entry. In bound volumes the cost is $24,000 and on microform

---

[7]J. McRee Elrod, "Universal Availability of Bibliographic Records," *IFLA Journal,* no. 4, 1978, pp. 347–350. This is a survey article of national bibliographies available through COM.

[8]Thanks to automation, libraries with a system such as OCLC may speed the process along, at least much of the time, by using the computer terminal to determine who has what. However, this is title by title, not by whole collections.

the cost is $18,000.[9] The dictionary catalog is continued in book form, although computer-produced, by *Dictionary Catalog of the Research Libraries* (New York: New York Public Library, 1972 to date, monthly with annual cumulations).

Library catalogs in Canada[10]

> *Canadians*. Ottawa: National Library of Canada, 1950 to date, quarterly with annual cumulations. A 10-year cumulation, 1968–1978, was published in 1978. Price on request.

The *Canadiana* has varied in scope, arrangement, and publication period. Today it is arranged by Dewey and classifies material published in Canada or of Canadian interest. It does not include everything received by the National Library of Canada, but is selective. It does list books, pamphlets, government publications, dissertations and theses and report literature—in this respect differing from many national catalogs.[11] At one time films were included, but as of 1977 this is a separate annual publication, appearing in *Film Canadiana*.

The scope of the bibliography is considerably less than that of the *National Union Catalog*. About 28,000 to 34,000 items are listed each year.

Library catalogs in Great Britain

> British Library. Department of Printed Books. *General Catalogue of Printed Books*. London: Trustees of the British Museum, 1959–1966, 263 vols. *Ten-Year Supplement, 1956–1965*, 1968, 50 vols. *Five-Year Supplement, 1966–1970*, 1971–1972, 26 vols.; *1971–1975*, 1978–1980, 13 vols. Prices on request.
>
> ————. *The British Library General Catalogue of Printed Books to*

[9]Herbert Mitang, "Library Cataloguing 10 Million Cards," *The New York Times*, January 1, 1980, p. 11. This is a brief story of the catalog. For an example of how book catalogs are used in a discipline, and the type available, see: Bonnie Nelson, "Anthropological Research and Printed Library Catalogs," *RQ*, Winter 1979, pp. 159–170.

[10]For a still useful discussion of *Canadiana*, see Marion C. Wilson's article of the same name in *Canadian Library Journal*, December 1977, pp. 417–421.

[11]*Canadiana* may be searched online through the National Library's machine-readable bibliographic file, CAN/MARC, which is on the CAN/OLE (Canadian On-Line-Enquiry) system. The system includes locations of scientific serials as well. Most large Canadian libraries have access to MARC tapes of the Library of Congress and the British National Bibliography through this or other online systems.

1975. London/New York: K. G. Saur, 1979 to date. In progress. 360 vols. $23,000. (Distributed in the United States by Gale Research.)

————. *Subject Index of the Modern Works Added to the Library of the British Museum in the Years 1881–1900*. London: Trustees of the British Museum, 1903. Five-year supplements have been published to date since the initial three-volume work was issued. Prices on request.

The British Library[12] is roughly equivalent to our Library of Congress, and its various catalogs are similar in purpose (if not in scope) to *The National Union Catalog*. The essential differences are:

1. The British Library is much older than the Library of Congress and has a considerably larger collection of titles dating from the fifteenth century up to the 1960s when the Library of Congress moved to embrace all world publications.

2. The British Library's catalog is not a union catalog and shows holdings only of the British Library.

3. The data for titles are somewhat more brief than those in *The National Union Catalog*.

4. Larger amounts of analytical material and cross references are included. For example, considerable attention is given to the analysis of series, and there are numerous cross-references from names of editors, translators, and other names connected with a title.

5. Keyword title entries are used; and in some ways this approach is useful because of the lack of a satisfactory subject catalog. The problem, of course, is that the title must reveal something of the contents.

6. Whereas *The National Union Catalog* can be considered very much a current bibliographical aid, the *General Catalogue,* because of its approach and infrequent publication, is more retrospective.

How much duplication is there between the massive British catalog and *The National Union Catalog*? Walford did a sampling and found that 75 to 80 percent of the titles in the British work are not in the American equivalent, and for titles published before 1800, 90 percent. Some estimate there are from 900,000 to over a million titles

---

[12]Under reorganization, the British Museum Library is now known as the British Library, but the basic bibliographies still retain the British Museum publication name.

in the British Library catalog not found in other national bibliographies. With increased interest in capturing worldwide titles in *The National Union Catalog,* the amount of duplication is bound to increase in the years ahead. Meanwhile, no large research library can afford to be without the British Library's *General Catalogue.*

The *Subject Index* is considerably less useful than its American counterpart. It is not issued until several years after the main entries in the *General Catalogue,* and large, rather than definitive, subject headings are used.

Just as *NUC* has its massive *Pre-1956 Imprints,* so will the British Library have an equivalent in the *British Library General Catalogue . . . to 1975.* The set of some 360 volumes incorporates in a single alphabet the *General Catalogue* plus the supplements. The set is to appear at the rate of six or seven volumes a month with completion scheduled for 1984. The first volume came off the press in 1979 and is reviewed in *The Times Literary Supplement* (April 4, 1980, p. 398).

NATIONAL AND TRADE BIBLIOGRAPHY

Most of the enumerative bibliographies found in libraries can be classified as national and trade bibliographies. The distinction between the types is not always clear, if indeed there is a distinction. There are numerous types and possible combinations. An equal number of possibilities exist for defining, categorizing, and argument. The important consideration is not so much where the bibliography falls in the sometimes esoteric reference scheme but, rather, how it is used.

The pragmatic function of a national bibliography is to tell the librarian what was, what is, and what will be available either by purchase or by possible loan from another library. The bibliographies give necessary bibliographical information (e.g., publisher, price, author, subject area, Library of Congress or Dewey numbers), which is used for a number of purposes ranging from clarifying proper spelling to locating an item by subject area. Also, the national bibliography is a primary control device for bringing some order to the 40,000 or more books published in the United States each year, not to mention similarly staggering figures for pamphlets, reports, recordings, films, and other items.

The process of compiling national bibliographies differs from country to country, but there is a basic pattern. Effort is made first to give a current listing of titles published the previous week, month, or quarter. These data are then cumulated for the annual breakdown of titles published and beyond that, for what is in print, what is out of print, and what is going to be published. (The same process applies to forms other than books.)

United States national and trade bibliography: Weekly and monthly

> *Weekly Record.* New York: R. R. Bowker Company, 1974 to date, weekly. $15.

> *American Book Publishing Record.* New York: R. R. Bowker Company, 1961 to date, monthly, $25. The annual cumulation, $53. *Cumulative, 1950–1977,* 1978, 15 vols. $1975. *Cumulative, 1876–1949,* 1980, 15 vols. $1975.

> *Cumulative Book Index.* New York: The H. W. Wilson Company, 1898 to date, monthly, with three-month, annual, and five-year cumulations. Service basis.

> *Forthcoming Books.* New York: R. R. Bowker Company, 1966 to date, bimonthly. *Subject Guide to Forthcoming Books,* 1967 to date, bimonthly. Combined subscription $45.

United States: Annual and biannual

(All titles published by the R. R. Bowker Company)

> *Publishers' Trade List Annual,* 1873 to date, annual. 6 vols. $59. *Books in Print,* 1948 to date, annual. 4 vols. $110. *Books in Print Supplement,* 1973 to date, annual, $58. *Subject Guide to Books in Print,* 1957 to date, annual, 2 vols. $79.50. *Paperbound Books in Print,* 1955 to date, biannual (January and October), 2 vols. $79.

> *Children's Books in Print,* 1969 to date, annual. $35. *Subject Guide to Children's Books in Print,* 1970 to date, annual. $35.

Booksellers call the national and trade bibliographies listed here "the tools of the trade." Librarians also regard them as such, and their purpose is evident from the titles. Essentially, the bibliographies list the books that can be purchased from American publishers (i.e., are in print), in what forms (hardbound, paperback), and at what prices. Depending on the individual trade bibliography, additional information is given as to the date of publication, the number of pages, the subjects covered, and other data necessary for proper and easy use of the bibliography.

Previously published titles

The most frequently consulted titles are *Books in Print (BIP)* and *Subject Guide to Books in Print*. More than 545,000 in-print books of all kinds (hardbounds, paperbacks, trade books, textbooks, adult titles, juveniles) are indexed by author and by title in *Books in Print*. Besides telling the user whether the book can be purchased, from whom, and at what price, the trade bibliography also answers such questions as: What books by William Faulkner are in print, including both hard-bound and paperbound editions at various prices? Who is the publisher of *The Old Patagonian Express*? Is John Irving's first novel still in print? (The fact that sometimes the inquiry cannot be answered is not always the fault of the questioner's spelling of the title or because the author's name is not correct or even close. *Books in Print,* through either filing errors or misinformation from the publishers, may fail to guide users to a title which they know to be correct.)

Almost every entry in *BIP* includes the author, coauthor (if any), editor, price, publisher, year of publication, number of volumes, Library of Congress card number and the International Standard Book Numbers (ISBN). The names and addresses of the nearly 8200 U.S. publishers represented in *BIP* are included. The listings provide answers to queries about publishers, although the librarian who needs more detail should consult reference works specifically intended for information about publishers, e.g., *American Book Trade Directory,* discussed later.

Issued in October of each year, *Books in Print* is supplemented by a single volume in April of the following year. Here publishers list some 40,000 titles newly published and not included in the basic *BIP,* as well as titles which are out of print or which they plan to issue before the next annual *BIP* volumes. These listings are arranged by author and by title as well as by subject; thus the *Books in Print Supplement* is also a supplement to *Subject Guide to Books in Print*. The *Supplement* includes an updated list of all publishers, with any address changes. For normal purposes, *BIP* is enough for most questions. When the original publishing date is more than one or two years old, when there has been a spurt of inflation, or when the librarian cannot find a title, a double-check in the *Books in Print Supplement* is wise.

The majority of titles listed in *BIP* are similarly found in *Subject Guide to Books in Print*. In the subject approach, no entries are made for fiction, poetry, or bibles. (Note, though, that the guide does list books *about* fiction under the name of the author of the fiction; criticism of Henry James, for example, is found under James.) The use of the subject guide, which virtually rearranges *BIP* under 62,000

Library of Congress subject headings, is self-evident. It not only helps in locating books about a given subject but may also be used to help expand the library's collection in given areas. If, for example, books about veterinarians are in great demand, the guide gives a complete list of those available from American publishers. An important point: The list is inclusive, not selective. No warning sign differentiates the world's most misleading book about veterinarians from the best among, say, 20 titles listed. The librarian must turn to other bibliographies and reviews for judgment and evaluation of titles in any subject area.

The massive *Publishers' Trade List Annual (PTLA)*, while less frequently used by reference librarians, fits in here because it is part of the bibliographical apparatus for tracing books in print. The *PTLA*, usually published in September, is a collection of U.S. publishers' catalogs in book form. The catalogs conform to a certain physical cut size but may be in hundreds of various typefaces, arrangements, and lengths. For convenience, the catalogs are bound in alphabetical order in six volumes. The set will vary in number of volumes from year to year. The first volume contains the index and a section reserved for small publishers who do not have enough titles to warrant a separate bound catalog. *PTLA* is the listings or catalogs of publishers represented in *Books in Print*. It is not complete, as some 8000 publishers have titles in *BIP* but only about 1800 in *PTLA*.

PTLA, beginning with the 1979 edition, includes a brief subject approach to the publishers' catalogs. There are about 65 subject and form categories which lead the reader to a publisher who concentrates on, say, reprints or textbooks or journalism and writing or law.

In terms of reference work, the subject index helps to give a broad picture of the publishers of certain types of materials. Other information which can be found in the *PTLA* includes (1) location of titles when the user knows only the name of the publisher (e.g., I know X publisher is famous for cookbooks, but what cookbooks?); (2) all titles in a publisher's series, such as a series on rivers of America or librarians I have known and loved; (3) the prices of various titles by one publisher of, say, dictionaries; (4) sometimes, although not always, a brief description of a book or books; and (5) added information about a publisher. The "Publishers Index" includes imprints, subsidiaries, affiliations, and so on.

New titles

How does one discover facts about books published last week or a month ago or, for that matter, books which are not yet out but are promised in the next few months? To put it another way, how does the librarian answer such questions as, "What recent books—I mean in the past few weeks or months—has [Y] written? I saw a review of [Y]'s last book somewhere, but I can't remember the title." Or, "I can't remember the author, but there is a good book recently on John Coltrane." Or, "What is the price, publisher, subject, and so on, of the [X] or [Y] title?"

If the question concerns a novel by Mario Puzo or Helen MacInnes, the librarian has no difficulty, because the book is familiar and, furthermore, is probably in the library or on order. The problem is with less-known titles, and here the librarian must turn to certain basic aids. The two most often used are the *Cumulative Book Index (CBI)* and the *American Book Publishing Record (ABPR)*. Both are monthly publications, and both list or index books recently published. A year's cumulation of either one will give the librarian a record of titles published that year in the United States (which is *ABPR*'s limited scope), or for the United States *and* the rest of the English-speaking world (which gives the *CBI* a quantitative edge over its competitor).

Beginners sometimes have difficulty in differentiating among the *CBI*, the *ABPR,* and *Books in Print.* The basic difference is that *Books in Print* gives information on available books that have been published in the previous year, or 5 or even 100 years ago. *CBI* and *ABPR* are concerned only with recording and indexing books as they are published. Their monthly or annual cumulations tell the librarian what books were issued last month or last year, but do not indicate whether they are still available from the publisher, that is, are still in print. (For working purposes, of course, the monthly or quarterly appearance of a title in either the *CBI* or *ABPR* is usually a safe indication that the reported book is still in print. Dependence on the annual cumulation may be more hazardous, and checking out the five-year volumes of the *CBI* or the *ABPR* cumulation for information on in-print titles is plain foolish.)

Although the *CBI* claims to be a "current index to books published in the English language," it hardly claims *all* English-language titles. Therefore, larger libraries will rely on more specific bibliographical aids for a wider sweep of English titles.[13] However, for most libraries the *CBI* coverage of American books, which is impressively complete for the majority of publishers, as well as of English-language titles, is quite enough to answer almost all reference queries.

---

[13]One such aid for English language titles: *International Books in Print: English Language Titles Published Outside the USA and the United Kingdom* (New York: K. G. Saur Publishing, Inc. 1979 to date, annual, 2 vols.) See p. 83.

Published since 1898, the familiar brown-covered *CBI* is to be found in almost all libraries, as are the monthly and annual cumulations. It has the advantage of being well known, accurate, and easy to use. Books are listed in one alphabet by author, title, and subject. The author, or main, entry includes pertinent bibliographic information, as well as useful data for catalogers and acquisitions librarians. The subject headings, which follow those established by the Library of Congress, are exhaustive. Although fiction is not included as a subject, one does find headings on science fiction, short stories, mystery and detective stories, and so on. There is also a good directory of publishers.

The publisher of *CBI* is able to list new titles monthly because "most publishers in the United States and Canada send copies of their books to the H. W. Wilson Company promptly," to quote a Wilson Company brochure, "and these are processed quickly and appear in the earliest possible issue of *CBI*. Therefore books are frequently listed in *CBI* before they appear in any other major bibliography." There is an understandable "sales pitch" here which is of interest because *CBI*'s rival does much the same thing in terms of listing new titles each month. One would not want to argue that *CBI* is faster to the mark with new titles than the *ABPR*, but only that the librarian who cannot find a title in one has the advantage of being able to check the other.

ABPR covers much the same ground as *CBI*, but differs in that (1) it limits listing to titles published in the United States; (2) it is arranged by the Dewey Decimal System, that is, by subject, and has an author and title index; and (3) it includes separate sections on juvenile and adult fiction and mass paperbacks. The information is much the same as found in *CBI*. Why take both services? Some librarians do not, giving preference to the long-established *CBI*. Larger libraries do take both, primarily as a double-check of one against the other for titles missed, for the different arrangements of material, or for the more inclusive coverage of English-language titles by *CBI*.

While the *CBI* cumulative volumes are limited to 2, 4, 5, or 6 years, the *ABPR* is more ambitious, now including 5- and 27-year cumulations. The 5-year cumulative volumes begin with the 1950–1954 edition, with the latest covering 1975–1979. Also, there are two cumulations which, combined, cover the years 1876–1977. The publishers say that in the sets there are close to 1.7 million author/title entries of books published in the United States, and while this does not represent the total output of American publishers (government works are excluded), it is a useful guide which may be employed with

The National Union Catalog for the years covered.[14] The main volumes of the cumulation are in Dewey Decimal classification order. The final volumes include three indexes: by author, by title, by subject. Also included here are revisions, additions, and changes which were missed in the main set.

The monthly issues of *ABPR* lead back to another service, the *Weekly Record*. Although more important to catalogers and acquisitions librarians, the *Weekly Record* is interesting to reference librarians because it records on a weekly basis what is published in the United States. About 700 to 800 new titles are listed each week by author.[15] Full bibliographic information is given for each, including Dewey and Library of Congress classifications and, often, descriptive cataloging notes. Most of the data is furnished by the Library of Congress and supplemented by the staff at Bowker.

The author arrangement limits the use for most reference purposes. However, every four weeks the contents of *Weekly Record* are rearranged by subject and cumulated as the aforementioned *ABPR*.

As a running record of what is going on in publishing, *Publishers Weekly* (New York: R. R. Bowker Company, 1872 to date) is required reading for reference librarians. This is the trade magazine of American publishers and, in addition, often contains articles, features, and news items of value to librarians. It is difficult to imagine an involved reference librarian not at least thumbing through the weekly issues, if only for the "PW Forecasts." Here the critical annotations on some 50 to 100 titles give the reader a notion of what to expect in popular fiction and nonfiction to be published in the next month or so.

A more definitive approach to what is going to be published is found in *Forthcoming Books.* Again, this periodical is likely to be of

[14]In a review of the 1850–1977 cumulation, Robert E. Bell points out: It should be noted that the listing in *ABPR Cumulative* does not totally replace the sources it is intended to cumulate. For example, a series of four Japanese print books by the distinguished Book Club of California were printed by the Grabhorn Press between 1959 and 1965. These were not subscription books, and copies of them can be found in the major libraries of the country. Each of the four is included in the *NUC*, but only one of them, *Ukiyo-e, The Floating World* (1962), appears in *ABPR Cumulative*. Other printings and publications of the Grabhorn Press met with the same uneven treatment. Thus a user needs to be aware that items not located in *ABPR Cumulative*, even though they do not fall into its list of exclusions, may need to be searched in *NUC*. (*RQ*, Fall 1979, p. 79.)

[15]Exact figures of the number of titles published in the United States are compiled in the early part of each year by *Publishers Weekly* and then updated, usually in the fall. For the past decade or so, the number of titles published here, including new titles and reprints and paperbacks, is between 40,000 and 42,000.

more value to acquisitions and cataloging than to reference, but it does answer queries about a new book or possibly about a book which the patron may have heard discussed on a radio or television program before it is actually published. The bimonthly lists by author and by title (not by subject) books due to be published in the next five months.[16] For a subject approach, one must consult the bimonthly *Subject Guide to Forthcoming Books.* One need not be an expert to realize that the two works would be much easier and faster to use were they combined.

While *Books in Print* lists paperbound titles, *Paperbound Books in Print* rearranges these same listings in a single volume, which is nicely divided into three separate indexes: title, author, and subject.[17] The 1980 compilation includes more than 160,000 books, with full bibliographical information about each. As a guide to a particular form, *Paperbound Books in Print* is invaluable in bookshops but is of more limited use in libraries. Librarians tend to use it as a double-check against *BIP,* particularly as not all new paperbound titles are in *BIP.*

Using the same information gathered from publishers for the compilation of *BIP, Paperbound Books in Print* is, in essence, a publisher's spin-off of the basic volume. It adds not only convenience for users and librarians but, it is hoped, profits for the publisher. Librarians must ultimately decide whether, once the basic volumes are acquired, the spin-offs are really necessary. The answer for large or special libraries is usually yes, because of added convenience. Small libraries might think again. Other fallouts of *Books in Print* are *Children's Books in Print* and *Subject Guide to Children's Books in Print.* Arrangement is by author and title, and an illustrator index is added. About 45,000 titles are included, with full bibliographical information, including grade levels. (If one wonders why *Books in Print* developed grade levels for some titles, the answer is that the publisher reasons that any information gathered is of possible use in another bibliographical form at a later date. Add a machine-readable database and computer to the compilation, as is the case for *BIP* and its spin-offs, and the process becomes relatively easy.)

[16]In *Books in Print,* as well as in some standard bibliographies which have borrowed from *Books in Print* or *Forthcoming Books,* one may find "ghost titles," i.e., books which were supposed to be published but were never issued. Such errors come from the *BIP* and *Forthcoming Books* policy of depending on publishers' early announcements—announcements which may later be amended but not always corrected in *BIP.*

[17]A major problem with the subject headings is their limited number, slightly over 450. Although an improvement over the 26 major categories in earlier volumes, the headings are still too general for most libraries, e.g., there are almost 30 pages of titles, without any subheadings, under United States history—here indicated, by the way, as "History—United States."

Separating out the 45,000 plus titles at the kindergarten through high school levels from *BIP* for the children's version is of some value for schools. Of considerably more use, however, is the subject arrangement; here the book is really new in that the *Subject Guide to Books in Print* headings (Library of Congress-based) are deleted in favor of over 8500 *Sears* headings, i.e., those found in *Sears List of Subject Headings,* 11th ed. (New York: The H. W. Wilson Company, 1977), headings based on the Library of Congress system but modified for small libraries. *Sears* offers subjects closer to the needs of children. As more than one reviewer has noted, however, the *Subject Guide to Children's Books in Print* has a major flaw—lack of adequate cross-references, i.e., *see* and *see also* suggestions.

In the supplementary series of Bowker "in-print titles" there is one of particular value: *Large Type Books in Print* which comes out each year in September. This lists more than 4000 titles by subject, with author and title indexes. Set in 18-point large type, the bibliography is a blessing for librarians looking for such titles. Note, too, it includes a shorter list of large-type magazines and newspapers.

Publisher spin-offs

Thanks to automation, and more particularly the computer and databases, it is possible to take a basic batch of data and cut and edit it in different ways to produce different books. This is called a "spin-off" and is a common element in reference books publishing today.

The inclusion of periodicals and other types of serials is now a common feature of several spin-offs from *Books in Print* which are combinations of listings found in *Books in Print* and *Ulrich's International Periodical Directory,* again all by computer. Among the Bowker titles in this group: *Business Books and Serials in Print, Medical Books and Serials in Print, El-Hi Textbooks in Print, Scientific and Technical Books and Serials in Print, Books in Series in the United States* (plus a supplement), *Religious Books and Serials in Print,* and so on. Modifications, changes, and additions are made, but the basic formula is the same—an author, title, and subject listing. Other publishers follow much the same procedure, and the practice is likely to grow as publishing becomes increasingly automated.

The question reference librarians have to ask is, Once we have the basic volumes (in this case *Books in Print* and *Subject Guide to Books in Print*) do we really need all the spin-offs? Is the convenience of having all titles of a similar type in one reference work worth the added price? For specialized, large libraries which would *not* have the more general *Books in Print,* the answer is yes. Convenience and added features are reasons enough to purchase the other volumes, although with a tight budget, these should be the first to go. In small-to-medium-sized libraries, the funds are better expended on reference works which do not duplicate one another.

Other national trade bibliographies

While the preceding discussion has been limited to two American publishers, the bibliographical apparatus for recording published titles and those still to be published is much the same throughout the United States and the rest of the world. Differences exist in scope and in emphasis, but essentially the purpose is the same, as one finds when one explores the current and retrospective bibliographies of other countries.

The most ambitious international bibliography, at least for those in English-speaking countries, is *International Books in Print* (New York/London: K. G. Saur Publishing, Inc., 1979 to date, annual, 2 vols.). This is an author/title (but not a subject) approach to English-language book titles published in countries other than the United Kingdom and the United States; e.g., India, The Netherlands, Japan, Israel, and Germany. Some 89 countries with 80,000 titles are found in the 1979 edition. (Even Canada is included, although many libraries have the more complete *Canadian Books in Print.*) Complete bibliographic information is included, down to the dollar price at the time of publication as well as a symbol for the country of publication.

For Canada there is *Canadian Books in Print* (Toronto: University of Toronto Press, 1968 to date, annual) and from the same publisher the annual *Canadian Books in Print: Subject Index* (1973 to date).

British Books in Print (London: J. Whitaker, 1974 to date, annual, 2 vols. Distributed in the United States by R. R. Bowker) lists about 290,000 titles from just over 9000 publishers. The author, title, and subjects are interfiled in one alphabet, and subjects are primarily those which surface when there is a keyword in the title. The subject approach is somewhat less than satisfactory.

For libraries with considerable involvement in English titles, the main work is supplemented by a monthly *British Books in Print on Microfiche* (1978 to date). The annual monthly microfiche editions are part of a chain which begins with the weekly *Bookseller* and the *British National Bibliography* (somewhat equivalent to the *Weekly Record* and the *Cumulative Book Index*) and the monthly *Whitaker's Books of the Month* and the quarterly *Whitaker's Cumulative Book List* (again, somewhat equivalent to the *American Book Publishing Record* and the *CBI*).

R. R. Bowker distributes a number of related titles. To give the reader a notion of such works, consider those available from Bowker: *Libros En Venta,* with supplements, is issued in Buenos Aires and is the standard work for Spanish books; *Catalogo dei Libri in Commercio* covers Italian works. Then there are *Indian Books in Print, Portuguese Books in Print, Australian Books in Print,* and even *New Zealand Books in Print.*

Just because there are numerous bibliographies, the beginner sometimes tends to forget the obvious. For example, having become involved with the trade bibliographies, one may overlook that old standby, *The National Union Catalog,* which is a favored place to look for retrospective titles. Asked to compile a bibliography of novels by English writer Anthony Powell, the librarian would first turn to *Books in Print* then to *CBI* and *ABPR,* to name only three sources which would list American and some English editions of Powell. Just to be certain, the librarian would then go to the English bibliographies. This procedure would be right and proper for a definitive list, but for a general rundown of Powell novels, it would be much simpler to consult the ongoing *National Union Catalog* and the *Pre-1956 Imprints,* with a double-check over the past six months or so in *CBI.* The librarian seeking books on a subject would accomplish much the same by looking into Library of Congress Catalogs: Subject Catalog, again with an update in *CBI* and/or *ABPR* and *Subject Guide to Books in Print.*

UNITED STATES RETROSPECTIVE BIBLIOGRAPHY

Most daily reference work is carried on with relatively current national and trade bibliographies. There are times, however, when one or more retrospective bibliographies are needed, i.e., bibliographies which list titles published not last week, month, or year, but from 10 to over 100 years ago. These bibliographies may be used to answer such questions as: Who is the author of *The Ballad of the Abolition Blunder-buss,* published in 1861? What is the correct title of a work on rattlesnakes by S. W. Mitchell, published in 1860? The person asking this type of question is likely to be a historian, literary scholar, librarian, or anyone else deeply involved in research of a given subject, place, or person.

In trying to fathom a retrospective bibliography, which is not always easy to do because of erratic arrangement, coverage, and purpose, the librarian is apt to overlook other approaches which are somewhat simpler. The first one is *The National Union Catalog* which, when the pre-1956 set is complete, will supply answers to all but the most elusive and esoteric titles.

Retrospective bibliography is not limited to the United States. In fact, it has reached scholarly, awesome proportions in England and on the Continent. Examples of the basic foreign retrospective bibliographies will be found in Sheehy and Walford. Regardless of national origin, retrospective bibliographies tell what was published where and by whom. They are a source of information about national, state, and local history and thus trace the cultural and scientific development of people in a given place and time.

In chronological order, the leading American retrospective bibliographies are:[18]

1500–1892 Sabin, Joseph. *Bibliotheca Americana. Dictionary of Books Relating to America from Its Discovery to the Present Time.* New York: Sabin, 1869–1892; Bibliographical Society of America, 1928–1936, 29 vols.

Molnar, John. *Author-Title Index to Joseph Sabin's Dictionary of Books Relating to America.* Metuchen, New Jersey: Scarecrow Press, 1974, 3 vols.

1639–1800 Evans, Charles. *American Bibliography: A Chronological Dictionary of All Books, Pamphlets and Periodical Publications Printed in the United States of America From the Genesis of Printing in 1639 Down to and Including the Year 1800.* Chicago: Printed for the author, 1903–1959, 14 vols. (Vols. 13 and 14 published by the American Antiquarian Society.)

Shipton, Clifford. *National Index of American Imprints Through 1800; The Short Title Evans.* Worcester, Massachusetts: American Antiquarian Society, 1969, 2 vols.

1801–1819 Shaw, Ralph, and Richard Shoemaker. *American Bibliography: A Preliminary Checklist.* Metuchen, New Jersey: Scarecrow Press, 1958–1963, 22 vols.

1820–1861 Roorbach, Orville. *Bibliotheca Americana.* New York: O. A. Roorbach, 1852–1861, 4 vols.

1820–1875 Shoemaker, Richard H., and others. *A Checklist of American Imprints, 1820* +, Metuchen, New Jersey: Scarecrow Press, 1964 to date. (Shoemaker died in 1970, and the plan is now to continue the series through 1875 with editors Scott Bruntjen and Carol Rinderknecht. As of 1981, the series was up to 1833.)

1861–1870 Kelly, James. *American Catalogue of Books, Published in the United States from January 1861 to January 1871, with Date of Publication, Size, Price, and Publisher's Name.* New York: John Wiley & Sons, Inc., 1866–1871, 2 vols.

[18]Original publishers are given for these titles, but most have been reprinted by one or more publishers and a number are available on microform.

1876–1910   *American Catalogue of Books, 1876–1910.* New York: *Publishers' Weekly,* 1880–1911, 15 vols.

1899–1927   *United States Catalog: Books in Print.* 4th ed. New York: The H. W. Wilson Company, 1928, 3164 pp.

The following titles are still being published and are discussed elsewhere. They are listed here by their beginning publishing date as an indication of what can be used for retrospective searching from 1928 to the present.

1872–   *Publishers' Weekly*
1873–   *Publishers' Trade List Annual*
1898–   *Cumulative Book Index*
1948–   *Books in Print*
1957–   *Subject Guide to Books in Print*

Sabin differs from all the other bibliographies listed here in that he includes books, pamphlets, and periodicals printed in the United States *and* works printed about America in other countries. The others are limited to titles published in the United States. An Oxford scholar, Sabin was an authority on rare books about America. He began his ambitious project (often called *Bibliotheca Americana*) in the early 1860s and lived long enough to see 13 volumes published by 1881. The next seven volumes were by Wilberforce Eames. R. W. G. Vail ultimately called a halt to the proceedings with the final volumes in 1936. Arrangement is by author, with some title entries and other entries by names of places. Entries include collation, usually the location of a copy, and a note on contents. There is no subject index. Each volume contains entries for one section of the alphabet up to the date of publication; hence, it is uneven in chronological coverage, particularly since cutoff dates of acceptable publications moved further and further back as the work continued. There is no guarantee that a work published in 1870, say, is listed here. The author must be known or the set is virtually worthless. However, once the author is identified, the information found is enough to warrant searching. Thanks to Molnar's index, it is now a relatively simple thing to consult the otherwise badly organized Sabin. The massive author-title index includes 270,000 entries.

Sabin is alphabetically arranged by author and has no chronologically logical approach. It thus tends to obscure the interrelationships between books and pamphlets printed at about the same time. Some improvement will come with the expected 45,000 separate listings of books or printed materials to supplement Sabin. Prepared by the John Carter Brown Library staff, this will be a chronological guide to materials published in Europe about America from the period 1493 to 1800 which are not listed in Sabin. The work is expected to be completed in the mid-1980s.

A work of love and considerable hardship for Charles Evans, his *American Bibliography* is a classic. It is considered the keystone upon which all retrospective American bibliography is built and is basic to any large collection. Arrangement is not alphabetical by author. It is chronological by dates of publication. If one does not know the date, or approximate date, there is an author, subject, and printer and publisher index to help. For each entry, there is the author's full name with birth and death dates, a full title, place, publisher, date, paging, size, and usually the location of one or more copies in American libraries.

The *National Index* is a required addition for anyone using Evans. It serves to eliminate nonexistent titles, or "ghosts" which Evans recorded without seeing a copy of the actual item. Furthermore, it adds over 10,000 titles discovered since Evans's set was published. The 49,197 entries are arranged alphabetically by author and short title, and there is reference to the original entry in Evans—if it is listed there. (The *National Index* is particularly valuable for use with the microcard reproduction of all nonserial titles listed in Evans and elsewhere and published in America before 1801. It is virtually an index to the tremendous set of nearly 50,000 individual books on microform.)

Shaw and Shoemaker continued Evans's initial efforts to 1820, and the gap between Evans and Roorbach is filled only partially. Each volume covers one year and gives the briefest author citation, along with a location for some copies. Addenda volumes include a title and author index for the full series.

Another set in the same series is *A Checklist of American Imprints,* which was to carry the same type of listing down to 1875 and the beginning of Kelly. From the 1821 volume on, this series differs from the 1801–1819 set in that locations are given for most of the copies and the compiler did check out the books listed. (In the earlier compilation, titles were primarily from secondary sources, with little attention given to checking the accuracy of those sources.) Since Shoemaker's death in 1970, the series has been carried on by Scott Bruntjen and Carol Rinderknecht and the publisher. There is a title and author index to the 1820–1829 series.

Until the *Checklist of American Imprints* is taken down through 1875, the Roorbach and Kelly bibliographies must be used. Roorbach is a contemporary bibliography similar in its intent to *Books in Print* but done with considerably less care. The arrangement is alphabetical by author and title, with information on the publisher; size; and usually, but not always, the price and date. Entries are frequently incomplete. From 1861 to 1870, Kelly serves the same purpose as Roorbach and gives the same type of incomplete information. Both Roorbach and Kelly, for example, list less than one-half as many titles per year as Evans, who was recording a much less productive period in American publishing. Although inaccurate and incomplete, the two bibliographies are the only reference aids of their kind.

In terms of retrospective searching, then, there is something more than a blank period from the time of the last Shoemaker volume to the beginning of the *American Catalog of Books* in 1876, i.e., from 1830 to 1876. Begun by Frederick Leypoldt as a trade bibliography of books in print, the *American Catalog* was published annually and later cumulated. Arrangement is by author and title with subject supplements. The information is generally reliable and comprehensive—but no more so than the publisher's catalogs from which the information came.

Competition from The H. W. Wilson Company's *United States Catalog* caused cessation of the *American Catalog* in 1910, and it did not begin publishing again until 1948 as *Books in Print*. The *United States Catalog* is really a cumulation of the *Cumulative Book Index* which began in 1898 as a type of *Books in Print* in competition with the *American Catalog*. There are four editions of the *United States Catalog*, but the most often used is the last, which lists all the books published in English in the United States and Canada in print in 1928. (Earlier volumes must be consulted for finding books out of print by 1928 and for fuller information on other titles.) By 1928, the increase in the number of titles published forced Wilson to abandon the *United States Catalog* in favor of cumulative issues of the *CBI*.

While this discussion may be too detailed for the beginner, it is an important part of bibliographic history and is included here to indicate the tremendous range of bibliographies needed when one becomes involved with other than current titles. For those who wish additional information in a pleasant, yet scholarly fashion, nothing could be better than George Tanselle's *Guide to the Study of United States Imprints* (Cambridge: Harvard University Press, 1971).

Book prices

American Book Prices Current. New York: Bancroft-Parkman, 1895 to date, annual. Publisher and price vary (approximately $80). Available online.

Book Aution Records. Folkestone, England: Wm. Dawson & Sons, 1903 to date, annual. Publisher and price vary (approximately $125).

Bookman's Price Index. Detroit: Gale Research Company, 1965 to date, annual. $74.

The average layperson's contact with retrospective bibliography is indirect, usually taking the form of trying to find a long-out-of-print book or, more likely, the answer to a question about the value of a book printed years ago. "What is my book, map, or broadside worth?" is a familiar question in many libraries. The three guides listed here are the most often used for an answer. The larger library will have them, not only to help the user but to assist in acquisitions when a question about a used-book dealer's asking price arises. Should the library pay X dollars for a title which last year cost Y dollars less at an auction? There are many variables for both the user and the library, but the guides indicate the logical parameters of pricing.

American Book Prices Current and *Book Auction Records* are collections of book prices paid at various auctions. The third, *Bookman's Price Index,* is based on prices garnered from antiquarian dealers' catalogs. The two first titles are frequently indexed over a period of a number of years. Hence, it is not always necessary to search each volume for a given title.

The American work lists items sold for $20 or more and includes books, serials, autographs, manuscripts, broadsides, and maps. Arrangement is alphabetical by main entry with cross-references. Each of the forms is treated in its own section. Sales run from the fall to the spring, hence each volume is usually numbered with two years, e.g., 1976–1977. Some 14 major auction firms, from Parke-Bernet Galleries to Christie, Manson & Woods Ltd., are included, as are a number of large individual sales of private libraries. The entries are cumulated about every five years, e.g., *American Book Prices Current. Index, 1975–1979* (New York: Bancroft-Parkman, 1980, 2 vols.). The cumulations give a quick overview of prices, but it should be noted that the two-volume set sells for $250. The publisher announced in late 1980 that the index will be online and that more than 100,000 titles and prices may be searched at the computer terminal. The hourly cost of the search was not announced.

Book Auction Records is the English equivalent of the American title, and while it duplicates some of the information found in that work, it includes a number of European auctions not covered elsewhere. Arrangement and form are similar to the *American Book Prices Current,* and there are periodic cumulations. Both titles suffer a time lag and normally are at least one year, and usually two years, behind the sales reported.

Bookman's Price Index differs from the other two titles in that it includes prices in catalogs of some 60 booksellers. Entries are listed in a standard main-entry form. Volume 20, issued in 1980 includes over 39,000 titles—almost twice the number found in the auction price lists. (The total number of titles priced now exceeds 650,000.) It also has the advantage of representing retail prices which may be somewhat higher than those at an auction where book dealers themselves are bidding.

The guides give only relative indications of price. The price requested by a book dealer or at an auction often represents the maximum. Someone selling the same copy of the book to a dealer must expect a lower price in order for the dealer to realize a profit. Other variables, such as condition and the demands of the current market, enter into pricing. On the whole, a librarian should refer such matters of pricing to an antiquarian book dealer. The most the librarian should do is show the price lists to inquirers, who can then reach their own conclusions.

Frequently the price of a book will turn on whether or not it is a first edition or has some other peculiar feature which sets it apart from the thousands of copies printed over the years. There are numerous guides, as well as detailed explanations of what constitutes a first edition, although the most valuable are the individual author bibliographies which give detailed information on such matters. These bibliographies are listed in the standard guides, from Sheehy to the *American Reference Books Annual.*

READER'S ADVISORY SERVICES[19]

Historically, reference service grew out of the need to give the individual particular attention. In the early years, answering specific queries and preparing bibliographies of the "best" of this or that were handled by the reference librarian. The reference desk was, and in many libraries remains, the primary point of contact the public had with the total collection. It was perfectly natural for persons seeking this or that book, as well as those seeking specific answers, to approach the reference librarian.

When the amount of public service work increased, it became apparent that the two duties would have to be divided. There was

[19]There is some debate whether this service still is formally a part of reference work or whether it is even called this by librarians in the 1980s. Some prefer such terms as "adult learning," but the fact remains that whatever it is called, the actual advice is a part of most library work, at least at the nonresearch level.

simply too much in both areas to expect one or two people to handle the questions well and quickly. Consequently, the reader's-advisory type of question had to be differentiated from the reference query. This was primarily a matter of separating two types of users. The first had some question in mind which would require a search in the reference collections or an extensive search for specific materials in the general collection. The second, who rightfully required special assistance, usually had some vague idea of certain areas in which they would like to read, possibly for specific information but more likely because of a simple interest in the subject.

In one sense, the reference librarian is constantly serving as a guide to readers in the choice of materials, either specific or general. This is particularly true as an adjunct to the search-and-research type of question. Here the librarian may assist the reader in finding a considerable amount of material outside the reference collection or may suggest the right book in that collection as an aid in searching.

At an informal stage, particularly in smaller and medium-sized libraries with limited staff, the reference librarian may help a patron to select a title. For example, someone may wander into the reference room looking for a good historical novel or a nonfiction work on the siege of Troy. The staff member will assist in finding the desired material, usually in the general collection.

Reader's advisory aids

> *Fiction Catalog,* 10th ed. New York: The H. W. Wilson Company, with four annual supplements, 1981–1984. $50.
>
> *Public Library Catalog,* 7th ed. New York: The H. W. Wilson Company, with four annual supplements, 1979–1982. $110.
>
> *The Reader's Adviser,* 12th ed. New York: R. R. Bowker Company, 1974, 1977, 3 vols. $29.50 each vol.

Of lists there is no end, and one of the more popular types centers on "best" books for a given library situation. The lists, despite certain definite drawbacks, are useful for the following:

1. Evaluating a collection. A normal method of evaluating the relative worth of a library collection is to check the collection at random or in depth by the lists noted here.
2. Building a collection. Where a library begins without a book but with a reasonable budget, many of these lists serve as the key to purchasing the core collection.
3. Helping a patron find a particular work in a subject area.

Most of the lists are arranged by some type of subject approach, and as the "best" of their kind, they frequently serve to help the user find material on a desired topic.

The advantage of a list is that it is compiled by a group of experts. Usually there is an editor and an authority or several authorities assisting in each of the major subject fields. However, one disadvantage of this committee approach is that mediocrity tends to rule, and the book exceptional for a daring stand, in either content or style, is not likely to be included.

Used wisely, a "best" bibliography is a guide; it should be no more than that. The librarian has to form the necessary conclusions about what should or should not be included in the collection. If unable to do this, the librarian had better turn in his or her library school degree and call it quits before ruining a library. When any group of librarians discuss the pros and cons of best-book lists, the opinion is always expressed that such lists are nice but highly dubious crutches.

Another obvious flaw, in even the finest special list, is that it is normally tailored for a particular audience. Finally, despite efforts to keep the lists current (and here Wilson's policy of issuing frequent supplements is a great aid), many of them simply cannot keep up with the rate of book production. No sooner is the list of "best" books in anthropology out when a scholar publishes the definitive work in one area that makes the others historically interesting but not particularly pertinent for current needs.

For a number of years the Wilson Company, with the aid of qualified consultants, has been providing lists of selected books for the school and public library. The consultants who determine which titles will be included are normally drawn from various divisions of the American Library Association. Consequently, from the point of view of authority and reliability, the Wilson lists are considered basic for most library collection purposes.

There are five titles in what has come to be known as the Wilson "Standard Catalog Series." They follow more or less the same organization, differing primarily in the scope evident from the title, e.g., *Children's Catalog, Junior High School Library Catalog. Senior High School Library Catalog,* and *Public Library Catalog.* The *Fiction Catalog* crosses almost all age groups, although it essentially supplements the *Public Library Catalog,* which does not list fiction. All the other catalogs have fiction entries.

Typical of the group, the *Public Library Catalog* begins with a classified arrangement of 8045 nonfiction works. Each title is listed under the author's name. Complete bibliographical information is given plus an informative annotation. The annotations not only are critical but often compare one edition of a title with another edition. The reference librarian who is trying to find a suitable book on astronomy for an adult user can either read the annotations or have the user read them and pick a title. In the second section, the books included in the classified arrangement are listed by author, title, and subject. The catalog ends with a directory of publishers. As with all the standard catalogs, the public library version is updated with annual supplements.

The *Fiction Catalog* follows the same format as the public library aid. In it there are 5056 titles with critical annotations. An additional 2000 titles will be included in the supplements. It is particularly useful for the detailed subject index which lists books under not just one area but numerous related subject areas. Furthermore, broad subjects are subdivided by geographical and historical area, and novelettes and composite works are analyzed by each distinctive part. Most of the titles are in print. Anyone who has tried to advise a user about the "best," or even any, title in a given subject area will find this work of extreme value.

The *Reader's Adviser* is among the best known of scores of general listings of "best" books. Planned originally for the bookseller seeking to build a basic stock, the three-volume set is now used extensively in libraries. There are close to 32,000 titles listed. The first volume concentrates on literature, bibliography, and reference; the second concerns drama and world literature in English translation; and the third is really a subject guide to reference books in that it includes a wide range of titles on many subjects, which might be used for reference. However, "reference" is used in its broadest context, which means there are standard biographies, science and history titles, travel books, and so on. Arrangement differs from volume to volume, although either subject or chronological order is followed, with titles listed and usually annotated. Particularly useful are the listings of major books of criticism, which are included for most authors.

These are only a few of literally hundreds of selection aids for the general and specialized collection. The scope of these books varies from 4285 titles arranged by Dewey classification in *Canadian Selection: Books and Periodicals for Libraries* (Toronto: University of Toronto Press, 1978, 1060 pp.) to about 200 titles listed in the highly selective *Chicano Perspectives in Literature* (Albuquerque, New Mexico: Pajarito Publications, 1976).

Since most of these titles are treated as both reference books and selection aids, it may be argued that the reference librarian should know them as well as the other bibliographies and guides. The answer to that is to turn to Sheehy, Walford, and the current reference-book review sources. Inevitably they examine and list the major bibliographies in the area of selection. Beyond knowing where to find such titles, the reference librarian is into another field, that of book selection.

BIBLIOGRAPHIES: PERIODICALS AND NEWSPAPERS

To this point, the primary focus has been on books, but national and trade bibliographies are also concerned with other physical forms of information. Library materials include not only books but periodicals, recordings, films, databases, etc.

> Titus, Edna Brown (ed.), *Union List of Serials in Libraries of the United States and Canada*, 3d ed. New York: The H. W. Wilson Company, 1965, 5 vols. $175.
>
> *New Serial Titles*. Washington: Library of Congress, 1961 to date, eight issues per year, cumulated quarterly and annually. $225.
>
> *New Serial Titles, 1950–1970*. New York: R. R. Bowker Company, 1973, 4 vols. $250. *New Serial Titles, 1950–1970. Subject Guide*. New York: R. R. Bowker Company, 1975, 2 vols. $138.50.
>
> *Ulrich's International Periodical Directory*, 1932 to date, annual. $69.50. *Ulrich's Quarterly*, 1977 to date, quarterly. $30.

A "serial" may be defined in numerous ways, but at its most basic it is a publication issued in parts (e.g., a magazine which comes out weekly) over an indefinite period (i.e., the magazine will be published as long as possible; there is no cutoff date). Serials may be divided in several ways, for example: 1. Irregular Serials; many types of these. 2. Periodicals. (*a*) Journals, from the scholarly and scientific to the professional; (*b*) Magazines, such as found on most newsstands; and (*c*) Newspapers. Some would not subdivide journals and magazines, while others would offer more esoteric subdivisions.

The approximate equivalent of *The National Union Catalog* for periodicals is the *Union List of Serials* and its continuation in *New Serial Titles*. *The National Union Catalog* lists serials, including periodicals, but only those acquired by the Library of Congress. The series for serials is a better guide, if only because more than one source is indicated for location and, more important, the serials, bibliographies, and union lists are limited solely to that form.

The base of the American series of union lists is the *Union List of*

Serials in Libraries of the United States and Canada, which includes titles published before 1950. It is continued by *New Serial Titles* on an eight-times-a-year basis. *New Serial Titles* is cumulated not only annually, but every 21 years, e.g., *New Serial Titles, 1950–1970.* Given the basic volumes and the almost monthly updating, the librarian is able to (1) locate in one or more libraries almost any periodical published from its beginning until today; (2) learn the name and location of the publisher; (3) discover the name, and various changes in the name, of a magazine; (4) check the beginning date of publication and, where applicable, the date it ceased publication and possibly the date it began publication again. This information is valuable for interlibrary loan purposes and for determining whether a library has a complete run of a magazine, whether the magazine is still being published, whether it has changed its name, and so on.

When someone finds an article through one of the library indexes in a journal or magazine which the library does not have, the librarian turns to one of the union lists to find the closest library where the magazine may be borrowed or the article copied. However, not all locations are given for a magazine. This has led to the development of regional, state, and even citywide periodical union lists. A regional list is composed of holdings of libraries in the immediate vicinity. Borrowing is easier and faster from a neighbor than from a distant library located through *New Serial Titles.* Ongoing and older local and regional union lists are found in Sheehy, Walford, and the *American Reference Books Annual.* The most frequently used lists are those published at the local, regional, or state level. These are known to any librarian who is in the least involved with periodicals.

The librarian searching for a periodical published before 1950 will turn to the basic unit in the periodical union lists, the *Union List of Serials in Libraries of the United States and Canada.* Here, alphabetically listed by title, are 156,499 serial titles held by 956 libraries in the United States and Canada. As defined by the compilers of this reference work, as with *New Serial Titles,* the primary meaning of "serial" is a periodical. Newspapers are not included nor are government publications, except for some periodicals and monographic series. As many serials change name, numerous cross-references to the main entry give complete bibliographical information on the title. Serials published in all countries are included. This sometimes confuses beginners. The list shows *holdings* of only American and Canadian libraries, but it includes titles *published* in all countries.

If a serial has been issued after 1950 but before 1971, the next place to look is *New Serial Titles, 1950–1970.* The 21-year cumulation contains the same type of basic bibliographic data found in the basic

Union List. The number of serials listed for only 21 years is almost half again the number of the basic list—220,000 titles held by 800 United States and Canadian libraries, with the addition of International Standard Serial Numbers (ISSN) and country codes. There is also a separate listing of cessations.

For information after 1970, the librarian should turn to the monthly, quarterly, and annual *New Serial Titles.* Here the full address of the publisher is usually given. (In the cumulations only the place of publication is generally indicated.) Also, the annual sales price is usually indicated.

Just as *The National Union Catalog* cannot be used for a subject approach to books before 1950 (when a separate subject service began), neither can it be used with periodicals. There is no subject entry to the *Union List of Serials.* However, there is a subject guide to *New Serial Titles,* and the 1950–1970 set arranges the 220,000 titles in a modified Dewey Decimal order of about 225 broad subject headings. Bibliographical information is given for each entry (usually the title, name of publisher, and ISSN number), although locations are not given. For this information, one must turn back to *New Serial Titles.*

The ongoing *New Serial Titles* also has a separate and twin publication to help with subjects, *New Serial Titles—Classed Subject Arrangement,* which begins with 1955. Lack of cumulations after 1970 makes this a difficult tool to use, and it would be much more valuable if it were combined with *New Serial Titles* as a subject index.

Standard guides

The basic periodical guide is *Ulrich's International Periodical Directory.* Revised and updated every year (until 1980 it was issued every two years), it provides bibliographical information for close to 75,000 periodicals. Unlike *Books in Print,* it is not limited to American publishers but includes titles from around the world. The titles are arranged alphabetically under about 385 broad subject headings, and there is a title index. A separate listing is provided for titles which have ceased publication since the last edition of the directory.

Reference librarians use *Ulrich's* to locate such basic information about a periodical as the address of the publisher, frequency of issue, year first published, and price. Beginning in 1980, the primary abstracting and indexing services for each subject area are included in the subject section. The problem is that information is dated almost as soon as the volume is published—a fault which, of course, cannot be overcome as long as periodical publishers change prices, names, locations, and so on, with alarming frequency.

Here *Ulrich's Quarterly* is of help. The supplement follows the same organization as the main volume; reports on new titles, changes in titles, cessations, and the like. There are some 1500 listings in each issue.

Sources of Serials (New York: R. R. Bowker, 1977 to date, irregular) arranges titles under the names of the publishers, and for each publisher a name and address is given. The entries are grouped by country, and within each country the publishers are listed alphabetically. Unfortunately, there is no title index and one must go back to Ulrich.

The Standard Periodical Directory (New York: Oxbridge Communications, 1964 to date, biennial) is another aid in that it lists and sometimes briefly annotates thousands of house organs, newsletters, reports, and so on, not found in *Ulrich's*. The seventh edition (1981–1982) lists some 25,000 magazines (less than half found in Ulrich's), but has 5000 newsletters; 4000 house organs; 7000 directories; and 20,000 bulletins, association publications, and other types of ephemeral materials. Here, however, the titles listed are limited to those published in the United States and Canada—about 64,000 in total. Entries give somewhat different types of information from that found in *Ulrich's* and include advertising rates, trim size, print methods, and so on. The availability of the title on microform is indicated. While not always accurate, the directory is a useful backup for *Ulrich's,* particularly as it includes types of work not found in the other directory.

The same publisher issues a number of spin-offs, e.g., *Directory of the College Student Press in America, Oxbridge Directory of Newsletters, Oxbridge Directory of Ethnic Periodicals,* and *Oxbridge Directory of Religious Periodicals.* These range from $25 to $40 each, compared with $105 for the *Standard Periodical Directory*—a price which is nearly double that for *Ulrich's.*

In addition to using *Ulrich's* for bibliographical data about a title or *New Serial Titles* for location of a serial, these and other serial aids can answer reference questions such as the following:

(1) What are the *basic* periodicals in chemistry, geography, art, needlework, and so on? Since *Ulrich's* and *New Serial Titles* have a subject approach, one can at least isolate old and new titles in subject areas. However, in both cases the lists are no more selective than *Subject Guide to Books in Print* and therefore are questionable selection aids, particularly as neither has annotations. For more specific results

the librarian should turn to selection tools such as *Magazines for Libraries* by W. A. Katz (4th ed. New York: R. R. Bowker Company, to be published in 1982) or other annotated specialized lists, such as *Periodicals for School Media Programs* (3d ed. Chicago: American Library Association, 1978, 420 pp.), which lists and annotates 500 titles for children and young people in grades K through 12. This is a carefully selected list which will be of use to many libraries.

There are a number of author guides to periodicals, that is to say, listings which indicate what editors are looking for in the way of manuscripts. Most of the guides are to help those writing for scholarly journals. For example, there is Marvin Sussman's *Authors' Guide to Journals in Sociology & Related Fields* (New York: Haworth Press, 1978, 214 pp.) which carefully lists 350 titles.[20]

(2) Where is *Time,* or *Ocean Engineering,* or *Indiana Slavic Studies* indexed? Such a question may be asked when the librarian or the user knows a particular periodical title is likely to give an answer to a query.

(a) The traditional source is *Ulrich's,* which lists one to four indexes or abstracting services for many, although not all, titles. However, *Ulrich's* analyzes only the basic services, and then not always well. For an analysis of the approach see Diana Wyndham's "An Evaluation . . ." *RQ,* Winter 1980, pp. 155–159.

(b) A useful addition to *Ulrich's* is Joseph Marconi's *Indexed Periodicals* (Ann Arbor, Michigan: Pierian Press, 1976). This volume lists, in alphabetical order by title, some 11,000 periodicals which have been indexed in major services. Usually two to four basic indexes are cited for each entry. No effort is made to be comprehensive (only 33 basic indexes are analyzed), and as a result, numerous indexes and abstracting services are not listed—particularly those of a specialized nature. On the other hand, within its scope the service is excellent and of tremendous value in most libraries.

(c) *Chicorel's Index to Abstracting and Indexing Services* (New York: Chicorel Library Publishing Corporation, 1978, 2 vols.) lists in alphabetical order 3 times the number of periodicals found in *Indexed Periodicals* and indicates, again, basic abstracts and indexing services in which they are listed. It is limited to the humanities and social sciences, and scientific and technological titles are covered only if they are indexed in standard social science and humanities services.

[20]For an annotated bibliography of author guides see Stanley P. Lyle, "Authors' Guides to Scholarly Periodicals," *Scholarly Publishing,* April 1979, pp. 255–262. The single best source to author guides: Margaret C. Patterson's *Author Newsletters and Journals* (Detroit: Gale Research Company, 1979).

Apart from minimal or even near-total coverage of indexes and abstracts, none of the above indicates whether the service indexes the title on a selective or on a complete basis. Aside from more esoteric, specialized titles, librarians who are familiar with the indexes and abstracts in their libraries can at least hazard a safe guess that a periodical dealing, for example, with education will be in an education index, a periodical dealing with business in *Business Periodicals Index*, etc.

(3) What does this abbreviation mean? Often the user and the librarian may be confused by an author or editor employing different abbreviations for the same journal. The best source to check to solve the problem: *Periodical Title Abbreviations* (3d ed. Detroit: Gale Research Company, 1981). This and the annual supplements cover some 35,000 abbreviations.

While irregular serials offer a major challenge to librarians, space does not permit more than a cursory glance at the subject. The basic guide: *Irregular Serials and Annuals* (New York: R. R. Bowker Company, 1972 to date, biennial). Following much the same pattern as *Ulrich's,* some 33,000 entries are arranged under 385 subjects with a detailed index. An irregular serial is a promise by a publisher to keep issuing such things as transactions, almanacs, proceedings of meetings, and the like, from time to time for an unspecified period. The publisher fails, or is unable, to state when the material is to be published—hence "irregular."

Serials: Newspapers

American Newspapers, 1821–1936 . . . reprint. Millwood, New York: Kraus Reprint Company, 1970, 791 pp. $90.

Ayer Directory of Publications (Formerly *N. W. Ayer & Son's Directory of Newspapers and Periodicals*). Philadelphia: Ayer Press, 1880 to date, annual. $62.

As neither the *Union List of Serials* nor *New Serial Titles* includes newspapers, how does one locate American newspapers in a given library? For those before 1936 the answer is *American Newspapers*. After 1936, and assuming the wanted newspaper is still being published, one may turn to the *Ayer Directory* to locate the city or town likely to have a run of the newspapers, usually in the local library.

The lack of a national union list may be accounted for as follows:

1. In the United States at least, the number of newspapers has decreased. There were 2461 dailies in 1916; today there are

no more than 1700 and the number is shrinking. The control problem, therefore, is nowhere near the control problem for magazines which, worldwide, now number over 150,000.

2. Current newspapers are filed, often indexed, and micro-formed by the state and by larger cities; therefore locating them, or parts of them, for interlibrary loan is usually a simple matter.

3. Lacking indexes to all but the largest newspapers, access is limited and demand is small for given newspapers of a given date on any national or international scale. (The local news-papers may be indexed and used locally or regionally, but seldom nationally.) For these and other reasons, the need for an up-to-date newspaper union list has never been pressing.

The location of American newspapers prior to 1821 is found in Clarence S. Brigham's *History and Bibliography of American Newspapers, 1690–1820* (Worcester, Massachusetts: American Antiquarian Socie-ty, 1947, 2 vols.). The list is not chronologically complete; where research is being done in a given geographical area, it is wise to check with libraries for local union lists of holdings of newspapers not included in the two major union lists.

The approximate equivalent to *Books in Print* and *Ulrich's* for newspapers is the *Ayer Directory of Publications*. It gives relatively complete information (from circulation and price to names of writers and editors) on daily, weekly, monthly, and less frequently published newspapers in the United States (including Puerto Rico and the Virgin Islands), Canada, the Bahamas, Bermuda, Panama, and the Philippines. Arrangement is geographical, first by state or province, then by city or town. Preceding each geographical section there is valuable reference material, including 69 clearly printed maps show-ing where the newspapers are published; market and economic data for each city and town; and summaries of population, agriculture, industry, and so on. This "bonus" makes *Ayer* a popular reference aid where the library (1) needs up-to-date information on a state or community that is not found in an almanac, encyclopedia, and so on; or (2) does not have the much more detailed *Rand McNally Commercial Atlas and Marketing Guide*. Classified indexes provide ready access to the publications by subject, type, name, editors, and so on.

In addition to newspapers, *Ayer* lists periodicals geographically by state, province, and territory. The reference librarian thus has a handy way of answering questions about the magazines and newspa-pers published in X community, the interests they represent, the existence of any foreign-language publications in the area, and so on.

(Also, for the would-be writer who wants to find a local publication, *Ayer* is of help.) Listing close to 23,000 titles of both newspapers and periodicals, *Ayer* is a good backup reference work for *Ulrich's*, at least for U.S., Canadian, and some territorial titles.

Basic guides for newspapers (and some periodicals) outside America are: *Newspaper Press Directory, Benn's Guide to Newspapers and Periodicals of the World* (London: Benn Brothers, 1846 to date, annual), and *Willing's Press Guide* (London: Willing, 1874 to date, annual). There are, also, special press directories covering everything from black newspapers to alternative newspapers listed in Sheehy, *ARBA*, and so on.

BIBLIOGRAPHIES: MICROFORM[21]

Guide to Microforms in Print: Author-Title. Weston, Connecticut: Microform Review, 1961 to date, annual. $79.50.

Books on Demand. Ann Arbor, Michigan: University Microfilms, 1975 to date, biennial. 3 vols. $73.50. (Plus paper bound annual supplement.)

For purposes of storage and convenience, most libraries with substantial holdings in periodicals and newspapers have both on microform. Books, particularly those hard to locate or out of print, are on microform as are various other printed works, from reports to government documents.[22] Most of the aids for locating these forms are employed in acquisitions, but there are times when the reference librarian should know at least the basic microform bibliographies.

Microform comes in two forms: the roll and the flat transparency or card. The familiar 35 mm reel or roll has been in libraries for so long that many librarians and users think only of this form when microform is mentioned. In the flat microform there are several basic varieties or types: (1) Microfiche, or fiche, is available in different sizes, but the favored is the standard 4 by 6 inches, with an average of 98 pages per sheet. Various reductions may either increase or

---

[21]The amount of material on microforms is impressive. See, for example, the 15-section unannotated bibliography, Michael R. Gabriel, *Micrographics 1900–1977, A Bibliography* (Mankato, Minnesota: Minnesota Scholarly Press, 1978). A relatively recent text is Michael Gabriel and Dorothy Ladd, *The Microform Revolution in Libraries* (Greenwich, Connecticut: JAI Press, 1980).

[22]Nancy M. Cline, "A Librarian's Perspective of the GPO and Micropublishing," *Microform Review,* Winter 1979, pp. 23–28. A clear discussion of what is likely to develop in the way of government documents on microform.

decrease the number of pages. (2) Ultrafiche, as the name implies, is an ultrafine reduction, usually on a 4- by 6-inch transparency. One card may contain 3000 to 5000 pages. (3) Micropoint is a 6- by 9-inch card which contains up to 100 pages of text in 10 rows and 10 columns.

COM (computer output microform) has a wide variety of uses in the library.[23] For example, as a role of film, it may appear as a substitute for the standard card catalog. Thanks to the easy generation of additions and corrections by computer, the film can be updated easily and at limited cost. The result is a current catalog which is similar to the standard book or card catalog, but is read with a machine.

Beyond the catalog, any current index or bibliography may take the same form, and for much the same reason; i.e., it can be updated quickly. For example, the *Magazine Index,* considered in the next chapter, is kept current by simply sending the library new COM reels instead of the standard printed form.

The equivalent of *Books in Print* for microform is the ever expanding *Guide to Microforms in Print.* It alphabetically lists over 70,000 titles from some 300 publishers, including international firms. Arranged by title and author in one alphabet, the guide lists books, journals, newspapers, government publications, and related materials. Sixteen different types of microform are considered, and the types, with explanation, are listed in the preface. Not all microforms are listed, for example, theses and dissertations. Another approach by the same company is *Guide to Microforms in Print: Subject* which lists the material under 135 broad Library of Congress headings. Certain types are classified by form; i.e., government documents, manuscripts, and so on. The publisher issues a type of *Publishers Trade List Annual* called *Micropublishers Trade List Annual.*

For ongoing microforms the publisher issues *Microform Review* (1972 to date, quarterly), which includes news of the field and detailed, critical reviews of more expensive microform publications. *Cumulative Microform Reviews,* 1972–1976 (1979, 619 pp.) is a reprint of over 300 reviews from the first five volumes of the magazine. Plans are for volumes every five years with cumulative indexes. *Microform Review* is augmented by *Microlist* (1975 to date, monthly), which updates *Guide to Microforms in Print* with an alphabetical listing of new microforms.

Microform is employed in a library for many reasons, one of the

---

[23]William Saffady, *Computer Output Microfilm* (Chicago: American Library Association, 1978). This is the best discussion of COM: includes material on most aspects of the art.

most frequent being its use as a substitute for books or other forms of printed material which are no longer in print, no longer available from a used-book dealer, or so prohibitive in cost as to make microform preferable. It would require a whole chapter to explain how librarians find out-of-print materials, but one approach is suggested by *Books on Demand.* This is a multivolume author, title, and subject catalog of about 100,000 out-of-print titles which may be purchased literally "on demand." The titles are available on microfilm or as hard-copy xerographic prints on the microform at an average cost of $15 to $20, depending on the number of pages. Other companies offer similar services as well as standard reprints of titles which the publisher thinks will be in sufficient demand. The reprints usually are listed in *Books in Print* as well as in a number of specialized guides.

PAMPHLETS

> *Vertical File Index.* New York: The H. W. Wilson Company, 1935 to date, monthly. $18.

A pamphlet is understood to be a publication of a few printed leaves, normally bound in paper. *The Weekly Record* does not list pamphlets under 49 pages, and such works are rarely included in the standard trade bibliographies. Individual libraries classify pamphlets as important to rebind and catalog separately or ephemeral enough to warrant no more than placement in a vertical file under an appropriate subject.

Recognizing the failure of most general trade bibliographies to list pamphlets, the Wilson Company has a bibliography devoted solely to this form. Issued monthly except in August, *Vertical File Index* is a subject approach to a select group of pamphlets. Selection is based on their probable use for the general library, not for the special, technical library.

Each entry includes the standard bibliographical information and a short descriptive note of content. A title index follows the subject list. Wilson does not recommend any of the works, many of which are distributed by companies and organizations for advertising and propaganda.

One of the headaches of ordering pamphlets is that they must be purchased from the publisher. No general book jobber will bother handling them. A free pamphlet may involve many dollars' worth of paperwork and time on the part of a librarian or clerk.

There are several sources of free or inexpensive materials which complement the *Vertical File Index.* One of the best, and discussed in the chapter on government documents, is *Selected U.S. Government Publications,* which includes many low-priced items. A source of free audiovisual materials is the *Educator Guides,* considered on p. 107. Then there is *Index to Free Periodicals* (Ann Arbor, Michigan: Pierian Press, 1976 to date, semiannual), which is primarily a subject approach to the contents of 50 magazines from business and nonprofit organizations. The articles, illustrations, and the magazines themselves offer further suggestions for similar types of material.

BIBLIOGRAPHIES: NONPRINT MATERIALS

"Nonprint" is not a precise descriptor. It has come to mean any communication material other than the traditional book, periodical, and newspaper. Nonprint is closely linked with terms such as the "new media," "audiovisual," "multimedia," "nonbook," and other expressions which indicate new approaches to reference work in particular and library services in general. Nonprint materials are an essential part of reference service, particularly in school libraries or, as they are called, "school media centers" or "learning centers."

When working with resources other than books, the reference librarian functions much as when working with the traditional media:

1. In schools, universities, and colleges, the librarian will be called upon by the teacher for information on media not only available in the library, but also that may be ordered, or even borrowed from other libraries.
2. The students will want information and advice about multimedia for the primary learning process.
3. The layperson's needs will be somewhat similar, although here most of the emphasis is likely to be on advice about films, recordings, and so on, within the library which may extend knowledge (or recreational interests) beyond the traditional book.

The reference librarian should be conversant with at least the basic bibliographies and control devices for the new media. Knowledge of bibliographies and sources is important for answering questions directly dealing with audiovisual materials: "Where can I find [such and such] a catalog of films, records, tapes?" "Do you have anything on film that will illustrate this or that?" "What do you have pertaining to local history on recordings or film?" In large libraries such questions might be referred to the proper department, but in small and medium-sized libraries, the questions usually will have to be answered by the reference librarian.

Guides and bibliographies[24]

> Rufsvold, Margaret. *Guides to Educational Media*. 4th ed. Chicago: American Library Association, 1977, 125 pp. Paperback, $5.
>
> Sive, Mary R. *Selecting Instructional Media: A Guide to Audio-Visual and Other Instructional Media Lists*. Littleton, Colorado: Libraries Unlimited, 1978, 268 pp. $16.
>
> National Information Center for Educational Media. *NICEM Media Indexes*. Los Angeles: University of Southern California, National Information Center, 1967 to date. Various services, prices. (Available online.)
>
> *Audiovisual Market Place*. New York: R. R. Bowker Company, 1964 to date, annual. $29.95.

There are no entirely satisfactory bibliographies for all nonprint materials—no *Books in Print*, no *Cumulative Book Index*, no *National Union Catalog*. And even the by-now-standard bibliographies leave much to be desired in organization and coverage. Lacking overall bibliographical control, the materials are difficult to track. The lack of such tools accounts in no small way for the development of media experts who are familiar with the many access routes, routes which the average harassed reference librarian has neither the time nor the inclination to follow.

The best single guide to bibliographies and media publishers' catalogs in this field is *Guides to Educational Media*. Arranged alphabetically by title of a published catalog, the guide clearly identifies each of the catalogs and annotates it to indicate audience, scope, number of entries, and special features. Close to 300 bibliographies on films, instructional materials, slides, videotapes, and the like are included. Entries are listed in an author, subject, and title index.

Mary Sive's *Selecting Instructional Media* is somewhat similar to the *Guides*. Selected media are arranged by subjects, and there are five indexes by subject, media, author, title, and instructional level. The

---

[24]There are numerous texts about media and libraries. A few examples: A. J. Casciero, *Introduction to AV* (Littleton, Colorado: Libraries Unlimited, 1981); Thomas L. Hart, ed., *Instruction in School Media Center Use* (Chicago: American Library Association, 1978).

main listing is by subject, but two other listings are by media and by comprehensive list including all elements. By using this with the *Guides,* the reference librarian will be sure to have fairly well covered the field, at least up to 1978. An updated version was slated for late 1981.

There are other general aids which profess to guide, but generally only list, with less than critical consideration, everything in sight. During the past 10 years there has been a mass of bibliographies and guides. Few of them are worth mentioning. The librarian should be careful in purchasing such titles. The quantity of rubbish and duplication is amazing.

The closest thing to *Books in Print* for audiovisual materials is the *NICEM Media Indexes.* The purpose of these indexes, which are really bibliographies, is to provide noncritical information on what is available in nonprint materials. And, although directed at elementary and secondary school needs, a good deal of the data is applicable to other types of libraries. Hence, it can be used to answer such queries as, What transparencies are available for geography? What educational films are here on animals? Environmental studies? And so on.

The *NICEM Indexes* are really a series of individual bibliographies, and *not* a single alphabetical subject/title index to the media. In 1981 the indexes listed over a half-million items in the following fields: 16 mm films (4 vols.), 35 mm filmstrips (3 vols.), audio tapes, video tapes, records, 8 mm cartridges, overhead transparencies (2 vols.), and slides. In addition to listings by form, the indexes include subject approaches with multimedia listings (recordings, films, and so on) for psychology, health and safety education, vocational and technical education, environmental studies, and free educational multimedia materials.

The volumes are arranged in different ways, although essentially each has separate subject and title indexes. Some volumes include directories of producers and distributors, and a separate volume is given over entirely to this type of directory information. Each entry gives essential information for tracking or ordering. While this is the single best bibliographical guide available to all the nonbook media, it has several drawbacks: (1) The lists are usually two or more years behind; (2) the subject headings are less than satisfactory and there are not enough cross-references; (3) the items are usually annotated, but the information is noncritical and of little help in selection; (4) the data are not always accurate. The reason for much of the difficulty is familiar enough: lack of funds. The indexes are a product of the nonprofit National Information Center for Educational Media. One advantage of having the various indexes online is that the librarian may search through the whole set at once, not through each of the individual volumes.

A more limited bibliography often found in libraries is the *Educator Guides* (Randolph, Wisconsin: Educators Progress Service, 1934 to date, annual, various prices). The unique feature is that all items listed are free. Each annual edition is totally revised and carries descriptive annotations for most items. The formats include film, filmstrips, and tapes; among the topics are guidance, social studies, science, and health curriculum materials. The guides are a valuable source of accurate answers to queries put by teachers as well as members of the community seeking free support materials for talks, lectures, or programs.

The *NICEM Indexes,* and especially the volume on producers and distributors, give information on who sells what. A more thorough listing is offered in the annual *Audiovisual Market Place,* which claims some 5000 listings under 25 subject headings. The librarian looking for information on, say, overhead projector manufacturers, distributors of films, or sources of slides will find the needed data under the subject or through a detailed index. A third section, of less use, includes periodicals, reference books, and a calendar of events.

A related title which gives an annual overview of media and education is *Educational Media Yearbook* (Littleton, Colorado: Libraries Unlimited, 1973 to date, annual). While this is prepared for elementary and secondary schools, much of the overview material is relevant to other types of libraries, and it is the single best summary of the year's activities in all aspects of media.

Reviews of the various media are found in numerous places. *Booklist,* previously mentioned as the "home" of "Reference and Subscription Books Reviews," has a good section on media and *Library Journal* now fills the gap, at least in part, left by the death of *Previews* in 1981. *Media Monitor* (Pearl River, New York: 1977 to date, quarterly) is an excellent personal effort edited and written by Mary Sive. There are many other reliable sources, although these three will be enough for most general situations.

Indexes to reviews

Media Review Digest. Ann Arbor, Michigan: The Pierian Press, 1970 to date, annual. 2 vols. $150.

A type of *Book Review Index* for films, videotapes, filmstrips, records, tapes, and other miscellaneous media. *Media Review Digest*

(MRD), until 1974 called *Multi Media Reviews Index*, analyzes reviews of the media appearing in over 150 periodicals. The 60,000 or so reviews are then indexed, with full citations, by type of medium reviewed. Some excerpts from reviews are given and an evaluative sign shows whether the review was favorable or not. Its use by a librarian is almost the same as for the indexes to book reviews, i.e., to check reviews, probably for purposes of buying or renting a given item. The information provided is full, and often includes descriptions of the material as well as cataloging information. The service has the major drawback of lack of currency. While one supplement a year is provided, it is late and the time lag is considerable. More timely is the *International Index to Multi-Media Information* (Pasadena, California: Audio Visual Associates, 1970 to date, quarterly), but this includes reviews from only 110 periodicals. It has a subject index, gives prices (not found in the *MRD*), and includes more review extracts. It lacks the full bibliographical information of the *Media Review Digest.*

BIBLIOGRAPHY OF BIBLIOGRAPHIES

> *Bibliographic Index: A Cumulative Bibliography of Bibliographies.* New York: The H. W. Wilson Company, 1937 to date, triannual with cumulations. Service basis.
>
> Besterman, Theodore. *A World Bibliography of Bibliographies.* 4th ed. Lausanne: Societas Bibliographica, 1965–1966, 5 vols. Supplemented by: Toomey, Alice. *A World Bibliography of Bibliographies, 1964–1974.* Totowa, New Jersey: Rowman & Littlefield, 1977, 2 vols.

A bibliography of bibliographies is, as the name suggests, a listing of bibliographies. One may find a bibliography on dogs at the end of a periodical article, an encyclopedia essay, or as part of a book on pets. If one lists these three bibliographies and adds a dozen to a thousand more, one has a bibliography of bibliographies—in this case, a listing of bibliographies, from various sources, about dogs. (In turn, each of the bibliographies constitutes a subject bibliography.)

The primary example of a bibliography of bibliographies is *Bibliographic Index.* Under numerous headings, one may find bibliographies about subjects, persons, and places. The entries represent (1) separate published books and pamphlets which are normally bibliographies in a specific subject area, e.g., *East European and Soviet Economic Affairs: A Bibliography* . . . ; (2) bibliographies which are parts of books and pamphlets, such as the bibliography which appears at the end of David Kunzle's book *The Early Comic Strip;* and (3) bibliographies which have been published separately or in articles in some 2200 English and foreign-language periodicals. Emphasis is on American publications, and to be listed, a bibliography must contain more than 50 citations.

The inevitable catch to many reference works is applicable here: (1) the bibliographies are not listed until from six months to a year after they are published, and (2) while books, and to a lesser degree pamphlets, are well covered, the index cannot be trusted to include many periodical bibliographies. Why? Because there are over 55,000 periodicals issued, often with bibliographies, and the index includes only 2200. The result is that the *Bibliographic Index* is usually a beginning point for the subject expert, or, most likely, a way for the expert to check to see whether anything has been missed in the mining of more detailed sources. General users are likely to find all they need in the way of bibliographies in the card catalog, *Subject Guide to Books in Print,* a subject index such as *Music Index,* or other general sources in the library. For the person between the expert and the generalist, *Bibliographic Index* is useful for finding hard-to-locate materials on less-known personalities and subjects.

A point to remember about any bibliography of bibliographies is that it is twice removed from the subject. Once a bibliography is located in *Bibliographic Index,* the next step is to find the bibliography itself. After that, still another step is required: the location of the particular article or book listed in the bibliography. At any point along the way, the user may be frustrated by not finding what is listed in the index or if finding it, by not being able to locate the desired information in the bibliography. With these stumbling blocks, it is no wonder that many reference librarians favor more direct sources.

Types of materials listed, along with the frequent difficulty in locating the final needed title, tend to restrict more limited bibliographies of bibliographies to specialists. The classic case in point is Theodore Besterman's *A World Bibliography of Bibliographies.* This fourth edition examines 17,000 separately collated volumes of bibliography in 40 languages published from the fifteenth century through 1963. Material is arranged alphabetically under 16,000 subject headings.

Besterman's basic volumes are updated by a supplement which lists 18,000 titles of published works or reprints. Here, an important point: Besterman and the supplement list only separate bibliographies and not those published as parts of articles, or in books, and so on, as is the practice of *Bibliographic Index.* For example, *Bibliographic*

Index lists bibliographies about Henry James wherever they may appear (as parts of articles, books, and so on); Besterman only includes titles devoted exclusively to bibliography—in this case Leon Edel and D. H. Lawrence's *A Bibliography of Henry James* (2d. ed. London: Rupert Hart-Davis, 1961). This is a 427-page definitive volume. One reviewer found, for example, that of 159 selected titles in the Besterman supplement only two appeared in *Bibliographic Index.*

SUGGESTED READING

Cave, Roderick, "Besterman and Bibliography: An Assessment," *Journal of Librarianship,* July 1978, pp. 149–161. A sympathetic yet critical look at the man and his work. Cave points out some of the important elements in a good bibliographic reference work, and suggests how revisions of Besterman's work may be improved. See, too, a tribute to another bibliographer, e.g., James G. Olle, "Arundell Esdaile," *Journal of Librarianship,* no. 4, October 1980, pp. 217–228.

Drolet, Leon, "Reference Readiness for AV Questions," *American Libraries,* March 1981, pp. 154–155. A brief, yet practical discussion of the basic reference works which are likely to be used in most libraries to locate AV materials.

Gorman, Michael, "Toward Bibliographic Control," *American Libraries,* various dates, pages. An ongoing column concerned with "the application of modern procedures and technologies to produce control and dissemination of documents." The author has a point of view, avoids jargon, and writes with amazing clarity and a sense of what is or is not important.

Hickey, Doralyn, "The American Librarian's Dream: Full Bibliographic Control." *Library Lectures,* no. 28–30, 1978, University of Tennessee, pp. 15–31. A unique exploration of bibliographic history in the United States in terms of how the system evolved in light of our particular social system. The author ends with some fascinating "questions for twenty-first century bibliography."

Leonhardt, T. W., "Fool's Gold in Your Attic . . .," *The Idaho Librarian,* January 1979, pp. 3–4. A brief, critical annotated bibliography of some inexpensive guides to help the librarian evaluate book prices.

Sable, M. H., "Systematic Bibliography as the Reflection of Reality," *International Library Review,* no. 1, 1981, pp. 17–24. A witty and heartfelt argument for the necessity for systematic bibliography. Along the way the author states the problems and possible solutions confronting today's bibliographer. A good introduction to systematic bibliography.

Walsh, Patricia (ed.), *Serials Management and Microforms,* Westport, Connecticut: Microform Review, Inc., 1979. A collection of articles on the benefits of microform and how it is applied to overcome problems with periodicals and other forms of serials. Uneven, yet a useful introduction.

Wellisch, Hans, "The Cybernetics of Bibliographic Control . . .," *Journal of the American Society for Information Science,* January 1980, pp. 41–50. A fascinating, although somewhat technical, discussion of universal bibliographic control and the hazards of document retrieval.

Winans, Robert B., "The Beginnings of Systematic Bibliography in America Up to 1800: Further Explorations," *Papers of the Bibliographic Society of America,* January 1978, pp. 15–35. A well-documented study of book catalogs. The "further explorations" refers to continuation of the study started by Jesse H. Shera, i.e., "The Beginnings of Systematic Bibliography in America, 1642–1799," in *Essays Honoring Lawrence C. Wroth,* Portland, Maine: Anthoensen Press, 1951, pp. 263–278.

CHAPTER FOUR

Indexing and Abstracting Services

AN INDEX REPRESENTS AN ANALYSIS, usually by name and by subject, of a document. As most books, magazines, reports and other sources are about a number of different things, it is necessary for the indexer to select key terms which are likely to be of most value to the user. Sometimes in the routine use of indexes. the librarian forgets that the material was laboriously prepared for them by indexers. One critic is correct when she notes: "The indexers are taking over the world. We're the only ones who know where the information is buried."[1]

In the quest to give the user more entries to information, there are an ever-increasing number of indexes and abstracts in various forms.[2] The beginner's primary challenge is to isolate and identify the titles commonly used in the reference process.

Leaving aside the individual book index, a reference librarian is

[1]Barbara Preschel, quoted by Alice Edmunds in "For the Professional Indexer a Book Needs That Listing in the Back," *Publishers Weekly*, August 14, 1978, p. 32.

[2]There are several thousand indexing and abstracting services in the United States. In England alone the estimate is close to 350, both in printed form and as machine-readable databases. Of these, 77 percent have been established in the last 20 years, as is also the case in the United States and other Western countries. See H. East, "UK Abstracting and Indexing Services . . ." *ASLIB Proceedings*, October 1979, pp. 460–475.

most likely to be concerned with the following types of traditional indexes:

1. Periodicals
   a. General indexes, covering many periodicals in a wide or specific subject field. *The Readers' Guide to Periodical Literature* is the most widely known of this type of index.
   b. Subject indexes, covering not only several periodicals but also other material found in new books, pamphlets, reports, and government documents. The purpose is to index material in a narrow subject field. Examples of this type of index are the *Applied Science & Technology Index* and *Library Literature*.
   c. Indexes to single magazines, either at the end of a volume or as separately published works. *The National Geographic Magazine Cumulative Index* (coverage from 1915 to date, entitled: *Handy Key to Your National Geographics*) and the *Scientific American Cumulative Index* are examples.[3]

2. Newspapers
   There is a growing number of newspaper indexes in the United States. Still, the number is not great, and the scarcity of indexes is made up for by individual libraries indexing local papers. The best-known newspaper index is *The New York Times Index*.

3. Serials
   There are indexes to reports both published and unpublished, government documents; proceedings of conferences and congresses, continuations; and other materials which can be defined as serials, i.e., any publication issued in parts over an indefinite period. Many of the subject periodical indexes include some of these forms, while other indexes such as *Resources in Education* are limited to indexing only reports.

4. Material in collections
   These indexes cover collections of poems, plays, fiction, songs, and so on. The *Speech Index* and *Granger's Index to Poetry* are examples.

5. Other indexes
   Here one might include everything from concordances to

---

[3]*Guide to Special Issues and Indexes of Periodicals* (New York: Special Libraries Association, various dates). Frequently updated, this is an alphabetical listing of nearly 1000 periodicals which indicates whether the periodical has its *own* index and also includes other features.

indexes of various forms, from *Book Review Index,* to collections of quotations, to indexes to patents or music. Scientific searching may include indexes which have specifications, formulas, standards, prospectuses, and so on. And machine-readable databases may deal exclusively with numbers or their equivalent. Usually these indexes are treated by reference librarians in terms of the subject covered rather than as indexes per se.

Abstracting services[4]

Abstracting services are an extension of indexes; they perform the same function in locating and recording the contents of periodicals, books, and various types of documents. They differ from indexes in that (1) by definition, they include a summary of the material indexed; (2) they tend to be confined to relatively narrow subject areas; and (3) the arrangement rarely follows the single author, subject, and sometimes title alphabetical arrangement of indexes. The abstract provides a clue to the relevance of the material and is valuable as a method of determining whether or not the user really wants the article, report, book, and so on. An index only gives a key to where the material is located and rarely indicates relevancy.

Most of the abstracting services aim at relatively complete coverage of a narrow subject area.[5] Coverage tends to be worldwide, with abstracts of foreign-language articles in English. The format varies from abstract to abstract, although normally the issues are arranged under broad subject headings, with appropriate author and some subject indexing.

The arrangement by broad subject classification sometimes confuses beginners. It is a blessing to experts who need only turn to the classification section of interest. The traditional index uses the specific rather than the broad approach, thus often requiring the searcher to go back and forth in the index to run down related subject headings. Most abstracting services have limited author and subject

[4]Bruce Manzer, *The Abstract Journal, 1790–1920: Origin, Development and Diffusion* (Metuchen, New Jersey: Scarecrow Press, 1977). A scholarly analysis of the growth and dissemination of the abstracting service.

[5]Technically. there are two types of abstracts. The "indicative" abstract indicates the type of article and the author's approach and treatment, but does not usually include specific data. The "informative," and most often used in works described in this text, summarizes enough of the data and findings to relieve the reader of the necessity of always reading the article. In neither case does the abstractor make any critical assessment.

indexes for the ongoing issues but prepare exhaustive annual author-subject indexes. The librarian unfamiliar with the subject will save time by turning to the annual cumulated index to discover the subject classifications under which this or that specific subject is likely to appear in the monthly abstracts.

A drawback even more severe for most abstracting services than for indexes is the delay time in publication. Whereas an average index may be 1 to 3 months behind material analyzed, the average abstract has a time lag of 9 to 15 months or more. The exception is the few online newspaper and business services which make a special effort to get certain materials abstracted and available before a week is out. However, for the majority of online abstracting services, the wait period, while not as great, is still longer than that of the standard index.

While any reasonably important journal may be covered by two or three different abstracting services in the United States, if time is a factor, the librarian should first consult standard indexes which may include the same titles but analyze them more quickly than the abstracting services.

EVALUATION

With the understanding that online index and abstracting services (i.e., bibliographic databases) should be evaluated as carefully as the traditional printed forms, although such evaluation is outside the scope of this chapter, the reader is asked to move to consideration of standard printed sources.[6]

An experienced indexer gives some practical advice on how to evaluate a book index:

> *To find out whether an index is good or bad, readers can sample a few pages of the text, then look in the index for entries that will lead to the information on those pages quickly and easily, and finish by doing the reverse, going from index to text. But a good index should not only work; it should also read well enough to give a reader a sense of the book.*[7]

Another point: Read the preface or introductory remarks. This

---

[6]Database format aside, much of what follows is equally applicable to machine-readable index or abstract services. Notes on evaluation of databases will be found in the second volume of this text.

[7]Alice Edmunds, "For the Professional Indexer a Book Needs That Listing in the Back," *Publishers Weekly*, August 14, 1978, p. 25.

is not always helpful, but at least it should give the reader a notion of what the index is about and, if nothing else, explain arrangement, abbreviations, and type of subject headings employed.

There are eight relative constants in the evaluation of indexes and abstracting services. They are:

1. The publisher

The most used indexes in all but special libraries are issued by The H. W. Wilson Company. The firm has an excellent reputation for producing easy-to-use, accurate indexes. One may argue with what is or is not included in one of these indexes, but the format and the depth of indexing are excellent. At the other extreme are the publishers of time-tested specialized and technical indexes such as *Science Citation Index*. In between are publishers about whom the librarian may know nothing and who seem to be offering (*a*) a duplication of another service or (*b*) a questionable venture into a new area. The librarian should check out the publisher, preferably by talking to subject experts and to other librarians who may have knowledge of the field and by reading reviews. Any or all of these safety checks will quickly reveal whom to trust and whom not to trust.

2. Scope[8]

The most essential evaluative point about an index or an abstract is that of coverage. Neither librarians nor users will consult an index unless they think it adequately covers the periodicals or other materials in the field of interest. Here one must consider obvious points: (*a*) the number and kind of periodicals indexed, especially whether the number is adequate for the field and whether the titles represent the best in the United States and, if necessary, abroad; (*b*) the inclusion of other material, since in some disciplines it will be necessary to consider not only periodicals but reports, books, monographs, and so on.

Few librarians or users are ever contented that index or abstract X or Y is totally satisfactory in scope. In general or in large, undivided disciplines, there is always the nagging doubt that this or that journal

---

[8]How can one judge if the index is even close to the right length (i.e., includes enough basic material to be useful) in a book? The American Society of Indexers believe a good index must have at least five pages for every hundred pages of text. The Society also suggests that if one fails to find cross-references, the index is as bad as the work which is limited simply to names and places.

(or type of book, or report, or other item) should be indexed rather than P or Q. In narrow, specialized subject areas, the question is usually resolved for the so-called core titles which everyone agrees are necessary, but arguments arise over what should be indexed in the fringe areas or in closely related disciplines.

When considering scope, related areas should be examined: (*a*) In an effort to include everything with the least amount of effort, the index may be virtually a concordance in that most keywords mentioned in the text are listed. The result is a bulky, often blind-alley, finding aid.[9] A fallout of this type of indexing is the equally frustrating practice of including after each work a number of undifferentiated page references. In a strong of, say, 20 page numbers after "Ostrich Eggs," the user has no idea which page reference is major, minor, or of absolutely no importance. (*b*) The text may be indexed, but there is no reference to plates, tables, diagrams, and so on. (*c*) There may be recurrent use of "see" entries instead of simply listing the place twice; e.g., "American Test Tube Concern, *see* ATTC." It would be much simpler to list the page under both the full name and the acronym, thus saving the reader flipping back and forth through the index.

3.   Duplication and gaps

A decade or so ago users complained of the lack of proper indexes or abstracts, but in the early 1980s the same people are complaining about too many services.

Ideally, index and abstract publishers would divide the disciplines in such a way that duplication of titles covered would be limited. They do not. Therefore the librarian must always ask the key evaluative question: How much duplication exists between X and Y service, and is the difference so much (or so little) that X should be chosen over Y?

Comparing duplication among indexes is a favored and beneficial study for librarians. There are numerous such reports; e.g., Goehlert found that among the 30 basic indexing and abstracting services in the social and political sciences there is a tremendous amount of duplication in what they index. Some 50 percent of the journals were indexed in 6 or more of the services, and 5 indexes would give access to 78 percent of the journals in the field. Knowing

---

[9]Humorist Stephen Leacock early wrote about what he called index non-entries. The 1942 sketch has been reprinted numerous times, but see pp. 419–422 of Norman Stevens, *Library Humor* (Metuchen, New Jersey: Scarecrow Press, 1971).

this, users tend to avoid esoteric indexes unless absolutely necessary. In fact, in the social sciences the experts turn to only 1 or 2 of the 30, and both are from the 5 which cover most of the journals.[10]

The methods of comparing duplication differ but primarily consist of (*a*) Checking what journals and monographs are indexed by both and (*b*) Checking the effectiveness of indexing by running the same search in both indexes.

4.   Depth of indexing

Indexing thoroughness varies considerably, and the publisher of a periodicals index should explain (but often does not) whether all articles in the relevant periodicals are indexed. Few indexes include short items, notices, announcements, and so on, but reputable ones should cite at least the main articles in terms of subjects covered, authors, and possibly titles. In a survey of 10 political science services, one study found that only 3 of the services actually indexed all possible articles. Depth of indexing for other services ranged from a low of 4.20 percent to a high of 96 percent.

The obvious—some would say deceptively obvious—way of recovering a maximum of information from a given document is to index it in considerable depth. This means assigning a maximum number of subject headings to the document (as well, of course, as author and sometimes title labels). The question is, What is the optimal depth of indexing? To put it more precisely, for a given collection of documents and a given population of users of those documents, what is the best number of index terms to assign to those documents on the average and for any single document.[11] Unfortunately there is no consensus, even among experts.

5.   Currency

The frequency of publication is a fair indication of the currency of the service. This is only a fair yardstick, because there are factors which cancel out publication frequency as a method of evaluation. For

[10]Robert Goehlert, "The Scope of Indexing Services in Political and Social Sciences," *RQ,* Spring 1978, p. 236. Others of this type show similar duplication in all indexing. See, for example, Jane Caldwell and Celia Ellingson, "A Comparison of Overlap: ERIC and Psychological Abstracts," *Database,* June 1979, pp. 62–67. For a detailed analysis of the overlap of the three scientific indexes, see B. Hawkins, et al., "Indexing Revisited," *New Library World,* June 1979, p. 106.

[11]M. E. Maron, "Depth of Indexing," *Journal of the American Society for Information Science,* July 1979, p. 224.

example, *The New York Times Index* is always two and sometimes three months behind in indexing the newspaper. The December 29 issue of *The New York Times* will not be in index form and available for library use until at least the following March. Other indexes may be as much as a year or more behind.

In another situation, the index or abstract does reach the library within the calendar period announced on its cover, but the material indexed is several weeks or months in arrears of the date on the cover. The lag between the time a periodical appears and the time it is picked up in the index is easy to check. Compare a few dates of indexed articles with the date on the cover of the index or abstract.

How often, if at all, is the index cumulated? Is there an annual volume which cumulates the weekly, monthly, quarterly, or other issues? Are there 5-year, 10-year, or other cumulations? For retrospective searching, the necessity for frequent cumulations is apparent to anyone who has had to search laboriously through, say, the bimonthly issues of *Library Literature* before the annual or the two-year cumulation appears.

6. Format

Employing "format" as a grab-bag term, the index or abstract must be considered in terms of *(a)* ease or difficulty of understanding or using the arrangement; *(b)* arrangement by alphabet, by subject, a classed form, or a citation form; *(c)* form, whether in dictionary form (i.e., in alphabetical order from, say, aardvark to zooplankton) or in separate divisions by subject, author, title, and so on; *(d)* readability of format, a particularly important point when one considers indexes published by computer printout; *(e)* completeness of the citation, with enough bibliographical information to identify the material and to locate it in the material indexed; and *(f)* accuracy of the bibliographical information.

7. Subject headings

The type, number, and form of subject headings used in an index or abstract are important. Many standard indexes rely on the Library of Congress subject headings, or Sears. Conversely, indexes for specific disciplines may develop their own subject headings, rely on keywords in the title, or adopt a plan suitable for the material being indexed or abstracted. Regardless of what type of subject-heading system is employed, there should be adequate *see* and *see also* references, a thesaurus of subject terms, or both.

The preceding brief paragraph only skims the most vexing problem of indexers, one which has resulted in a considerable body of theoretical and practical literature. (See, for example, any issue of *The Indexer,* the official journal of The American Society of Indexers.)

8. Description

When one turns to abstracts, there is the added dimension of whether the abstract adequately describes the document. The readability factor may be high or low, depending on how the abstracts were prepared (by the author of the indexed item, by the publisher, or by both—in other words, whether the author's abstract has been edited judiciously or by "automatic" methods such as keyword scanning).

In order truly to test an index for inclusion in a library, a considerable amount of time and effort is required, as well as some expertise in comparative analysis. Consequently, the majority of librarians rely on reviews, the advice of experts, or both—particularly when considering a specialized service. The benefit of learning evaluation techniques is as much to show the librarian how indexes or abstracts are (or should be) constructed as it is to reveal points for acceptance or rejection.

The best evaluative summary is suggested by users' attitudes toward indexes. Among the preferences shown by users:

> (a) *accuracy;* (b) *ease of use;* (c) *layout and presentation;* (d) *choice of subject index headings;* (e) *optimum use of cross-references;* (f) *overall effectiveness in practical use;* (g) *minimum amount of "noise."*[12]

SEARCHING AN INDEX

In searching an index one has to match the search subjects or concepts in the user's own words to those entry points or searchable elements in the index. "The match between concepts and entry points determines the quality of the search results. What are these entry points? They divide roughly into uncontrolled and controlled vocabularies."[13]

Most printed indexes employ *controlled vocabularies;* that is to say, the subject headings are predetermined and the article is matched

[12]K. Boodson, "Subject Bibliographies in Information Work," *The Indexer,* April 1976, p. 21. This is a good summary article on abstracts and indexes.
[13]Susan M. Johnston, "Choosing Between Manual and Online Searching . . ." *ASLIB Proceedings,* October/November 1978, p. 386.

against the authority list of subject headings and/or thesaurus to find the headings which come closest to describing the contents. Hence controlled indexing tends to be rigid. Occasionally, the given subject headings will be incapable of expressing the required concepts, and then new headings are considered.

The other broad approach is the use of *uncontrolled vocabulary*, where words from the title, abstract, and even the text may be searched by the user. This is a much more flexible system but usually not suitable to printed indexes, and is associated with online, machine-readable databases where the computer can quickly search out the keywords. The online database offers more types of entry points and the added bonus of coordinating those different entry points; i.e., the librarian can combine different terms or words to get necessary results. The manual searcher cannot do this but may interpret information given under one entry point to identify possible other references.

Subject searching

Even a cursory look at the index in a number of books will show a frightening degree of individuality. No two book indexes are alike, and there is little consistency of subject headings even within a single index. Here it is worth pointing out that a book index and the standard index for periodicals differ, because the former is concerned with analyses of the work of only one or perhaps two or three authors while the latter must give consistency to the work of thousands of writers.[14]

Users begin in the index with terms they use and know. They must learn to adapt to the index, which may take quite a different view of the phrase or word. What subject heading has the cataloger assigned to an article, which will allow one to find what is needed? Normally the subject is broad enough, well enough known that few problems arise. The librarian simply flips over the pages (or if at a computer, employs a thesaurus, printed or online) to find the subject heading(s) needed. Here and there are cross-references which will refer the user to a related subject heading or to one that the indexer thought more appropriate.

Everyone is familiar with this search pattern—as they are with the sometime problem of trying to find the elusive subject heading which should be, but is not, in the index. At this point one begins to

[14]There are other differences, of course. A major flaw with too many book indexes is that they simply use names and no subjects.

think in synonyms; that is, if X is not a subject heading, has the indexer used Y or P? Then one starts looking for Y, and failing that goes for P. Ahh, here it is.

Even more aggravating is the fact that not all indexes use the same subject headings. For example, one may be going along nicely with "field crops" only to find that another service prefers "farm produce" as a subject heading for the same thing while a third uses "agricultural products." Failure to check out all three may result in failure to find what is needed—and even that may not be enough, for the next publisher may use "agriculture and agricultural products."

All of this may involve flipping through various issues of volumes of the index. When trying to find elusive subject headings, always begin with a late cumulative volume of one or two or more years. If a term is entirely new, begin with the latest issue of the index and work backward.

There are shortcuts:

(1) Library of Congress Subject Headings (Washington: Library of Congress, various dates). Frequently updated, this familiar two-volume work lists the standard Library of Congress subject headings, with cross-references, synonyms, and other bits of advice and help to aid the user in running down a subject heading. Turn first to the suspected heading, and if it is not there, the chances are good there will be some reference to a related heading.

(2) Sears List of Subject Headings (New York: The H. W. Wilson Company, various dates). This is the rough equivalent of *(1)* for smaller libraries. Here the Library of Congress headings are used, but much abridged and simplified.

(3) Cross Reference Index (New York: R. R. Bowker Company, 1974). Here, under 8000 main-term subject headings, the compiler shows the headings and their variations as employed in *Library of Congress* and *Sears* (above) as well as *The Readers' Guide to Periodical Literature, The New York Times Index, Public Affairs Information Service,* and *Business Periodicals Index.* There are numerous *see* and *see also* references.

(4) Subject Cross Reference Guide (Princeton, New Jersey: National Library Service, 1975). Here the subject headings are limited to the *Readers' Guide,* but the compiler has listed them with all their variations since 1900.

Another shortcut is to go first to the card catalog and see which subject heading is employed there, as well as cross-references. Note, too, that at the bottom of most catalog cards are "tracings" or additional subject headings which may help in finding what is needed.

GENERAL PERIODICAL INDEXES

The Readers' Guide to Periodical Literature. New York: The H. W. Wilson Company, 1900 to date, semimonthly (September–June), monthly (July and August). $62.

Magazine Index. Los Altos, California: Information Access Corporation, 1978 to date, monthly (ROM reader and cumulated film). $640 to $1480, depending on library budget. (Online, $45 an hour.)

Popular Periodical Index. Camden, New Jersey: Popular Periodical Index, 1973 to date, semiannual. $15.

Access. Evanston, Illinois: J. G. Burke, 1975 to date, three issues a year. $75.

British Humanities Index. London: Library Association, 1962 to date, quarterly and annual cumulations. £60.

Canadian Periodical Index. Ottawa, Ontario: Canadian Library Association, 1948 to date, monthly. Rates on request.

During the past five or six years, there has been an interest in indexing more popular periodicals. Today there are two indexes which analyze almost all the magazines likely to be considered as popular; that is to say, sold at the corner drug store or found in many homes. These indexes include the traditional *Readers' Guide to Periodical Literature* and the not-so-traditional, relatively new *Magazine Index.* On the periphery other publishers cover ground not considered by the *Readers' Guide.* Three such indexes are: *Access, Popular Periodical Index,* and *New Periodicals Index.*

How many of these popular periodical indexes are likely to last out the 1980s is a major question. Meanwhile, a large proportion of periodical indexes used in small and medium-sized American libraries, as well as in the largest research library on a more limited scale, originate from The H. W. Wilson Company. The Wilson indexes are celebrated for their ease of use and have become a model of the best in indexing. Many of the company's publications are sold on a service basis. Since the larger, better-financed libraries often use more services, they usually pay more than the small libraries for the same index. This service arrangement is explained in any current H. W. Wilson catalog.

The Readers' Guide is by far the most popular periodical index in the United States, Canada, and most of the English-speaking world. Its success is due both to the excellent indexing and the selection of periodicals indexed—a selection which concentrates on relatively high-circulation, well-read magazines. There are now about 177 titles indexed by author and by subject. Book reviews are in a separate section and are arranged alphabetically by author. There are, too, headings for the criticism of drama, opera, ballet, and musical comedy. Where applicable the headings are found in the other H. W. Wilson indexes, and the book review section is a permanent feature of nearly all their indexes.

Issued twice a month, the *Reader's Guide* is an excellent source of relatively current materials and is one of the first places a librarian would turn for information on a news event of a month or so ago. There are useful quarterly and annual and two-year cumulations. *The Cumulative Index to Periodical Literature* (Princeton, New Jersey: National Library Service, 1976) is a cumulation which covers 1959–1970. This permits the user to search one index rather than eight of the *Readers' Guide*. Unfortunately, it has another name and another publisher and sometimes is not understood by the inexperienced person to be no more than a cumulative version of the *Readers' Guide*.

An *Abridged Readers' Guide* is available, which indexes only 59 titles but follows the same general indexing procedures as the senior version. It is published monthly, rather than every two weeks, and is only about one-half the annual price of the larger work. Its use in libraries is questionable, in that it is much better for even the smallest library to have the larger index, which is more frequent and indexes three times as many periodicals.

The great advantage of the indexes for general use is the arrangement. Author and subject entries are in a single alphabet. The subject headings, as in all the Wilson indexes, are consistent and easy to locate. Furthermore, numerous cross-references make the indexes a model for rapid use. Each entry contains all necessary information to find the article. Abbreviations are held to a minimum, and they are clearly explained in the front of the index.

Selection of periodicals for the *Readers' Guide* (and the other Wilson indexes) is determined by a committee and by polling librarians. When asked to consider a title to be added or deleted, the publisher reminds users of the purpose of the service to "index U.S. periodicals of broad, general and popular character." A deciding factor is the determination of whether or not the indexed material will be of any "reference value" to the users. Here "reference" is used to mean a work to assist in ready-reference questions and to a lesser extent specific search queries. The general coverage of essentially popular and semipopular magazines makes it of little or no real use for detailed research questions.[15]

---

[15]James S. Healey and Carolyn M. Cox, "Research and the Readers' Guide . . .," *The Serials Librarian,* Winter 1978, pp. 179–190. The authors found the *Guide* is rarely used for serious research.

The *Readers' Guide* offers a device for selection of periodicals. Many libraries purchase only those titles indexed here, or at least a high percentage of the periodicals budget goes to *Readers' Guide* titles before other magazines are considered. One may argue the merits of such a system, but it does exist.

There is rarely a consensus on what is omitted or included in the *Readers' Guide*, and it is a continuing three-way debate between publishers of magazines left out, librarians who want something in or out, and the committee and publisher, who are trying to please everyone. For example, in 1977 the committee added 60 new titles, dropped 43. Of the 43 deleted, at least 9 had to be reinstated because of the howl of protest by the index subscribers, not to mention the publishers.[16]

Parallel to the acquisitions procedure for periodicals is the question of how long the library should retain titles indexed in the *Readers' Guide*. Research indicates that in most libraries the user is likely to concentrate on using the past five years of the *Readers' Guide;* i.e., seek material in magazines of the past five years. This leads most librarians to agree that in small and medium-sized libraries retention of titles indexed in the *Readers' Guide* for more than five years is a waste of space. When people do want earlier issues, there should be a fast and efficient way to find them in larger area libraries or through various other regional and national networks.[17]

There is only one serious challenge to the *Readers' Guide*. This is the *Magazine Index*, which not only includes all the titles indexed by the *Readers' Guide* but has about 200 more. The challenge is muted by the cost of the *Magazine Index*. Service charges vary but run from $640 to $1480, compared to the $50 charge for the *Readers' Guide*.

The *Magazine Index* is available in most libraries through a microfilmlike reader. Each month the publisher sends the library an updated reel of film which cumulates previous month's listings. The film is mounted in the machine, and when someone wants to look up an item, a simple, motorized system makes it possible to view the wanted area almost immediately.

[16]Discussed by Brian Aveney and Rod Slade, "Indexing of Popular Periodicals: The State of the Art," *Library Journal*, October 1, 1978, pp. 1915–1923. The nine deleted and then returned to the *Guide* include: *Harper's Bazaar, Mademoiselle, Redbook, Saturday Evening Post, Science, Senior Scholastic, Seventeen, Sky and Telescope,* and *Vogue.*

[17]Healey, op. cit., p. 188. The authors point out a little-discussed corollary of maintaining long runs of little-used periodicals: "To make space [for titles], either reader space or shelf space has to be removed. . . . As seats get fewer, so do patrons served. As fewer patrons are served, the library loses more of its reason for existence."

The *Magazine Index* has several advantages over the *Readers' Guide:* (1) It indexes more titles, some 375 as compared to 180. (2) There are short, supplementary annotations for articles the title of which does not clearly indicate content. (3) There is a built-in consumer feature which makes it possible to check material on specific brands and models. (4) Because it is updated as a complete unit at least once a month, one need only use the reading machine, and there is no need to consult various volumes and cumulations. The cumulation will cover five years, and after that, when each new month is added, a month's listing will be dropped. Printed versions of the deleted material are promised. For example, as each month of 1982 indexing is added, that month of 1977 indexing is deleted from the microform edition. In December 1982, the library receives the printed volume for 1977.

Book reviews are coded in the index by the grades A through F. Each grade represents a reviewer's opinion, and it is a simple matter to count the number of A or C grades to ascertain the probable level of acceptance of a given work by at least the critics found in the 370-plus magazines indexed. In days past, *The Book Review Digest* used to grade reviews, but the system was dropped. Now it reappears, for better or for worse, in the *Magazine Index.* Note, too, that the same grading system is applied to records, film, theatre, restaurant reviews, and so on.

The drawbacks, aside from the forbidding price: (1) Started in 1978, it does have retrospective indexing back to 1976, but is of no value for materials prior to 1976. (2) The reading machine, although simple enough to use, does require another approach to using an index, which some people find forbidding.

The index is also available at a computer terminal at $45 an hour; and the company will furnish the library with an individual computer tape service at $400 a year. "Perhaps the most intriguing feature of the product . . . is the computer tape service. Since LC subject headings are used, MI indexing can be merged into any computer-based catalog to incorporate indexing for the magazines received by a given library or system."[18] In other words, for the first time it is possible to merge, say, books and periodical articles on "aardvarks" or "nuclear power" under a single subject heading in a computer-based catalog.

A companion service by the same publisher, considered in the section on newspapers, is *The National Newspaper Index.* This functions

---

[18]Aveney and Slade, op. cit., p. 1923.

in much the same manner, in that it is made available to libraries both online and as microfilm which is cumulated and is read with a reader.

There are several other indexes which augment the *Readers' Guide*. "Augment" is perhaps the wrong word, as the raison d'être of these indexes is the inclusion of periodicals which for one reason or another have been excluded by the selection committee for the *Readers' Guide*.

The earliest of the indexes of omission is the *Popular Periodical Index*, which includes about 30 titles not found in the Wilson index. Some examples: *Analog, TV Guide, Mother Jones,* and *Playboy*. The librarian-publisher, Robert Bottorff, includes subject headings for reviews, motion pictures, recordings, and so on. Where a title does not describe content, the editor often adds a word or line or two explaining what the article is about. While this is hardly a full abstract, enough information is given to make the index particularly useful.

Access is another general index. It includes over 154 titles, with particular emphasis on popular music, travel magazines, science fiction, and arts and crafts titles. It is particularly strong in its coverage of city and regional magazines. Its value to librarians is as a wide net, in the indexing of really popular titles which are not in *Readers' Guide*, e.g., *Playboy, T.V. Guide, Creem, Mother Jones,* and so on. Originally published by Gaylord Bros., Inc., it is now issued by its editor. The index added to its coverage in mid-1980 with the announcement that it had incorporated *The Monthly Periodical Index* (1978 to 1980).

Ideally, libraries might take all the general periodical indexes. Where a choice must be made, selection is not difficult. First would come *Readers' Guide*, followed by *Popular Periodical Index* (as much for the low price as for the excellent selection of titles), then the equally general *Access*.

Magazine Index would be a choice for any library with the budget large enough to support the service, although it would not be a substitute (at least for many years yet) for the *Readers' Guide*, which has an invaluable cumulative service to 1900 and is so familiar to so many users. And, where possible, *Magazine Index* should be available online, along with the still-to-be-considered *New York Times Information Bank*.

Canadian and British indexes

Libraries in Canada and England normally use the *Readers' Guide*, although both have rough equivalents to it. Having suffered a division, the *British Humanities Index* is somewhat less ambitious than the *Readers' Guide*. From 1915 on, it was called the *Subject Index to Periodicals,* but after 1962, it omitted titles in the fields of education (taken up by *British Educational Index*) and technology (now in *British Technology Index*). Medical sciences and business were also cut out. What remains is a serviceable and relatively general guide to British journals covering such subjects as politics, economics, history, and literature. Unlike the *Readers' Guide,* it is of limited use in the area of current materials, because it is published only quarterly with annual cumulations. By the time the *British Humanities Index* and the corresponding periodicals reach North America, the timeliness factor is nil.

The *Canadian Periodical Index* is an approximate equivalent to the *Readers' Guide.* It is an author-subject index to about 137 Canadian magazines, including French titles. Owing to an added interest in Canadian periodicals among Canadian readers and libraries, the *Index* has increased the scope of its indexing. It now includes special sections for poems and short stories as well as book and motion picture reviews.[19]

Retrospective periodical indexes

Poole's Index to Periodical Literature, 1802–1906. Vol. 1, 1802–1881, Boston: Houghton, 1981; vols. 2–6 (supplements 1–5), 1882–1907, Boston: Houghton Mifflin Company, 1888–1908 (6 vols. reprinted in 7 vols., Gloucester, Massachusetts: Peter Smith Publisher, 1963).

This was the first general magazine index, and the forerunner of the *Readers' Guide.* It was the imagination of William Frederick Poole, a pioneer in both bibliography and library science, that made the index possible. Recognizing that many older periodicals were not being used for lack of proper indexing, he set out, after one or two preliminary starts, to index 470 American and English periodicals covering the period 1802 to 1881. Having completed this work, he issued five supplements which brought the indexing to the end of 1906.

The modern user is sometimes frustrated upon realizing that the total approach is by subject of an article. The author index to some 300,000 references in the main set and the supplements is supplied by C. Edward Wall, *Cumulative Author Index for Poole's*

[19]Anne B. Piternick, "Financing the Canadian Periodical Index," *Canadian Library Journal,* August 1978, pp. 271–274. A general discussion of costs and pricing applicable to many indexing services.

Index . . . (Ann Arbor, Michigan: Pierian Press, 1971, 488 pp.). The index is computer-produced and not entirely easy to follow, but it is a great help to anyone seeking an author entry in *Poole*.

With all its faults, Poole's work is still a considerable achievement and an invaluable key to nineteenth-century periodicals. The last decade of the century is better treated in *Nineteenth Century Readers' Guide to Periodical Literature*, 1890–1899, with supplementary indexing 1900–1922 (New York: The H. W. Wilson Company, 1944, 2 vols.). Limited to 51 periodicals (in contrast to Poole's 470), this guide thoroughly indexes magazines by author and subject for the years 1890 to 1899. Some 14 magazines are indexed between 1900 and 1922.

The term "retrospective" in this section is fairly well limited to nineteenth-century periodicals, although it should be remembered that "retrospective index" indicates any index which covers a period other than the present. In this sense, all indexing is retrospective. But to stay with nineteenth- through twentieth-century retrospective indexes, there are three computer-generated guides which are suitable for tracing periodicals in history, political science, and sociology. These are: *Combined Retrospective Index to Journals in History, 1838–1974*, an index to 234 history journals in the English language arranged by subject, with two author-index volumes; *Combined Retrospective Index to Journals in Political Science, 1886–1974*, an index to 179 journals; and *Combined Retrospective Index to Journals in Sociology, 1895–1974*, an index to 118 titles. All are published by the Carrollton Press, Arlington, Virginia, and range in price from $550 to $985. (The combined price in 1977: $2075.) As these are computer-generated, the page format is quite different from that of The H. W. Wilson Company indexes. Subjects are indicated by a keyword in the left-hand margin, followed by the full title of the article, followed by the author's name and the year, volume, journal name, and page. The primary difference is that the journal is given a code number, and to find the full title, one must turn to that number at the end of each volume. Although this set of indexes has extreme retrospective value, it should be noted that the cutoff date is 1974. Therefore, many of the titles already have been and are being indexed in standard indexes.

SUGGESTED READINGS

Bakewell, K. G. B., "Why are There So Many Bad Indexes," *Library Association Record*, July 1979, pp. 330, 331. A short checklist of faults found in indexes and a key to evaluation.

Harrod, Leonard M. (ed.), *Indexers on Indexing*. New York: R. R. Bowker Company, 1978. Reprints more than 50 articles from the English periodical, *The Indexer*, the basic publication for information on Anglo-American indexing problems and practices.

Marshall, Joan K., *On Equal Terms: A Thesaurus for Nonsexist Indexing and Cataloguing*. New York: Neal-Schuman Publishers, Inc., 1977. Not only does the author note the presence of sexist subject headings but she offers solid principles for bringing about a needed change. For an earlier, pioneer work on discrimination in subject headings, see Sanford Berman, *Prejudices and Antipathies* (Metuchen, New Jersey: Scarecrow Press, 1971). See, too, William J. Pease, "Black Subjects, White Subjectivity," *California Librarian*, April 1978, pp. 40–45.

Phillips, Linda, and E. A. Raup, "Comparing Methods for Teaching Use of Periodical Indexes," *The Journal of Academic Librarianship*, January 1979, pp. 420–423. University librarians offer a method of teaching the use of indexes through the program method and offer useful sample pages from their programmed booklet.

Preston, Gregor, "Coping With Subject Heading Changes," *Library Resources & Technical Services*, Winter 1980, pp. 64–68. The author suggests methods of overcoming the problem of having both obsolete and new subject headings in a card catalog and, in so doing, points up the problems of subject headings in closed catalogs and tries to answer the question, How can new subject headings be discovered?

Regazzi, John, "Evaluating Indexing Systems: A Review after Cranfield," *The Indexer*, April 1980, pp. 14–21. A clear overview of the various evaluative methods employed to judge an index or an indexing system.

Svenonius, Elaine, "Directions for Research in Indexing, Classification, and Cataloging," *Library Resources & Technical Services*, January/March 1981, pp. 88–103. A detailed discussion of how indexing is employed in bibliographic control. The author asks questions about methods of evaluating and comparing indexes, concepts of abstracting, and the need for more information on the index process.

The Society of Indexers, *A Select Reading List on Indexing*. London: The Society, 1978. A guide to close to 100 basic books and articles on indexing. Many are English, but almost all are of interest to Americans and readers in other countries.

CHAPTER FIVE

Indexing and Abstracting Services: Various Forms

S O FAR WE HAVE CONSIDERED only the general periodical index, but there are numerous other forms. Let us begin with the more specialized subject index.

The librarian soon learns when to turn to subject indexes. For example, for most popular music queries the general periodical indexes might be enough, but for someone looking for material in depth they are inadequate. Knowing this, the librarian reaches for *Popular Music Periodicals Index* (Metuchen, New Jersey: Scarecrow Press, 1974 to date, annual), which indexes 61 periodicals featuring rock, country, jazz, blues, and other types of popular music. The index is primarily subject, with a separate author index. Related to this, but at the classical and "serious" music level would be *Music Index* (Detroit: Information Coordinators, 1949 to date, monthly), which includes references to articles in over 300 periodicals.

The natural progression from the general index to the subject index may be more direct when the user or the librarian has a question which is quickly associated with a subject and with an index. Yet it is not quite that simple. A high school student who asks for an article on the American Civil War should be referred to almost any year of *Readers' Guide*. The same student, or, for that matter, the teacher or subject expert, who is doing a detailed paper on the Civil

War will require not only more periodicals likely to have such material, but more sophisticated approaches. Then one might turn to several indexes, but more likely the one which concentrates on American history, i.e., *America: History and Life.*

By now it should be apparent that the subject indexes are of major importance in libraries, and it is with a few of these that the next section is concerned.

SUBJECT INDEXES

All the following are published by The H. W. Wilson Company:

> *Humanities Index.* 1974 to date, quarterly. Service.[1]
> *Social Sciences Index.* 1974 to date, quarterly. Service.
> *General Science Index.* 1978 to date, monthly. Service.

The H. W. Wilson Company issues three indexes which bridge the general to the specific subject, edited specifically for the student, average public library user, and the nonexpert who wants more depth in a subject than found in the *Readers' Guide* but not as much specialization as in the subject indexes such as *Business Periodicals Index.*

The *Humanities Index* analyzes 254 English-language periodicals. The single index is by subject and author, with the usual section for book reviews. It has several unique features: (1) Opera and film reviews are listed under appropriate subject headings, i.e., "opera reviews" and "motion picture reviews"; (2) poems may be located both by the author's name and under a section, "poems"; (3) the same procedure is followed for short stories; and (4) there is a section for theatre reviews. Given these divisions, the work is valuable for checking current critical thought on a wide variety of subjects in the humanities—here taken to mean archaeology and classical studies; folklore; history; language and literature; literary and political criticism; performing arts; philosophy; religion and theology; and, according to the publisher, "related subjects."

The *Social Sciences Index* covers about 260 English-language periodicals in anthropology, area studies, psychology, public administration, sociology, environmental science, economics, and related

---

[1] Actually both the *Social Sciences* and the *Humanities Index* go back much further. Originally they were one; i.e., *Social Sciences and Humanities Index* (1965–1974), and prior to that the index was called *International Index* (1907–1965). Many research libraries have both sets.

areas. There are author and subject entries with a separate section for book reviews.

The *General Science Index* completes The H. W. Wilson Company semi–subject approach to general indexing. It is an effort to be more popular than their *Applied Science and Technology Index,* more specialized than what is found in Readers' Guide. About 90 English-language general science periodicals are indexed by subject. As in the *Applied Science and Technology Index,* there is *no* author approach other than in the citations to book reviews, which are listed by authors of the books. The subject headings are selected for the nonspecialist, and where specialized subjects are employed, there are adequate cross-references. Fields covered range from astronomy to zoology. An interesting point here is that there is duplication between this and other Wilson indexes. *Readers' Guide* has 20 of the titles found in the *General Science Index,* another 12 are in the related *Applied Science* title and several others are in *Biological and Agricultural Index.* Duplication of this type is likely to continue, as it is difficult, if not unreasonable, to expect the publisher to delete titles simply because they appear elsewhere.

Specific subject indexes

All the following titles are published by The H. W. Wilson Company:

> *Applied Science and Technology Index.* 1958 to date, monthly. Service.
>
> *Art Index.* 1929 to date, quarterly. Service.
>
> *Biological and Agricultural Index.* 1964 to date, monthly. Service.
>
> *Business Periodicals Index.* 1958 to date, monthly. Service.
>
> *Education Index.* 1929 to date, monthly. Service.
>
> *Index to Legal Periodicals.* 1908 to date, monthly. $85.
>
> *Library Literature.* 1934 to date, bimonthly. Service. (Note: Cumulative volume, 1921–1932, published in 1934.)

The following are non-Wilson Company publications:

> *F&S Index of Corporations and Industries. F&S Index International. F&S Europe.* Cleveland: Predicasts, 1960, 1967, 1979 to date weekly, $265 to $350 for each service. [Online, PTS (Predicasts, Inc.) *F&S Indexes,* $90 an hour.]
>
> *Public Affairs Information Service Bulletin.* New York: Public Affairs Information Service, 1915 to date, twice a month, including

cumulations and annual. Rates on request. (Online, $60 an hour.)

The Business Index. Los Altos, California: Information Access Corporation, 1979 to date, monthly, $1860. [Note: The "online" time rate here and throughout this and other chapters is usually based upon charges made by Dialog in mid-1981 or by the exclusive vendor for the database. Other vendors have different price structures. The point is to indicate in a relative fashion the difference between print and online costs.]

The basic subject indexes found in most American and Canadian libraries are published by The H. W. Wilson Company, and follow much the same format and approach as do Wilson's aforementioned general indexes. There are several hundred subject indexes and abstracting services from other publishers. They concentrate on more specialized areas than those covered in the Wilson entries.

When considering subject indexes, three facts must be kept in mind:

1. Many are broader in coverage than is indicated by such key title words as "Art" or "Education." Related fields are often considered. Therefore, anyone doing a subject analysis in depth often should consult indexes which take in fringe-area topics.

2. Most of the subject indexes are not confined solely to magazines. They often include books, monographs, bulletins, and even government documents.

3. A great number are not parochial but international in scope. True, not many foreign-language works are listed, but anything in English is usually noted, even if issued abroad.

Because of this wider base of coverage, many libraries are doubtful about including such indexes. What good is it to find a particular article in a specialized journal and then be unable to obtain the journal? The library should be in a position either to borrow the journal or to have a copy made of the article. If it is not, it had better look to improving its services. Also, even without the pertinent items indexed, the indexes do serve to give readers a broader view of the topic than they might get from only a general index.

There is little point in describing each of the Wilson subject indexes. For the most part, their titles explain their scope and purpose. The user may be either the specialist or the generalist—journals and periodicals for both are indexed. Most indexed titles are American, but there are representative selections from other countries in other languages. The number indexed ranges from 185 to over 300.

The approach is much the same; that is, the author and subject entries are in a single alphabet and there are the usual excellent cross-references. (Some indexes, such as the *Applied Science and Technology Index,* have only a subject approach.) Subject headings are frequently revised, and in most services book reviews are listed in a separate section. Each index has its peculiarities, but a reading of the prefatory material in each will clarify the finer points.

Applied Science and Technology Index is complemented by the *General Science Index* and *Biological and Agricultural Index.* The index analyzes about 300 English-language periodicals by subject. In addition to the sciences, it covers such areas as transportation, food, and a wide variety of engineering titles. The *General Science Index* has been considered; the *Biological and Agricultural* work is the opposite in that it is more subject-oriented than either of the others. Here emphasis is on 185 periodicals in biology and more detailed aspects of agriculture. The normal search pattern for anyone but a subject expert would be the *General Science Index* to the *Applied Science and Technology Index* to the last title.

There are several hundred, perhaps even thousand, indexing and abstracting services in science, and almost every discipline and subsection of a scientific or technological area has its own service(s). The basic ones are considered in the second volume of the text, primarily because most of them are now in machine-readable form for online searches.

Art Index is the only one of its type in the Wilson family, although numerous art titles are covered in the *Humanities Index.* It indexes more than 200 periodicals and museum publications. The definition of "art" is broad and includes areas from films and photography to architecture and landscape design. Related indexes would include the machine-readable database (as well as hard-copy) *ARTbibliographies Modern* (Santa Barbara, California: ABC-Clio, 1973 to date, semiannual), which abstracts 500 periodicals, as well as books and over 1000 exhibition catalogs. As the title suggests, the scope is limited to modern art, i.e., 1800 to the present. *RILA (Repertoire International de la Littérature de l'Art)* (Williamstown, Massachusetts: Clark Art Institute, 1973 to date, semiannual) considers some 300 journals for its abstracting service and covers 3000-plus books, catalogs, dissertations, and so on in all aspects of art.

Business Periodicals Index covers 272 titles (about 30 from outside the U.S.) with indexed items by subject, not by author. Subjects are so all-inclusive as to make this almost a general index, and it is used as such by librarians who cannot find enough material in the basic services. For example, one may be looking for an article on reading and television, only to find that an analysis of the subject (from the point of view of sales of books and television sets) has been indexed in *Business Periodicals Index* although hardly considered in the more likely *Library Literature*. Still, the index is used primarily for finance, business technology, and economics.

The basic *F&S Index of Corporations and Industries* covers about "750 financial publications, business-oriented newspapers, trade magazines and special reports." About the same number is indexed in the other two parts. For each entry there is a brief description of content, and a black dot indicates the importance of the piece.

Actually, the *F&S Index* is in three parts, although sold as separate indexes. The first covers the United States, while the other two are self-explanatory in coverage. Each is sold separately, comes out weekly, and is cumulated quarterly. Within each of the indexes the reader will find two sections.

The first section "Industries and Products," is a subject-heading approach to a wide variety of topics, from population to energy. Groupings are in a hierarchical system, and automotive brakes, for example, is a subgroup of motor vehicle parts. Fortunately, the major subject divisions are given in alphabetical order in the cumulative alphabetical guide—and each issue has a table of contents which allows ready access to the subjects.

The second part of the index is alphabetical by the name of the company; and where the company is vast, there are subheadings. This is easy to follow and presents no momentary problem as does the first section. There is also a "Source Materials" section which gives the full address of publishers whose works have been indexed, along with the handy price for a single issue.

Available both in print and online, the index is timely and about as basic for business information as any index. It is a beginning point for a serious query concerning business or economics, and particularly for data on a special industry, corporation, company, and so on.

The Business Index is a specialized version of the *Magazine Index*. It comes with a reader and a monthly update on computer output microfilm. Some 325 periodicals are indexed, as well as major books noted, and there is cover-to-cover indexing of *The Wall Street Journal, Barrons,* and the business section of *The New York Times.* Brief annotations are usually included where needed. One may question whether it is a real competitor of the Wilson index, because it is priced at $1860 a year compared to a service charge for the Wilson entry which is only in two or three figures.

Canada has its own version of the business index, limited primarily to analyses of Canadian publications: the *Canadian Business Periodical Index* (Toronto: Information Access, 1975 to date, monthly).

Index to Legal Periodicals may be used in connection with a business query. It offers access to material in almost 430 publications. It differs from many of the other indexes in that it analyzes books, yearbooks, annual institutes' publications, and the like. It has the standard subject and author index but adds an index for law cases, and case notes are found at the end of many subject headings. While a good deal of this is technical, the careful librarian will find material here which is equally suitable for the involved layperson, and it can be of considerable help in almost any field which is remotely connected with the law or a legal decision.

Publishers of the *Magazine Index* offer the same type of computer output microfilm and reader for a legal service: *Legal Resource Index* (Los Altos, California: Information Access Corporation, 1980 to date, monthly). This is more specialized than the Wilson entry, concentrating on contents of 600 legal periodicals and newspapers. Another version, little more than a printout of the monthly COM, is *Current Law Index,* issued monthly, with quarterly and annual cumulations. The latter is $300 a year, compared to from $1560 to $1720 for the COM version. This service is available online (at $90 an hour) as are several other major, better-known and more varied indexes for law libraries discussed in the second volume of the text.

Education Index covers material in 326 publications, and while it concentrates on periodicals, it does analyze some books, reports, and the like. All aspects of education are considered, and numerous allied fields are touched upon, such as language and linguistics and library science. It has a strong competitor in *Current Index to Journals in Education,* which is considered in the next section.[2]

The *Canadian Education Index* Repertoire Canadien Sur L'Education (Toronto: Canadian Education Association, 1965 to date, five a year) is a bilingual author-subject index to some 200 periodicals and some monographs. Coverage is limited to education and to things exclusively Canadian, whether topics or authors. It includes sections which index book and media reviews.[3]

---

[2]Andrea J. Sward, "CIJE," *Database,* December 1979, pp. 22–27. A comparison between *Education Index* and *CIJE* (see p. 27) indicates that the library with *CIJE* probably needs to use *Education Index* only rarely because *CIJE* "in most cases would yield almost complete coverage from 1969 until the most recent update."

[3]This is discussed at some length in: Deborah C. Sawyer, "The Canadian Education Index," *Canadian Library Journal,* August 1978, pp. 277–281.

Library Literature offers a subject and author entry to articles which have appeared in about 200 library-oriented periodicals. One will find citations for books, pamphlets, dissertations and theses, and audiovisual materials. It gives the librarian a fairly complete look at the current literature. Of added help are two abstracting services: (1) *Library and Information Science Abstracts* (London: Library Association, 1969 to date, bimonthly. Distributed in the United States by Oryx Press, Phoenix, Arizona). Whereas *Library Literature* is in the traditional alphabetical subject-author arrangement, the abstracting service depends on a classification system for the arrangement of material. Some 400 journals are indexed, and the service abstracts selected reports, theses, and other monographs. Thanks to an author and subject index, even the novice has no real difficulty in locating material. The service also is available online.

An even more sophisticated approach is offered in (2) *Information Science Abstracts* (Philadelphia: Documentation Abstracts, Inc., 1966 to date, bimonthly). The emphasis is on technical periodicals, books, reports, proceedings, and similar materials. And of the some 4500 abstracts issued each year, a vast proportion deal with aspects of automation, communication, computers, mathematics, artificial intelligence, and so on. It is a service particularly suited to the needs of the researcher and the librarian in a large system. Arranged under broad subject headings, the abstracts are well-written and complete. Each issue has an author index, and there is an annual subject index.

One non-Wilson subject index which is found in most libraries is the *Public Affairs Information Service Bulletin*. This has the advantage of relative currency. The *Bulletin* (or *PAIS*, as it is usually called) is issued twice a month and cumulated four times a year, with a final annual volume which may be purchased separately. Coverage is primarily of material in political science, government, legislation, economics, and sociology. Periodicals, government documents, pamphlets, reports, and some books in such areas as government, public administration, international affairs, and economics are indexed. About 800 journals and some 6000 other items (from books to reports) are indexed each year. Valuable additions are a "Key to Periodical References" and a list of "Publications Analyzed." Both serve as a handy checklist and buying guide for the library.

While works analyzed are limited to those in English, coverage is international. Arrangement is alphabetical, primarily by subject. A few of the entries have brief descriptive notes on both contents and purpose. Beginning in 1972, *PAIS* issued a second index, *Foreign Language Index,* which offers much the same service as the *Bulletin.* Here about 400 journals are indexed along with 2000 non-journal items. The essential difference is that the quarterly index considers the same subject areas in a number of foreign-language journals, books, reports, pamphlets, and the like.

Online the two are combined and called *PAIS International*. They are available from 1976 for the *Bulletin* and from 1972 for the *Foreign Language Index*.

Another approach in printed form is possible. For example, *The Cumulative Subject Index to the PAIS Annual Bulletin 1915–1974* (Arlington, Virginia: Carrollton Press, Inc., 1975, 15 vols.) arranges almost 60 years of *PAIS* in a single subject index, thereby accomplishing in printed form one of the services of a machine-readable database. It is similar to machine-readable indexes for retrospective searching, although it has the disadvantage of not being updated monthly as a database would be. If the publisher should want to keep the set up to date, it would have to be republished each year with the preceding year's subjects integrated into the main set. This appears economically prohibitive. Also, the user of the index still must go to the original *PAIS* index to find specific entries. The cumulative index indicates only issues of the *PAIS* where the subject is covered, not the precise citation itself.

Anyone using *PAIS* should be familiar, too, with the *Index to U.S. Government Periodicals* (Chicago: Infordata International, 1974 to date, quarterly). This indexes some 160 to 200 titles issued by various departments and agencies of the federal government. It is discussed in the chapter on government documents, as are other indexes in this area.

While technically one should classify the *Catholic Periodical and Literature Index* (Haverford, Pennsylvania: Catholic Library Association, 1950 to date, bimonthly; service) as a religious index, actually it is much broader in scope. It indexes by author, subject, and title between 130 and 150 periodicals, most of which are Catholic, although they vary widely as to editorial content. In fact, many of the titles could be classified as general magazines. Also, the index includes analyses of books by and about Catholics. There are sections for book reviews, movie reviews, and theater criticism. Although this is of limited value in many libraries, it should be a consideration for public and college libraries serving a Catholic population.[4]

---

[4]Indexes concerned primarily with religion are not numerous, at least in English. The basic work is *Religion Index One: Periodicals*; formerly, *Index to Religious Periodical Literature* (Chicago: American Theological Library Association, 1949 to date, semiannual), a Protestant-oriented title. The nondenominational *Religious and Theological Abstracts* (Myerstown, Pennsylvania: J. C. Christman, 1958 to date, quarterly) is equally useful.

ABSTRACTING SERVICES

While subject indexes are much used, abstracting services, are preferable because: (1) they include a brief summary of the contents of an
article, book, report, and so on, allowing the librarian to decide
whether or not to read the entire document; and (2) arrangement
normally is more complex but in such a way as to favor the needs of
the subject expert. On the other hand, as they do require abstracts,
the services tend to take longer to publish and may be later than the
normal index—though this is not always the case.

Representative abstracting services

Psychological Abstracts. Washington: American Psychological Association, Inc., 1927 to date, monthly. $315. (Online, $65 an
hour.)

America: History and Life; Part A, Article Abstracts and Citations.
Santa Barbara, California: American Bibliographical Center-
Clio Press, 1964, three issues per year. Service rate, $155 to
$560. (Online, $65 an hour.)

Comprehensive Dissertation Index, 1861–1972. Ann Arbor, Michigan: University Microfilms. 5-year cumulations, 1973, 1977; and
annual volumes. The annual cumulations consist of 5 volumes,
$450. (Online, $55 an hour.)

These three abstracting services are representative of what is
available in the humanities, science, and the social sciences. More
technical scientific abstracts and indexes are considered in the second
volume of this text.

Psychological Abstracts is familiar to many people, primarily
because, as with a few other subject abstracting services (such as
Resources in Education), it can be used in related areas of interest. For
example, an important section concerns communication which, in
turn includes abstracts on language, speech, literature, and even art.
Anyone involved with, say, the personality of an engineer or an artist
would turn here, as would the better-educated layperson seeking
information on everything from why a companion talks in his or her
sleep to learning about why people do or do not read.

The abstracts are arranged under 16 broad subject categories
from physiological intervention to personality. This allows the busy
user to glance quickly at a subject area of interest without being
bothered by unrelated topics. As a guide to the less experienced,

there is an author and a brief subject index in each issue. The subject approach is expanded and modified in the cumulative indexes published twice a year. (When in doubt about a subject, turn first to the cumulation, not the individual issues.)

The online version goes back to records from 1967 to date. In an effort to attract online users, the online service as of 1980 contains more references than found in the printed version.

America: History and Life: Part A, Article Abstracts and Citations[5] covers articles on U.S. and Canadian history in 2000 scholarly journals throughout the world. Approximately 5000 to 6000 abstracts are published each year, as well as about the same number of brief descriptions from local and specialist historical publications. The classified arrangement ends with a subject and author index. The "subject profile index" expands the subject approach to the classified abstracts in four areas: subject, geography, biography, and chronology. An article on Cornwallis's campaign for Virginia, for example, would be listed: subject: Revolutionary War; biography: Cornwallis; geography: Virginia; chronology: 1781. Under these and other headings, the article analyzed appears in the subject index an average of four or five times, providing insurance against a user's not finding a work.[6]

Most abstracting services not only analyze periodicals and books but often include dissertations. However, only the *Comprehensive Dissertation Index* concentrates exclusively on the form—a form which covers all disciplines and interests. Dissertations are important for the reference librarian seeking specific, often unpublished, information about a given subject, place, or person. Since most dissertations contain extensive bibliographies and footnotes, they can be used as unofficial bibliographies for some relatively narrow areas. Before a librarian begins a broad search for bibliographies in any area, these lists should be checked. There is a good chance that some student has already completed the bibliography sought or at least has done enough work to indicate other major sources.

A problem with dissertations is that most libraries will not lend them. Policy differs, but the excuse for not lending is that (1) there is

[5]Part B is *Index to Book Reviews* (covering over 100 scholarly United States and Canadian journals of history); Part C is *American History Bibliography (Books, Articles and Dissertations);* Part D is *Annual Index.* The whole series is often simply called *America: History and Life.* All three are available on the online database.

[6]The publisher, ABC-Clio, has two other humanities indexes on databases (as well as in printed form): *ARTbibliographies Modern* and *Historical Abstracts,* which covers world history except for the United States and Canada, covered in *America: History and Life.*

only one copy and it cannot be replaced or (2) a microfilm copy may be purchased from University Microfilms, who just happen to publish the index. The second explanation is most often the case, and today a library requiring a dissertation must usually purchase the microfilm, or a printout copy at a slight additional cost.

The "control" of dissertations by University Microfilms leads one critic to comment: "It is interesting to speculate whether . . . the document service is supportive of the abstracting and indexing service, or vice versa. Does *Dissertation Abstracts* sell microfilm, or does the microfilm service sell *Dissertation Abstracts?*"[7] Either answer leaves the user in a position of dependence on University Microfilms, whereas before their interest in microfilming dissertations it was possible to receive most of them by interlibrary loan.

How does one trace the dissertation? The answer is twofold. The first place to go is *Comprehensive Dissertation Index.* The index set is divided into the sciences, social sciences, and humanities, and each of these broad categories has subdivision, for example, biological sciences, chemistry, and engineering. One locates the volume(s) likely to cover the subject and then turns to the finer subject heading where one will find a list of dissertations by full title and name of the author. Entry is possible by author too; i.e., the final volumes of the main set and the supplement are author index volumes. After each entry there is a citation to *Dissertation Abstracts,* where the librarian then turns for the full abstract.

Dissertation Abstracts International is a separate set from the index, but is issued by the same publisher. Like the index, it appears in three parts.[8] Until the annual index is issued, the monthly issues of *Dissertation Abstracts* must be searched individually. Each of the three sections has its own index. It is published monthly, and the arrangement by broad subject headings and then by narrow subject areas is similar to that of the index. Each entry includes a full abstract. Note: The abstracts are not available online and must be examined in the printed volumes.

A computer-generated index, the *Comprehensive Dissertation Index,* suffers from the fault of many such works. Unless the key-word(s) or phrase(s) appear in the title, the dissertation may be "lost," as the subject index simply lists the work by those keywords.

[7]Anne Piternick, "Financing of Canadian Abstracting and Indexing Services," *Canadian Library Journal,* December 1977, p. 453.

[8]For a discussion of its policy concerning listing of European dissertations, see Jean Herold's review of the set's "Section C," *Reference Services Review,* April/June 1979, pp. 65–66.

ERIC/IR: Specialized information service[9]

U.S. Educational Resources Information Center. *Resources in Education*. Washington: Government Printing Office, 1966 to date, monthly. $42.50. (Online, $25 an hour.)

Current Index to Journals in Education. Phoenix, Arizona: Oryx Press, 1969 to date, monthly, semiannual cumulations. $150. (Online, $25 an hour.)

Many of the current abstracting and indexing services are only one part of fuller information systems which not only publish indexes and abstracts, but offer other services. This may be illustrated by ERIC/IR, or, in full, Educational Resources Information Center/ (Clearinghouse for) Information Resources. The system includes (1) an index and an abstracting service available both in printed form and on database for online retrieval; (2) an ongoing subject vocabulary, represented in the frequently updated *Thesaurus of ERIC Descriptors;* (3) a dissemination system which depends primarily on reproducing the material indexed on microfiche and distributing that microfiche to libraries; and (4) a decentralized organizational structure for acquiring and processing the documents which are indexed and abstracted.

The first abstract part of ERIC is *Resources in Education,* which lists reports and associated items and for each includes a narrative abstract of 200 words or less. The abstracts are written by the authors. Approximately 400 to 500 reports are submitted to ERIC each month, but at least 50 percent are rejected, often as much for lack of typing skills as for content. The reports have to be reproduced on microfiche and if not typed properly cannot be properly reproduced; hence rejection. Selection is made at one of 16 clearinghouses—each considers only a particular subject and has experts able to evaluate the submitted material.

The actual type of material includes research and technical reports (about one-third); published proceedings, dissertations, preprints and papers presented at a conference; and another one-third consists of curriculum guides, educational legislation, lesson plans, and the like. The key to access includes both a subject and an author index as well as an index by institution. The index is cumulated semiannually and annually.

---

[9]*A Bibliography of Publications about the Educational Resources Information Center* (Washington: Government Printing Office, December 1978). This lists and briefly explains over 260 works about the service. A cursory glance at any issue of *Library Literature* will show other articles, books, reports, etc. concerning ERIC.

The second method of tapping ERIC is through *Current Index to Journals in Education*. This is an index to some 775 periodicals in education, which results in about 1700 citations each month. Although published by a commercial film, the indexing is provided by the 16 clearinghouses. The first part of the index is much like *Resources in Education* in form; that is, items are abstracted and arranged numerically by the accession number.[10] The second part is the subject index, which, again, follows the style of *Resources in Education*. There are also an author index and a fourth section in which the indexed journals are arranged alphabetically by title, and the table of contents for each is given, with accession numbers for articles.

One outstanding feature of ERIC, although a usual one among similar documentation systems such as that developed by the National Aeronautics and Space Administration, is that some 80 percent of the documents abstracted in *Resources in Education* are available on microfiche.[11] In most large libraries, the user finds the required citation in *Resources in Education* and then, instead of laboriously looking for the item abstracted, simply turns to the microfiche collection, where the items are arranged by accession number. This, then, is a total information system and not the normal two-step bibliographical reference quest in which one finds the abstract or the indexed item and then must try to find the document, journal, book, or what have you, which the library may or may not have available.

Ideally, the total information system would be offered with the second ERIC finding tool, *Current Index to Journals in Education*. It is not. Why? Because here the index and abstracts are for journal articles, and the journals themselves have to be searched. The cost of putting each article on a microfiche card, not to mention copyright problems with publishers, makes the cost of a total information service prohibitive.[12]

---

[10]Andrea Sward, "CIJE," *Database*, December 1979, pp. 22–27. This, among other things, is a discussion of the content, length, and value of the *CIJE* abstracts which have varied over the years in length and content. The majority of entries are much briefer than those found in *Resources in Education*, and they often may be no more than a few words.

[11]*Directory of ERIC Microfiche Collections* (Washington: Government Printing Office, September 1978). This is a state-by-state listing of libraries where the microfiche may be viewed.

[12]At the same time, University Microfilm, among others, does offer about 55 percent of the journal articles as reprints. The "Source Journal Index" in each issue indicates which of the journals is cooperating with UM. However, the cost of reprints is considerably more than the microfiche available for the other part of ERIC.

Thanks to its wide coverage of subject areas, its relative low cost, and its position as a teaching device for online searches, ERIC is favored by people in both the humanities and the social sciences. In various frequency-of-use studies, it is often rated first or among the top two or three databases most often used in libraries.[13]

INDEXES TO CURRENT EVENTS

In any reference library, one of the most time-consuming, sometimes futile, types of search is for current material on recent events. How is one to answer the question concerning a presidential appointment of a week or a month ago, trace current sporting records, or find information on a prominent woman who died only last week?

The first general index source is *The Readers' Guide to Periodical Literature* which is issued every two weeks and may be no more than four to six weeks behind in actually indexing some current news periodicals. A subject rather than a general aid, with somewhat more of a time lag, is the semimonthly *Public Affairs Information Service Bulletin*.

The natural inclination is to turn to a newspaper index. This is of limited use, because the standard print indexes are several months behind. There are two exceptions: (1) the *National Newspaper Index* (to be discussed shortly) is on a microfilm role and is updated once a month. However, this is so expensive as to be out of the question for most libraries. (2) *The New York Times Information Bank,* as well as several other indexes, is available for online searches. Here the material is updated once each week, with really current headlines updated every 24 hours. Again, cost may be prohibitive for all but the largest of libraries.

Of these two answers to the problem of recency, the online service is the most satisfactory. This is the direction in which the long-term solution to data on current events is going. In the library, in private and government organizations, the computer terminal will be used more and more in the 1980s to find data which are no more than a few hours or a few days old. One of the great blessings of the new technology is its ability, given enough funding, to short-circuit the long delays associated with printed indexes and abstracting services.

---

[13]See various issues of *Online;* e.g., October 1977, p. 62; July 1978, p. 63. Depending on type and size of the library, the favored databases (which translates into favored printed subject indexes as well) are: *ERIC, Psychological Abstracts, NTIS* (National Technical Information Service), *Medlars,* and *Social Science Citation Index.*

Lacking a computer terminal, how does one locate material published yesterday, or a week or a month ago, if the average index is so far behind or so expensive? There are several approaches: (1) The least satisfactory is simply to go through current issues of magazines related to the subject or to examine the latest issues of newspapers. (2) A somewhat more rewarding step is to consult the weekly summaries of events, such as *Facts on File,* which, if nothing more, give the date of the event. (3) One may consult with the local newspaper, radio, or television news bureau. There is always the "expert" in the community who may have exactly the information needed. (4) The last suggestion, and ultimately the best solution of all, is for the librarian to keep advised of current events by careful reading of at least one newspaper each day and the weekly news magazines, and also to keep an ear open for community events. Obviously the "one" newspaper should include the local publication(s), and, where possible, the closest thing we have to a national newspaper, i.e., *The New York Times.*

Sources for last week's events

Facts on File, a Weekly World News Digest, with Cumulative Index. New York: Facts on File, Inc., October 30, 1940, to date, weekly. $330.

Keesing's Contemporary Archives. London: Keesing's, July 1, 1931, to date, weekly (represented in the United States by Charles Scribner's Sons). $130.

Canadian News Facts. Toronto: Marpep Publishing, January 1, 1967, to date, biweekly. $125.

Congressional Quarterly Weekly Report, 1943 to date. Washington: Congressional Quarterly, Inc., 1943 to date, weekly. $560.

While all of these may be employed for searching events which took place last week, it should be noted that none (as of late 1981) is available online. Several publishers indicate this may be changed by the mid-1980s.

Of all the services, *Facts on File* tends to be the most prompt (the U.S. mails permitting), and normally only a few days elapse between the last date covered and receipt of the publication. Emphasis is on news events in the United States, with international coverage related for the most part to American affairs. Material is gathered mainly from the major newspapers and condensed into objective, short, factual reports. The index is arranged under broad subject headings, such as "World affairs," "Finance," "Economics," "National affairs," and so on. This is a bit confusing; but fortunately, every two weeks, each month, and then quarterly and annually, a detailed index is issued which covers previous issues. There is also a *Five-Year Master News Index,* published since 1950. The latest edition, covering 1976–1980, was published in 1981. The publisher notes a "few ways" the service may be used: Check dates in the index; skim the weekly issues to prepare for current affairs tests; read Supreme Court decisions in the Digest; scan the "U.S. and World Affairs" column for ideas for short papers. And there are countless other uses, although the most frequent call is for specific current data.

In *Keesing's Contemporary Archives,* emphasis differs from *Facts on File* in two important respects. The scope is primarily the United Kingdom, Europe, and the British Commonwealth. Detailed subject reports in certain areas are frequently included (the reports are by experts and frequently delay the weekly publication by several days), as are full texts of important speeches and documents. However, *Keesing's* does not cover in any detail many ephemeral events, such as sports, art exhibitions, and movies, which may be included in *Facts on File*. Arrangement is by country, territory, or continent, with some broad subject headings, such as "Religion," "Aviation," and "Fine arts." Every second week, an index is issued which is cumulated quarterly and annually.

Following much the same procedure and format as *Facts on File, Canadian News Facts* differs in its scope and its frequency; it appears every two weeks rather than weekly. The news digests vary from 8 to 12 pages, and are concerned almost exclusively with Canada. While it would be a first choice for Canadian libraries, *News Facts* would be well down the selection scale for all but the largest libraries in the United States.

While both *Keesing's* and *Facts on File* are sources of information on general news events, there are some specialized weekly services which assist the reference librarian. Among the best of those giving detailed reports on government activities is the *Congressional Quarterly Weekly Report*. Issued by a private firm, not by the government, it presents in condensed form all congressional and political activities of the previous week—not only those relating to Congress. Bills, acts, names of members of congress, how they voted, committee action, major legislation, and related subjects are covered in full and are competently indexed and summarized in a "fact sheet" procedure. Since the service is indexed in *Public Affairs Information Service Bulletin,* it may be approached through two indexes.

Newspaper indexes[14]

The New York Times Index. New York: The New York Times, 1851 to date, semimonthly, with quarterly and annual cumulations. $278. (Online, $80 to $110 an hour.)

Newspaper Index. Wooster, Ohio: Bell & Howell, 1972 to date, monthly, with quarterly and annual cumulations. Individual indexes, $275 each. (Online, $80 an hour.)

Index to the Christian Science Monitor. Wooster, Ohio: Bell & Howell, 1949 to date, monthly. $90. (Online, via other services.)

The Wall Street Journal Index. Princeton, New Jersey: Dow Jones Books, Inc., 1950 to date, monthly. $150. Annual vol., $150. Combined monthly and annual. $245. (Online, via other services.)

The *National Newspaper Index.* Los Altos, California: Information Access Corporation, 1979 to date, monthly. $940 to $1880. (Online, $75 an hour.)

The Times. London: Index to the Times, 1906–1977, bimonthly and quarterly; 1977 to date, monthly, $250. (Distributed in the United States by Research Publications, Woodbridge, Connecticut.)

Canadian Newspaper Index. Toronto, Ontario: Micromedia Ltd. 1977 to date, monthly. $395. (Online, price varies.)

Only a decade or so ago there were few national newspaper indexes. Today the number is increasing for two reasons: (1) There is an urgent need and demand for facts which are current (less than a day or two old) and found in national newspapers. (2) The computer has allowed rapid processing and availability of the index at a terminal.

Still, of the 500 to 700 estimated newspaper indexes, all but a half-dozen or so are files maintained by individual newspapers or libraries. Eventually these local indexes may be connected through the computer to a national system, but that is years away.[15] Meanwhile,

---

[14]Susan Cherry, "Yesterday's News for Tomorrow," *American Libraries,* November 1979, pp. 588–592. This is an excellent summary of the various newspaper indexes available as of early 1980.

[15]Then, too, as James Rettig observes, the increased cost of indexing local newspapers is reducing rather than encouraging such indexes. Discussing the indexing of the *Dayton Daily News,* Rettig notes: "A recent estimate of the total annual labor and materials cost for the index came to approximately $6000. Statistics show it was used approximately 180 times a year, at a cost of about $33 per use. . . . The index was discontinued." *American Libraries,* February 1980, p. 86.

the librarian—given the appropriate funds—does have access to major newspapers at a computer terminal. Unfortunately, as indicated, the printed versions of the same indexes are months behind. So, for most libraries the marvelous opportunities for almost instant tapping of yesterday's newspaper remains more theory than reality.

Three major indexes are available both online and in variations of the printed form. It is primarily with the printed form that this section is concerned. The online aspects of the services are discussed in the second volume of the text.

No matter what its form, the best-known newspaper index in the United States is the one published by *The New York Times.* A distinct advantage of *The New York Times Index* is its wide scope and relative completeness.[16]. Although the United States does not have a truly national newspaper, the *Times,* in its effort to cover all major news events, both national and international, comes close to being a daily national newspaper. The *Times Index* provides a wealth of information and frequently is used even without reference to the individual paper of the date cited. Each entry includes a brief abstract of the news story. Consequently, someone seeking a single fact, such as the name of an official, the date of an event, or the title of a play may often find all that is needed in the index. Also, since all material is dated, the *Times Index* serves as an entry into other, unindexed newspapers and magazines. For example, if the user is uncertain of the day ship X sank and wishes to see how the disaster was covered in another newspaper or in a magazine, the *Times Index* will narrow the search by providing the date the event occurred.

The New York Times Index is arranged in dictionary form with sufficient cross-references to names and related topics. Events under each of the main headings are arranged chronologically. Book and theater reviews are listed under those respective headings.

Some libraries subscribe only to the annual cumulated *Index.* This volume serves as an index and guide to the activities of the previous year. Thanks to the rather full abstracts, maps, and charts, one may use the cumulated volume as a reference source in itself.

Beginning in 1978, the index began quarterly cumulations, thus saving the user the necessity of poring over each individual issue. While a great help, this still requires, near year's end, the use of three separate volumes plus the bimonthly issues. The annual cumulation is fine, but it is late; normally it is not published for six to seven months after the end of the year.

---

[16]Grant W. Morse, *Guide to the Incomparable New York Times Index* (New York: Fleet, 1979, 72 pp.). This is an invaluable guide for someone who plans to use earlier issues of the *Times Index.* The author explains organization, search strategies, and the like.

Currency is the major difficulty. The bimonthly issues do not appear in a library for two to three months after the period indexed. The situation is not likely to improve, although the online service for the index offers 24-hour and 1-week indexing of the same material.

Using an approach similar to that of the *Magazine Index,* the publishers of the *National Newspaper Index* offer the service on microfilm, which is updated once a month and loaded into a reader. Thanks to this system, it is not necessary to consult various volumes, supplements, and cumulations, as it is for *The New York Times Index.* The cost will make most librarians pause.

The publishers include indexing to *The New York Times,* the *Christian Science Monitor,* and *The Wall Street Journal.* A tremendous advantage to this system is that it is possible to search three newspapers at one time; i.e., the indexing is combined. Emphasis is primarily on subjects, but one may also search the index by title and by-lines.

The *National Newspaper Index* comes out once a month, compared with twice-a-month issues from *The New York Times,* but the important difference is that the monthly index is just that—up to date and not two to three months behind publishing schedule. The result, at least as of this writing, is that the *National Newspaper Index* is considerably more timely than its rival. There is still a two-to-three-week lag between the time the film is available and the last index entry. *The New York Times Index* has the advantage of including major abstracts which are not found in the other index and, aside from currency, is better for reference.

As with the *Magazine Index,* the newspaper index is available for search online—in fact, it can be searched in conjunction with the *Magazine Index,* so one looks for a subject not only in a newspaper but in a magazine. This service is called *NewsSearch.* The database gives access to four printed services: *The National Newspaper Index, Magazine Index, Legal Resource Index,* and *Management Contents.*

Libraries in different geographical areas from those represented by the two major national indexes will subscribe to one or more regional titles. The Bell & Howell *Newspaper Index* (also available online) began as a single unit, but by now is really no more than individual indexes to individual papers. Included in the series: *Chicago Sun Times, Chicago Tribune, Denver Post, Detroit News, Houston Post, New Orleans Times-Picayune, San Francisco Chronicle, Los Angeles Times,* and *Washington Post.*

The individual, computer printout indexes are issued monthly with quarterly and annual cumulations. Four-year cumulative indexes are available for 1972 through 1975 and 1976 through 1979, for the

Chicago Tribune, Los Angeles Times, New Orleans Times-Picayune and *Washington Post,* but not for the others in the series. Each index is in two parts. The first section is the subject index, and while there are no abstracts, the title of the article is enough for most purposes. When it is not, the publisher may add a few words of description. The second part is a personal name index.

Each of these indexes serves a useful purpose in the library, although, like *The New York Times Index,* each is from two to three months or even more behind in publishing.

Issued since 1958, the index to *The Wall Street Journal* is in two parts, "Corporate News" and "General News," with brief summaries of the events. As in *The New York Times Index,* enough information is usually found in the summaries to cancel the need to go to the newspaper. While of primary interest for business and economic studies, the paper is more general in its news coverage than the title or its previous history indicates. It frequently carries articles in depth about national problems other than those linked to economics.[17] (Note: This index also is available from Bell & Howell, as is the index to *Barron's.*)

The monthly *Christian Science Monitor Index* has been issued since 1960, but retrospective indexing to 1950 is available (the paper began publishing in 1908). Although the newspaper is biased on its editorial page, its reporting of the general news is considered to be extremely objective. In fact, many libraries that draw the line at subscribing to any religion-supported newspapers make an exception of the *Monitor.* Consequently, the index is extremely useful as an adjunct to *The New York Times Index.*

The *Monitor Index* cites stories carried in its three editions: Eastern, Western, and Midwestern. The approach is primarily by subject, and no effort is made to annotate the items as the *Times Index* does. It has one distinct advantage over the other indexes—a much lower price. It is available online via *The New York Times Information Bank* and *Newsearch.*

NewsBank (Greenwich, Connecticut: NewsBank, 1970 to date, monthly) is an index, by subject, to about 100 major American newspapers not covered by the other services. The library receives not only the printed index but a set of microfiche cards with the

---

[17]The index to *The Wall Street Journal* is available online as part of the *Dow Jones News/Retrieval System.* This includes *Barron's* and the *Dow Jones News Service.* The independent service is the most current of the group—is updated literally by the minute—but data is maintained in the file for only 90 days. Also, it is part of the online *Newsearch.*

articles from the newspapers. The service is sold in parts (such as subjects which fall only in the arts) or as a total. A person, interested in urban renewal, for example, can compare how the subject was handled by Eastern and by Western newspapers as well as, of course, examine the material itself.

The *Canadian Newspaper Index* offers a relatively current subject and name index to Canada's leading newspapers: *Montreal Gazette, Toronto Globe and Mail, Toronto Star, Vancouver Sun, Winnipeg Free Press, Calgary Herald,* and the *Halifax Chronicle Herald.* The online version corresponds to the printed index.

The index published by *The Times* of London is in dictionary form with sufficient cross-references to names and related topics. It has brief abstracts which provide dates; facts; and, often enough, material for ready-reference work which does not require the user to consult the newspaper itself. In addition to indexing the newspaper, it indexes related *Times* publications. It, too, appears several months after the publications have been issued and cannot be used for really current searching.

Which index?

Most medium and large public and academic libraries have *The New York Times Index,* followed by the index to *The Washington Post.*[18] It is too soon to say how successful the *The National Newspaper Index* will be, but it is likely to be a serious contender against *The New York Times* title—at least if it can lower costs. Far behind come other indexes, and many libraries have their own in-house service for the local papers.

In a survey of 80 large and medium-sized research, university, and college libraries, it was found that the mean number of papers in libraries was 127 and of this number, from 41 to 60 percent are domestic.[19] Selection of American newspapers is based on the needs of the public, faculty, and students, although aside from the national newspapers (*The New York Times* to *Los Angeles Times*), the choice tends to be confined to the immediate locality or region.

Television news is now available in micro form and in the years ahead may also be part of the video tape or disc collection. A pioneer in this field is *CBS News Index* (New York: Microfilming Corporation of America, 1975 to date, quarterly with annual cumulation). Access is

---

[18]*The New York Times Index* has 4700 to 4800 library subscribers, while *The Washington Post* has 450 subscribers and the *San Francisco Chronicle,* about 100. Cherry, op. cit., p. 590.

[19]Joel A. Rutstein, "The Role of Newspapers as an Information Resource: A Survey of Academic Libraries," *The Library Scene,* March 1978, pp. 17–21.

offered on microfilm or microfiche to verbatim transcripts of daily television broadcasts as well as special programs such as "60 Minutes" and "CBS Reports." The index is primarily a subject approach, but does offer entry by name and location and personal names. There is a one- or two-phrase description of the program. The quarterly edition is prompt, out no later than one month after the end of the quarter. In addition, the annual edition precedes *The New York Times* annual by at least three months.

INDEXES TO MATERIAL IN COLLECTIONS

Essay and General Literature Index. New York: The H. W. Wilson Company, 1900 to date, semiannual. $45. (Five-year cumulations, $115.)

Short Story Index. New York: The H. W. Wilson Company, 1975 to date, annual. $25. (Irregular, 1953 to 1973; basic volume, 1953, plus six supplements, 1956 to 1978, various prices.)

Granger's Index to Poetry. 6th ed. New York: Columbia University Press, 1973, 2223 pp. $99. *Supplement 1970–1977,* 1978, 653 pp. $59.50.

Play Index. New York: The H. W. Wilson Company, 1953 to date. (Irregular; basic volume, 1954, plus four additional volumes. $10 to $28.)

Anthologies and collections are a peculiar blessing or curse for the reference librarian. Many of them are useless, others are on the borderline, and a few are worthwhile in that they bring the attention of readers to material which otherwise might be missed or overlooked. Regardless of merit, all collections may serve the reference librarian who is seeking a particular speech, essay, poem, play, or other literary form. In reference, the usefulness of anthologies is dependent on adequate indexes.

This type of material is approached by the average user in one of several ways. He or she may know the author and want a play, a poem, or other form by that author. The name of the work may be known, but more than likely it is not. Another approach is to want something about X subject in a play, poem, short story and so on.

Consequently, the most useful indexes to material in collections are organized so they may be approached by author, subject, and title of a specific work. Failure to find a particular title in an anthology or collection usually means it has been published independently and has still to find its way into a collective form. The card catalog certainly should be checked; if it fails to produce an answer, standard bibliographical tools, such as the *Cumulative Book Index* and *Books in Print,* should be consulted.

Indexes to materials in collections serve two other valuable purposes. Most of them cover books or other materials which have been analyzed; and since the analysis tends to be selective, the librarian has a built-in buying guide to the better or outstanding books in the field. For example, the *Essay and General Literature Index* picks up selections from most of the outstanding collections of essays. The library that has a large number of these books in its collection will have a good representative group of works.

The second benefit, particularly in these days of close cooperation among libraries, is that the indexes can be used to locate books not in the library. Given a specific request for an essay and lacking the title in which the essay appears, the librarian may request the book on interlibrary loan by giving the specific and precise bibliographical information found in the index.

Aside from sharing a similar purpose of locating bits of information from collections, anthologies, and individual books and magazines, this type of reference aid tends to center on the humanities, particularly in literature. There is little need for such assistance in the social sciences and the sciences, or where the need does exist, it is usually met by an abstracting or indexing service. While the titles listed here are the best known, new entries appear each year. They range from guides to science fiction to information on handcrafts, costumes, photographs, and such. Once the form is recognized, the only basic change is in the topics covered and the thoroughness, or lack of it, in arrangement and depth of analysis.

The single most useful work in libraries as an entry into miscellaneous collections of articles is the *Essay and General Literature Index.* It is valuable for general reference questions, in that the analyzed essays cover a wide variety of topics. There are usually about 20,000 analytical subject entries to the contents of some 1500 collected works on every subject from art to medicine. While the indexing emphasis in on subjects, the index is useful for approaching an author's work via his or her name as well as for locating criticism of the author's individual efforts.

The *Essay and General Literature Index* is also a type of buyer's guide to collections, in that subscribers each month receive a list of the books to be indexed. (A necessary companion volume for the large library with a complete run of the index is *Essay and General Literature*

Index: Works Indexed 1900–1969. This 70-year list cites all the 9917 titles that have been analyzed in the seven permanent cumulations.)

The useful addition to *Essay and General Literature Index* is *Canadian Essay and Literature Index* (Toronto: University of Toronto Press, annual, 1975 to date). This differs from the American title in several ways: (1) In addition to analyzing contents of about 90 books, it indexes some 40 periodicals; (2) all publications are from Canada, although content is not limited to Canadian interests; (3) in addition to essays, the contents of books and periodicals are analyzed for book reviews, poems, plays, and short stories. All material is integrated into a single author-title-subject index, with only essays and book reviews in separate sections. Finally, the indexing lags by about two years; i.e., the 1982 volume covers 1980; the 1980 volume, 1978, and so on.

The elusive short story may be tracked down in the *Short Story Index.* Now published annually, the *Index* lists stories in both book collections and periodicals. A single index identifies the story by author, by title, and by subject. The subject listing is a handy aid for the reference librarian attempting to find a suitable study topic for a student who may want to read an entire book on the Civil War or life in Alaska. The names of the books and the magazines analyzed are listed. More than 3000 stories are considered each year. There are four-year cumulations and the one for 1974–1978 (issued in 1979) indexes approximately 13,500 stories from 930 collections. About 3000 of these appeared in periodicals.

Short Story Index: Collections Indexed, 1900–1978 (published in 1980) is a complete author, title, and editor index to the seven volumes of the *Short Story Index.* There are over 120,000 separate listings, and complete bibliographic information—which allows the librarian to locate the collection in which the story appears—is given with the author or editor entry. One disadvantage: there is no subject approach, and for this the user must return to the basic set.

Another index to short stories in collections is the *Chicorel Index to Short Stories in Anthologies and Collections* (New York: Chicorel Library Publishing Corp., 1974, 4 vols.). The basic set is updated every two or three years; e.g., a two-volume work covering 1977–1978 was issued in 1979. There are related works with a narrower focus. For example, *Index to Science Fiction* (Boston: G. K. Hall & Company, 1978, 608 pp.) is an author and title index to more than 2000 anthologies and collections.

Indexing both individually published plays and plays in collections, *Play Index* is a standard reference work. The basic part is an author, title, and subject index. The author entry for a play "contains the full name of the author, title of the play, a brief descriptive note, the number of acts and scenes, the size of the cast, and the number of sets required." There are numerous other helpful devices, ranging from symbols for plays suitable for elementary school children to prizes a play has won. A cast analysis, making up the second section, helps the reference librarian locate plays by number of players required. The other sections key the plays to collections from which they have been taken.

Another index to plays in collections is the multivolume *Chicorel Theater Index to Plays in Anthologies and Periodicals, Discs and Tapes* (New York: Chicorel Library Publishing Corp., 1970 to date, annual). This index differs from the others in that it includes plays in periodicals as well as in anthologies. A feature is its lists of plays available on records or tapes. Arranged in one alphabet, the *Index* covers the title of the play, author, editor, translator, and so on.

The sixth edition of *Granger's Index to Poetry* follows previous editions in arrangement and approach. Close to 800 poetry anthologies are analyzed in three sections, each alphabetically arranged, which cover title and first line, author, and subject. Each of the anthologies is listed with full bibliographical information. The supplement provides the same indexing for poems in 119 anthologies published between 1970 and 1977. This differs from the main work in that the editors have expanded the subject headings, included more collections of poetry by women and minorities and checked primary acquisitions for small and medium-sized libraries.

Not only is *Granger's* useful for tracing elusive poems, but the first-line approach is a resource for quotations which may not be included in standard quotation books.

An equally good reference work in this area is John Brewton's *Index to Poetry for Children and Young People: 1970–1975* (New York: The H. W. Wilson Company, 1978, 472 pp.). This offers title, subject, author, and first-line approaches to 110 collections, and supplements the original 1942 index. There are now two supplements to the 1942 title, and a third supplement is likely in 1983. *The Index of American Periodical Verse* (Metuchen, New Jersey: Scarecrow Press, 1973 to date, annual) is an author and title (or first-line, if no title) index to a broad variety of magazine verse by both well-known and less-known writers. *Chicorel Index to Poetry in Anthologies and Collections in Print* (New York: Chicorel Library Publishing Corp., various dates) was up to six volumes by 1980. New volumes are issued as needed to cover current anthologies. The anthologies (not first lines) are indexed by broad subjects, and the poems and authors in the anthologies are indexed by author and title.

Related to poetry first lines and verses are songs, and, in fact, some people confuse the two. A help here is *Popular Song Index* (Metuchen, New Jersey: Scarecrow Press, 1975; Supplement, 1978). This is an index of titles and, more important, first lines from about 400 collections published between 1940 and 1975. Other material is included, although the first-line approach is the most useful for reference questions. This supplements the classic Sears' title, *Song Index* (various publishers, 1926, 1934), which with the initial volume and the supplement indexes about 20,000 songs by title, first line, authors' and composers' names, and so on.

In the same area: *Index to Children's Songs* (New York: The H. W. Wilson Company, 1979, 318 pp.) which is a title, first-line, and subject index to 5000 songs in 298 children's books published between 1909 and 1977. Note that this has a subject approach which can be useful. There are numerous reference works related to music, and there is even a method of helping someone discover the origin of a haunting tune or melody.[20]

Concordances

There is one other form of index which is "basic" in most libraries, and that is the concordance. A concordance is an alphabetical index of the principal words in a book, or more likely, in the total works of a single author, with their contexts. Early concordances were limited to the Bible; a classic of its type, often reprinted, is Alexander Cruden's *Complete Concordance to the Old and New Testament . . .* , first published in 1737.

The laborious task of analyzing the Bible word by word, passage by passage, is matched only by the preparation of early concordances to Shakespeare. Fortunately, the advent of the computer considerably simplifed the concordance effort (for both editorial and production purposes). Today there are concordances to not only the Bible and Shakespeare, but almost every major writer. Examples include concordances to F. Scott Fitzgerald's *The Great Gatsby*, James Joyce's *Finnegans Wake*, the complete poetry of Stephen Crane, and the plays of Federico Garcia Lorca.

A concordance is used in a library for two basic purposes: (1) to enable students of literature to study the literary style of an author on

---

[20]Denys Parson. *The Directory of Tunes and Musical Themes.* (London, 1975) offers a code to melodies. One hums the melody and the book helps the user identify the song. For a thorough, sometimes amusing discussion of this unique work, see Harry Bauer, "Breaking the Sound Barrier . . ." *RQ*, Winter 1978, pp. 156–159.

the basis of use or nonuse of given words; and (2) more often, to run down elusive quotations. With one or two key words, the librarian may often find the exact quotation in the concordance. This approach presupposes some knowledge of the author.

Quotations

Bartlett, John. *Familiar Quotations,* 15th ed. Boston: Little, Brown and Company, 1980, 1540 pp. $24.95.

Stevenson, Burton E. *The Home Book of Quotations, Classical and Modern,* 10th ed. New York: Dodd, Mead & Company, Inc., 1967, 2816 pp. $40.

The Oxford Dictionary of Quotations. 3d ed. New York: Oxford University Press, 1979. 907 pp. $29.95.

Indexing "who said what" is the role of the book of quotations. Actually, these books are not so much indexes as distinctive forms unto themselves, defying ready classification. Having found the quotation, for example, the average user is satisfied and does not want to go to the source, as he or she might do when using the standard index to materials in collections. Be that as it may, a frequent question in any library is either, Who said the following? or What do you have in the way of a quote by or about X subject? Any of the standard books of quotations may provide the answer. "May" is used here advisedly, for frequently the quotation is not found in any of the standard sources, either because it is so unusual or, more than likely, because it is garbled. When the patron is not certain about the actual wording, another approach is by subject.

By far the most famous book of quotations is Bartlett (as *Familiar Quotations* is often called). A native of Plymouth, Massachusetts, John Bartlett was born in 1820 and at sixteen was employed by the owner of the University Bookstore in Cambridge. By the time he owned the store, he had become famous for his remarkable memory, and the word around Harvard was, "Ask John Bartlett." He began a notebook which expanded into the first edition of his work in 1855. After the Civil War, he joined Little, Brown and Company, and he continued to edit his work through nine editions until his death in December 1905.

The work is updated about every 10 to 12 years, and the fifteenth edition, published in 1980, includes more than 450 new authors. Most of these are contemporary and thanks to a famous word or two have made their way to fame in the standard work. A few are historical and represent a new look at history; e.g., the fifteenth edition has several more representatives of the early women's movement than has the fourteenth. The total is now some 2500 individuals including such new entries as Woody Allen; Pope John Paul II; and a late-comer, George Sand. The number of quotes is claimed to be near 23,000, or some 2500 more than the last edition. As with past efforts, the editors favor establishment figures, e.g., Milton Friedman has a solid page of quotes, but there are considerably briefer entries from Dorothy Parker, Mick Jagger, and the Beatles.

Although Bartlett and the other sources contain similar material, many quotation works are needed; often what will be found in one may not be found in the others.

The Oxford Dictionary of Quotations is another popular book of this type found in many libraries. The third edition represents the first substantial revision since the original 1941 publication, and of the three basic books of quotations, the Oxford has the advantage of being the most current. According to the admirably written preface, selection is based on what is most familiar to a majority of people—and in this case, while the bias is English, most of the quotations represent a considerably more international tone and will be equally well known to educated Americans. The editor points out that a team of some 20 advisers "voted for or against every suggested addition, thus providing the editors with at least a sample poll for that popularity which had seemed the only valid criterion."[21]

Briefly, the difference between Bartlett, Oxford, and Stevenson (a common identification of *The Home of Quotations, . . .*), aside from content, are:

1. *Arrangement.* Stevenson is arranged alphabetically under subject. Bartlett is arranged chronologically by author. In this, Bartlett differs from almost every other anthology of quotations. Oxford is alphabetically by author.

2. *Index.* All have thorough indexes by subject, author, and key words of the quotation or verses. Stevenson does not repeat the subject words employed in the main text in the index.

3. *Other features.* Stevenson has brief biographical data on authors. Bartlett features helpful historical footnotes, sometimes tracing the original quotation normally associated with one individual back to another person or time. The Oxford has a separate Greek Index.

Each year seems to produce more compilations of quotations, most of which disappear without any great loss. Regardless of overall

[21]J. I. M. Steward quoting the editor in "Tags for the Times," *The Times Literary Supplement,* November 30, 1979, p. 61.

quality, many librarians prefer to collect such works because the quotation query is so popular and no one can ever be sure where a quotation may appear. Note, for example, the difficult query section in each issue of *RQ*. A major part of each column consists of elusive quotations, which may be traced to an even more elusive book of quotations.

Examples of relatively new works are *The Dictionary of Biographical Quotation of British and American Subjects* (New York: Alfred A. Knopf, 1978, 860 pp.).[22] Here famous people are given the opportunity to talk about other famous people; e.g., Edith Sitwell is quoted as saying she enjoyed talking to Virginia Woolf, "but thought nothing of her writing. I consider her a beautiful little knitter." And F. Scott Fitzgerald said of Gertrude Stein: "What an old covered wagon she is." Then there is *The Quotable Woman 1800–1975* (Los Angeles: Corwin Books, 1977, 539 pp.) in which is found Zelda Fitzgerald's remark on love: "I don't want to live—I want to love first, and live incidentally." This is a collection of 8000 quotations by some 1300 women. Arranged chronologically, it has a fine subject and author index, which not only cites quotations but gives the author's full name, dates, nationality, relationships to other notables, contributions, and honors. Why such a reference work? To give women a fair quota, because according to the compiler, only 5 percent of the total number of famous words in Bartlett's comes from women and only 1 percent in the Oxford book. (Once the gap is discovered, there is no shortage of titles; e.g., in 1979 Thomas Y. Crowell published *Feminist Quotations,* and more reference works of this type are promised.)

Currency normally does not loom so large for indexes of quotations as it does for other reference books; still, a useful up-to-date title covering quotations of the previous year is *What They Said in 197—* (Beverly Hills, California: Monitor Books, 1969 to date, annual). Published about mid-year after the closing year, this compilation includes about 550 pages of "direct quotations from speeches, news conferences, interviews, etc." Quotations are grouped by subject, and there is a detailed subject-author index. Full citations are given, and an added bonus is the full identification of the author by position, rank, title, and so on.

The problem with quotations is that one may read one or two in passing, forget the source, and then try to rediscover them. For example, here are two marvelous insults which may or may not be

---

[22]For a review of this work and general comments on books of quotations see William Safire, "A Useful, Browseworthy Compendium," *The New York Times Book Review,* December 24, 1978, pp. 1, 14.

found in a standard book of quotations. They would be lost for all time until you, or a friend, remembered the source.

J. P. Mahaffy's reply to a rudely interrupting, incontinent student at Trinity College, Dublin: "At the end of this corridor you will find a door marked GENTLEMEN, but don't let that stop you," and Dorothy Parker's retort to a young actress's muttered "Age before beauty" as the latter stood aside for her: "And pearls before swine." These are insults for the recipient to take home and think about.[23]

SUGGESTED READING

Boehm, Eric H., "Twenty-Five Years of History Indexing . . .," *The Indexer,* April 1978, pp. 33–42. A description of the evolution of *Historical Abstracts* and *America: History and Life* by the president of ABC-Clio, publishers of both services. Concludes with basic recommendations applicable to most indexes.

Borko, Harold and Charles Bernier, *Indexing Concepts and Methods.* New York: Academic Press, 1978. A basic text on both the theory and the practical aspects of indexing. Particularly useful, as there are numerous "how-to-do-it" chapters of considerable help to anyone learning "how-to-use" an index.

James, Barbara, "Indexing The Times," *The Indexer,* October 1979, pp. 209–211. An easy-to-understand account of the steps necessary in indexing the London *Times.* Particularly good, as it gives the reader an idea of the human element much involved in indexing. (Note: other issues of *The Indexer* carry splendid articles on the art.)

Safire, William, "The Triumph of Evil," *The New York Times Magazine,* March 9, 1980, pp. 8–10. An amusing yet factual account of trying to trace a common quotation to its original source and the failure of traditional reference works such as Bartlett to give the proper source.

Sisson, Jacqueline, "Case History of the Compilation of a Large Cumulative Index," *The Indexer,* October 1977, pp. 164–175. A step-by-step description of how one person planned a cumulative index covering 1901–1940.

---

[23]D. J. Enright, "The Obscenity Scene," *The Times Literary Supplement,* August 25, 1978, p. 946. Also, different quotations works often cite different sources for the same quotation, e.g., see the letter to the editor on this subject "Living, Eating, and Attribution" in *The Times Literary Supplement,* September 12, 1980, p. 995, where an author finds numerous people who said the same thing; i.e., "One must eat to live and not live to eat." Among those quoted by different quotation works: Moliere, Plutarch, Cicero, and Socrates.

SOURCES OF
INFORMATION

PART
III

CHAPTER SIX

Encyclopedias:
General and Subject

T HE EIGHTEENTH CENTURY was the Age of Enlightenment, when Diderot, eternal optimist, believed it
possible to capture knowledge in his great
Encyclopédie. The Enlightenment, although a land-
mark in the history of knowledge, remains, as Hugh
Kenner puts it, as "a mystical experience through
which the minds of Europe passed." Kenner then goes on to cleverly
summarize the content and purpose of an encyclopedia:

> *We carry with us still one piece of baggage from those far off days, and
> that is the book which nobody wrote and nobody is expected to read, and
> which is marketed as* The Encyclopaedia: Britannica, Americana,
> Antarctica *or other. The* Encyclopaedia . . . *takes all that we know
> apart into little pieces, and then arranges those pieces so that they can be
> found one at a time. It is produced by a feat of organizing, not a feat of
> understanding.* . . . *If the Encyclopaedia means anything as a whole, no
> one connected with the enterprise can be assumed to know what that
> meaning is.*[1]

[1]Hugh Kenner, *The Stoic Comedians* (Berkeley, California: University of California
Press, 1974, pp. 1, 2). I am grateful to Joelle Ross for bringing this essay on
encyclopedias and Flaubert to my attention. It is a fine introduction to the author and
to the philosophical (not to mention comic) side of reference works.

The complaint is common, although in some ways it is to miss the point of the modern encyclopedia. Today the general set serves a variety of purposes, but essentially it is to capsulize and organize the world's accumulated knowledge, or at least that part of it that is of interest to readers. Through detailed articles and brief facts, an effort is made to include a wide variety of information from all fields.

Encyclopedias may be divided into two or three categories: (1) by format—there are the general and subject sets of 4 to 24 volumes (such as the *World Book*) and the smaller works of 1, 2, or 3 volumes (such as the 1-volume *New Columbia Encyclopedia*); (2) by scope—here the division is either general (the *World Book*) or by subject (*International Encyclopedia of the Social Sciences*); (3) by audience—the general work may be for a child, teenager, or layperson. If a subject set, it is likely directed to an expert or near-expert in that subject field. There are other methods of dividing and subdividing encyclopedias, many of which will be evident as the reader progresses through this chapter.

By definition an encyclopedia is "A literary work containing extensive information on all branches of knowledge, usually arranged in alphabetical order."[2] "Extensive" is not "all," but the concept of total coverage is inherent in the myth of the encyclopedia, a myth best summarized by Diderot, who stated his classic set's overall purpose as "to collect all knowledge scattered over the face of the earth . . . so that our children, by becoming more educated, may at the same time become more virtuous and happier."[3]

The admirable belief in the efficacy of encyclopedias is no more. Diderot's noble thoughts have been modified by a more complicated attitude toward education and certainly by the recognition that there is too much information being generated daily to allow any single encyclopedia the boast of containing "all knowledge scattered over the face of the earth."

Purpose

No matter which type of encyclopedia is published, it usually will include detailed survey articles, often with bibliographies, in certain fields or areas; explanatory material, normally shorter; and brief informational data such as the birth and death dates of famous

[2]*The Oxford English Dictionary* (London: Oxford University Press, 1933, vol. 3), p. 153.

[3]Stephen J. Gendzier (ed.), *Denis Diderot's Encyclopedia* (New York: J & J Harper Editions, 1969), p. xv. For a more current discussion of the famous Diderot work see Robert Darnton, *The Business of Enlightenment*. (Cambridge, Massachusetts: Harvard University Press, 1979).

people, geographical locations, and historical events. This scope makes the encyclopedia ideal for reference work, and the general set is often the first place the librarian will turn for answering questions.

The bibliographies at the end of articles may help the reader to find additional material in a given subject area. The importance of adequate bibliographies is particularly well recognized at the juvenile level (augmented by the use of study aids) and at the specialist's level (by highly developed bibliographies in narrow subject areas). Many encyclopedias now offer a variety of study guides which indicate related articles the student might employ to put together, with the help of other books, a truly creative paper rather than a carbon copy of an encyclopedia article.

To clear up a common misunderstanding, no general encyclopedia is a proper source for research. (This does not include specialized works.) It is only a springboard. Furthermore, in presenting material with almost no differentiation, the general encyclopedia is not completely accurate or up to date; important facts must be double-checked in another source, if only in a second encyclopedia.

At the child's level, another purpose is often falsely advanced. An encyclopedia, no matter how good, is not a substitute for additional reading or for a collection of supporting reference books. In their natural enthusiasm, some salespeople and advertising copy-writers are carried away with the proposition that an encyclopedia-oriented child is an educated child.

Publishers

How good is this encyclopedia? Before considering that vital question, as well as the one of cost, one must ask: Just what choice do I have in the purchase of a set? The real, as opposed to the theoretical, choice among various general encyclopedias is radically limited by the number of publishers. Four firms with annual sales of over $300 million control approximately 95 percent of the general encyclopedias published for all age groups in the United States. They are:

(1) Encyclopaedia Britannica Educational Corporation. The Chicago-based publisher, largest of the four, issues *Encyclopaedia Britannica, Compton's Encyclopedia and Fact Index, Britannica Junior Encyclopaedia, Compton's Precyclopedia, Young Children's Encyclopedia, Great Books of the Western World, The Annals of America,* and so on. Among other holdings are G. & C. Merriam Company, publisher of Webster's dictionaries; Frederick A. Praeger, Inc.; and the Phaidon Press, Ltd. They also distribute, but do not publish, the *Random House Encyclopedia.*

Estimates in 1980 are that the Britannica does about $250 million worth of business a year. Year after year the company maintains its leading position not so much on the quality of its products, which is uneven, but through advertising. Among the 10 book publishers who spend $1 million or more in major-media ad campaigns, the company tops the list. In 1977, for example, they spent $5.138 million, most of which was devoted to newspaper and magazine advertisement. Grolier, the second-place encyclopedia firm, spent $2.5 million the same year.[4]

(2) Grolier Incorporated. The New York firm publishes *The Encyclopedia Americana, The Encyclopedia International, The New Book of Knowledge, Encyclopedia Canadiana,* and *The Catholic Encyclopedia,* and distributes a number of other sets. It also has controlling interest in Scarecrow Press and Franklin Watts. Sales are close to the *Britannica* in volume.

(3) Macmillan Educational Corporation. Although a large publishing house, it is only fourth in sales of encyclopedias. The only two major sets are *Collier's* and the *Merit Students Encyclopedia.* However, Macmillan publishes a number of related works ranging from the *Encyclopedia of Philosophy* to the *Harvard Classics* and has an interest in Brentano's bookstore, Berlitz language schools, and so on.

(4) Field Enterprises. The Chicago firm sells more than half the encyclopedia units in the United States, and its *World Book* is by and large the most popular among the children's and young people's sets. Like Macmillan, the firm is involved in numerous other business interests, varying from department stores to newspapers. The firm also publishes *The World Book Dictionary* and *Childcraft.*

(5) Others. Here one might include one or two firms whose sets are passable, in that they have been approved by librarians and, more particularly, the Reference and Subscription Books Review Committee of the American Library Association. For example, Funk & Wagnalls (a division of Standard Reference Library), whose *Funk & Wagnalls New Encyclopedia* is an acceptable set, as is the Arete *Academic American Encyclopedia.* Then, too, there are foreign-based works such as *Everyman's Encyclopedia* from J. M. Dent & Sons.

The librarian who comes across a set whose publisher is not one of the four or five most reputable should take more than average care to double-check the work's authority and, for that matter, everything else about the set.

[4]*Media Industry Newsletter,* June 5, 1978, p. 3.

A basic reason for the less-than-competitive situation is the high cost of producing an encyclopedia. The latest venture, the *Academic American Encyclopedia,* cost several million to publish. The *Britannica's* changeover to a new approach in the fifteenth edition is said to have cost the firm $40 million, and Random House invested some $7 million in its one-volume title. Comparatively, the English firm of J. M. Dent & Sons issued a revised sixth edition of their famous *Everyman's Encyclopaedia* in 1978. The revision cost over $2 million, or the equivalent for Dent of nearly double one year's total manufacturing expenditure for all publishing.[5]

EVALUATING ENCYCLOPEDIAS

Thanks to a familiarity with evaluation, librarians make up their own minds—primarily by daily use of the sets. That daily use inevitably will be a practical test of some, if not all, of the evaluative measures applied to encyclopedias.

What does one consider? The scope, authority, and writing style; recency; viewpoint and objectivity; format, arrangement, and entry; index; and cost.[6]

Scope

The scope of the specialized encyclopedia is evident in its name, and becomes even more obvious with use. The scope of the general encyclopedia is dictated primarily by two considerations.

Age Level   The children's encyclopedias, such as the *World Book,* are tied to curriculum. Consequently, they include more in-depth material on subjects of general interest to grade and high schools than does an adult encyclopedia such as the *Britannica.* Recognizing that the strongest sales appeal is to the adult with children, most encyclo-

---

[5]The basic sets continue to be published year after year. The only major casualty of the 1970s was Grolier's *American Peoples Encyclopedia* and the English *Chambers's Encyclopaedia.* There were several other minor deaths, such as *The Child's World.* These are listed and annotated by Kenneth Kister in his *Encyclopedia Buying Guide.*

[6]The American Library Association, i.e., "Reference and Subscription Books Reviews" (*Booklist,* December 1, 1978, p. 632–634) lists 12 criteria to use "in measuring the worth of an encyclopedia." They are authority, arrangement, subject coverage, accuracy, objectivity, recency, quality, style, bibliographies, illustrations, physical format, and special attributes. All of these are considered here under somewhat different headings.

pedia publishers aim their advertising at this vulnerable controller of the family pocketbook. All the standard sets claim that an audience ranging from grades 6 to 12 can understand and use their respective works. This may be true of the exceptionally bright child, but the librarian is advised to check the real age compatibility of the material before purchase, not merely the advertised age level.

A consequence of attempting to be all things to all age levels is twofold: (1) Even in many adult encyclopedias, the material is shortened for easier comprehension by a child; and (2) the effort at clarity frequently results in an oversimplified approach to complex questions.

Emphasis If age level dictates one approach to scope, the emphasis of the editor accounts for the other. At one time, this varied more than it does today; one set would be especially good for science, another for literature. Today, the emphasis is essentially a matter of deciding what compromise will be made between scholarship and popularity. Why, for example, in most adult encyclopedias, is at least as much space given to the subject of advertising as to communism? This is not to argue the merit of any particular emphasis, but only to point out that examining emphasis is a method of determining scope.

Authority

The first question to ask about any reference book is its authority. If it is authoritative, it normally follows that it will be up to date, accurate, and relatively objective. Contributors and publishers constitute the authority for encyclopedias.

Authority is evident in the names of the scholars and experts who sign the articles or are listed as contributors somewhere in the set. There are three quick tests for authority: (1) recognition of a prominent name, particularly the author of the best recent book on the subject; (2) recognition of a field known to the reader, and a quick check to see whether leaders in that field are represented in the contributor list; and (3) finally, determination of whether the author's qualifications (as noted by position, degrees, occupation, and so on) are related to the article.

An indication of the encyclopedia's revision policy and age can be ascertained from knowledge about the authors. Some contributors may literally be dead, and while a certain number of deceased authorities is perfectly acceptable, too many in this category indicates either overabundant plagiarism from older sets or lack of any meaningful revision.

The authority of material in an encyclopedia received particular attention in 1979 when a writer for *The Progressive* magazine claimed that at least some of the material he researched on the hydrogen bomb came from Volume 14, page 655, of the *Americana.* Here Dr. Edward Teller not only explains but gives a diagram which shows the steps in the explosion of a hydrogen bomb. Using the ready availability of material as a defense, *The Progressive* protested a court order, later lifted, against the magazine publishing the piece.[7]

Writing style

When the writing style of today's encyclopedia is considered, none of the general sets is for the expert. As the former editor of the *Britannica* puts it: "Perhaps the most critical editorial policy that was established [was] our absolute certainty that general encyclopaedias are inappropriate source books for specialists in their own areas." Basically, everything should be comprehensible to the person Preece calls "the curious intelligent lay reader." For the *Britannica,* at least, this is an about-face since the time when not only advertising but the articles themselves proclaimed the scholarly and pedantic nature of many of the contributions.

Recognizing that the purchasers are laypersons, who considerably outnumber the scholars, encyclopedia firms tend to operate in a relatively standard fashion. Contributors are given certain topics and outlines of what is needed and expected. The manuscript is then submitted to one or more of the encyclopedia's editors (editorial staffs of the larger encyclopedias range from 100 to 200 full-time persons), who revise, cut, and query—all for the purpose of making the contributor's manuscript understandable to the average reader. The extent of editing varies with each encyclopedia, from the extreme for the children's works (where word difficulty and length of sentence are almost as important as content) to a limited amount for big-name contributors.

Serving as a bridge between contributor and reader, the editor strives for readability by reducing complicated vocabulary and jargon to terms understandable to the lay reader or young person. The purpose is to rephrase specialized thought in common language without insulting that thought—or, more likely, that eminent contrib-

---

[7]In that the court order was the first prior restraint on publishing ever ordered in the United States, it received wide attention, particularly because of the defense that nothing in the article was secret—it was readily available in libraries. For a good summary of the arguments pro and con, see *Quill,* June 1979.

utor. In the humanities and the social sciences, this often works, but only as long as the contributing scholar is willing to have his or her initials appended to something that will not cause a colleague's criticism.

Kenner summarizes the author-editor-publisher situation, and in so doing makes another point which earnest encyclopedia salespeople may not appreciate:

> A hundred contributors, or a thousand, each responsible for squinting at creation through a single knothole, can work in utter isolation, very likely in a hundred different cities, each on his self-contained pack of knowledge; and these packets an editor with a flow chart may coordinate . . . by appending cross-references, and organize only by filing each in its alphabetical place. . . . Open the Encyclopaedia Britannica itself, and the first topic on which you will receive instruction is the letter A . . . and the fourteenth is the Aardvark. This is sublimely nonsensical, like conversation in Wonderland. . . . The mark of the encyclopaedia, then, is its fragmentation. . . . And nobody, consequently, is talking to anyone else. Least of all is the contributor talking to the reader, for there is no way in which the contributor can form the least idea who the reader is. The only entrance requirement is that the reader be able to use the alphabet.[8]

Recency: Continuous revision

As most large encyclopedia companies issue new printings of their sets or individual volumes each year it is necessary to constantly update the work. This has been made considerably easier through word processing and automation procedures which allow the editors to enter new material, delete, and correct without completely resetting the whole article or section.

No matter what the technological procedures may be for updating new printings of an encyclopedia, the librarian should know: (1) Few general encyclopedias use the "edition" as an indication of the relative currency of the work. For example, the *Britannica's* fourteenth edition was just that from about 1929 until the fifteenth edition in 1974. (2) Most encyclopedias do revise material with each printing, and a printing normally is done at least once or twice or even more often each year. The relative date of the printing will be found

---

[8]Kenner, op. cit., pp. 2, 3. In discussing Flaubert's *Bouvard et Pecuchet,* Kenner points out that fascination with the fact is relatively new, that Socrates trifled with reason but it took Swift in *Gulliver's Travels* to discover that "humanity has encountered Facts." p. 26.

on the verso of the title page, but this in itself means little. (3) There is no accurate measure of how much of any given encyclopedia is revised with each printing or how often it is done, but most large publishers claim to revise about 5 to 10 percent of the material each year. For example, in a 1979 advertisement Macmillan claims that of the over 21,000 articles in the *Merit Students Encyclopedia,* "over 1300 articles have been added, completely rewritten or updated and more than 2200 text pages have been revised." This is about 6 to 7 percent revision, and common enough for most publishers. The annual changes are known as "continuous revision."

Continuous revision is a major sales point for publishers involved with selling sets to libraries. They rightly reason that no library is going to buy a new set of the same encyclopedia (loss or damage aside) unless there has been substantial revision. In advertising the *Academic American Encyclopedia,* the publisher claims "revision plans include an annual 20% updating of the content."

One need only check a subject, place, or individual one knows to see if the set has the latest information in the entry. Illustrations are useful. Check fashions, automobile designs, and portraits of major political figures to gauge currency.

Publishers vary considerably in attention given to revision. In his guide to encyclopedias, Kister uses 10 basic entries to check encyclopedias for currency. These range from "abortion" and "Eritrea" to "solar energy." He found fully 50 percent of the entries "not current" in the *Britannica* as compared with only one "not current" in *Collier's* and two "not current" in *Americana.* A check of other topics indicates that the *Britannica* has not (as of early 1981) made any major revisions in its basic set since 1974, and therefore the library with the 1974 printing would be foolish to trade it off for a so-called new printing.

Viewpoint and objectivity

How objective and fair are encyclopedia articles? Back in 1964, a Columbia professor, Harvey Einbinder, detailed almost article by article the errors and the lack of objectivity in the fourteenth edition of the *Encyclopaedia Britannica.*[9] The attack was so devastating as to be at least one reason for the publishers revising the complete set.

---

[9]Harvey Einbinder, *The Myth of the Britannica* (New York: Grove Press, Inc., 1964). The analysis is still worthwhile for students who wish to study detailed criticism of a reference work. In the otherwise good Britannica article on "Encyclopaedias," the pertinacious Einbinder is not even mentioned—an understandable oversight for the *Britannica.*

(Einbinder was never given credit for this massive push toward revision. *Britannica* officials publicly refused comment on his book.)

As general encyclopedias are profit ventures, they aim to please everyone, insult or injure no one. Despite sometimes pious claims of objectivity on grounds of justice for all, the real reason often is commercial. For example, it was not until many years of active prodding by women that encyclopedia publishers made a conscious effort to eliminate or curb sexual bias.

One reason for the sudden awareness of rights of women: a recognition by the sales department that many women buy encyclopedias. Still, slips do happen; e.g., in an index for *The New Twentieth Century Encyclopedia* (London: Hutchinson, 1979), the index for "Eve" has the entry, "*See* Adam."

Blatant racial and sexual bias has been eliminated from most of the standard encyclopedias, but particular subject areas remain points of contention. It is instructure to trace controversial material through several sets. One discovers marijuana is everything from a "killer of youth" to an "apparently harmless" drug for relaxation.

How is the encyclopedia to be objective when such controversial issues as capitalism and communism, civil rights and segregation, conservatism or liberalism are involved? There are two approaches here. One is to ignore the differences entirely, depending on a chronological, historical approach. The other is an effort to balance an article by presenting two or more sides. The reader should expect at least a projection of different views, either by the contributor or by the editor.

Another aspect of the question of viewpoint is what the editor chooses to include or to exclude, to emphasize or deemphasize. Nothing dates an encyclopedia faster than antiquated articles about issues and ideas either no longer acceptable or of limited interest. An encyclopedia directed at the Western reader can scarcely be expected to give as much coverage in depth to, let us say, Egypt as to New York State. Yet, to exclude more than passing mention of Egypt will not be suitable either, particularly in view of ancient history and the emergence of Africa as a new world force. The proportion of one article to another plagues any conscientious encyclopedia editor, and there probably is no entirely satisfactory solution.

Arrangement and entry

The traditional encyclopedic arrangement is the familiar alphabetical approach to material, with numerous cross-references and an index. Most major sets follow this tradition. Average users are accustomed to the alphabetical order of information, or the *specific entry*. Here, the information is broken down into small, specific parts.

Index

Most general encyclopedias are alphabetically arranged, and some publishers have concluded that with suitable *see* and *see also* references, the arrangement should serve to eliminate the index.

The argument for an index is simply that a single article may contain dozens of names and events which cannot be located unless there is a detailed, separate index volume. A good index is an absolute necessity.

Format

A good format considers the size, typeface, illustrations, binding, and total arrangement. Among the components to consider when evaluating format are the following:

Illustrations (photographs, diagrams, charts, maps, etc.)   Nothing will tip off the evaluator faster as to the currency of the encyclopedia than a cursory glance at the illustrations. Even illustrations of the 1980s will not be suitable unless they relate directly to the text and to the interests of the reader. The librarian might ask: Do the illustrations consider the age of the user, or do they depend on figures or drawings totally foreign to, say, a twelve-year-old? Do they emphasize important matters, or are they too general? Are they functional, or simply attractive? Are the captions adequate?

The reproduction process is important. Some illustrations have a displeasing physical quality, perhaps because too little or too much ink was employed, or the paper was a poor grade, or an inadequate cut or halftone screen was used.

Illustrations are particularly useful in children's and young people's encyclopedias. The *World Book,* for example, has a well-deserved reputation for the timeliness and excellence of both its black and white and numerous colored illustrations. At the same time, an abundance of illustrations is a tip-off that an encyclopedia is (1) primarily for children and young people, or (2) primarily a "popular" set or one-volume work purposely prepared for a wide appeal. Neither objective is to be censured, but the librarian seeking out an encyclopedia superior for ready-reference is likely to be more interested in the amount of text (and how it is presented) than in the number of illustrations.

Maps are an important part of any encyclopedia and vary in number from 2300 in *World Book* to 1175 in *Britannica* to slightly over 250 in the one-volume *Columbia*. Many of the maps are prepared by Rand McNally or C. S. Hammond and usually are good to excellent. In the adult sets the major maps are usually in a separate volume, often with the index. The young adults' and children's encyclopedias usually have the maps in the text, and if this is the case, there should be reference to them in the index and cross-references as needed. The librarian should check how many and what types of maps are employed to show major cities of the world, historical development, political changes, land use, weather, and so on. The actual evaluation of the maps is discussed in the chapter on geography.

Size of type The type style is important, as is the spacing between lines and the width of the column. All these factors affect the readability of the work.

Binding It should be suitable for rough use, particularly in a library. Conversely, buyers should be warned that a frequent method of jacking up the price of an encyclopedia is to charge the user for a so-called deluxe binding which often is no better, and in fact may be worse, than the standard library binding.

Volume size Finally, consideration should be given to the physical size of the volume. Is it comfortable to use? Equally important, can it be opened without strain on the binding?

The sheer weight of a single volume, heretofore the concern chiefly of librarians who had to wrestle with giant folios or the prosaic bound volume of newspapers, is worth considering. More and more publishers seem to favor larger and heavier one-volume encyclopedias.

Cost

Prices vary from set to set, depending as much on the basic publisher's price as on the honesty of the salesperson who may raise the cost considerably by advising a different binding (which can boost the price by as much as $100 or more) or attempting to include in the sale a wide variety of other titles. For example, one may buy the *Britannica* alone, but a good salesperson usually will end up selling the buyer *Great Books of the Western World* or *The Annals of America* or anything that the customer is willing to purchase which is available from Britannica.

Another factor is the library discount. Most publishers grant healthy discounts to libraries, if only to boast that the set is in a library and therefore must be "approved" by those who know about such matters. For example, in 1981 the *Britannica's* lowest retail price was $899, but librarians could purchase the same set for $629 or less.

Comparatively, the most expensive accepted set for the individual to buy is the *Britannica,* the least expensive *Compton's* at $419 (1981 prices). On average an adult set will be between $400 and $450. The price, of course, increases with inflation. All of this has led many individuals to buy secondhand sets from bookdealers, often at 50 to 60 percent less than the initial cost, or purchase sets at discount from some dealers. A more radical and increasingly common solution is to eschew the general set for a less-expensive (under $100) one- or two-volume set. Finally, some adults simply avoid the general set and invest in more specialized subject sets such as the *Encyclopedia of Philosophy.*

Sales practices

Traditionally, the general encyclopedia has been sold door to door, often by less than forthright salespeople. With the 1970s emphasis on consumer protection, the U.S. Federal Trade Commission began a systematic crackdown on encyclopedia sales practices. Misrepresentation of everything from the real purpose of the sales pitch to the cost of the set was proved by the FTC. The result was twofold: (1) The law now allows the purchaser a cooling-off period of three days during which time a signed contract may be voided. This gives the customer an opportunity to check the true price of the set, often through the library, and decide such things as whether or not other books are wanted in addition to the encyclopedia. (2) The salesperson must clearly state the purpose of the call, thus giving the potential customer (or victim) an opportunity to shut the front door. There are other rules and regulations which have also badly cut into the sales efforts of the encyclopedia publishers.

The publishers have met the challenge in various ways, from completely ignoring the regulations to the more practical approach of changing sales procedures. The latter is likely to be the trend of the future, and more and more sets are now available from bookstores; e.g., many of the basic titles may be purchased, usually at a 20 percent or more discount, from large book dealers in New York and throughout the United States. The publisher of the new *Academic American* set deliberately decided to sell the set through stores in order to avoid the door-to-door-sales stigma.

Another approach is to use direct mail, and most of the larger publishers now have active mail campaigns supported by the familiar television and magazine advertising. Making the set directly available from the publisher not only saves on salespeople's commissions but allows the publisher to lower the price of the set.[10]

Reviews: Indirect evaluation

The single best source of retrospective reviews and evaluation of the basic 36 plus general English-language encyclopedias is Kenneth Kister's *Encyclopedia Buying Guide* 3d ed. (New York: R. R. Bowker Company, 1981) which is revised every three years. This experienced librarian and teacher systematically analyzes each set or work by such standards as reliability, recency, clarity, and objectivity and by type of readers. (In addition, Kister has an impressive group of advisors, listed in the preface, who helped to analyze the sets.) The same points are considered for each title and, again, these are listed in the preface. They range from articles on Afghanistan to hypnosis to x-rays to William Styron. Particularly useful is Kister's comparative technique in which he balances one encyclopedia against another, to come to a conclusion about which is best for what individual or library situation. A chart offers a quick overview of the titles, and Kister has a fine chapter on "Finding the Right Encyclopedia." There also is a section in the third edition devoted to library rating of encyclopedias (mentioned in this chapter) and bias in young people's sets. While written for the average layperson, the guide is of value to librarians and certainly can be trusted to help answer the query What encyclopedia would you recommend?

Less useful for a survey of 20 general sets, all of which are found in Kister, is the American Library Association's 40-page booklet *Purchasing an Encyclopedia: 12 Points to Consider* (Chicago: American Library Association, 1979). Here the information is concise and follows a set pattern of evaluation. Unfortunately, it is dated, and there is little or no attempt to compare one set with another.[11]

Ongoing reviews of new sets or revisions or new editions will be

---

[10]For a background article on the reasoning behind these changes in sales practices see "Grolier Unveils Unusual Selling Tactics . . ." *Publishers Weekly,* January 23, 1978, pp. 287, 288. Libraries continue to purchase most general works directly from the publisher (often, to be sure, through library representatives who usually do not make door-to-door sales). The subject and one-volume titles are increasingly available from book jobbers and wholesalers.

[11]The booklet appeared first in *The Booklist,* December 1, 1978, pp. 631–641, and December 15, 1978, pp. 708–715, but the information was for sets of from one to three years old. Hence the 1979 publishing date is not a true guide to the relative timeliness of the material. Kister is less than pleased with the results and makes some telling points in his short review of the work. *See Library Journal,* December 15, 1979, p. 2632.

found in the regular "Reference and Subscription Books Reviews" section of *Booklist*. In a previous discussion of these reviews it was noted that they are objective, lengthy, and usually reliable.

Other sources of current encyclopedia reviews include the basic review periodicals discussed elsewhere, all of which include evaluations of new editions or new sets. Another good source, at least annually, is the careful consideration of encyclopedias in the *American Reference Books Annual*.

Consumer advice

The librarian has several ways of meeting the request for information about a given set:

1. Give no advice. Several major public libraries, fearful of repercussions from salespersons and publishers, adamantly refuse to advise on the purchase of this or that set. Such a refusal is unprofessional and highly questionable.

2. Give limited advice. Normally, the procedure here is to give the inquirer several reviews of the set or sets under question, leaving the final decision to the user. Of particular assistance in this respect are the "Reference and Subscription Book Reviews" in *The Booklist* and Kister's *Encyclopedia Buying Guide*.

3. Go all out with an endorsement or a condemnation. Privately, of course, many librarians do just this. Such opinionated statements may have some nasty repercussions, particularly when the question is between sets that are approved by ALA and are more or less even in quality.

Of the three, the second option is best. If the set is not readily recognized by either publisher or reputation, the librarian should not hesitate to point out that the chances are it is a poor buy from the standpoint of both cost and quality. The librarian should be prepared to support this statement with reviews; or lacking reviews (either because the set is too new or such a "dog" as not to have been noticed), there should be no hesitation about standing on one's own professional knowledge of the set. If nothing can be found about it in print (and who is familiar with many of the works which pass for encyclopedias in supermarkets and in questionable advertisements?), the librarian should explain that the opinion may be personal, but the odds are all against the set being of good quality.

Many public librarians avoid recommending their own favorite titles. Instead they refer the person to one of the standard review compilations and to encyclopedias in the library which can be examined. Actually, the presence of a work in the library is a tacit stamp of approval by the librarian. Asked in a survey if they ever recommended "your favorite encyclopedia," 47 replied "never," 20 said "sometimes," and only 2 replied "always."[12] The reluctance to give advice is not so much a decision taken by the individual reference librarian, as it is policy of the library. Many libraries have policy statements which specifically state that the librarian is to give no advice on such matters.

Replacement

Most libraries replace an encyclopedia every two to five years. In practical terms this usually means that the one of the most used sets (*World Book, Americana, Britannica,* and *Collier's*) is replaced with a revised set every two years, the next most used very three years, the next every four years, and so on. Where the library is medium or large the two-to-four-year-old sets are sent to the branches, put in the general reading room, or duplicated in heavily used parts of the library, such as the young adults' area. When a set is more than five years old it should be discarded. Note that the older sets may be quite suitable for home use, but not for libraries, where the reader expects to find the most up-to-date information. Ideally, and where budgets allow, all the four to five basic sets should be replaced every one to two years; but these days that is rarely possible.

Replacement depends upon whether the publisher actually revises the set from year to year. Where this is apparently not done, or done at a rate of less than 5 percent revision annually (such as the case of the current *Britannica*), it is pointless to replace the set unless it is worn. Therefore the amount of continuous revision carried on by the publisher should be checked carefully.

ADULT ENCYCLOPEDIAS

The New Encyclopaedia Britannica, 15th ed. Chicago: Encyclopaedia Britannica Inc., 30 vols. $899 (with discount to libraries, $629).

The Encyclopedia Americana. New York: Grolier Incorporated, 30

---

[12]Ken Kister, "Encyclopedias and the Public Library: A National Survey," *Library Journal,* April 15, 1979, p. 893.

vols. $750 (discount to libraries, $499). Note: The publisher on the title page is Americana Corporation, a subsidiary of Grolier.

There are few multivolume adult encyclopedias; therefore the choice is limited. The basic sets found in most public, secondary school, and college and university libraries include (1) *The New Encyclopaedia Britannica,* (2) *The Encyclopedia Americana,* and (3) possibly an English or Canadian set, such as the *New Caxton Encyclopaedia* or *Encyclopedia Canadiana.*

Some librarians will include *Collier's* as an adult set, although probably it is more suitable for teenagers, and others will constantly use the young adult and children's *World Book* for ready-reference work with adults.

In homes the choices are about the same, although many adults will wisely settle for the *Funk & Wagnalls New Encyclopedia* under $150, compared with over $800 for the *Britannica*) or use the multipurpose *World Book,* or purchase a second-hand set at a large discount. Another good choice is a one- or two-volume work, which is a "best buy" in terms of comparative cost.

Which of the sets is best?

(1) Public librarians believe that of the some 40 general sets now available, the *World Book* is the most in demand—certainly the most effective for reference work in the library. Close behind is the *Americana,* and much lower on the usability ladder are the *Britannica, Collier's* and *Compton's.* The *World Book* has always been a favorite among librarians, even though book reviewers and encyclopedia critics have praised the *Britannica* more—at least for adult use. Working librarians find that the *World Book* can be used for adults better than the *Britannica* in many situations .[13]

(2) Library school teachers follow somewhat the same pattern. A survey indicates that of 31 schools replying to a questionnaire about encyclopedias all included the *World Books,* 29 the *Americana,* all the *Britannica,* 30 *Collier's,* and 25 *Compton's.* The teachers rank the *Britannica* higher than most public librarians.[14]

The Britannica

The best-known encyclopedia in the Western world is the *Britannica.* First published in 1768, it underwent many revisions and changes

---

[13]Kister, op. cit. The study compiles the results of replies from 77 public libraries of various types and sizes throughout the United States.

[14]John C. Larsen, "Information Sources Currently Studied in General Reference Courses," *RQ,* Summer 1979, p. 345.

until the triumphant Ninth edition in 1889. This was the "scholar's edition," with long articles from such contributors as Arnold, Swinburne, Huxley, and other major English minds of the nineteenth century. The Ninth was followed by the equally famous Eleventh. [Note: Both of these are discussed in considerable detail in a *New Yorker* article. See "Suggested Reading," Koning, Hans.]

After several changes caused by economic difficulties, the set came to the United States and by 1929 appeared as the Fourteenth edition. By that time, the long essays had been reduced and divided, although the set continued to be sold (as it is even today) on the reputation built with the Ninth and Eleventh editions.

The first total revision of the Fourteenth edition of the *Britannica* appeared in 1974. Between 1929 and 1974 the Fourteenth edition had undergone continuous revision, but 45 years of this practice had resulted in a less than satisfactory set. The decision was then made to rewrite the entire *Britannica*.

Of all the general sets, the *Britannica* is the largest, with 43 million words, compared with 31 million for the *Americana* and 21 million for *Collier's*. It also ranks first in illustrations and number of contributors and has the dubious distinction of being the most expensive, $899 compared with $750 for the *Americana*. For sheer volume of information, it is required in libraries.

The *New Encyclopaedia Britannica* is new on two counts: (1) The Fifteenth edition of 1974 represents, even today, the first total revision of one of the basic five or six general encyclopedias in many decades. (2) The arrangement of the set is "new" in that it is in three parts, which accounts for some librarians referring to it simply as *EB3*.

The parts include (1) the *Micropaedia*, 10 volumes containing some 12,000 short entries in alphabetical order, (2) the *Macropaedia*, 19 volumes of essay-length articles; and (3) the *Propaedia*, a single-volume so-called outline of knowledge. There is no index volume, but the publishers claim the *Propaedia* serves as a topical index to 15,000 items in the other two parts; and there are frequent index references in the *Micropaedia* to longer articles in the *Macropaedia*.

What all this comes down to is two distinct, although related, encyclopedias. The *Micropaedia* is a ready-reference work, whereas the *Macropaedia* is the typical, time-tested topical set. Actually, either one may be used without the other, although there is the major problem of finding bits of material in the longer *Macropaedia* items. The result is that many librarians simply use the *Micropaedia* for fast-fact queries and ignore the other parts. The *Propaedia* is so difficult to use that it tends to gather dust in libraries. It is a single volume arranged by broad subjects. The idea is to outline human knowledge, to show relationships between ideas, persons, and events.[15]

Failure of the *Britannica* to rank higher in a survey of public librarians is due to the peculiar arrangement of the set and lack of a standard index volume. As one librarian put it: The *Britannica* "is not a good source for quick reference, because the index is not specific enough." And another librarian noted that while the *Britannica* remains first for credibility, the "current format is difficult to use."[16]

The failure or success of the arrangement is one thing, but few question that the *Britannica* (or at least the 19-volume *Macropaedia*) remains the best single source of long, scholarly, and authoritative articles. It has more notable contributors than any other set, has a wider coverage of both topics and geographical areas than other sets, and remains the basic general encyclopedia in the field. It is an absolutely essential requirement in public, college and university, and secondary school libraries.

The Americana

The Encyclopedia Americana is based on the seventh edition of the German encyclopedia *Brockhaus Konversations Lexikon*. In fact, the first published set (1829 to 1833) was little more than pirated, translated articles from the German work. It was asserted in 1903 that the *Americana* was a wholly new work, but still many of the articles were carried over from *Brockhaus*. The set was reissued in 1918 with changes and additions, although still with material from *Brockhaus*. It claims to be the oldest "all-American" encyclopedia in existence, although the claim is a matter more of chronology than of accuracy.

As the title implies, the strength of this work is the emphasis on American history, geography, and biography. This encyclopedia unquestionably places greater emphasis on this area than any of the other sets, and it is particularly useful for finding out-of-the-way, little-known material about the United States. However, general coverage of the United States is matched in other major encyclopedias.

The writing style is clear, the arrangement admirable, the index good, and the general format (including illustrations and type size) adequate. A helpful feature is the insertion of summaries, resembling

---

[15]For a detailed favorable discussion of the *Propaedia* and how it should work, as well as its relationship to the Syntopicon (the index of sorts to *Great Books of the Western World*) see Arthur V. Coyne, "Ideas for Indexing . . ." *The Indexer,* April 1979, pp. 136–140.

[16]Kister, op. cit., p. 891. The *Britannica* apparently is working on a separate index volume.

a table of contents, at the beginning of multiple-page articles. The set is edited for the adult with a high school education. It is not suitable (despite zealous copywriters) for grade school children.

There has been no new edition since 1920, but the continuous revision policy has kept at least the major items up to date. The encyclopedia falters now and then on the accuracy of biographical data (which make up over 40 percent of the contents). In technical and social areas the lack of a total revision is sometimes evident.

Supermarket sets

Funk & Wagnalls New Encyclopedia. New York: Funk & Wagnalls, 27 vols. $77 (in heavy-duty binding, $139).

There are numerous adult (and children's and young people's) encyclopedias sold in supermarkets and other such retail outlets. Usually there is a separate display with a notice that the first volume is a certain price (normally under $5 and often even free) and each additional volume another price. Many, too many, are the traditional "rip-off," in that the total price for a set may be well over $100 and the work itself dated, inaccurate, and often not even suitable for the audience it claims. Librarians are sometimes asked about such works, and the general warning is that, with the exception of *Funk & Wagnalls,* the supermarket set is probably a bad buy. The would-be purchaser is better off with a one- or two-volume work or even a second-hand standard set.

As one of the few sets not published by the major four encyclopedia publishers, this work has received the approval of the American Library Association and Ken Kister. Anyone who looks at it carefully will conclude that it is one of the best buys for the average family where a set may not be used often. The material is relatively current, well organized, and easy to use. There is a good index and adequate, although sometimes badly selected, illustrations. While it is no competitor with the major sets for a library, it might well serve as a second set for the library faced with budget problems.

Popular adult and high school sets[17]

Collier's Encyclopedia. New York: Macmillan Educational Corporation, 24 vols. $579 (with discount to libraries, $467).

[17]"Popular" is used here to differentiate writing styles among the various encyclopedias as well as basic editorial approaches. A "popular" set, in contrast with the *Britannica* and *Americana,* is frankly edited for the student or adult with less interest in knowledge in depth.

Encyclopedia International. New York: Grolier Incorporated, 20 vols., $288 (with discount to libraries). Note: Sometimes the set is sold by independent dealers as the *New Age Encyclopedia,* but the content is precisely the same as in the International—as is the price.

Academic American Encyclopedia. Princeton, New Jersey: Arete Publishing Company, 1980. 21 vols., $400 (with discount to libraries).

There are at least three encyclopedias which legitimately claim to be of equal value to adults and to young people. The reader-suitability level claimed by the publishers is from about 12 or 15 years of age to adult. The claim is accurate, and all the sets are much better suited to young people and less-well-educated adults than the *Britannica, Americana,* and so on.

For comparison, let us begin with *Collier's* and the *International.* The *Academic* will follow because it is still too new to determine how it will work in a daily reference situation.

Both *Collier's* and the *International* differ from the *Americana* and the *Britannica* in a particular emphasis on popular, concise writing. The articles are easy to read and either set may be consulted by either the layperson or the expert who may want an overview of a difficult area. Arrangement is specific entry and both have good-to-fine indexes.

Public librarians rank *Collier's* almost on a level with the *Britannica* for usefulness, and, in fact, find it easier to consult than the *Britannica* for ready-reference questions. It has another advantage for reference work: it is among the most up-to-date of the standard adult–young people's sets. The publisher makes a point of continuous revision unmatched by the other publishers.

In terms of words, *Collier's* has 21 million, ranking third behind the *Britannica* and the *Americana.* However, it is in first place when it comes to the index, with the best index volume of any of the sets. Another feature of the final volume is the excellent section on bibliographies. Titles are arranged under broad subjects and subdivided. Most entries are current, and the reading lists offer adults and students a satisfactory supplement to material found in the set. (Incidentally, the bibliographies can be useful to librarians looking for material in sometimes hard-to-locate subject areas.)

Most of the illustrations are in black and white, and many (too many in the view of some critics) are dated, in that the backgrounds and primary figures remind one of a 1950s moving picture. But they are well placed in relation to the text, and the few colored illustrations are excellent.

Whereas *Collier's* is one of the top three choices for adult–teenage encyclopedias for libraries and individuals (the others, of course, are the *Britannica* and *Americana*), much further down the list is the *International*. While the Grolier set is directed to about the same audience, although with a more simplified approach which makes it suitable for some children, it is not up to the quality of *Collier's*.

The *International* is not revised as consistently as *Collier's*, and while the material is accurate and clear, it is too often dated. For example, check the bibliographies which refer to titles by now (1980) out-of-print and not even found in many libraries. In aiming at a popular audience, the *International* excels *Collier's*, at least if one believes that the average teenager, older child, or adult is more involved with persons and places (which constitute a full 50 percent of the entries in the *International*) than with *Collier's* more balanced coverage of science, arts, and literature.

On the plus side the set has useful study guides at the beginning of major articles. The guides refer the reader to related topics as well as outline the main features of the article. Another useful feature is the inclusion of definition of difficult terms. Most of this approach is duplicated in the basic children's sets but is unusual for teenage–adult works.

Academic American Encyclopedia[18]

The first general new set of the 1980s, the *Academic American* is a 21-volume work directed to young adults and adults. Financially backed by a Dutch publishing firm, it was produced in America and is edited for an American, or at least an English-speaking, audience.

The promoters of the set see their primary competition in the adult area, i.e., against the *Americana* and *Britannica*. There is some justification for this, in that the reading difficulty of the set is about the same as that of the *Britannica* or *Americana*. At the same time, the short entries and the focus on illustrations places it squarely in the young adult–adult area.

The publisher claims the set contains 9 million words (compared with 21 million in *Collier's* and 9.5 million in the *International*). There are some 32,000 articles, somewhat more than the 25,000 for *Collier's*,

[18]Kenneth Kister, "The Making of the Academic American Encyclopedia: An Interview with the Publisher," *Wilson Literary Bulletin*, March 1980, pp. 436–441. See, too: N. R. Kleinfield, "Arete Encyclopedia Misses Sales Target," *The New York Times*, March 11, 1981, p. D5. The set was recommended by the ALA. See: *Booklist*, July 1, 1981, pp. 1402+.

because the *Academic* puts particular stress upon the specific short article. Illustrations are close to 17,000—about the same number as in *Collier's* but about 4000 more than in the *International*. The *Academic* index volume boasts 250,000 entries, about half of what is found in *Collier's* (400,000) but double the number in *International*. The vital retail price is $400 for the *Academic,* compared with $579 for *Collier's* and $288 for the *International*.

The *Academic* has several advantages over both other sets: (1) It is new, and the publisher rightfully claims that the 2400 contributors offer a fresh approach to information. A spot-check indicates most of the data is up to date (as of 1979). The publishers assert they will revise 20 percent of the material each year. (2) More than 40 percent of the articles have current bibliographies. (3) The illustrations—and the majority are in color—are some of the best available in any set. (4) Science and technology are better represented than in the other sets—with the publisher claiming that 35 to 40 percent of the content is in these areas. In July 1981 the American Library Association approved the set. Kister is impressed and has recommended it to readers.

CHILDREN'S AND YOUNG ADULTS' ENCYCLOPEDIAS

Compton's Encyclopedia and Fact Index. Chicago: Encyclopedia Britannica, Inc., 26 vols. $419.

Merit Students Encyclopedia. New York: Macmillan Educational Corporation, 20 vols. $579 (discount to libraries, $286).

World Book Encyclopedia. Chicago: Field Enterprises Educational Corporation, 22 vols. $399 (with discount to libraries, $336).

There are many more young adult and children's encyclopedias than adult works, primarily because publishers realize that the majority of sets are purchased for younger people, not for adults. In fact, even the *Britannica* is advertised as suitable for young people.

The most popular, most widely accepted encyclopedia for children and young adults is the *World Book*. It is equally valuable for reference work with adults. Next one would rank *Compton's,* followed by the *Merit Students*.

The triumph of the *World Book* is not an accident but a careful combination of many elements, not the least of which is a nice balance between timely illustrations and text. As one critic puts it: "With the emphasis today so much on visual presentation, encyclopaedias sometimes also become clotted up with faded, off-putting prose styles which somehow seem to creep in by default. The *World Book* is always admirably clear."[19]

Compton's has fine illustrations equal to *World Book's,* and both are ahead of *Merit.* By word count *World Book* has 10 million words, *Compton's* 8.6 million and *Merit* 9 million. The price of the three sets varies.

All have indexes. *Compton's* indexing differs in that there is no single index volume, but an index and a study guide appear at the end of each volume. The advantage to this for libraries is that a single index is not tied up with one user, but the disadvantage is obviously that one must turn to 24 indexes instead of one for information. *World Book* and *Compton's* have elaborate cross-references and can readily be used without the index. The cross-references in *Merit* are less evident, and the index contains no references to illustrations.

The three sets have much in common. Differences are minimal in coverage, illustrations, and even format. The essential differences may be summed up briefly:

1. *World Book* is better organized than the other two, and information is easier and quicker to find.

2. The style of writing in the three is graded, i.e., the articles begin with relatively easy material and definitions and grow progressively more difficult and sophisticated. Still, the style is better in the *World Book* than in its competitors. In depth of coverage, *Compton's* is best, while *Merit* scores heavily in individual articles which are written specifically for given grade levels.

3. The strong point of *Compton's* is its "Fact" index at the end of each volume. Combining an index with brief information on subjects not included in the main work, it serves as an excellent ready-reference source for both children and adults. *World Books's* specific arrangement and massive cross-references make it equally good for ready-reference work. *Merit* lags behind both.

4. All three are constantly being revised, but *World* has a more active revision policy, which it shows in the more up-to-date statistical data and in the illustrations. Close behind is *Merit* which, in the past few years, has made a more aggressive

[19]Nicholas Tucker, "Checking the Facts," *The Guardian,* May 29, 1979, p. 11. For a detailed review, generally favorable, see "Reference and Subscription Books Reviews," *Booklist,* May 1, 1979, pp. 1383–1385.

move to update material. Lagging behind the other two is *Compton's.*

In an optimistic yet cautious move, the *Reader's Digest* entered the children's field in 1978 with a set far short of the normal 20 to 22 volumes, yet more than the traditional one-volume work, i.e., *The Reader's Digest Library of Modern Knowledge.* Boasting 1408 pages, with almost double that number of illustrations (including 250 maps), the set consists of three volumes neatly divided into the World of Nature, the Human World, and the Everyday World.

Another departure is abandonment of the strict alphabetical, specific-entry arrangement in favor of broad essays subdivided into about 1800-word parts. Here, the set follows the same procedure as the *Random House Encyclopedia.* Each chapter begins with a summary statement, which is sometimes more journalistic than factual and is the weakest part of the set. The section concludes with an alphabetical glossary of names and technical terms.

One may find ready-reference material in a number of ways: (1) At the end of the third volume there is a comprehensive index to the set. (2) Each volume begins with a detailed table of contents, including a diagram to show interrelations. (3) The chapter titles are printed at the top of every alternate page, with subheadings on top of the opposite page.

While the arrangement is not ideal for reference work, it does challenge the concept that all encyclopedias must avoid long, broad entry forms. True, the numerous subdivisions sometimes defeat the overall purpose, but at least it is an effort to show readers the relationships among various facts. The argument then turns to the ease of use versus the philosophy and the librarian must decide which is most important. Given other sets for this age group—and others are needed for ready-reference purposes—this is a complementary work which may lapse in ease of use, but wins a large plus for its satisfactory way of linking concepts.

Preschool and children's encyclopedias

Britannica Junior Encyclopaedia. Chicago: Encyclopaedia Britannica, Inc., 15 vols. $199.

New Book of Knowledge. New York: Grolier Incorporated, 21 vols. $360 (discount to libraries, $264).

Young Students Encyclopedia. Middletown, Connecticut: Xerox Educational Publications, 22 vols. $149.

Information with entertainment is the key to the success of the preschool and children's encyclopedias for ages five to about twelve. They are constructed around the curriculum, with attention to vocabulary level and a style to carry the reader through the material.

By far the best of this group is the *New Book of Knowledge*, which compares favorably with the *World Book*, *Compton's*, and *Merit*. It exceeds its competitors on all counts: It has close to 7 million words and 9000 articles (*Britannica:* 5 million words and 4100 articles; *Young Students:* 1.5 million words and 2400 articles). The *New Book of Knowledge* has almost twice as many illustrations as the *Britannica*, and close to 5 or 6 times the number in the *Young Students*. Among preschool and children's sets, the *New Book of Knowledge* leads in coverage, authority, recency, objectivity, and other criteria for evaluating encyclopedias. It is a favorte among public librarians with 18 out of 71 votes, compared with 3 votes for *Britannica Junior* and 1 for the *Young Students*.[20] It and *Britannica Junior* are the two sets most discussed in library schools.[21]

The *Young Students Encyclopedia* is edited by the staff of *My Weekly Reader* for students from seven to thirteen years of age. The set has some 4500 illustrations and 2400 articles which are qualitatively commendable, but considerably fewer than those found in the standard, better-known titles. It is one of the few inexpensive works recommended in the American Library Association's "Reference and Subscription Books Reviews" for home use, as is the annual yearbook. Considering this recommendation, it would be a good choice after the *New Book of Knowledge*, and it certainly would be preferable to the much older and dated *Britannica Junior*.

The encyclopedia firms all offer preschool types of encyclopedias. The best-known is *Childcraft—The How and Why Library* (Chicago: Field Enterprises Educational Corporation, 15 vols., $169). The set includes stories and factual material about practically everything of interest to a young child, from animals and art to the body. With excellent illustrations and well-thought-out texts, the volumes are useful for preschool and early grades.

Another entry is *Compton's Precyclopedia* (Chicago: Encyclopaedia Britannica, 1977, 16 vols., $149); on the order of *Childcraft*, it is designed to introduce the child (ages four through ten) to basic learning experiences. The average reading level is second or third

---

[20]Kister, op. cit., p. 891.

[21]John Larsen, "Information Sources Currently Studied in General Reference Courses," *RQ*, Summer 1979, p. 344.

grade, the material is presented in a story-telling, light fashion, and the set is more of a collection of readings than a true encyclopedia.[22]

Libraries might want one or two of these sets, but they would be used for casual reading, not for reference work with children. None is a substitute for a good encyclopedia.

Encyclopedia supplements: Yearbooks

There are two basic purposes for the encyclopedia yearbooks, annuals, or supplements. They are published annually to (1) keep the basic set up to date and (2) present a summary of the year's major events. A third, less obvious, purpose is to increase sales; it is comforting for the buyer to realize that the set will never be outdated (a questionable assumption, but one used by almost every encyclopedia salesperson).

The yearbooks range in price from $12.95 (*World Book Year Book*) to $15.95 (*Britannica Book of the Year*) and are usually available only to purchasers of the initial sets. They are all attractively printed, and they generally feature numerous illustrations.

The supplements are not related to the parent set except in name. The arrangements are broad, with emphasis on large, current topics. Most of the material is not later incorporated into the revised basic sets—a positive and negative consideration. On the positive side, a run of the yearbooks does afford a fairly comprehensive view of the year's events. On the negative side, the library is wise to keep a run of the yearbooks because the revised parent set cannot be depended upon to contain the same material, or at any rate, not in such depth. Consequently, someone looking for more than basic facts on a given topic really should search not only the main encyclopedia, but a number of the yearbooks also.

Aside from the age of the audience for which each is prepared, significant differences between the various yearbooks are difficult to discover. In this, they resemble the daily newspaper. One reader may prefer the slant or emphasis of one newspaper over another, but both papers are drawing from the same general materials. Nor is the analogy as far-fetched as it may seem. In the annuals particularly, the predominantly newspaper-trained staffs of the larger encyclopedia firms have a holiday. Format, content, and the ever-important emphasis on up-to-date, often exciting events reflect more than a scholar

---

[22]"Reference and Subscription Books Reviews," *Booklist,* November 1, 1979, pp. 453–456. This is a detailed review of the *Compton's* set. The reviewers point out many features of this particular type of encyclopedia that may be of value to children's librarians and involved parents; useful as a general discussion of the genre.

behind the final book; they reveal an emphasis on what makes the daily newspaper sell, at least as seen from the standpoint of the ex-newspaperman.

In libraries, it is sufficient to purchase yearbooks for encyclopedias not replaced that year. If more than a single adults' and children's yearbook is to be purchased, the nod will go to the work preferred by the librarian and the patrons of the library. As long as the preference is within the standards set for encyclopedias, it is a matter more of taste than of objective judgment, and any one of the accepted publishers will serve as well as another.

While Kister discusses yearbooks, in his *Encyclopedia Buying Guide*, the most detailed appraisal will be found in the *Reference and Subscription Books Reviews* special section, "Encyclopedia Yearbooks . . .," *The Booklist*, March 15, 1981, pp. 1049–1054. Seven works are considered, but only from publishers whose main sets have been approved by the reviewers.

ONE- AND TWO-VOLUME ENCYCLOPEDIAS

The Lincoln Library of Essential Information. Columbus, Ohio: Frontier Press Company, 1924, 2 vols. $99. (Note: The 1980, 4th edition was published as the *New Lincoln Library Encyclopedia;* but in 1981, the publisher says, the set will revert to its original name and two volumes instead of the three in the 1980 edition.)

The New Columbia Encyclopedia. 4th ed. New York: Columbia University Press, 1975, 3052 pp. $79.50 (Distributed by J. B. Lippincott).[23]

The Random House Encyclopedia. New York: Random House, Inc. 1977, 2856 pp. $71.45.

The decline in favor of the general multivolume encyclopedia, rising production and advertising costs, and an effort to meet the challenge of a public which no longer has the patience to read detailed accounts of anything has resulted in an increasing emphasis on one- or two-volume general encyclopedias. Typically, the one- or two-volume work is arranged alphabetically and lacks an index, which in this case is not needed. The information is stripped down to facts, and the specific-entry form is almost universal.

[23]This work is often discounted, as are the other one-volume sets. Barnes & Noble advertised the *Columbia* in early 1980 for $29.50, and for once the copywriter is correct: It is "an incomparable bargain" in encyclopedias.

Kister notes that of the "36 general encyclopedias currently (1978) in print in the U.S., 14 (or 40 percent) are now in the one or two volume category."[24] In another survey he found that librarians are not anxious to embrace the single- or two-volume works, primarily because they do not seem to find them as useful for reference work. In his query to 77 librarians, Kister found that the *New Columbia, Lincoln Library,* and *Random House* are used only sometimes for reference work and largely in that order of preference. He notes that the "cool attitude toward one volume encyclopedias, particularly the better ones . . . was unexpected."[25] This is not likely to change, because even for ready-reference work the standard sets, from the *World Book* to the *Britannica,* have the advantage of superior size. The *New Columbia* claims to have more words than any of its competitors (6.6 million compared with 3.5 million in the *Lincoln Library* and 3 million in the *Random House*), but this is far behind the 10 to 43 million in the larger sets.

For home use, the one-volume works are economical and, compared with multivolume sets in the same general price range, are a better buy. The information is exact, well presented, and more reliable than that in the similarly priced "supermarket" sets. Where cost is a factor, the librarian should always inform the prospective purchaser of these one-volume works, encouraging a personal comparison of reviews or of the encyclopedias themselves.

Depending on nuggets of information rather than exposition, the 10½ pound *New Columbia Encyclopedia* has more than 50,000 articles; 66,000 cross-references; some 400 integrated illustrations, including maps of all major countries; and approximately 6.5 million words. While the content is hardly up to the 14 million words and 102,000 entries in the Britannica's *Micropaedia,* it compares favorably with the content in almost all young adults' and children's sets.

Qualitatively, the *Columbia* is a valuable ready-reference aid. The fourth edition gives added attention to third-world countries, science, social sciences, and the humanities. The strongest area is biography. Biographical sketches will be found here for individuals not included, or at best only mentioned, in the standard multivolume sets.

First issued in 1924, *The Lincoln Library of Essential Information* is in two volumes, with information arranged under 12 general subject fields, from the English language to biography and miscellany. The

---

[24]Kister, op. cit. Other reasons for favoring the one-volume set, at least among publishers: the cost of updating is minimal; as it is priced low, the volume of sales is encouraging; and it is easily marketed through regular channels rather than depending on a large sales force.

[25]Kister, op. cit., pp. 891, 892.

index is detailed enough to overcome the basic problem of arrangement, which is not ideal for ready-reference work. Among its many good features are its several hundred charts and tables, bibliographies, quality illustrations, a good atlas of the world, and broad coverage of general knowledge. The articles are well written and can be easily understood by a junior high or high school student. As the material is arranged under broad sections with over 25,000 different entries, coverage tends to be brief, factual, and unopinionated.

The difficulty with the *Lincoln* is its revision policy. Although it claims a policy of constant revision, a cursory glance at the 1980 printing will show it is best on current events, but slower on updating standard material in the social sciences, arts, and humanities. The specific-entry short items are more likely to reflect the year's past events than are the longer, more detailed survey articles.

The *Random House Encyclopedia* is in two parts: (1) "Colorpedia," which consists of seven main sections, subdivided into short articles and extensively illustrated with four-colored photographs and drawings. The sections move from the universe through man and machines. (2) Alphapedia is similar to the *Britannica's* Micropaedia and consists of 25,00 short, specific entries, often referring the reader to the Colorpedia for more information. Directed to the average family, the writing style is lively, the material generally easy to understand and the thousands of illustrations judiciously placed to clarify the written material.

A major problem with the Colorpedia section is lack of an index. As in the *Britannica* system, there are cross-references from the Alphapedia to the essay section, but they are hardly workable. The result amounts to two distinct parts or sets with little relation to one another.

An interesting aspect of the work is that it is really an English product, conceived and written in England. The financial backing came from America. The resulting coproduction is evident to anyone familiar with English writing style and writers.

FOREIGN-PUBLISHED ENCYCLOPEDIAS

Most reference questions can be quickly and best answered by an American encyclopedia, but there are occasions when a foreign-language work is more suitable. Obviously, a foreign encyclopedia will cover its country of origin in considerably more depth than an American work will. The same will also be true for such items as biographies of nationals, statistics, places, and events.

Even for users with the most elementary knowledge of the language, several of the foreign works are useful for their fine illustrations and maps. For example, the *Enciclopedia Italiana* boasts some of the best illustrations of any encyclopedia, particularly in the areas of the fine arts. A foreign encyclopedia is equally useful for viewpoint. Some American readers may be surprised to find how the Civil War, for example, is treated in the French and the German encyclopedias, and the evaluation of American writers and national heroes is sometimes equally revealing of how Europeans judge the United States. More specifically, the foreign encyclopedia is helpful for information on less known figures not found in American or British work; for foreign-language bibliographies approach, for detailed maps of cities and regions; and for other information ranging from plots of less known novels and musicals to identification of place names.

French

La Grande Encyclopédie, rev. ed. Paris: Larousse, 1972–1978, 21 vols. (Distributed in the United States by Maxwell Scientific, Inc. $1597.)

The name Larousse is as familiar in France as the *Encyclopaedia Britannica* is in the United States. Pierre Larousse was the founder of a publishing house which continues to flourish and is responsible for the basic French encyclopedias. In fact, "Larousse" in France is often used as a synonym for "encyclopedia."

One problem, as with most European encyclopedias, is the alphabetical arrangement. Any student who had had a brush with a foreign language realizes that while the Latin alphabet is employed, there are variations in letters; Spanish, for example, has two letters not found in English, *ch* and *ll*. There are also marked differences in common names. John turns up as Giovanni, Jan, Juan, Johannes, or Jehan. Consequently, before abandoning a foreign encyclopedia for lack of an entry, the user should be certain to look for the entry in terms of the language employed.

Larousse continues with the policy of short specific entries, but it does give some rather extensive treatment of major subjects. For example, the length of articles for countries and leading personalities often equals that found in American works.

La Grande Encyclopédie comprises 21 volumes. There is a 400,000-item reference index. The Larousse titles, which include several subject encyclopedias, are particularly renowned for the excellent illustrations, often in full color. And each page of the *Encyclopedia* includes photographs, charts, maps, diagrams, and the like. Regardless of one's command of French, everyone will enjoy the illustrations—even the smaller ones—which are noteworthy for their sharpness.

In an otherwise highly unfavorable analysis of foreign encyclopedias, Einbinder considers tbe French work a "splendid encyclopedia" with "lucid prose" and a "dazzling profusion of color photographs." The excellence of the set is due, he believes, to such diverse matters as the French passion for learning, the lack of adequate public libraries, and "the importance of the baccalauréat examination."[26]

German

> *Brockhaus Enzyklopädie,* rev. 17th ed. Wiesbaden: Brockhaus, 1966–1975, 20 vols. $1200. *Supplement,* 1975–1976, 4 vols. Total: 24 vols.

First issued as *Frauenzimmer Lexikon* (between 1796 and 1808), an encyclopedia primarily for women, *Brockhaus* got off to a bad start. The original publisher, possibly because of his limited sales, gave up the financial ghost; in 1808, Friedrich Brockhaus purchased the set and issued the last volume. A wise man, Brockhaus continued to offer his volumes not as scholarly works, but as books guaranteed to give the average man (or woman) a solid education. In this respect, he was years ahead of the times—in fact, so far ahead of his American and English counterparts that they freely borrowed his text, if not his sales techniques. As noted earlier, the Brockhaus works were the basis for the early *Americana* and *Chambers's.*

Brockhaus extended his popular formula to cutting back articles to little more than dictionary length. In this respect, he followed the European form of specific entry. Consequently, all the Brockhaus encyclopedias—and there is a family of them—are an admixture of dictionary and encyclopedia. (The family includes the basic 24-volume set, the revised 12-volume set, and a 1-volume work, among others.)

As might be expected, the longer articles, some of them over 100

[26]Harvey Einbinder, "Encyclopedias: Some Foreign and Domestic Developments," *Wilson Library Bulletin,* December 1980, pp. 258, 259. The author concludes a brief survey of foreign sets with some highly critical remarks about American works.

pages, are on European countries. In many respects, the Brockhaus encyclopedia is considerably more provincial than the *Larousse;* and while it is an excellent source of material on German history and personalities, it can be passed up for other items.

Because of its scope, the *Brockhaus* is useful in large research libraries or where there is a German-speaking populace, but it is probably near the bottom among choices of all the foreign-language encyclopedias.

Italian

> *Enciclopedia Italiana di Scienze, Lettere ed Arti.* Rome: Instituto della Enciclopedia Italiana, 1929 to 1939, 36 vols., appendices I-III, 1938 to 1962, 5 vols. $2285.

Lavishly illustrated with black-and-white and superb color plates, the Italian encyclopedia is best known for its artwork. For this, it can be used profitably by anyone; and somewhat like the *National Geographic* magazine, it will afford hours of browsing time even for the person who does not understand a word of the language in which it is written.

At perhaps a more important level, it has an outstanding reputation for detailed articles in the humanities. All the articles are signed, and there are a number of bibliographies. One good example is the article on Rome, which runs to almost 300 pages and has close to 200 photogravure plates illustrating nearly every aspect of the city, present and past.

Grande Dizionario Enciclopedico UTET (Turin: Unione Tipografico-Editrice, 1966–1975, 20 vols.) is a more popular Italian set with short entries and massive numbers of colored illustrations. It is useful for ready reference because of the extensive index.

Russian

> *Bol'shaia Sovetskaia Entisklopediia,* 3d rd. Moscow: Sovetskaia Entisklopediia, 1980, 30 vols. plus index. (*The Great Soviet Encyclopedia.* New York: The Macmillan Company, Inc., 1973 to date—in progress. Prices varies.)

This set may be taken at two levels. It is passable, i.e., no better or worse than most other works, for factual material, particularly in the sciences. It is controversial when dealing with the social sciences, and as one critic puts it, "it mirrors the intellectual sterility and political conformity of Soviet life" in its political, historical, and arts viewpoints. It has numerous anti-Zionist and anti-Jewish views.[27]

As most American readers will use the English translation, several points are worth making: (1) An index is published after each five volumes, with a complete index to the whole set scheduled in 1981–1982. Each new interim index cumulates previous entries and intergrates additional encyclopedia content. For example, in 1979 the publisher issued the index to volumes 1 through 20. (2) The index is necessary because of the unusual alphabetical arrangement of each volume, caused by differences between the Russian and Latin alphabets. For example, the first translated volume contains entries for "Aalen Stage" and the "Zulu War of 1879." (3) The quality of the translation is good. The American version differs from the Russian in that cost considerations made it necessary to delete the fine maps in the original Russian version.

The *BSE* is the basic encyclopedia for the Soviet schools and for families, being somewhat equivalent in scholarship to the older version of the *Britannica*. The entire set has more than 21 million words and over 100,000 articles. Including both the specific-entry and the broad-entry forms, the set is a combination of routine dictionary and gazetteer items, with detailed, many-paged articles covering every aspect of Soviet interest.

Spanish

> *Enciclopedia universal ilustrada Europeo-Americana (Espasa).* Barcelona: Espasa, 1907 to 1933, 100 vols; including annual supplements, 1934 to date. (Distributed in the United States by Maxwell Scientific, Inc. $3250.)

Usually cited simply as *Espasa*, the *Enciclopedia* is a remarkable work. First, it never seems to end. Forgoing continuous revision or new editions, the publishers continue to augment the 80 volumes (actually 70 basic volumes with 10 appendixes) with annual supplements, which are arranged in large subject categories and include an index. (The term "annual" must be taken advisedly, as the supplements generally are not issued until three to five years after the period covered. For example, the 1969–1970 volume came out in 1975.)

[27]Ibid.

Second, *Espasa* has the largest number of entries—the publishers claim over 1 million. Since they evidently do not count on "authority," none of the articles is signed, although they are signed in the supplements after 1953. Again, as in the German and French encyclopedias, the emphasis is on short entries of the dictionary type. Still, there are a number of rather long articles, particularly those dealing with Spain; Latin America; and prominent writers, scientists, artists, and so on who claim Spanish as a native tongue. The longer articles are often accompanied by extensive bibliographies which can be used to find definitive studies usually not listed in other sources. The illustrations and paper are poor, and even the colored plates of paintings leave much to be desired.

SUBJECT ENCYCLOPEDIAS

Now that the general encyclopedia seems to be on the decline, the subject work is gaining added favor with both librarians and individual buyers. It is part of a media trend which has resulted in the increased development of specialized periodicals, recordings, and even radio and television programs for narrow segments of the population. The reasoning of publishers and producers is that it is no longer possible or profitable to reach out to everyone. The best approach is to prepare a work for a select group, normally a group with both a high interest in the subject and a medium-to-high income to purchase the book.

Publishers of subject encyclopedias follow the special audience philosophy. The result generally is encouraging for reference librarians, particularly when (1) a ready-reference question is so specialized or esoteric it cannot be answered in a general encyclopedia or (2) a user needs a more detailed overview of a subject than found in a single general-encyclopedia article. The more limited the library budget for both reference work and general titles, the more reason to turn to subject encyclopedias. One may have a limited amount of material on, for example, modern China, but many questions can be readily answered with the one-volume *Encyclopedia of China Today* rev. ed. New York: Harper & Row, 1980.

As the general encyclopedia fades gently away, there is an ever-increasing number of specialized sets or one-volume works. Publishers rush in to fill needs and keep up with current ideas. An excellent example: *Harvard Encyclopedia of American Ethnic Groups* (Cambridge, Massachusetts: Harvard University Press, 1980). Here are some 100 essays on ethnic groups, from Afro-Americans and Yankees to Zoroastrians. And there are close to 30 essays on broader topics such as assimilation, ethnicity, and so on.

Encyclopedias and handbooks

There is a thin line between the subject or specialized encyclopedia and the traditional handbook. The handbook, as discussed in a later section, is a collection of a miscellaneous group of facts centered on one central theme or subject area, e.g., *Handbook of Physics* and *Handbook of Insurance*. An encyclopedia tends to be more discursive, although the dictionary, specific-entry type may simply list brief facts. A handbook is usually a means of checking for bits of data to assist the user in work in progress. Also, a handbook presupposes some knowledge in the field. A subject encyclopedia normally assumes that interest, more than knowledge, is the point of departure. If one must draw distinctions, a handbook is a working tool, whereas a subject encyclopedia is more a source of background information which eventually may help the user to formulate a project or a work.

The differences between the traditional encyclopedia and the handbook are not always so evident. The title is not necessarily a clue. The distinction seems to be that a handbook is usually conceived in the old German *Handbuch* sense of being a compendious book or treatise providing guidance in any art, occupation, or study. The encyclopedia may supply equal guidance, but the information therein tends to be more general, less directly involved with use in an actual working situation. The encyclopedia, then, is primarily for retrospective research. The handbook is primarily for ongoing help or guidance.

Evaluation

Much the same evaluative techniques are used for subject encyclopedias as for general sets. Even with limited knowledge of the field covered, librarians may judge the set for themselves, although they are more likely to depend on reviews or subject experts for evaluation of the expensive works. Subject sets are evaluated in scholarly periodicals, which discuss them at greater length than standard reviews do.

Once it is determined the encyclopedia is good, the librarian must ask which and how many readers will use the work. The subject encyclopedias will fill gaps in the collection of art, science, or more esoteric subjects. For this reason, a subject encyclopedia is often a better buy for small and medium-sized libraries than multiple sets of general encyclopedias.

Examples

Space does not permit a full discussion of the numerous, many quite superior, subject encyclopedias. Here the focus is on works which are best known and likely to be found in many medium-to-large libraries. Most, although not all, have been published relatively recently. This rather arbitrary approach gives at least a cursory glance at the direction of subject-encyclopedia publishing.

Art

> *Encyclopedia of World Art.* New York: McGraw-Hill Book Company, 1959–1968, 15 vols. $995.

The *Encyclopedia of World Art* is the finest set available among encyclopedias devoted entirely to art. It includes art of all periods and has exhaustive studies of art forms, history, artists, and allied subject interests. Arranged alphabetically, it contains many shorter articles which answer almost every conceivable question in the field.

An outstanding feature exists in the illustrations. At the end of each volume, there are 400 to 600 black-and-white and colored reproductions. They, as well as some colored plates in the main volumes, are nicely tied to the articles by suitable cross-references and identification numbers and letters.

Education

> *The Encyclopedia of Education.* New York: The Macmillan Company, 1971, 10 vols. $250.

This is the basic encyclopedia in education, having more than 1000 articles which examine the history, theory, and philosophy of education. All are written by subject experts and are not only authoritative but also clear and literate. There are detailed bibliographies and an excellent index.

In view of the broad area covered by the term "education," the set may be helpful to persons in related fields. It nicely supplements, for example, the better-known *International Encyclopedia of the Social*

Sciences, as well as the *Dictionary of the History of Ideas.* While most emphasis is on American education, there are comparative articles which consider education and related topics throughout the world.

History

> Adams, James T. (ed.), *Dictionary of American History,* rev. ed. New York: Charles Scribner's Sons, 1976, 7 vols. and index. $370.
>
> *The New Cambridge Modern History.* New York: Cambridge University Press, 1957–1976, 14 vols. $550.

It is questionable whether separate history encyclopedias are needed for small or medium-sized libraries, expecially if the library has complementary reference works such as the *Dictionary of American Biography* and the *Atlas of American History.* Larger libraries will want the more specialized encyclopedias, many of which are described in the basic bibliographical guide to this area, *Harvard Guide to American History* (rev. ed.; Cambridge, Massachusetts: Belknap Press of Harvard University Press, 1974, 2 vols.).

Among works published beyond these shores, the best modern history is the multivolume *New Cambridge Modern History,* which begins with the Renaissance and closes shortly after World War II.

In addition to its *Modern History,* the same press has issued *The Cambridge Ancient History, The Cambridge Economic History of Europe, The Cambridge History of the Bible, The Cambridge Medieval History,* and a number of other multiple-volume sets which are standard reference aids in larger research libraries. All enjoy a scholarly reputation; and although each can be criticized for this or that, they are basic and among the most authoritative in the field.

There is nothing quite like the Cambridge volumes for American history. The closest thing is the standard overview of American history for the layperson and the expert, the *Dictionary of American History.* Revised in 1976, it now includes 6045 entries by over 1400 contributors. The revision carries the history through the early 1970s and has new or revised sections on American Indians, Afro-Americans, women, and so on. The title derives from the fact that a vast number of the articles are brief, but this is more a matter of editing than of depth or scope. Actually, major periods are simply broken down into much smaller parts than are normally found in an encyclopedia, and then treated as separate, specific entries. This approach is ideal for reference work. There are no biographical entries, although names mentioned in articles are in the index volume. The publisher issues numerous related works, such as the *Encyclopedia of American Economic History* (New York: Charles Scribner's Sons, 1979, 3 vols.) which is almost a history textbook on the subject. Some 72 articles, often many pages in length, are systematically divided by history, chronology, social framework, and the like. There is a useful index and glossary.

Library Science

ALA World Encyclopedia of Library and Information Services. Chicago: American Library Association, 1980, 616 pp. $85.

Encyclopedia of Library and Information Science. New York: Marcel Dekker. 1968 to date. Irregular, 36 vols., in progress. Various prices, $45–$55 per vol.

There are several encyclopedias, handbooks, and dictionaries for library and information science, including *The American Library Association Yearbook,* which gives an annual rundown on much of the material covered in the one-volume ALA encyclopedia. The difference is scope. The encyclopedia covers the world, as the title indicates. Still, the type of data is much the same, e.g., fundamental principles, statistical data, historical background, and late developments. There are about 160 articles, including some fine overall viewpoints, such as Jesse Shera's piece on the philosophy of librarianship and Charles Bunge's perceptive survey of reference services. In addition, there are close to 200 biographical sketches, primarily of dead notables.

The multivolume, still-to-be-completed set from Dekker is more exhaustive and sometimes gives scores of pages to an entry which is no more than a paragraph or two in the ALA work. Because of its long-range publishing history, much of the material in earlier volumes is dated. Also, the contributors vary considerably in ability and the set is quite uneven—the good is excellent, the bad is just that. Nevertheless, it is a valuable aid for any librarian who is seeking basic background information on almost any conceivable subject related to the profession.

Literature

The Cambridge History of English Literature. New York: Cambridge University Press, 1907 to 1933, 15 vols. $620.

Cassell's Encyclopaedia of World Literature. New York: William Morrow & Company, 1973, 3 vols. $47.95.

There is an overwhelming amount of material concerned with literature and related areas such as drama and poetry. As with history, the general encyclopedia usually contains enough material for all but the expert. Special sets are useful for the particular or unusual query which is so narrow in scope that it cannot be answered by a general source.

The two encyclopedias listed here are representative of the "classics" in the field, and are available in most medium and large academic and public libraries. And even in small collections, there is usually a place for *Cassell's*. First published in 1953, this standard work, consisting of two volumes of biographical data and an opening volume which is devoted to the histories of different literatures and essays on general literary subjects, touches on almost every facet of the subject. The advantage of this set is that is covers all literature, not just American and English entries, and the two-volume biographical work includes a wide variety of writers from many lands.

The Cambridge History of English Literature is the basic set in its field. While quite properly considered a "history" rather than a typical encyclopedia, its wide coverage means it is often used in libraries as a type of encyclopedia. If nothing else, it illustrates the difficulty of categorizing some reference works. (See the previous discussion of encyclopedias and handbooks.) The discussion in the first volume opens with the earliest literature and closes with cycles of romances. The twelfth through fourteenth volumes carry the history to the twentieth century, and the fifteenth volume is a detailed index. Each chapter is written by an expert and ends with an extensive bibliography.

Music

> *The New Grove Dictionary of Music and Musicians.* 6th ed. New York: Macmillan Company, 1980, 20 vols. $1900.

Compiled at a cost of over $7 million, the 20-volume *New Grove* is unquestionably the standard set in the field of music. Like its predecessors, it is extremely reliable, drawing on the experience and skills of over 2500 contributors.

While of value to reference librarians primarily for the detailed articles on pre-twentieth-century music and musicians, the latest edition now includes detailed information on modern musical life, covering not only the contemporary classical composers and performers, but also those from popular music, including the vast area of folk music.

There are some 22,500 articles with over 3000 illustrations, which, according to the publisher, occupy about 7 percent of the page space. In addition, there are several thousand musical examples.

Of particular value, in addition to the detailed material on music and the long biographical sketches, are the many bibliographies. Not only are these found at the end of articles but in numerous cases they are separate entries, e.g., "Germany and Austria: Bibliography of Music to 1600." There is equal emphasis on lists of works by various composers.[28] Still, in many reviews of the set there is a consensus that the high points are the biographies. These are the best of their type to be found in any reference source, and a first choice for reference libraries.

The $1900 price tag will give any librarian pause, particularly as sets of this type sold a few years ago for several hundred dollars. Still, this is the trend, and several multivolume subject encyclopedias are well above $800 and moving toward $1000 to $2000.

Philosophy

Dictionary of the History of Ideas. New York: Charles Scribner's Sons, 1973–1974, 5 vols. $255.

Encyclopedia of Philosophy. New York: The Macmillan Company, 1973, 4 vols. $125.

Both works have a wider use than may be indicated by the titles. The *Encyclopedia of Philosophy* is truly encyclopedic and covers philosophy in the broadest sense. The *Dictionary of the History of Ideas,* which has a wider scope, considers almost every aspect of the human condition and history. Both may be used profitably to augment the sometimes scanty treatment of philosophy in general sets and to give another dimension to ideas found in subject sets such as the *International Encyclopedia of the Social Sciences.*

Religion

New Catholic Encyclopedia. Washington: Catholic University of America, 1967. 17 vols. $450. Supplements 1967 to date, irregular. $60 each.

---

[28]Allen Hughes, "Grove Music Dictionary Doubles Its Size," *The New York Times,* October 20, 1980, p. C13. A short history of the editing of the new set. For an even more detailed appraisal see Charles Rosen "The Musicological Marvel," *The New York Review of Books,* May 28, 1981, pp. 26–33.

The Encyclopedia of American Religions. Wilmington, North Carolina: McGrath Publishing Company, 1979, 2 vols. $135.

The *New Catholic Encyclopedia* is so well known, so close to a general set, that it should at least be mentioned. In fact, it is well enough known to be generally accepted in most libraries, and certainly in most Catholic school libraries from high school through the university. Its 17,000 articles by close to 5000 scholars (many of whom have no affiliation with the church) are models of objectivity. The set is quite obviously strongest in the areas of religion, theology, and philosophy; but in literature and history, it compares favorably with more general encyclopedias. In an average reference collection, its primary value would be for the philosophy and comparative religious articles, as well as for many biographical pieces not often found elsewhere. Moreover, it has excellent illustrations and bibliographies and a fine index.

The supplements, issued about four to five years apart, are a collection of articles which augment and update those in the basic set. Unlike many other encyclopedia supplements, an effort is made to tie the additions to the basic work by constant citation to the original articles. They are required for anyone with the original set.

Prepared by the editorial staff of the *Catholic Encyclopedia,* a more general work is the *Encyclopedic Dictionary of Religion* (New York: Corpus Publications, 1979. 3 vols.). While limited to Christian groups, the signed articles are exhaustive and as objective as they are clear. The set is an ideal reference work for a quick definition of terms, concepts, and happenings and identification of persons, events, and so on.

Edited and written by an ordained minister, the *Encyclopedia of American Religions* is unique in that it is a one-person work, and is a 16-year effort to categorize and explain some 1200 religions and beliefs. The primary value of the work is reliable information on more obscure groups—of the 17 large categories, 10 are Christian, but 7 are not and vary from the Krishna groups to those involved with UFOs. It is particularly useful for reference, as there is an exhaustive index by names of groups, people, places, and even publications.

Science

The Cambridge Encyclopedia of Astronomy. Cambridge: University of Cambridge Press, 1977, 481 pp. $35.

Encyclopedia of Bioethics. New York: Macmillan & Free Press, 1978, 4 vols. $200.

McGraw-Hill Encyclopedia of Science and Technology, 4th ed. New York: McGraw-Hill Book Company, 1977, 15 vols. $850 ($765 to schools and libraries).

McGraw-Hill Yearbook of Science and Technology. New York: McGraw-Hill Book Company, 1962 to date, approximately 500 pp. $29.50 ($22.50 to owners of main set).

A History of Technology. New York: Oxford University Press, 1954–1979, 7 vols. Price varies per volume.

Each of the sciences and applied sciences has its own encyclopedias, and these cover topics from astronomy to zoology. There are hundreds listed in *Guide to Reference Books,* and the much more selective *Reference Books for Small and Medium-Sized Libraries* (with 1048 total entries) annotates close to 10 encyclopedias, dictionaries, and related handbooks.

Representative of the group is the *Cambridge Encyclopaedia of Astronomy,* a reference work one can consult for quick facts or read almost cover to cover. It is arranged by broad topic, hence the attraction of reading it as a survey of astronomy. Ready reference is added by a detailed index and a fine glossary. There are fine color and black and white illustrations which augment the well-written text.

The well-planned sequence of chapters, written by Cambridge astronomers, moves from the different types of stars to final chapters on telescopes, cosmology, and major developments in the field. It is an excellent example of a specialized encyclopedia which challenges and informs the layperson without being too simple or too difficult. This is not to say all or even most works in the broad field of science and technology are similar in editorial approach, although many do favor the essay rather than the specific entry arrangement and can be read in part or in whole as much for pleasure as for information.

Edited and written by leading teachers of the history of science, the *History of Technology* covers the development of applied science from the earliest times down through the middle of the twentieth century. Additional volumes will be published to update the initial set. The style is for the educated layperson; the illustrations are good, the index useful, and the overall approach makes it ideal for answering in-depth queries about everything from building to insights into major technological and economic problems. Many of the volumes can be read from cover to cover and serve not only as basic reference works but as equally basic background for laypersons and experts alike.

Bioethics is concerned with the life sciences and ethical questions from abortion to genetics and patients' rights. Few encyclopedias cover these areas well, so the set is useful for larger libraries, particularly those dealing with social-scientific questions. The close-to-300 articles, which may be 700 or 12,000 words long, are written by experts who make an honest effort to present both sides of any argument. A current bibliography follows each of the alphabetically arranged articles. The style is for the educated layperson, and there is a good subject index.

In the field of science, the best all-around general encyclopedia is the McGraw-Hill entry. (The set is periodically revised and kept updated with the *McGraw-Hill Yearbook.*) There are some 7800 articles, which move from broad survey types to specific shorter entries for specialized areas. Each volume is nicely illustrated, and there are numerous graphs and charts.

The style of writing is unusually clear, and the set may be used both by young adults (such as high school students) and by experts who may be seeking an overview of a field they know little about. Thanks to the arrangement and the index, the set is particularly useful to the librarian for ready-reference questions, especially those which call for brief definitions of terms which may be foreign to the librarian or the user.

The *McGraw-Hill Yearbook of Science and Technology* reviews the past year's work in science and includes a section on "Previews of 198–," a look at the year to come in 8 to 10 articles. *Science Year* (Chicago: Field Enterprises Educational Corp., 1965 to date, approximately 400 pp.) is issued by the publishers of *World Book* and is directed to children and young adults. There are usually 2 general science essays, 15 to 20 special reports on the year's activities, and 50 to 75 shorter articles under general topics, including biography. The many illustrations and the index make this an ideal purchase for libraries serving young people. An equally good annual is offered by the Britannica: *Yearbook of Science and the Future* (Chicago: Encyclopaedia Britannica, 1968 to date, approximately 450 pp.). This volume contains an average of 16 feature articles and some 30 topical sections. There is an excellent index—one of the best of the group—and bibliographies. The *Britannica* also issues the related *Medical and Health Annual* (1976 to date), which is a semipopular summary of the year's activities for the nonspecialist.

Social sciences

International Encyclopedia of the Social Sciences. New York: The Macmillan Company, 1968, $935. *Biographical Supplement,* 1979, 820 pp. $75.

This is unquestionably the single-subject encyclopedia of most use and greatest interest in libraries; and although is predates the 1977 cutoff it is too important to exclude. Its coverage includes subjects most often central to reference questions and, more particularly, to those calling for a limited amount of research or requiring an unbiased overview of a given area. Some 1500 scholars from 30 countries have contributed lengthy, comparative, analytical articles on all aspects of the social sciences, including anthropology, economics, geography, history, law, political science, psychology, sociology, and statistics. In addition to articles on various subject matter, the set includes some 600 biographies.

The set is arranged alphabetically, and there are copious cross-references and a detailed index. All these features make it extremely easy to use for reference work. Of particular interest is the arrangement of related articles under a single heading; for example, there are 12 contributions under "Learning"; under "Leadership," related articles on psychological aspects, sociological aspects, and political aspects are included in a group.

In 1979 the set was supplemented with a volume containing 215 biographies primarily of dead social scientists. In the biographies, the contributors have provided basic data on developments in the social sciences, so the work may be used as both a biographical reference and an update of sorts to the original set.

SUGGESTED READING

Collison, Robert, *Encyclopaedias: Their History Throughout the Ages.* 2d ed. New York: Hafner, 1966. This remains the basic history in the field, but *see also* Collison's brief history in *The New Encyclopaedia Britannica, Macropaedia* (Chicago: Encyclopaedia Britannica, 1974, vol. 6); Sidney Jackson's "Towards a History of the Encyclopedia . . ." *Journal of Library History,* no. 4, 1977, pp. 342–358; [Another chapter in the author's history is continued under the same general title in *International Library Review* no. 1, 1981, pp. 3–16]; Francis Witty, "Medieval Encyclopedias," *Journal of Library History,* no. 3, 1979, pp. 274–296.

Grayson, Martin, and David Eckroth, "The Making of an Encyclopedia . . ." *Journal of Chemical Information and Computer Sciences,* August 1978, pp. 117–122. A history of the background and planning of the 3d edition of the Kirk-Othmer *Encyclopedia of Chemical Technology.* The article gives a good overview of what is required to edit a technical work and is useful for a summary of modern computer composition procedures which are equally applicable to other works.

Kister, Kenneth, "Encyclopedia Publishing," *Library Journal,* April 15, 1978, p. 822+. An overview of the past, present, and likely future of the encyclopedia as a business venture. Many American firms today can continue to prosper due to heavy sales outside the United States.

Koning, Hans, "The Eleventh Edition," *The New Yorker,* March 2, 1981, pp. 67–83. A noted writer views the 11th edition of the *Britannica* as the last gasp of "an unthreatened world." Along the way he gives a highly satisfactory history of the set and points out some humanistic methods of reviewing an encyclopedia.

Leonov, Valerij P., "On the Concept of the Automated Encyclopedias." *International Forum on Information and Documentation,* vol. 4, no. 1, 1979, p. 1+. A relatively easy-to-follow discussion on automation, with a nod to fiction writers who have constructed various types of sets. *See also* Dagobert Soergel, "An Automated Encyclopedia . . ." *International Classification,* No. 1, 1977, pp. 4–10 and No. 2, 1977, pp. 81–89.

Meredith, Joseph C., "The Encyclopedia of Library and Information Science . . .," *Canadian Library Journal,* December 1980, pp. 411–419. A carefully documented review (there are 52 footnotes) of a subject encyclopedia. The reviewer is inclined to think the set is more a collection than a reference work. In making his point he employs numerous methods of evaluation which might be used in examining other special sets.

Preece, Warren, "Toward a New Encyclopedia," *Scholarly Publishing,* October 1980, p. 14+; January 1981, p. 141+. The former editor of the *Britannica* looks to the past and to the future of encyclopedia publishing. He makes several suggestions for improving the general sets, and takes a hard look at how the electronic revolution is likely to modify encyclopedia and reference publishing.

Roberts, J. M., "Enlightenment on the Market," *The New York Review of Books,* February 7, 1980, pp. 49–51. This is a detailed review of the aforementioned Robert Darnton, *The Business of Enlightenment.* (See footnote No. 3.) The reviewer discusses the publishing history of the French *Encyclopédie* and gives insights into today's notions about encyclopedias in general.

Wilmers, Mary-Kay, "Next to Godliness," *The New Yorker,* October 8, 1979, pp. 145–163. A lively history of the first popular, inexpensive, English *Pears' Cyclopaedia.* The author outlines its history, and explains how the editorial changes in the work over the years reflected the changes in the Victorians' attitudes about themselves and their world.

Young, Percy, *George Grove 1820–1900: A Biography.* New York/London: Macmillan, 1980. A sympathetic study of the man who managed to inflame a generation of concertgoers with his enthusiasm, as well as editing the basic reference work in music.

CHAPTER SEVEN

Ready-Reference Sources:
Almanacs, Yearbooks,
Handbooks, Directories

M UCH TO THE DELIGHT of book publishers, many people are involved with facts, with trivia, with anything that requires a minimum of attention or analysis. One result of this mania has been a new interest in the fact book or, more formally described, "ready-reference source."

Commenting on the involvement with facts, columnist Russell Baker observes that much is written about "hard" facts. He then questions what the adjective means.

> *Facts have no molecular structure and can, therefore, be neither hard nor soft. . . . Keeping that in mind, consider your newspaper report that some hard facts are beginning to emerge. I have already disposed of the absurd possibility that these facts can be hard, soft, scratchy, oily, etcetera. . . . Your newspaper is merely stating that some facts, possibly long existent, have now come to its attention. These facts are, of course, not hard. They may, however, be interesting, dull, amusing, important or trivial to you, depending upon your interests.*[1]

Having disposed of the "hard" facts Baker then goes on to make a point about evaluting facts found not only in newspapers but in reference works.

[1]Russell Baker, "Coffee, Toast and Calipers," *The New York Times,* November 3, 1979, p. 21. (The syndicated column will be found in many other newspapers on this day.)

Misinformation . . . appears frequently in the press (and reference works), but it is not a false fact, since it is not a fact at all. It is merely an error or, if published with intent to deceive, a lie, or if published with intent to hoodwink, a hoax. A fact cannot be false.

Facts approach infinity in number, and as any reference librarian will tell you, so do the reference titles which deal with the numberless facts. So do ready-reference questions, which, mercifully, can normally be answered with a half-dozen or so of the thousands of possibilities. Answers to fact or ready-reference queries are usually found in the forms to be discussed here and in the next chapter: almanacs, yearbooks, handbooks, and directories.

ALMANACS AND YEARBOOKS

Although almanacs and yearbooks are distinctive types or forms of reference work, they are closely enough related in both use and scope to be treated here as a single class of ready-reference aid. Aside from the general almanac, e.g., *World Almanac,* and the general yearbook, e.g., *Britannica Book of the Year.* the subject almanac and the yearbook are similar and often used for much the same purpose in reference.

Definitions

Almanac   An almanac is a compendium of useful data and statistics relating to countries, personalities, events, subjects, and the like. It is a type of specific-entry encyclopedia stripped of adjectives and adverbs and limited to the skeleton of information.

As most special subject almanacs are published on an annual or biannual schedule, they are sometimes called yearbooks and annuals. Traditionally, the almanac per se was general in nature; the yearbook and the annual were more specific, that is, were limited to a given area or subject. No more. There are now subject almanacs and encyclopedia yearbooks which are as broad in their coverage as the general almanac.

Yearbook/Annual   A yearbook is an annual compendium of data and statistics of a given year. An almanac will inevitably cover material of the previous year, too. The essential difference is that the almanac will also include considerable retrospective material—material which may or may not be in the average yearbook. The yearbook's fundamental purpose is to record the year's activities by country, subject, or specialized area. There are, to be sure, general yearbooks and, most notably, the yearbooks issued by encyclopedia companies. Still, in ready-reference work, the most often used type is usually confined to special areas of interest.

Compendium   A compendium is a brief summary of a larger work or of a field of knowledge. For example, the *Statistical Abstract of the United States* is a compendium in the sense that it is a summary of the massive data in the files of the U.S. Bureau of the Census. As almanacs and yearbooks have many common qualities, they are sometimes lumped together as "compendiums."

Purpose

Recency   Regardless of form and presentation, the user turns to a yearbook or an almanac for relatively recent information on a subject or personality. The purpose of many of these works is to update standard texts which may be issued or totally revised only infrequently. An encyclopedia yearbook, for example, is a compromise—even an excuse—for not rewriting all articles in the encyclopedia each year.

Brief Facts   Where a single figure or a fact is required, normally without benefit of explanation, the almanac is useful. A yearbook will be more useful if the reader wishes a limited amount of background information on a recent development or seeks a fact not found in a standard almanac.

Trends   Because of their recency, almanacs and yearbooks, either directly or by implication, indicate trends in the development or, if you will, the regression of civilization. Scientific advances are chronicled, as are the events, persons, and places of importance over the previous year. One reason for maintaining a run of certain almanacs and yearbooks is to indicate such trends. For example, in the 1908 *World Almanac,* there were 22 pages devoted to railroads. The 1977 issue contained about 3, while television performers rated close to 10 pages. The obvious shift in interest of Americans over the past 50 years is reflected in collections of yearbooks and almanacs. More important for the historian, many of these early works are convenient sources of statistical information otherwise lost. Old ready-reference books have a definite monetary value. For example the Argosy Bookstore (New York) advertised a run of the *World Almanac* for 1899 through 1933. The asking price for the 35 volumes: $450.

Informal Index Most of the reliable yearbooks and almanacs cite sources of information, thus can be used as informal indexes. For example, a patron interested in retail sales will find general information in any good almanac or yearbook. These publications in turn will cite sources, such as *Fortune, Business Week,* or *Moody's Industrials,* which will provide additional keys to information. Specific citations to government sources of statistics may quickly guide the reader to primary material otherwise difficult to locate.

Directory and Biographical Information Many yearbooks and almanacs include material normally found in a directory. For example, a yearbook in a special field may well include the names of the principal leaders in that field, with their addresses and perhaps short biographical sketches. The *World Almanac,* among others, lists associations and societies, with addresses.

Browsing Crammed into the odd corners of almost any yearbook or almanac are masses of unrelated, frequently fascinating bits of information. The true lover of facts—and the United States is a country of such lovers—delights in merely thumbing through many of these works. From the point of view of the dedicated reference librarian, this purpose may seem inconsequential, but it is fascinating to observers of human behavior.

GENERAL ALMANACS AND YEARBOOKS

General almanacs

The Hammond Almanac.[2] Maplewood, New Jersey: Hammond Incorporated, 1970 to date. $6.95; paper, $4.50.

Information Please Almanac Atlas & Yearbook. New York: Simon & Shuster, Inc., 1974 to date. $7.95; paper, $3.95.

The People's Almanac. Garden City, New York: Doubleday & Company, 1975 to date, irregular. $19.95; paper, $9.95.

The Reader's Digest Almanac and Yearbook. New York: W. W. Norton & Company, 1966 to date (various publishers). Paper, $5.95.

[2]This work may hold the world's record for the most changes in a title within a short time; it began as *The New York Times Encyclopedia Almanac* in 1970 and was continued from 1973 to 1975 as the *Official Association Press Almanac* and from 1976 to 1978 as *The CBS News Almanac.* The new name came in 1979.

Whitaker's Almanack. London: Whitaker, 1869 to date. (Distributed in the United States by Gale Research Company, Detroit.) $28.

The World Almanac and Book of Facts. New York: World Almanac, 1868 to date (various publishers). $7.95; paper, $3.95.

All the titles listed here are basic general almanacs found in most American libraries. For general use and importance, they might be ranked as follows: (1) *World Almanac* (2) *Information Please Almanac* (3) and *Whitaker's Almanac.* The order of preference is based on familiarity. Sales of the *World Almanac* now exceed the combined sales of its two principal competitors, *The Hammond Almanac* and *Information Please Almanac.* The latest edition is 10 percent new compared with the previous edition. It includes precise factual data on people, places, events, and other information ranging from postal zip codes to 25,000 sports facts. There are even income tax advice and maps of various foreign cities. Putting aside for a moment *The People's Almanac* and *The Hammond Almanac,* some comparisons may be made among the top three general titles.

With the exception of *Whitaker's,* all are primarily concerned with data of interest to American readers. In varying degree, they cover the same basic subject matter, and, while there is appreciable duplication, their low cost makes it possible to have at least two or three at the reference desk. The best one is the one which answers the specific question of the moment. Today, it may be the *World Almanac,* and tomorrow, *Whitaker's.* In terms of searching, though, it is usually preferable to begin with the *World* and work through the order of preference stated in the previous paragraph.

All almanacs have several points in common: (1) They enjoy healthy sales and are to be found in many homes; (2) they depend heavily on government sources for statistics, and readers will frequently find the same sources (when given) quoted in all the almanacs; and (3) except for updating and revising, much of the same basic material is carried over year after year.

Of the three works, *Whitaker's,* the English entry, is by far the most extensively indexed (25,000 entries), followed by the *World Almanac* (9000 entries). *Whitaker's* is distinctive in that, as might be expected, it places considerable emphasis on Great Britain and on European governments. For example, the 1980 edition has close to 90 pages of an almost complete directory of British royalty and peerage, with another 150 pages devoted to government and public offices. Other features include an education directory, lists of leading newspapers and periodicals, and legislative data. Each year the almanac includes special sections on items in the news, such as pollution, test-tube babies, and current painting exhibitions. Salaries of prominent civil servants and public officials came to be a feature when Whitaker started the almanac. He asked for salaries; they were not given, so he printed what he thought the employees were worth. The entire subject of Great Britain is dismissed in the American almanacs in less than a dozen pages. Where *Whitaker's* and the American books meet, however, is on standard information about events of the year, foreign countries, and international statistics. *Whitaker's* places more emphasis on emerging nations.

Whereas there is little real duplication between *Whitaker's* and the American works, the almanacs published on this side of the Atlantic are similar to one another in scope if not arrangement and emphasis. The cousins of the *World Almanac* feature discursive, larger units on such subjects as the lively arts, science, education, and medicine. *Information Please Almanac* expanded its contents to include medicine, the economy, political and world developments, and so on. It has 16 pages of colored maps. *Information Please* gravitates more to the methods of encyclopedia yearbooks than to the standard form set by traditional almanacs. The subtitle "yearbook" emphasizes this focus as does the advertising, which stresses it is the "most complete, up-to-date, easiest-to-use reference book for home, school, and office." While "most" is questionable, it is certainly excellent. It is considerably more attractive in makeup (larger type, spacing) than the *World*. Most almanacs come in both hard and soft covers; libraries normally buy the hardbound editions.

The essential question about these titles is, Are they all needed? It may be answered by ascertaining the amount of duplication among them, the ease of finding facts through the index, and the amount of data in each entry. In one study, where the accuracy and completeness of answers were tested in major areas, the author concludes that *"Information Please* and *World* together would appear to provide most of the information. If we add *Hammond* we gain some helpful data that neither *Information Please* not *World* includes, such as foreign museums, current art trends. . . . *Reader's Digest* also includes some information not found elsewhere . . . but it provides significantly less hard data than the other three almanacs."[3]

[3]Julia E. Miller and Jane G. Bryan, "Wealth of Information, . . ." *Reference Services Review*, July/September 1979, pp. 77, 78. Compared are *Information Please, World, Reader's Digest* and *Hammond*. In a survey of 28 different libraries in the Philadelphia area, the authors found the majority of libraries had *World, Information Please,* and *Hammond,* in that order; but only two had the *Reader's Digest*. The article is a good one as a model for comparative studies of other types of reference works—which the editor of RSR promises will follow in the 1980s.

A special case may be made for *Whitaker's,* which covers Europe in more depth than any of the American works, and for the much publicized *People's Almanac.*

The entry from *Reader's Digest* is by far the least expensive, even in paper, and has some of the flavor of the old-time *Farmer's Almanac.* Divided into some 40 main sections, from "Home and Family" to animals to medicine and health, it concentrates on large areas of interest rather than specific facts. The information is of the magazine's familiar "how-we-do-it" variety and includes everything from tips on gardening to first aid. It has by far the most illustrations, primarily photographs on numerous pages, and it has the standard maps, although in black and white. The emphasis on illustration, peculiar to this almanac, underlines the popular appeal. There is a quite thorough index, and, although of limited value for standard almanac data, it is extremely useful for out-of-the-way statistics; chronology; and, as noted, practical tips and advice on getting through the day. It is low on the list of required almanacs.

The *People's Almanac,* like its companion *The Book of Lists,*[4] represents the collaboration of novelist Irving Wallace, his son David, and his daughter Amy, who maintain a staff of about 14 to gather and check the facts for the best-selling 1500-page paperback. The editor rightly claims that the almanac can be read for pleasure or for looking up facts, the latter simplified by an adequate index. The index is necessary because, as in most almanacs, the 32 or so major categories follow no particular order.

Because the 1975 effort was so successful, a second volume was issued in 1978, and plans are to continue new works every three to five years. The almanac differs from the traditional form in numerous ways. Each volume is completely (or almost) different in content from the previous one, so that the 1978 title is a new work. The material is presented in essay form, with a number of charts, tables, maps, and the like. The essays, written by professional authors, are conversational and entertaining. Topics of the sections range from data on presidents to gossip about Hollywood. There are numerous,

[4]*The Book of Lists No. 2* (New York: William Morrow & Company, 1980). The first of these works came out in 1977, but the second is a completely new work; i.e., all the lists are different from those in the first book. Each volume has hundreds of lists, such as the most insulting letters in history. Many lists represent the opinions of experts; some are culled from other reference works. In using the work, it is important to differentiate between opinion (best motion picture actresses of all time) and fact (7 people who died laughing). The difference is not always clear. Never lacking ideas, the team issued a third member of its family in early 1981, i.e., *The People's Almanac Presents The Books of Predictions* (New York: Morrow, 1981), a compilation of prophecies and forecasts.

quite fine biographical sketches. While some of the information can be found elsewhere, it is a brand of trivia difficult to locate. Hence the title is useful for most reference collections and should also be purchased in multiple copies for the general reading section.

Not everyone agrees with this summation, and some find it difficult to reconcile a "reference" work with digs about how famous people have been exhumed or notes on desserts. The mad collection, some critics claim, is no more than another sign of the decline and fall of reference service. As one reviewer summarized the *People's Almanac:*

> *Within its self-proclaimed intentions, it succeeds. Is it, then, being cranky and Colonel Blimpish to suggest that reference books need not be "amusing"? It will, suffice for them to be accurate and accessible. Reference books per se are changing as a result of the information explosion and the sophisticated electronic compilation of data. The 1979 edition of the* Information Please Almanac *insists that it is more* relevant, *and a proof, acknowledging the popularity of pocket calcula-tors, drops square-root tables in favor of answers to questions about specific personal needs.*[5]

The questions of equal billing for amusement and facts in a reference book is not likely to be easily resolved, but the two need not be harshly divided. A careful examination of many encyclopedias will show article after article more amusing than enlightening. One wonders if enjoyment and education need exclude one another, but that, to be sure, is another argument.

General Yearbooks

> *Facts on File Yearbook.* New York: Facts on File, Inc., 1940 to date, annual. $57.50.
>
> *The Annual Register of World Events.* London: publisher varies; 1761 to date, annual. (Distributed in the United States by St. Martin's Press, Inc. $37.50.)

The best-known general yearbooks are those issued by encyclo-pedia publishers, and they are discussed in Chapter 5 on encyclopedi-as. For ready reference, the two titles listed here are the most often used, mainly to check dates, events, and personalities in the previous year's news. (Equally useful is the cumulated *New York Times Index.*)

[5]Eden R. Lipson, "Nonfiction in Brief," *The New York Times Book Review,* January 28, 1979, p. 16.

Facts on File Yearbook is a complete year's cumulation of the data in the weekly *Facts on File* gathered under four broad categories: world affairs, United States affairs, other nations, and general. The American section makes up about 50 percent of the work, while about 10 percent of the whole is given over to general information—facts on the economy, labor, education, the arts, sports, crimes, and so on. The reporting is objective and the writing style clear. For ready reference, the *Facts on File* annual is particularly good because it has an excellent, detailed index with specific entries for every item mentioned.

By virtue of its longevity and its broad coverage of the past year's events, the *Annual Register* is a basic work in larger libraries. Published in England, it is divided into 16 sections. It gives more attention to world events than its American counterpart does. The first part is a survey of the highlights of the year's past events and developments in each country. Another section is concerned with international organizations, religion, science, and so on. The quality of the writing in the *Register* is excellent, and the work has the added advantage of evaluating the year's events. There is an adequately detailed index.

REPRESENTATIVE SUBJECT ALMANACS AND YEARBOOKS

Almost every area of human interest has its own subject almanac, compendium, or yearbook. In a text of this type it is pointless to enumerate the literally hundreds of titles. What follows, then, is a representative group of subject almanacs and compendiums and, more particularly, those "basic" or "classic" works which cross many disciplines and are used in some libraries as often as the familiar index, encyclopedia, or general almanac.

Government

Statesman's Year-Book. New York: St. Martin's Press, Inc., 1964 to date, annual. $16.95.

International Yearbook and Statesman's Who's Who. Surrey: Neville House, 1953 to date, annual. $105.

Europa Yearbook. London: Europa Publications, Ltd.(distributed in the United States by Gale Research Company), 1926 to date, annual, 2 vols. $150.

U.S. National Archives and Record Service. *United States Government Manual.* Washington: Government Printing Office, 1935 to date, annual. $7.50.

The Almanac of American Politics. New York: E. P. Dutton, 1972 to date, biennial. $19.95; paper, $10.95.

Congressional Quarterly Almanac. Washington: Congressional Quarterly Inc., 1945 to date, annual. $82.

Municipal Yearbook. Washington: International City Management Association, 1922 to date, annual. $36.

Book of The States. Chicago: Council of State Governments,1935 to date, biennial. Inquire for price.

It is somewhat arbitrary to separate out most of these yearbooks from the "general" category, particularly as they all relate directly to the type of material found in encyclopedia annuals and, for example, *Facts on File Yearbook.* The major difference in emphasis. The government titles stress the standard, statistical, and directory types of information, which change only in part each year. The aforementioned general yearbooks stress the events of the past year.

Published for over a century, the *Statesman's Year-Book* provides current background information on 166 nations. Along with a general encyclopedia and an almanac, it is a cornerstone for reference work in almost any type of library. It has a distinct advantage for ready-reference work—it is the most up-to-date of the group discussed here and can be relied on for currency. It has a superior index.

The *Year-Book,* grouping countries alphabetically, begins with comparative statistical tables and information on international organizations. With the 1978–1979 edition, more effort was made for balance of coverage, with the result that the third-world countries are now better represented than in earlier volumes. Still, the 1981 edition shows a heavy emphasis on England and Europe. The quantity of information varies in proportion not so much to the size of the country as to the definite Western slant of the reference work. For example, in the 1976–1977 edition, over 190 pages are given over to the United States, some 60 to Canada, and equally full coverage to Commonwealth countries. Many of the so-called third-world nations are limited to less than 10 pages.

The book arranges the information systematically. Typical subheadings for almost every entry are: heads of government, area and population, constitution and government, religion, education, railways, aviation, and weights and measures. There are excellent brief bibliographies for locating further statistical and general information and numerous maps showing such things as time zones and distributions of natural resources.

Given this basic yearbook, one might ask why others are needed. The answer is that while several yearbooks duplicate information, they have additional useful data. The *International Yearbook and Statesman's Who's Who* provides more of the directory type of information than does the *Statesman's Year-Book,* and adds 10,000-plus entries in a biographical section. However, the *Statesman's Year-Book* has bibliographies not found in the *International,* the index is much better, and the data tends to be more current.

The *Europa Yearbook* also covers much of the same territory as its competitors but it has several advantages: (1) Timeliness is a major factor. Not all the material is updated (an anticipated weakness in yearbooks), but most of it is relatively current, and both volumes begin with a page of late information on election results, cabinet changes, deaths, and the like. The work is almost as timely as the *Statesman's Year-Book* and ahead of the *International.* (2) In the number of words and amount of information it leads both. (3) The first volume covers the United Nations; special agencies, including international organizations by subject and European countries. (4) The second volume covers non-European countries. There is a uniform format throughout. Each country begins with a short introductory survey, followed by a statistical profile, the constitution, government, political parties, diplomatic representatives, judicial system, religion, the press, publishers, radio and television, trade and industry, transportation, and higher education—as well as miscellaneous facts peculiar to that country. This wider coverage, particularly of the media, gives it a substantial lead for ready-reference queries over the other two works. The balance among countries is good, with an average of about 100 pages for the USSR, slightly over 50 for Italy and France, and only one for Andorra.

Europa is far from perfect; the flaws continue despite its long publishing history. For example, the index in the first volume is only for the UN and international organizations. One must turn to the second-volume index for material on Europe. There is no composite index.[6]

A fourth basic yearbook of this type, found in larger libraries, is the *Political Handbook of the World* (New York: McGraw-Hill Book Company, 1927 to date, annual). After a checkered publishing history, under various publishers and formats, it appears to be on an annual basis again. Covering much the same material as the other

[6]Elizabeth Hyslop, "What in the World and Who in The World? The Europas," *Reference Services Review,* December 1979, pp. 53–57. The author poses four possible reference-desk questions and then tries to find the answers in various publications. In so doing she points up an excellent method of evaluating and comparing not only annuals but reference works in general. Small yet essential differences between the titles are established nicely.

yearbooks, it has a unique feature: signed essays on political development in each country as well as an overview of current political issues for the previous year. The *Handbook* is used as much for ready reference as for the essays, which are timely, acute, and most helpful when a user is trying to find current, objective material on a country's government.

Current World Leaders (1957 to date) a periodical published in Santa Barbara, California, comes in parts, and is most valuable for the three-times-a-year "Almanac." Here the publisher lists key officials of all independent states and in international organizations. Arranged by country, the entries follow a pattern and are a quick way of updating material from the aforementioned handbooks. Another part of the series, issued every two months, is *Biography & News*, with a listing of "Official Government Changes" updating the current *Almanac.*

Turning from the international scene to the United States, the American equivalent of the yearbooks mentioned is the *United States Government Manual.* In one sense this is an expansion of what is found in the *Statesman's Year-Book*, and has equivalents in Britain, France, Germany and other western countries. The basic purpose of the *Manual* is to give in detail the organization, activities, and chief officers of all government agencies within the legislative, judicial, and executive branches.

Each of the agencies is discussed separately, and the units within each organizational pattern are clearly defined. Now and then, charts and diagrams are employed to make matters a bit clearer. The style is factual, yet discursive enough to hold the interest of anyone remotely involved with such matters.

A useful feature of each year's issue is the list of agencies transferred, terminated, or abolished. Full particulars are given. This, by the way, is justification for holding several years of the *Manual* on the shelves. All too often, someone will want information on a certain agency which can be found only in earlier editions.

Civics and history students find the *Government Manual* an excellent source of factual material for papers. Adults use it for names and addresses of officials. *Documents to the People* (Chicago: American Library Association, 1972 to date, quarterly) updates the *Manual* from time to time.

The single best retrospective source of information on congressional and, to a degree, executive and judiciary action is the annual *Congressional Quarterly Almanac.* Covering activities of the previous year, it includes information on all major legislation, how congressmen voted, highlights of the Supreme Court, basic Presidential messages, and the like. There are numerous charts and graphs to speed along the ready-reference process, and the whole is brought together by a complete index.

Current information on candidates for national office is easy to come by, and their records can be checked in the *Congressional Quarterly Almanac.* At a local, state, or municipal level, the League of Women Voters (among other groups) publishes biographical and evaluative material on candidates.

The Almanac of American Politics, another title often found in libraries, is a mass of topical information and statistics. The 1000-plus pages include brief sketches on all the senators, representatives, and governors of the nation. It is filled with map details and statistical information about the federal, state, and local governments. It also includes highly personal predictions about politics and politicians.[7] As most of the almanac is divided by "states and districts," it is a handy way to check for names of officials at most levels of government. (See, too, the related *Congressional Staff Directory.*)

The *Municipal Yearbook* offers an annual review of developments in U.S. cities, looking at statistics and trends comparatively, without always giving specific data for specific cities. There are several sections, including those on trends, employment and finance, management issues, public safety, and the environment. The overall view of American cities is visually aided by graphs, charts, and tables and is useful to ascertain trends and to get averages for this or that. However, only the directory section can be used for specific cities. Here, there is a directory of municipal officials for cities over 2500. It is the most valuable part of the book for reference work, particularly as, beginning with 1974, it gives the telephone numbers of city halls.

Data for a state or city are usually found in local annual or biennial guides, frequently known as "blue books." These vary in scope and depth of presentation but are of major importance for all libraries; e.g., even the smallest library will want the manual for its state. If there is any question about the title or frequency of such a manual or annual, the librarian should contact the state library or any official in the governor's office. The local manuals are invaluable for biographical information on state legislators, data on various agencies, and the like.

For a broader look at state policy, the favored reference work is

---

[7]Francis X. Clines, "Almanac of Politics . . .," *The New York Times,* November 13, 1979, p. B15. A short article about how the almanac is edited by its founder Michael Barone. Clines claims that at the time President Carter "had two copies of the 1978 edition, one on his desk in the Oval Office and the other tucked in a drawer aboard Air Force One, back to back with a dictionary and a thesaurus."

aptly named *Book of the States.* Both content and arrangement vary with each biennial number. Generally, there are articles on the past, present, and future state of the states, but in reference work it is employed primarily for relatively recent directory data, such as the names of principal state officers. Statistical data is supplied on a wide variety of subjects. Although biennial, there are annual supplements updating names of officials.

Many professions have their own yearbooks, and librarians are no exception. Two worth brief mention are *American Library Association Yearbook* (Chicago: American Library Association, 1975 to date), a running report on events, legislation, and professional activities of concern to librarians; and the *Bowker Annual of Library & Book Trade Information* (New York: R. R. Bowker Company, 1965 to date), a compendium of data and information. In addition to articles are numerous statistics and information of the directory type not found in the *ALA Yearbook.* The two complement rather than compete with one another.

Statistical data[8]

U.S. Bureau of the Census. *Statistical Abstract of the United States.* Washington: Government Printing Office, 1879 to date, annual. $12; paper, $5.

United Nations Statistical Office. *Statistical Yearbook.* New York: United Nations Publications, 1949 to date, annual. $41.

Historical Statistics of the United States, Colonial Times to 1970. Washington: Government Printing Office, 1976, 1200 pp.

International Encyclopedia of Statistics. New York: Macmillan Free Press, 1978, 2 vols. $100.

American Statistics Index. Washington: Congressional Information Service, 1973 to date, annual with monthly and quarterly supplements. Approximately $1000 (online, $90 an hour).

Statistical Reference Index. Washington: Congressional Information Service, 1980 to date, annual with monthly and quarterly supplements. Approximately $1000 (online, $90 an hour).

[8]Almost all the statistical sources considered here are involved with compilation of economic and social statistics. Scientific and technological statistical data is sometimes considered, although it is gathered and indexed in more specialized sources, such as National Technical Information Service. The basic bibliography in the total area is *Statistical Sources* (Detroit: Gale Research Company, 1962 to date. Irregular). The 1980 edition lists more than 20,000 sources under about 12,000 subjects.

Statistics are concerned with the collection, classification, analysis, and interpretation of numerical facts or data. The reference librarian meets the statistical question when the user opens a query with "How much?" or "How many?" Depending on whether the query is motivated by simple curiosity or by a serious research problem, the sources of possible answers are as numerous as the hundreds of reference works dealing peripherally or exclusively with statistical data.

The reference librarian's most difficult problem remains in isolating the source of an answer to the esoteric, specialized statistical query. Almost as hard is translating the query into the terminology of the statistical source. Given the numerous sources and the specialized terminology, it is no wonder that in larger libraries the expert in statistics is as important as the subject bibliographer. Normally, this librarian is located in the government documents or the business section. Statistical reference work is highly specialized; all that can be done here is to indicate the basic general sources with which the beginner should be familiar. Fortunately, the basic works are sufficient for most general questions.

One of the best sources of answers to general statistical questions is any of the almanacs or encyclopedias which, in turn, draw on the second general source, the *Statistical Abstract of the United States,* for most of their data. A third source that may be used when the others fail (usually for lack of currency) is the group of indexes, from *The New York Times Index* to *Public Affairs Information Service Bulletin* to the *Business Periodicals Index.*

The *Statistical Abstract of the United States* is divided into approximately 35 major sections; each is preceded by a summary which explains terminology and clearly states sources and origins of data. Broad topics include education, public lands, vital statistics, population, and almost any conceivable area likely to interest either the expert or the layperson. There is an excellent index which is particularly strong on the subject approach.

A large proportion of statistics is from government sources, although close to 75 private firms and organizations supply material. As these are identified, the *Statistical Abstract* is a worthwhile guide to major statistical services outside the government. Most of the data are presented in tabular form. The text is issued annually, and each of the tables is updated by one year. For comparison, figures are usually retained for several previous years.

The level of unemployment, the number of persons on welfare, crime statistics, the amount of aspirin produced, the distribution of television sets and bathrooms in American homes—these are just a few of the various facts which can be ascertained through the *Statistical Abstract.* Statistics for cities and other small geographical units are used infrequently, and as a consequence, there are a number of other reference titles for small units. Among the most used are *County and City Data Book* (1952 to date, irregular) and the *Congressional District Data Book* (1961 to date, biennial). Also issued by the Bureau of the Census, they offer a local approach to the same type of data found in the more general *Statistical Abstract.*

Some notion of the general public interest in statistics may be found in the relatively recent publication of a number of popular spin-offs of the *Statistical Abstract,* such as the *Pocket Data Book, USA* (1967 to date, biennial) and *We, The Americans* (1967 to date, irregular), both published by the Bureau of the Census in a popular form, with many colored charts, diagrams, and the like. At the other extreme, almost every government department and bureau publishes its own specialized statistical data in such reports as the U.S. Office of Education's *Digest of Educational Statistics* (1962 to date, annual) and the U.S. Department of Housing and Urban Development's *Statistical Yearbook* (1966 to date, annual).

Historical Statistics of the United States, Colonial Times to 1970 is revised over the years. The present edition includes data for more than 12,500 time series grouped in tabular form. It gives comparative figures on statistics, ranging from the average wage over the years to the number of residents in a given state or territory. Most material is on the national level but a few sections cover regions and smaller areas.[9]

The majority of Western nations follow the pattern established by the American government in issuing equivalents of the *Statistical Abstract* and specialized statistical information. For example, England has *Annual Abstracts of Statistics* (London: Her Majesty's Stationery Office; 1854 to date). On an international level the best-known equivalent is the United Nations *Statistical Yearbook,* which covers basic data from over 150 areas of the world. The information is broken down under broad subject headings ranging from population to transportation, and no effort is made to single out units of government smaller than national.

[9]Barry Tarshis, *The Average American Book* (New York: Atheneum Publishers, 1979) is based on many of these statistical sources and is a popular approach to what is essential about Americans, from 40 percent of American teen-agers believing in Sasquatch to the fact that most Americans are getting taller and becoming more conservative in their politics.

The United Nations issues an often updated *Directory of International Statistics* (New York: United Nations Publications, 1973 to date, irregular) which lists the various UN organizations and their publications in this area. There is a subject approach and, in these days of automation, an inventory of data bases.

Another useful international statistical compilation, the *Demographic Yearbook* (New York: United Nations Publications, 1948 to date, annual), follows the same general pattern as the *U.N. Statistical Yearbook,* breaking down data by 250 to 300 geographical areas rather than by specific countries. Distribution of population, death rate, number of marriages and divorces, and numerous other demographic characteristics are considered. For historical research it is useful to know that the 1976 volume has a cumulative index to the set.

For smaller libraries, most of these UN works may be skipped—but in their place is highly recommended the UN's *Statistical Pocketbook* (New York: United Nations Publications, 1976 to date, annual). This is a summary of national data and is particularly useful because material is found under each member country. Statistics on education, population, trade, and so on, are clearly given and relatively current. A second section treats large subjects by region.

The International Encyclopedia of Statistics features scholarly articles which cover the development of modern statistical methods and describe methodologies. There are 75 articles on statistics, another 42 on the social sciences and statistics, and several biographies, as well as extensive bibliographies. Some of the material is from the *International Encyclopedia of the Social Sciences,* but is updated. A detailed index completes the two-volume work, a basic guide for beginners in statistics and research, of particular value to those in the social sciences and mathematics.

A much more specific approach is offered by the *American Statistics Index,* whic analyzes social and economic statistical data from over 500 government sources and some 800 to 900 periodicals. In a year, close to 8000 different articles, reports, studies, and the like will be abstracted. It is particularly concerned with publications from the Bureau of the Census, Bureau of Labor Statistics, Department of Agriculture, the National Center for Educational Statistics, and the National Center for Health Statistics.

The work is in two parts. The first, as in many abstracting services of this size (e.g., recall the index volume to *Dissertation Abstracts*) is the index. Here one can find statistical data by subject, title, issuing agency, and so on. The second is the abstracts of the material located through the index.

The librarian should turn first to the index by subject, title, and so on, for a key to the second part containing the abstracts. Full bibliographical information is given for each item, and it is usual to list and describe the tables and articles appearing in the individual issues of the periodical, report, study, and so on. Each item is abstracted.

Once a citation is located, the document can be found through the Superintendent of Documents number or the name of the periodical. Also, the publisher offers microfiche of almost all the material indexed—an impressive amount, about 900,000 pages a year.

The publisher supplements the index with the *Statistical Reference Index*, which has the same approach but casts a wider net, in that it covers nongovernment statistical reports; periodical articles; and data from nonprofit associations, corporations, university and independent research centers, and even state governments. Statistics cover business, financial, industrial, social, political, and environmental data. The publisher claims that in an average year about 2600 items are indexed. Emphasis is on currency.

The arrangement is similar to the other work; i.e., there is an abstract section and a separate index with briefly annotated entries keyed to the abstracts.

There are quarterly and annual cumulations. The beginner should begin with the cumulations before attempting to use the more frequent issues.

Two other points: Both services are sold either separately or with microfiche copies of everything indexed. The microfiche is highly desirable, as many of the items indexed are difficult to locate in the average library. And, finally, both are available online. Because of the complexity of the printed indexes, this is one more case where an online computer search is much simpler than the average search of the printed volumes.[10]

HANDBOOKS AND DIRECTORIES

The next large group of ready-reference sources consists of handbooks, manuals, and directories.

Because it is difficult to distinguish between the average handbook and the average manual, the terms are often used synonymously, or the confused writer solves the definition problem by again using the term "compendium" for either or both.

---

[10]Lynn Green, "American Statistics Index," *Online*, April 1978, pp. 36–40. This is a clear discussion of both the printed and the online version of the service. The online database began at the same time as the printed work.

Purpose

The primary purpose of handbooks and manuals is as ready-reference sources for given fields of knowledge. Emphasis normally is on established knowledge rather than recent advances, although in the field of science, handbooks that are more than a few years old may be almost totally useless.

The scientific handbook in particular presupposes a basic knowledge of the subject field. A good part of the information is given in shorthand form, freely employing tables, graphs, symbols, equations, formulas, and downright jargon, which only the expert understands. Much the same, to be sure, can be said about the specialized manual.

Scope

With some exceptions, most handbooks and manuals have one thing in common—a limited scope. They zero in on a specific area of interest or a subject. In fact, their particular value is their depth of information in a narrow field.

There are countless manuals and handbooks. New ones appear each year, while some old ones disappear or undergo a name change. It is obviously impossible to remember them all. In practice, based on ease of arrangement, lack of substitute, or amount of use, librarians adopt favorites.

There are scores of general handbooks and manuals. There are thousands dedicated to specific subject areas and subsections of those areas. A cursory glance at *Guide to Reference Books* will make the point, and in the *American Reference Books Annual,* many of the subject areas include a section for handbooks.The following representative group was selected because of wide use in libraries.

General handbooks and manuals

> *Guinness Book of World Records.* New York: Sterling Publishing Company, 1955 to date, annual. $15.95; paper, $9.95.
>
> Kane, Joseph N. *Famous First Facts,* 4th ed. New York: The H. W. Wilson Company, 1981, 1360 pp. $55.

There are numerous fact books edited primarily to entertain, to settle arguments, to meet the insatiable needs of trivia collectors, and to provide people with the "first" to the "best" to "the worst" of everything. Most of these are at least accurate and provide the librarian with still another entrance into the sea of facts. Of the scores of such titles now available, the ones listed here are representative.

Parenthetically, they are termed "handbooks and manuals," although they might just as well be classified as almanacs, yearbooks, or whatever. Defying rigid categorization, they provide a fast means of isolating facts otherwise buried in an encyclopedia.

The leader among the steadiest-selling fact books is, of course, the world-famous *Guinness Book of World Records*. With over 30 million copies now in print, it is among the best-selling books of all times, even threatening to rival the sales records of almanacs.[11] The title has gained fame and leadership by recording representations of the tallest, fattest, longest, smallest, and similar record-making data. Divided into sections and well-indexed, the *Guinness Book of World Records* gives figures on records of human achievement, space, the arts, scientific world, animal and plant kingdom, and so on. One reviewer notes that "Although much of the information is at best trivial (baby carriage pushing, fastest wedding, car wrecking, etc.), the work has been extremely popular . . . with those who wish to settle arguments, win bets, or establish new records."[12]

The success of the book has resulted in numerous spin-offs, or what the publisher calls "Guinness Family of Books." Typical titles: *Guinness Sports Record Book, Guinness Book of Extraordinary Exploits,* and *Guinness Book of Surprising Accomplishments.* [See *Books in Print* (1981 — 1982), where titles in this series take up a complete column.] Most are fine for general reading and of some value in reference work.

Kane's *Famous First Facts* is the joy of the librarian seeking out-of-the-way information on such vital issues as who invented the toothbrush or can opener, when a man first jumped off the Brooklyn Bridge, who was the first woman senator. Despite its obvious catering to the fact fiend and its limitation to events in the United States, it has value for the scholar or researcher attempting to establish a fact. The material is arranged alphabetically by subject, with an excellent index listing the facts geographically, chronologically, and by personal name.

Awards/Prizes

> *Awards, Honors and Prizes.* 4th ed. Detroit: Gale Research Company, 1978, 1980, 2 vols. $50, $65.

The standard two-volume work for awards and prizes is the much revised *Awards, Honors and Prizes.* The 1978–1980 edition has

---

[11]The world's all-time best-selling book (after the Bible) is the *World Almanac.* It averages about 1 million copies a year.

[12]"Reference and Subscription Books Reviews," *The Booklist,* September 1, 1978, p. 76.

about 7400 awards in a wide variety of fields, from literature and science to public affairs and business. Three important aspects of these volumes: (1) The first lists American and Canadian awards; the second is international. (2) Listings are alphabetical by the name and subject, and there are subject and geographic indexes. (3) The awards are described in full with names and addresses of sponsors. However, names of winners are *not* given. For that, one must turn to other sources. Much the same procedure is followed in the *World Dictionary of Awards and Prizes* (Europa. Distributed by Gale, 1979), but here the names of recent recipients are given.

Literature

> Magill, Frank N. *Masterplots.* Englewood Cliffs, New Jersey: Salem Press, 1949 to date. Various prices (12 vols. 1976 edition, $295).

As far back as the Middle Ages, there were so-called cribs to assist students studying for an examination or working on a paper. There is nothing new about the medium and, in its place, it is a worthwhile form of publishing. A reference librarian may have mixed views about the desirability of such works for students, but that is a problem which students, teachers, and parents must work out together. It is an error to deny a place on the reference shelf to valuable sources, regardless of how they may be used or misused.

Plot summaries and other shortcuts to reading are often requested by students. By far the most famous name in this area is Frank N. Magill's *Masterplots,* a condensation of almost every important classic in the English language. Not only are the main characters well explained, but there is also a critique of the plot which gives good, bad, and other points about it. Somewhat over 2000 books are considered and there is easy reference to about 12,000 characters.

The basic set is supplemented by additional works such as *Cyclopedia of Literary Characters.*[13] Issued first in 1963, this surfaces in new printings from time to time but is the same 1963 work. Books are arranged alphabetically by title, and the principal characters are discussed in order of significance. Some 17,000 characters from about

---

[13] Another of these is closer to *Book Review Index* or *Current Book Review Citations* than the standard Magill products, i.e., *Magill's Bibliography of Literary Criticism* (Englewood Cliffs, New Jersey: Salem Press, 1979. 4 vols.). This lists the work of 613 authors but does not give plots. It does refer the user to periodical articles, books, and parts of books where one can find critical remarks about the specific title by the author. As this set sells for $200 and as most reference is to criticism published between 1960 and 1970, the combination of cost and scope put it out of range of most libraries.

1300 novels and dramas are considered. A name index helps the librarian locate the elusive character.

Magill's Literary Annual (1977 to date, annual)[14] is a two-volume effort to keep up with current titles. Some 200 books, arranged by title, are discussed. Plots, per se are not given, although the quite good critical remarks certainly help the reader to deduce plot, character, style, and so on. The 200 include both fiction and nonfiction, and a title and author index makes it easy to locate the books. Also, there is an annotated categories index. The unanswered question: What criteria are employed to isolate the 200 American titles from the over 40,000 published? Some indication is given but not enough to warrant complete trust in the editor.

There are numerous versions of the plot/character shorthand approach to literature. Most bookstores, for example, have *Monarch Literature Notes* (New York: Monarch Press, various dates). The over 75 titles in this series are 35- to 75-page pamphlets outlining the plot, character and criticism of a particular work or the place of a writer in history. They are closely related to senior high school and college English courses. Teachers frown upon such cribs, and few libraries provide this type of service.

Occupation

U.S. Department of Labor. *Occupational Outlook Handbook*. Washington: Government Printing Office, 1949 to date, biennial. $9.50.

Although vocational guidance in larger libraries is usually not a part of the reference service, it is very much so in medium-sized and small libraries, and certainly in schools.[15] When occupational and professional advice is given to students by trained counselors, there inevitably is a fallout of young men and women seeking further

---

[14]Until 1977, this was known as *Masterplots Annual* and included only 100 titles. The new title, except for expansion of coverage, is much the same as the older series. Under the name *Survey of Contemporary Literature* (1977, 12 volumes), the publisher has reissued the *Masterplots Annual* from 1954 through 1976. This includes 2300 books, of which about half are fiction and 400 or so biography. Arranged alphabetically by title, the set ends with an author index.

[15]Rita Green and David Erwin. "Acquisition Aids for a Vocational Technical Media Center," *Florida Libraries*, January/February 1980, pp. 14–16, is a good overview of vocational material, applicable to other types of library situations. See, too, M. K. Cook, "Career Education: A Guide to Basic Sources," *Reference Services Review*, October/December 1979, pp. 45–52; as well as an article in the same issue (pp. 59–64) on résumé-writing aids by Carolynne A. Sanders.

materials—either for personal reasons or, often, for preparing class papers. The rush has become so general that even the smallest library is likely to include a considerable amount of vocational material in the vertical file.

When working with students or, for that matter, with adults, a certain amount of probing and patience is normally required. The user may have only a vague notion of the type of information desired, and may be quite uncertain about particular interests and the possibility of turning those interests into a channel of work. Here the *Occupational Outlook Handbook* is especially useful. Close to 700 occupations are discussed in terms likely to be understood by anyone. Each of the essays indicates what the job is likely to offer in advancement, employment, location, earnings, and working conditions. Trends and outlook are emphasized to give the reader some notion of the growth possibilities of a given line of work. Unfortunately, the writers are often no more accurate in their predictions than economists and racehorse followers. An effort to update the title is made through *Occupational Outlook Quarterly* (Washington: Government Printing Office, 1957 to date, quarterly). The periodical contains current information on employment trends and opportunities.

Specific employment opportunities are suggested in the *College-Placement Annual* (Bethlehem, Pennsylvania: College Placement Council, 1970 to date, annual), which lists needs of about 1300 corporate and governmental employers who normally employ college graduates. Listings are alphabetical by employer, with directory-type information about the employer and the types of jobs offered, if only in a general way. There is an extensive geographical and occupational index. Although primarily a recruiting device, the annual is extremely useful for students who wish to get some idea of the number and types of employers in a given field.

A related work is the *Dictionary of Occupational Titles* (4th ed. Washington: Government Printing Office, 1977), which classifies and briefly describes about 20,000 jobs. The 5-pound, 1300-page fourth edition is useful for people looking for ideas about employment, particularly curious high school and college students. They may then turn to the *Occupational Outlook Handbook* for details on most, although not all, jobs. Nine-digit code numbers identify positions including such things as dog bather, bomb loader, and batperson—all unlikely to make the index of the handbook.

As in most reference works, a conscious effort is made to eliminate racist and sexist terminology. The 12-year editing of the new edition resulted in elimination of sex and age references contained in more than 3000 occupations in the previous third edition.

It once was that a batboy was someone who made sure that baseball sluggers had the proper wood in their hands. Now that someone is a bat handler. The old dictionary had separate listings for waiter and waitress. That presented a problem to the editors of the new dictionary, since they wanted to eliminate the ageism and sexism from their work. They struck a compromise: waiter-waitress.[16]

Many libraries have files of occupational material. Sources of often free and inexpensive pamphlets are numerous, including such standard sources as *The Vertical File Index* and *The Encyclopedia of Associations,* discussed elsewhere. The latter work lists free material the associations are more than anxious to distribute. Specific sources include *Current Career and Occupational Literature 1973–1977* (New York: The H. W. Wilson Company, 1978), which lists and annotates about 2500 titles for people in grades K through adult, and *The National Career Directory* (New York: Arco, 1979), which covers about 2000 careers alphabetically by career name. Both titles include material from associations, government publications, professional groups, and so on.

How to pass a test is a major type of question in libraries. Sample tests and the manuals on how to prepare for such tests can be divided by age level and by type. Usually questions concern (1) tests which will be given to gain admission into a university or college,(2) tests administered in the classroom, or (3) tests for various jobs.

The familiar Arco Publishing Company sample tests, which cover examinations for everything from bridge tender and garbage inspector to librarian and teacher, are found in most bookstores and many libraries. The equally popular Barron's Educational Series includes such titles as *How to Prepare for American College Testing* and *Verbal Aptitude Workbook for College Entrance Examinations.* Cowles Regnery is another publisher of many such titles, and the three hardly exhaust the list.[17]

Some public libraries now offer specific information on local or national employment opportunities. Along with employment offices, they receive computerized job information lists from the Department of Labor's Employment Service. The Department offers other publications, such as the monthly "Occupations in Demand." The librarian will actively seek information on jobs in the community, keep a file of

---

[16]"A Dictionary of Jobs," *The New York Times,* December 18, 1977, p. 29.

[17]For a short bibliography of such titles, see John Fluitt and David L. Payne, "How to Take Tests: Needed Library Holdings," *The Southeastern Librarian,* Spring 1979, pp. 21, 22.

everything from current want ads to pamphlets and clippings on employment, and serve as an information center for the person seeking employment.

Rules of order

Robert, Henry. *Robert's Rules of Order*. Morristown, New Jersey: Scott, Foresman Company, 1970, 594 pp. $24.95; paper, $9.95.

Every library gets constant questions about formal organizational rules of order—*Robert's Rules of Order* will answer these queries.

So well known as to warrant only a mention, the *Robert's Rules* is a compendium of data on how to conduct a meeting, how to organize and run an assembly, how to do just about anything where a group of people are meeting and wish to let reason rather than riot govern. The book is a standard guide for both government and informal meetings and organizations. There are many less-involved titles, such as Alice Sturgis's *Standard Code of Parliamentary Procedure* (New York: McGraw-Hill, 1966), but none has the distinguished history and reputation of *Robert's*.

Etiquette

Post, Emily. *The New Emily Post's Etiquette*. NewYork: Funk and Wagnalls, 1975, 978 pp., $11.95.

Although believed passé by some schools of social thought, the rigid rules of etiquette detailed by Emily Post and others continue to enjoy popularity as at least indicators of when to pick up chicken with the fingers and how to address an envelope to a member of Congress. Actually, over the years the Post work has become rather liberal, and reflects new trends in current good manners. A welcome addition to later revisions: the necessity of teaching children to behave in a relatively civilized fashion. A companion, a rival, another approach will be found in the equally much revised *Amy Vanderbilt's Etiquette* (Garden City, New York: Doubleday, 1978, 879 pp.) Some swear there is much difference between the two, others are not so sure. Parenthetically, neither book is now revised by the authors whose names are part of the titles. Letitia Baldridge updates the Vanderbilt guide, and Elizabeth Post is responsible for the title first issued in 1922.

Almost everyone does agree that there is a 1980s entry which conflicts with both Post and Vanderbilt. This is *Charlotte Ford's Book of Modern Manners* (New York: Simon & Schuster, 1980). The author "leans over backwards to accommodate today's relaxed standards while making no bones about her training and preferences. . . . We learn how to be polite to answering machines. . . . In addition, she is tolerant of the use of doggie bags in fine restaurants, the institution of divorce, the problems of living together without marriage."[18] Most libraries will want Post, Vanderbilt, and Ford, for reference and for circulation.

Secretarial practice

> *Webster's Secretarial Handbook.* Springfield, Massachusetts: G. & C. Merriam Company, 1976, 546 pp. $9.95.

Books on secretarial practice have a dual reference function. First, they assist the professional secretary who needs some background information. Therefore at least one or two of the handbooks should be duplicated in the general collection, so they can be taken home and studied. Second, because of the thorough, relatively simple approach to problems of English, letter writing, style, and so on, they are helpful to the student preparing papers or the layperson wanting to write a correct letter.

A typical secretarial guide is the *Webster's Secretarial Handbook.* Written by a dozen specialists, it provides information of essentially the how-to-do-it type on almost every secretarial activity from using a calculator to planning a meeting. The best section is the one devoted to business English. A detailed index makes the book useful for quick-reference queries.

Librarians tend to have favorites in this area, particularly because many of the handbooks equally serve to answer questions about spelling, taking minutes of meetings, preparing reports, basic rules of grammar and punctuation, and so forth. Among other equally useful titles found in many libraries are the following: L. I. Hutchinson, *Standard Handbook for Secretaries* (New York: McGraw-Hill Book Company, various dates, frequently revised); Lillian Doris, *Complete Secretary's Handbook,* 3d ed.(Englewood Cliffs, New Jersey: Prentice-Hall, Inc. 1970).

Science

> *Handbook of Chemistry and Physics.* Cleveland: Chemical Rubber Company, 1913 to date, annual. $57.95.

---

[18]Doris Grumbach, "Nonfiction in Brief," *The New York Times Book Review,* March 30, 1980, p. 10.

Considered the bible of chemists and physicists, the *Handbook of Chemistry and Physics* is, as the subtitle explains, "a ready-reference book of chemical and physical data." The data are readily accessible, as they are organized in a way that groups similar and related materials commonly needed in research. Much of the information is in tabular form and, like the rest of the annual, is constantly updated to include reference material in such developing areas as solar radiation and cryogenics. Although using it requires some basic knowledge of chemistry and physics, it is as familiar to beginning students as to experienced researchers.

ADVICE AND INFORMATION

A common problem that arises in reference service is when to give information, when to give advice, and when to give neither. Normally, the emphasis is on information, not advice. The distinction is important, because in some librarians' minds, advice and information are confused when medicine, law, or consumer information is sought by the layperson. Most librarians are willing to give consumer data, even advice (as this author believes they should about reference books and related materials), but some hesitate to give out data on medicine and law.

There is no reason not to give information about law or medicine. This does not mean the librarian is giving advice. The trend today is to welcome legal and medical queries. Still, doubts may arise in the following forms:

(1) "I may be practicing law (medicine) without a license." The answer is that there is no case of a library or a librarian being named as defendant in a legal suit on this ground. The librarian has no liability to fear.[19] Of course, the librarian should not try to diagnose the situation or offer treatment (legal or medical), but simply provide the information required—no matter how much or in what form.

(2) "I don't know enough about law (medicine) to find required information." The answer is that there are now numerous books, articles, pamphlets, and television and radio tapes available for the layperson. These are reviewed in most of the standard reference review media. Furthermore, as with any subject area, the librarian soon becomes familiar with how to evaluate a title for reliability,

---

[19]Norman Charney, "Ethical and Legal Questions in Providing Health Information," *California Librarian,* January 1978, pp. 25–33. This should be required reading for library students and any librarian who hesitates to give out medical information.

currency, style of writing, and the like. As for finding the data, again, this is not difficult when one becomes accustomed to using a few basic reference works.

Medicine

> *Physicians' Desk Reference.* Oradell, New Jersey: Medical Economics Company, 1947 to date, annual. $15.
>
> *Medical Books for the Layperson.* Boston: Boston Public Library, 1977 to date, irregular. Request.
>
> Rees, Alan (ed.). *The Consumer Health Information Source Book.* New York: R. R. Bowker Company, 1981. 500 pp. $35.

The development of the consumer and health education movements in the United States has meant increased attention to medical information for the layperson. At one time, reference librarians hesitated to answer any type of medical question. That attitude is rapidly disappearing, although a few librarians still believe medical reference questions should not be answered, or only in a noncommittal way, such as sending the person to the card catalog or popular index or the shelf with the medical books. No other help is given, because the librarian fears possible complications.

Today, there is an active movement among public, school, and even some college and university libraries to develop community health information centers, health-lines, or whatever they may be called.[20]

Many doctors approve of the new interest in medicine by laypersons, and unless it is an unusual situation or community, the librarian is not likely to meet difficulty from the doctors. In fact, since 1977, doctors have worked with a "consensus development" program to involve consumers, lawyers, librarians, and others in deciding the appropriate applications of medical capabilities. The idea of the panel is to help make decisions in light of conflicting points of view.

> *There are a lot of things in medicine about which there is no agreement. "The practicing physician faced with a patient may read an article in a medical journal, or consult a specialist, or look up a medical text. If the advice is conflicting, how does he decide what to do? And how does he keep up with new developments? Medical textbooks are the basis for many*

---

[20]See, for example, Eleanor Goodchild, "CHIPS-Consumer Health Information Programs and Services in Los Angeles," *California Librarian,* January 1978, pp. 19–24; the proceedings of the METRO "Medical Materials for the Reference Librarian who is not a Medical Librarian" (New York: METRO, 1978).

treatment decisions, and they're out of date before they're even published."[21]

Many librarians take an active interest in medical information. In 1979, Case Western Reserve started a program to transform area public libraries into health information dissemination centers. One library-based medical query service for laypersons in CHIN (Community Health Information Network) in Massachusetts, which links the medical library at Mt. Auburn Hospital in Cambridge with area public libraries. Ellen Gartenfeld, director of this government sponsored network, addressed herself to the fear of giving medical information:

As long as librarians don't pretend to be doctors, there's really no problem for them. . . . I don't apply any other cautions. . . . You know, we're not providing "do-it-yourself" medicine: we're supporting people in their interaction with their health professionals. . . . The time has come for librarians to develop [medical advice] skills and provide this service. If we don't, someone else will, and we'll have allowed another of our responsibilities to go to some other kind of new information professional.[22]

A now relatively common approach for giving medical information is by telephone and prerecorded tapes. A typical example is in Maryland, where some 250 tapes are available on everything from birth control and breast cancer to vasectomy and alcoholism. The user dials; the tapes play.[23]

Telemedicine, another effort to bring medical advice to laypersons, consists of experts taking over a cable television channel. Usually at least one local channel is available for nonprofit civic use and often originates in a library.[24]

Newspapers now carry regular columns with medical advice. One of the best: Jane E. Brody's "Personal Health," a weekly feature

[21]Jane Brody. "Consensus Program Praised by Doctors," *The New York Times*, September 23, 1979, p. 49. Medical librarians are not always sure about offering medical help to the public; e.g., see Cathy Schell, "Preventive Medicine: The Library Prescription," *Library Journal*, April 15, 1980, pp. 929–931.

[22]"Medical Information Taboos," *Library Journal*, January 1, 1978, p. 7. This is quoted from an editorial by editor John Berry which is a solid justification for giving out medical information at the reference desk. An article on the system by Ms. Gartenfeld is in the October 1, 1978 issue of *Library Journal*, pp. 1911–1914.

[23]For a detailed explanation of this system, although in another library area, see Susan Branch. "Health-Line: A New Reference Service," *RQ*, Summer 1979, pp. 327–330. For a report on a similar service, see Donald J. Sager, "Answering the Call for Health Information," *American Libraries*, September 1978, pp. 480–482.

[24]For a discussion of a proposed channel of this type, see Bob Brewin's television column in *The Soho Weekly News*, January 24, 1980, p. 7.

in *The New York Times*. Brody often lists lists books of value to laypersons.

Granted that access to medical information is increasing (although, in the author's view, considerably less than necessary), the next important consideration is understanding. The user must be able to decipher the texts. This can be ensured by (1) purchasing books written for laypersons; (2) purchasing medical dictionaries which give solid, clear definitions; and (3) purchasing or having access to technical information which is not beyond the understanding of the better-educated or the more involved layperson.

There are a number of standard medical dictionaries; among those most often found in libraries is *Dorland's Illustrated Medical Dictionary* (Philadelphia: Saunders, 1900 to date). Frequently revised, this is the work of over 80 consultants, who review all entries and the numerous illustrations. *Stedman's Medical Dictionary* (Baltimore: William & Wilkins: 1911 to date) is another often-revised work which has some of the more up-to-date entries.

There are an equal number of anatomy titles. Among the more popular works one of the best is *The Way Things Work—Book of the Body* (New York: Simon & Schuster, 1979). The presentation is clear without being over simple, and the body descriptions are divided into numerous short sections, each illustrated with diagrams and drawings. Diseases are considered.

Popular medical reference works can now be found in almost every bookstore in both paperback and hardback, written for numerous age levels and degrees of sophistication and education. They are listed in numerous standard bibliographies, of which the best for the medium-to-large collection is *Medical Books for the Layperson*. It is frequently updated and supplements are issued, so it is relatively current. Material is carefully selected and annotated, and there is a subject index. Another useful, annotated guide is Art Ulene, *Help Yourself to Health* (New York: Putnam, 1980), which lists items, including many free or inexpensive titles, under subjects such as asthma, aging, alcoholism, and so on.

The best all-around title for libraries is Alan Rees, *The Consumer Health Information Source Book*. It has the advantage of currency (published in early 1981) and of being edited for librarians. After a brief introduction on consumers and health information, there follows an annotated listing of basic reference works as well as pamphlets, audiovisual, and other types of materials. There is a good title and subject index.

There are numerous useful lists published from time to time in library periodicals, e.g., John Cornier's "Medical Texts for Public Libraries," *Library Journal*, October 15, 1978; *Illinois Libraries*, June,

1976, the complete issue of which is given over to reference work and medical titles; and *California Librarians,* January 1978. *Reference Books for Small and Medium-Sized Libraries* (Chicago: American Library Association, 1979) lists and annotates about 18 basic titles.[25] Published by a group of doctors, *Medical Self Care* (1978 to date, quarterly) is a 65- to 75-page periodical devoted to objective information on health works for the layperson. It is by far the best place for the librarian to turn for ongoing reviews, and a run of the magazine serves as a solid source of information on previously published titles.

The Encyclopedia of Alternative Medicine and Self Help (New York: Schocken Books, Inc., 1979, 243 pp.) is a bit out of the ordinary in that there are sections on such things as acupuncture, chiropractice, and yoga. These are just the topics the harassed librarian is likely to be asked to explain, and its direct, simple, yet factual approach makes this a good reference work. A useful feature is a symptom index.

The best-known and most often found pharmacology work in a library is the *Physicians' Desk Reference.* Frequently referred to as the *PDR*, it provides information on over 2500 drug products. White it is objective, the publisher does note that the "information is supplied by the manufacturers," and is not checked by a disinterested source. Still, over the years, the *PDR* has proved reliable. Brand, generic, and chemical names are given, so, with a little experience, one can easily check the content of this or that drug. (A generic and chemical name index is a major finding device.) For each item, the composition is given, as well as such data as side effects, dosage, and contraindications. One section pictures over 1000 tablets and capsules, with product identification. The neatly divided six sections are arranged for easy use.[26]

Another much-used basic work, equally technical although suitable for certain library situations, is the *Merck Manual of Diagnosis and Therapy* (Rahway, New Jersey: Merck Sharp & Dohme, 1899 to date). Published for many years as a manual for physicians. It is equally clear to laypersons with patience and a medical dictionary at

[25]There are many bibliographies in this area, but a particularly useful one is Joanne Callard et al., "Minimum Cost for Medical Reference," *Oklahoma Librarian,* July 1980, pp. 4–6, which suggests a core list of medical books for public libraries. For nonbook material, see Lucienne Maillet, "Media for Consumer Health Care," *Previews,* October 1979, pp. 2–10. This is an annotated listing primarily of films and cassettes.

[26]*The United States Pharmacopeia* (Easton, Pennsylvania, 1820 to 'date) is the basic technical handbook in the field. It gives detailed instructions on purity and strength of compounds, and is among the better-known titles in this area. Beginning in 1980, the *Pharmacopeia* and the *National Formulary* are published in one volume. The publisher also issues the *United States Pharmacopeia Dispensing Information* (1955 to date, annual), which describes types of drugs and how to use and dispense them. It is particularly useful for information on side effects of drugs.

hand. Illness and diseases are described in relatively nontechnical language, symptoms and signs are indicated, and diagnoses and treatment are suggested.

Some indication of the wide number and types of titles for laypersons can be given by listing only a few works now available—works which should be found in most reference libraries: *The Best Doctors in the U.S.* (New York: Simon & Schuster, 1979, 460 pp.) is a listing with explanation of 2500 of the most highly respected and able doctors in every major medical and surgical specialty in the United States. The compilation is accurate and fair. *Encyclopedia of Health and the Human Body* (New York: Franklin Watts, Inc., 1977, 426 pp.) is typical of scores, if not hundreds, of handbooks and encyclopedias which present accurate medical information for laypersons, in this case younger people. A more specific title, *Good Housekeeping Family Guide to Medications* (New York: Hearst Books, 1980, 320 pp.) is a well-written guide for the person who wants to know more about prescribed drugs than told by the physician. An equally valuable title in this area is James W. Long, *The Essential Guide to Prescription Drugs* (New York: Harper & Row, Pubs., Inc., 1980, 863 pp.). The revised 1980 edition has numerous charts which show summaries of drug effects on hearing, sleep, mood, vision, and so on.

Law

Librarians often are more reluctant to give out reference information about law than about medicine. Some believe they will be placed in legal jeopardy. A more prevailing view (for medical data as well) is that many people do not have the education to cope with technical legal data.

The librarian should not try to act as an attorney (anymore than act as a doctor), but it is important to give information when requested. To do anything else is to act as censor, or so this author believes. Furthermore, not to give such information is to help keep many people who desperately need assistance in the dark about the law.

At a METRO seminar on librarians and the law, Robert Sheehan remarked that today all librarians are to some extent law librarians. Among the causes for the growing demand for legal information, he names "such diverse stimuli as government contracts and grants, television programs, and the sprawling growth of government regulation and administrative law."[27]

---

[27]Alice Norton, "Lex: Law Advice for Public and Academic Librarians," *Library Journal,* February 1, 1978, p. 313.

An example of the growing role played by general librarians in legal questions is the Brooklyn Public Library, which provides free legal aid to people over 60. The program began in late 1978 and is supported by advice from the Legal Aid Society and limited to those below a certain income.

Detailed discussion of even basic legal reference works[28] is beyond this text—they are normally considered in government documents and law information courses in library schools—but some indication will be given of layperson approaches to the law; titles that can be used by librarians. First, a brief look at the problems involved in giving users legal information.

All librarians are likely to face both personal and ethical difficulties when asked for legal assistance. When people are trying to solve their own legal problems by using standard law books or popular titles, there is, as in medicine, the problem of the librarian's knowledge of the subject matter. Here, however, the problem is complicated, as there are few popular legal works and most people want the standard texts, statutes, interpretations, cases, and the like. This requires more than a passing familiarity with legal research. Also, lawyers are sometimes quick to take exception to anyone, even their peers, giving out legal help, and librarians are sometimes nervous about recriminations from attorneys.

The real question, however, concerns the practice of law. Is the librarian who gives legal information actually practicing the law? The answer is a categorical no. As with medical information, the response to a query, the location of the necessary data, is not practicing law or medicine. Even in a law library open to the public, the trained legal librarian is unlikely to be charged with unauthorized legal practice. As one law librarian puts it: "The risk as far as the librarian is concerned is probably slight, for it is unlikely that anyone will bother to take us into court for the unauthorized practice of law and the tort cause of action is tenuous and difficult to establish."[29]

The problem is for the person who does not understand how to use the information. How, then, does the librarian avoid risk?

[28]Robert Q. Kelly, "State of the Art Survey of Legal Reference Sources," *Reference Services Review*, January/March 1978, pp. 13–20. This is a solid annotated guide to basic titles in the field. For a more casual approach, with a brief history of a leading publisher of popular law books, see "Those Sue-It Yourself Manuals," *Time,* December 8, 1980, p. 112.

[29]Robin K. Mills, "Reference Service vs. Legal Advice: Is It Possible to Draw the Line?" *Law Library Journal,* Spring 1979, p. 192. For a general coverage, see Kathleen Coleman, "Legal Reference Work in Non-Law Libraries. A Review of the Literature," *Special Libraries,* January 1981, pp. 51–58; "Youth and the Law," a special issue of *Emergency Librarian,* January-April 1981.

Though he was speaking of the law, Mills's advice is equally applicable to medical situations:

> *The posting of notices urging those who need legal assistance to consult an attorney is a good idea. . . . Staff members . . . should be carefully instructed as to how to deal with members of the general public who are handling their own legal problems. It is virtually impossible to develop a reliable test or standard to be applied to determine where the line should be drawn between giving legal information and legal advice, for the facts vary so much from one request to the next. . . . To avoid the appearance of giving legal advice (the librarian) should encourage the patron to find the answer. . . . It is best to do this by showing the books needed . . . and demonstrating their use. . . . It might be wise to make available . . . a basic legal bibliography text or an internally developed guide for the layman.*[30]

There are several helpful guides for the nonlawyer, but the best and by far the most consulted is Miles Price and Harry Bitner, *Effective Legal Research* (various publishers and dates). Often updated, it offers an easy-to-understand, nonjargon approach to the literature of law. Important sections on basic reference works are of particular value. Referred to as "Price and Bitner," it is both a beginning point and a constant companion for the librarian.

One of the best overviews, with subjects arranged in alphabetical order, is D. M. Walker's *The Oxford Companion to the Law* (Oxford: Oxford University Press, 1979). Compiled by a Glasgow professor of law, the 1366 pages are inclined to focus on English law, but it does have sections on other countries, and most of the entries are as applicable to the United States and Canada as to England. It is particularly valuable for short, clear definitions and for historical background.

There are some reliable laypersons' guides to the law. None are likely to reach the classical proportions of *Black's Law Dictionary* or a set of *The Revised Statutes of the United States*, but they do answer most basic questions not requiring formal legal action.

Henry Shain's *Legal First Aid* (New York: Funk & Wagnalls, 1975) was written as a handy guide for the average reader. It includes six sections dealing with the origins of the law, marriage and divorce, civil lawsuits, and other legal matters. Charts at the end of chapters summarize, state by state, laws governing the topics discussed.

Typical of more limited, yet equally popular, approaches to legal

---

[30] Ibid.

rights is Shana Alexander's *State-by-State Guide to Women's Legal Rights* (Los Angeles: Price, Stern, Sloan, 1975, 224 pp.), which includes essays on adoption, marriage, divorce, and so on, with state-by-state summaries of the law expressed in lay terms.

Consumer aids

> *Consumer Complaint Guide.* New York: Macmillan Information, 1979, 200 pp. $12.50, paper $5.95.

The reference librarian is usually asked one of three questions about consumers and consumer protection: (1) "What is the best product for my needs?" (2) "To whom can I complain, or to whom can I turn for information, about a product or service?" (3) "How can I protect myself from poor-quality products or services?" No one reference source answers all queries, although several are of particular value in locating possible sources.

Combining director and consumer information is the *Consumer Complaint Guide.* The bulk of this often-revised work is a list of firms, with full addresses and names of executives, that produce consumer goods. There are over 8000 product names—often with cross-references from a trade name to the actual name of the manufacturer. The first part includes an essay on consumer practices and law as well as information on how to make a complaint. There are other basic sources for answering the question, Who manufactures or produces this product? The basic sources, considered a bit later, include: *Standard & Poor's Register,* which lists names of officials in companies; and *Thomas' Register of American Manufacturers,* which does the same and offers a method to run down the primary manufacturer of a product.

Easier to use is the *Trade Names Dictionary,* 2d ed. (Detroit: Gale Research Company, 1979, 2 vols.), which lists 130,000 names of products, as well as their 30,000 or so manufactures and distributors with their addresses. Here will be found brand and trade names in boldface type. Arranged in one alphabetical sequence, the user may easily find who manufactures or produces what (each entry has a brief description of the product). Also, information and full addresses are given for associate companies.

When one turns from directories to product evaluation, there are two basic periodicals which should be in every library: *Consumer Reports* (Mount Vernon, New York: Consumers Union of United States, 1936 to date, monthly), the best-known and most quoted source for objective tests of all types of consumer products, and

Consumer Bulletin (Washington, New Jersey: Consumers' Research, Inc., 1931 to date, monthly), with reports of the same type. Both issue annual summaries in paperback, which should be kept at the reference desk.

A related work is the quarterly *Consumers Index to Product Evaluations* (Ann Arbor, Michigan: Pierian Press, 1973 to date, quarterly.) which extracts reviews of consumer products from 75-or-so periodicals and arranges citations to the reviews under 14 subject headings. The index is valuable when the user cannot find satisfactory data in *Consumer Reports* or the *Consumer Bulletin.*

The *Magazine Index* or, for that matter, many of the general periodical indexes serves to guide users to stories, articles, and even critical pieces on various consumer items. The *Magazine Index* has a special section on "Product Evaluations," which is issued later as a loose-leaf service. This, in turn, becomes the base for *America Buys: The Index to Product Information* (Los Altos, California: Information Access Corporation. 1981 to date, annual), an index to some 40,000 products cited in the publisher's periodical and *National Newspaper Index.* In fact, this is little more than another version of the *Consumers Index to Product Evaluations* but with a much wider coverage. It remains to be seen whether it will be as useful as its competitor.

DIRECTORIES

Directory-type information is among the most often called-for in libraries, particularly public libraries. People are trying to locate other people, experts, and organizations through addresses, phone numbers, zip codes, correct titles, correct spelling of names, and so on.

Staff-produced directories can be found in almost all libraries, augmenting the standard reference works—from the city and telephone directory to the Zip code directory. Here are such items as frequently requested phone numbers, the names of individuals and agencies in the community, sources of help for difficult questions, often-requested names of state and federal officials, and a wealth of other miscellany. The Chicago Public Library reference staff, for example, listed the staff-produced files as the most useful source of data for daily reference work—matched only by the *World Book Encyclopedia* and the *World Almanac.*

Definition

The *A.L.A. Glossary of Library Terms* defines a directory as "a list of persons or organizations, systematically arranged, usually in alphabetical or classed order, giving addresses, affiliations, etc., for individuals, and address, officers, functions and similar data for organizations." The definition is clear enough for a directory in its "pure" form; but aside from the directory type of information found in biographical sources, it should be reiterated that many other ready-reference tools have sections devoted to directory information. Yearbooks and almanacs inevitably include abundant amounts of directory-type material.

Purpose

The purpose of directories is implicit in the definition, but among the most frequent uses is to find out (1) an individual's or a firm's address or telephone number; (2) the full name of an individual, a firm, or an organization; (3) a description of a particular manufacturer's product or a service; or (4) "Who is . . ." for example, the president of the firm, or the head of the school, or responsible for advertising, or in charge of buying manuscripts.

Less obvious uses of directories include obtaining (1) limited, but up-to-date, biographical information on an individual—whether he or she is still president, chairperson, or with this or that company or organization; (2) historical and current data about an institution, a firm, or a political group—when it was founded, how many members it had; (3) data for commercial use, such as selecting a list of individuals, companies, or organizations for a mailing in a particular area; e.g., a directory of doctors and dentists serves as the basic list for a medical supply house or a dealer in medical books; and (4) random or selective samplings in a social or commercial survey, for which they are basic sources. Directories are frequently employed by social scientists to isolate certain desired groups for study. And so it goes. Because directories are intimately concerned with human beings and their organizations, they serve almost as many uses as the imagination can bring to bear on the data.

Scope

Directories are easier to use than any other reference tool, chiefly because the scope is normally indicated in the title and the type of information is limited and usually presented in an orderly, clear fashion.

There are many ways to categorize directories, but they can be broadly divided as follows:

Local Directories These are limited primarily to two types:

telephone books and city directories. However, in this category may also be included all other types issued for a limited geographical audience—for example, directories of local schools, garden clubs, department stores, theaters, and social groups. The distinction is more academic than important.

Governmental Directories This group includes guides to post offices, army and navy posts, and the thousand and one different services offered by federal, state, and city governments. These directories may also include guides to international agencies.

Institutional Directories These are lists of schools, foundations, libraries, hospitals, museums, and similar organizations.

Investment Services Closely related to trade and business directories, these services give detailed reports on public and private corporations and companies.

Professional Directories These are largely lists of professional organizations such as those relating to law, medicine, and librarianship.

Trade and Business Directories These are mainly lists of manufacturers' information about companies, industries, and personal services.

Additional directory-type sources

The almanac and the yearbook often include directory-type information, as do numerous other sources of directory information:

1. Encyclopedias frequently identify various organizations, particularly the more general ones which deal with political or fraternal activities.
2. Gazetteers, guidebooks, and atlases often give information on principal industries, historical sites, museums, and the like.
3. A wide variety of government publications either are entirely devoted to or include directory-type information. Also, some works are directories in name (*Ulrich's International Periodical Directory* and the *Ayer Directory of Publications,* for example) but are so closely associated with other forms (periodicals and newspapers) that they are usually thought of as guides rather than directories.

The basic listing of directories is the *Directory of Directories* (Detroit: Gale Research Company, 1977 to date). The annual publication lists more than 5000 new or revised titles under about 15 broad subject categories from business to professional and scientific. There is a detailed subject and a title index. Information for each entry includes the name of the directory, the publisher, address and phone number, and a full description of the work. The publication is updated twice a year by *Directory Information Service,* which follows the same pattern of arrangement and entry, listing new titles or basic changes.

As with other reference works, some of the same information can be found in another Gale publication, *Encyclopedia of Associations.* One simply turns to the subject index, locates associations in the subject area, and then goes to the entries to see whether or not the associations issue directories. The *Directory Information Service,* which describes nearly 2000 new services each year, also acts, in another way, to update the *Encyclopedia of Associations.* The two services are so interdependent that the library with one will want both.

City directories

The two most obvious, and probably the most used, local directories are the telephone book and the city directory. The latter is particularly valuable for locating information about an individual when only the street name or the approximate street address is known. Part of the city directory includes an alphabetical list of streets and roads in the area, giving names of residents (unless it is an apartment building, when names may or may not be included). The resident usually is identified by occupation and whether or not she or he owns the home. Some city directories, but not all, have reverse telephone number services, i.e., a "Numerical Telephone Directory." If you know the phone number, you can trace the name and address of the person who has the phone.

The classified section of the directory is a complete list of businesses and professions, differing from the yellow pages of the telephone book in that the latter is a paid service which may not include all firms. Like the telephone book, city directories are usually issued yearly or twice yearly.

Most city directories are published by the R. L. Polk Company of Detroit, founded in 1870, which issues over 800 publications. In addition to its city directories, it publishes a directory for banks and direct-mail concerns.

A number of ethical questions arise regarding the compilation and use of the city directories. For example, bill collectors frequently call large public libraries for information which can be found only in the city directory, such as reverse phone numbers and addresses and names of "nearbys," that is, the telephone numbers of people living next door to the collector's target. Some librarians believe such information should not be given over the telephone. They argue that this helps the collectors in an antisocial activity and an invasion of privacy.

> *The Virginia Beach Public Library, for example, has a policy which clearly limits giving such information over the phone. The right of privacy also includes the information contained in city directories. City directories are available in each branch for use by the public, but no information from a city directory may be given over the phone by any library staff member.*[31]

This policy may be commendable in spirit, although question-able in practice as it simply makes it more difficult, but not impossible, to use the directories. The author of this text would say the librarian is there to supply information, not to question how or by whom it is used. Several large urban libraries are currently examining their policy in this regard, and most now do give the information over the phone.[32]

Telephone directories

With enough telephone directories, many of the specialized directories might be short-circuited. A telephone book will give the address of a friend, business contact, hotel, and so on, in almost any community. The location of potential customers or services is a frequent purpose for using the familiar yellow pages. And from the point of view of a historian or genealogist, a long run of telephone books is a magic key to finding data on elusive individuals.

Most libraries have at least the local telephone directory and usually those for larger cities in the immediate area. As the library becomes bigger, so does the collection. The 360 major current Bell Company telephone directories for urban communities and regions in the United States run to 40 feet of shelf space. One microphoto company, Bell & Howell, offers a solution to the space problem with a collection of microfiche cards for the 360 telephone books. This device reduces the 40 feet to a space 8 by 16 inches.

[31]Elizabeth Futas, "Library Acquisition Policies and Procedures (Phoenix, Arizona: Oryx Press, 1977, p. 364).

[32]I am grateful to Mike Donovan of the Portland, Oregon, Public Library for

Under the generic title "the people's yellow pages," there is a series of directories published at the local level to help people find vital information on food co-ops, collectives, drug information centers, political action groups, health advice, and so on. These directories fit into any library reference pattern. An example of this is *The New York Women's Yellow Pages* (New York: St. Martin's Press, 1978, 525 pp.). Under such topics as children, rape, and the law are essays and an annotated directory of local sources, as well as bibliographic listings. The information is equally accessible through subject and organization indexes. This type of "yellow pages" is replicated in major cities, e.g., *The San Francisco Bay Area People's Yellow Pages,* 5th ed. (San Francisco: People's Yellow Pages, 1981).

A relatively new development in telephone listings is *The National Directory of Addresses and Telephone Numbers* (New York: Bantam Books, 1977 to date. Irregular), listing over 55,000 addresses and telephone numbers in the United States.[33] Sometimes called "the green pages" because of its green stock, the paperback is a blessing to librarians who cannot afford multiple directories. At only $14.95, it is a best buy because it is a source of answers to such questions as the address of the Teamsters' national headquarters, the phone number of a public library in Seattle, or the zip code of a government agency.

The directory lists basic information under nine major headings: government, politics, and diplomacy; education, foundations, religious denominations; business service; transportation and hotels, and the like. The typical entry includes the zip code, street address, and telephone number.[34] The editor, Stanley Greenfield, imposed certain limitations on the listings. Usually, they are for places in communities of over 50,000, for businesses with annual sales of $10 million or more, and hotels with at least 300 beds. The listing is updated irregularly, but at least often enough to keep the material timely and accurate.[35]

A related title is *Dial 800* (New York: Dial 800 Publishing Company, 1978 to date, annual). Now less than 100 pages but sure to grow, it lists toll-free numbers (i.e., those prefixed by 800) arranged alphabetically by subject from abortion to x-ray equipment. The

background information on the city directory and its uses.

[33] Apparently the publisher plans to reissue this about every three years. The 1980–1981 edition was published in late 1979, and the 1982–1983 number is planned for late 1981. A hard-cover edition is available from Sterling at $28.99.

[34] "Story Behind the Book," *Publishers Weekly,* December 5, 1977, p. 34.

[35] There are numerous specialized directories; e.g., *The Librarian's Phone Book* (New York: R. R. Bowker, 1980) lists 51,412 numbers of librarians, heads of library networks, academic department librarians, etc. *The Federal Yellow Book* (Washington: Washington Monitor, 1979) lists 25,000 federal employees.

service is supplied by companies anxious for business (from movers to airlines and hotels) and by government.

Most libraries provide some type of telephone reference service and use many types of reference works, including telephone books. While the heaviest telephone service is in public libraries, a study at the University of California at Berkeley revealed that during a two-month period, 3282 calls were received. "Of these, some 3195 were answered in less than three minutes each. The remaining 87 ranged from three minutes to 75 minutes each."[36]

Larger libraries have separate sections for phone reference, usually out of view of the public; the smaller and medium-sized libraries usually perform the service from the main desk.

The problem of the telephone ringing when the reference librarian is helping someone else may be solved by installing a phone answering service. The American Telephone Company will install the device to record questions. The librarian then can call back with the answer or some indication of when the answer will be found. Another advantage is that the library is in service 24 hours a day; i.e., calls may be received at any time, although answered during the regular open hours.

Government directories

> U.S. Congress Joint Committee on Printing, *Congressional Directory*. Washington: Government Printing Office, 1809 to date, annual. $8.50; paper, $6.50.
>
> U.S. Postal Service, *Directory of Post Offices With Zip Codes*, Washington: Government Printing Office, 1955 to date, annual.

A basic reference source for questions regarding government is the *United States Government Manual,* discussed earlier in this chapter. Equally important is the *Congressional Directory.* This is a who's who for Congress but includes considerable other information. In some 20 sections there are biographical sketches of the Supreme Court justices, items on members of congressional committees, names of foreign representatives and consular offices in the United States, members of the media who cover Congress, and the chief officers of departments and independent agencies. Used with the *United States Government Manual,* the *Directory* will answer virtually any question concerning individuals involved with the federal government at any major level.

---

[36]Gary S. Sampson. "A Staffing Model for Telephone Reference Operations," *Special Libraries,* May/June 1978, p. 220.

A useful supplement to the *Congressional Directory* is the *Congressional Staff Directory* (Indianapolis: Bobbs-Merrill, 1959 to date, annual). Here one will find names of people currently in key government positions along with, in some cases, brief biographical sketches.[37]

Where does one find information on former members of Congress no longer listed in the *Congressional Directory*? If relatively well known, they will be listed in such sources as the *Dictionary of American Biography* (if deceased) or a good encyclopedia. But for short, objective sketches of all senators and representatives who served from 1774 to 1971, the best single source is *Biographical Directory of the American Congress, 1774–1971* (Washington: Government Printing Office). There is a handy first section which includes officers of the executive branch, e.g., the cabinets from George Washington through the first administration of Richard Nixon. There is also a chronological listing by state of members of the First through the Ninety-first Congress. Among the most-used directories and biographical sources for men and women in government is *Who's Who in American Politics* (New York: R. R. Bowker Company, 1967 to date, biennial).

The *Directory of Post Offices* lists post offices with their zip codes by state and county. This source can be useful for more than its obvious purpose, e.g., when someone trying to locate a small community in the United States does not have an exhaustive gazetteer or an atlas at hand. By now, zip code information can be found in almost any general reference book, including most of the almanacs and in a more concise form in the annual *National Zip Code Directory* (Washington: Government Printing Office, 1975 to date).

Associations and foundations

Encyclopedia of Associations. Detroit: Gale Research Company, 1956 to date, biennial, 3 vols. Vol. 1, $110; vol. 2, $95; vol. 3, $110 (online, $55 an hour).

The Foundation Directory. New York: Columbia University Press, 1960 to date, irregular. $40 (online, $60 an hour).

---

[37]The names and telephone numbers of members of Congress, or any major federal officials is now providing business for several publishers. For example, the Carroll Publishing Company issues *The Federal Executive Directory*, with some 30,000 key names, updated every two months. For a discussion of this see "Washington Business: Keeping Track of the Bureaucrats" *The New York Times,* January 4, 1981, pp. F6, F7. See, too, a bibliographic essay on this subject; Lucinda D. Conger, "Biographical Information and Other Government Secrets," *RQ*, Spring 1981, pp. 282–290.

Termed "one of the most useful and essential titles in any library's reference collection,"[38] the *Encyclopedia of Associations* is a single work in three volumes. The basic volume describes some 14,000 U.S. organizations under 17 broad subject categories, including each group's name, address, chief executive, phone number, purpose and activities, membership, and publications (which are often directories issued by the individual associations). There is a key word alphabetical index, but the second volume is really an index to the first in that it lists all the executives mentioned in the basic volume, again with complete addresses and phone numbers. A second section rearranges the associations by geographical location. The third volume is a periodical publication which is issued between editions and keeps the main setup to date. With this set, the librarian can easily retrieve information by subject, by the name of the association, and by the name of executives connected with the association, and generally can keep up with name changes as well as new organizations.

A number of the associations are foundations, but the seeker of information on foundations and more particularly on their grants should turn to *The Foundation Directory*. The 1978 edition, the seventh, lists 3138 foundations by state, with their purpose and activities, administrators' names, and grants available. Only foundations having minimum assets of $1 million and making total grants of $100,000 in the last year of record are listed. (Individual grants are usually less than $100,000). There is an index by subject, by cities, by donors, and by foundation name.

The work is supplemented by the publisher's *The Foundation Grants Index* (1972 to date, annual). Here one will discover precisely what type of grants are given and by which organization; or, as the publisher puts it; "Discover the grant making interests of nearly 400 foundations through the grants they actually made." There are brief details of money given to nonprofit institutions for a certain type of work or research. The information is in the "grant listing" (an alphabetical-by-state arrangement of some 400 of the grant foundations). The listing can be approached through a subject index, a keyword index, and an index of recipients of grants. About 15,000 grants are indexed each year.

The *Annual Register of Grant Support* (Chicago: Marquis Academic Media, 1969 to date) has the advantage of listing grants in numerous areas of interest for both individuals and institutions. Under 11 main categories, from the humanities to physical science,

[38]"Reference and Subscription Book Reviews," *Booklist*, April 1, 1979, p. 1239.

the grants are listed with detailed information on who gets how much for what type of work. The whole is approached through subject, geographic, personnel and organization, and program indexes. The later editions include introductory material on how to write grant applications.

Education

> *The World of Learning.* London: Europa Publishing Company (distributed in the United States by Gale Research Company), 1947 to date, annual, 2 vols. $130.

The amount of interest in college and university education requires that a library of almost any size have a basic reference collection in this area plus a series of college and university catalogs or, at least, ready information about where such catalogs may be obtained. Even the best of the directories cannot give the bits of information a potential student seeks and can find only in a particular catalog.

The lack of proper advisory services in some high schools makes it particularly important that at least one member of the reference department be familiar with helping teenagers (and their parents) find information on colleges and universities. Such items as cost, entrance requirements, size of school, and strengths and weaknesses of faculty are covered in part in many other directories.

There are several less specialized, less detailed directories, particularly of a popular type found in most bookstores and even on newstands. The best known is *Lovejoy's College Guide* (New York: Simon & Schuster, Inc., 1952 to date, biennial) which outlines, state by state, the various qualifications, offerings, and so on, of American schools. There are also Lovejoy guides to vocational schools and prep schools. While uneven in presentation and arrangement, the various guides are at least as well known to many students as are those published by Barron and by Peterson.

A series of annual volumes published by Marquis Academic Media of Chicago offers up-to-date statistical data and directory-type information for U.S. and Canadian schools. They include the *Yearbook of Higher Education* (1968 to date); *Yearbook of Adult and Continuing Education* (1974 to date); *Yearbook of Special Education* (1974 to date); and *Standard Education Almanac* (1968 to date). The latter two concentrate on elementary and secondary education with a nod to higher education.

The British-published *World of Learning* gives basic data on educational institutions throughout the world, including the United States. The first volume begins with a discussion of international education and scientific and cultural organizations and continues with the country-by-country listing, completed in the second volume. There is a good index. Standard information (address, function, and so on) is given for each country and institution, here interpreted to mean not only universities and colleges but libraries, research centers, museums, art galleries, and even learned societies. There is a listing of professors at all major universities. This is a directory approach, not a discursive discussion of world education; but informative and considered "basic" in most larger libraries.

Libraries and publishing

The American Library Directory. New York: R. R. Bowker Company, 1923 to date, biennial, $54.95; bimonthly updating service, $50.

Directory of Special Libraries and Information Centers. Detroit: Gale Research Company, 1963 to date, biennial, 3 vols. $290.

The American Library Directory is included here to indicate that there are directories for virtually every profession. Published since 1923, it provides basic information on 33,000 public, academic, and special libraries in the United States and Canada. Arranged by state and city or town, the listings include names of personnel, library address and phone number, book budgets, number of volumes, special collections, salaries, subject interests, and so on. It has many uses, from seeking addresses for a survey or for potential book purchasers to providing necessary data for those seeking positions in a given library. (Information, for example, on the size of collections and salaries will sometimes tell the job seekers more than can be found in an advertisement.) There is a separate section on interlibrary loan, i.e., a listing of more than 300 networks, consortia, and other cooperative groups—again, listed by state or province. A spin-off of the directory is *The Librarian's Phone Book* which lists almost all the names in the directory in alphabetical order with their libraries, cities, states, and telephone numbers. The 1981 edition includes about 51,000 phone numbers.

Special libraries receive considerably more detailed treatment in the *Directory of Special Libraries and Information Centers.* This work lists over 14,000 units which either are special libraries or have special collections, including a number of public and university libraries.

Arrangement is alphabetical by name, with a not very satisfactory subject index. (Subject headings are furnished by the libraries, and as this approach is uncontrolled, it tends to be erratic.) The second volume is the geographic-personnel index, and the third is a periodic supplement covering new material between editions. A spin-off of the basic set is the *Subject Directory of Special Libraries and Information Centers,* a five-volume work which simply rearranges the material in the basic set by subject area; e.g., volume one covers business and law libraries; volume four, social sciences and humanities libraries. Within each volume is the same material found in the basic set. The advantage is that the library may purchase a single volume for about $64 rather than invest $290 in the whole work.

Three related directories from R. R. Bowker are more likely to be used by librarians and book people than by laypersons. These are: (1) *American Book Trade Directory* (1915 to date, biennial) which lists booksellers, wholesalers, and publishers state by state and city by city, with added information on Canada and United Kingdom and Ireland. The 1980 edition included over 20,000 retail book dealers. To keep the service updated, the publisher, beginning in late 1979, provides address, telephone, and personnel changes every two months. The cost: $50 a year. (2) *Magazine Industry Market Place* (1980 to date, annual) lists the major magazine publishers with data on subject matter, personnel, and the like. There is other information and a concluding section of 20,000 addresses and telephone numbers of those listed in the main work. (3) *Literary Market Place* (1940 to date; annual; paper, $26.95), the standard in the field, gives directory-type information on over 10,000 firms directly or indirectly involved with publishing in the United States. It furnishes an answer to a frequently heard question at the reference desk: "Where can I get my novel [poem, biography, or other work] published?" Also, it is of considerable help to acquisitions librarians, as it gives fuller information on publishers than do bibliographies such as *Books in Print* or *Cumulative Book Index.* Among other things, it has a section, "Names and Numbers," which lists 17,000 executives and firms in publishing, with their addresses and phone numbers.

The *Literary Market Place* includes names of agents whom the writer might wish to contact. However, it presupposes some knowledge of the publisher and fails to answer directly the question: Does this publishing house publish fiction or poetry, or other things? For this, the beginner should turn to several much-used allied titles: *Writer's Market* (Cincinnati, Ohio: Writer's Digest, 1929 to date, annual), with a section on book publishers that includes not only directory-type information but paragraphs on types of materials wanted, royalties paid, and how copy is to be submitted. The remainder of the nearly 1000-page directory gives similar information for thousands of periodical publishers to whom free-lance writers may submit material. *The Writer's Handbook* (Boston: The Writer, Inc., 1936 to date, annual) gives some of the same information, but at least one-half of each annual volume is devoted to articles on how to write, and its listings are not as complete as those in *Writer's Market*. Writers who wish information on small presses should consult the *International Directory of Little Magazines and Small Presses* (Paradise, California: Dustbooks, 1965 to date, annual).

SUGGESTED READING

Capp, Bernard, *Astrology and the Popular Press; English Almanacs 1500–1800.* London, Faber & Faber: 1979. A scholarly history of the English almanac as a guide to trends in popular culture of the period. Useful for its lengthy bibliography.

Corbin, John, "Abiding by the Law: Legal Materials in Public Libraries," *Wilson Library Bulletin,* February 1981, pp. 419–422. Some practical advice on how to handle law questions and how to organize a popular legal collection.

Isaacson, David, "The Reference Librarian as General Fact-totem," *Wilson Library Bulletin,* April 1980, pp. 494–500. A witty, yet factual examination of the role of the reference librarian as a ready-reference person and the need to develop much wider, deeper types of reference services. Along the way the author examines some popular fact titles.

McCallum, Sue, "Legal Research for Non-Law Librarians," *Government Publications Review,* no. 3, 1979, pp. 263–274. The author discusses relevant legal publications most likely to be employed by the librarian in an academic or public library. Most emphasis is on government publications.

Robertson, Nan, "The Achievements of Women? You Could Look it Up," *The New York Times,* May 12, 1981, p. C11. A brief article which annotates some dozen reference works (primarily almanacs and handbooks) which have been published to celebrate the achievements of women.

Schell, Cathy, "Preventive Medicine: The Library Prescription," *Library Journal,* April 15, 1980, pp. 929–931. A survey of how medical information is used in various types of libraries, particularly, public libraries. The author suggests that medical library resources should be an important consideration in serving the public, which is not now sufficiently the case.

Spillman, Nancy, "Bright Ideas for Consumer Educators," *Previews,* September 1979, pp. 2–8. An annotated listing of multimedia materials (from charts to video).

Stowell, Marion, "Revolutionary Almanac Makers, . . ." *The Papers of the Bibliographical Society of America,* no. 1, 1979, pp. 41–61. A scholarly, lively discussion of the publishers of colonial American almanacs.

Taylor, Betty, "Consumer Access to Health and Legal Professional Information," *Florida Libraries,* September/October 1980, p. 8. A general discussion of the problems involved with giving information to laypersons on legal and medical questions.

Walker, Gregory, "Describing and Evaluating Library Collections," *Journal of Librarianship,* October 1978, pp. 219–231. Actually, this is a study of directories of library resources. The author considers editorial problems in compiling such a directory. In so doing, he makes many points applicable to the construction of other types of directories.

Walters, Ray, "Paperback Talk . . . The Lowdown on Facts," *The New York Times Book Review,* February 12, 1978, pp. 29, 30. A brief article on how fact books are compiled, their sales records, and their appeal to Americans.

CHAPTER EIGHT

Biographical Sources

B IOGRAPHY, as *The Oxford English Dictionary* defines it, is "the history of the lives of individual men" and—although it may shock the male who wrote this definition—women. Addressing himself to the full-length book biography, Harold Nicholson gives a further definition which seems applicable for reference work:

> A biography must be "history," in the sense that it must be accurate and depict a person in relation to his times. It must describe an "individual," will all the gradation of human character, and not merely present a type of virtue or of vice. And it must be . . . written in grammatical English and with an adequate feeling for style.[1]

Some readers delight in poring over biographical reference sources, but few of the reference works quite measure up to Nicholson's high standards. They are compilations of data which are satisfactory for locating an address, finding information on achievements, or discovering a birth or death date.

---

[1]Harold Nicholson, *Biography as an Art*, James Clifford (ed.), (New York: Oxford University Press, 1962), p. 197. For a basic history of biography, consult any major encyclopedia or the cited essay.

EVALUATION

How does the librarian know whether a biographical source is reliable? There are a number of tests.

Selection Why is a name selected (or rejected) for the various biographical reference aids? The method for the several who's who entries is discussed later, but the process is relatively easy to establish for biographical aids limited to a given subject or profession: the compiler includes all the names that qualify for the scope of the work, as in *American Men and Women of Science* or *World Authors.* In both cases, the widest net is cast to include figures and authors likely to be of interest. There are limitations, but they are so broad as to cause little difficulty for the compiler. As one moves from subject and profession to the famous, eminent, or renowned on a national or international scale, the choices become increasingly difficult.

While admittedly the choices for other than subject and professional biographical aids are relative, all the editors of reputable works do establish some objective guidelines; e.g., *Who's Who in America,* includes many "arbitrarily on account of official position." This means that a member of congress, a governor, an admiral, a general, a Nobel Prize winner, or a foreign head of government is automatically included; and numerous other categories, as well, ensure a place in the volume. The *International Who's Who* is certain to give data on members of all reigning royal families. The *Dictionary of American Biography* takes a more negative approach—one must first be dead to be included; after that requirement is met, the editor begins making selections.

Then, too, there are some automatic exclusions. In the case of subject biographical reference works, the exclusion is usually evident in the title: one does not look for poets in *Who's Who in American Art* or *American Men and Women of Science.*

There are levels of exclusiveness; it may be somewhat more difficult to get into *Who's Who in America* than *Who's Who in American Art.* For the former listing, it is a matter of "Don't call us, we'll call you" and depends on some public achievement. Others depend only on membership in a group or profession; it is difficult to stay out of such titles as *Who's Who in the United Nations* if one happens to work there, or *Who's Who in Golf* should one be a professional or a well-known amateur. A listing depends upon one's filling out forms for a given title. Failure to do so may mean failure to be included unless one is such a famous U.N. employee or golfer that the editor digs out the information.

An organization called "Who's Who Biographies," makes a

point of getting its members in as many biographical reference works as possible. Some ability is required, although just about anyone who joins the nonprofit organization is guaranteed a place in one or more biographical dictionaries.

Accepted members (hence candidates for a biographical directory) include a Brooklyn woman who is an expert on supplying winning lines for contests, a Manhattan writer and Star Trek meetings organizers and a private detective who was accepted and nominated as the group's world program director for polygraph science.[2]

Length of Entry   Once a name is selected, another question presents itself: How much space does the figure warrant? five or six lines? a page? The purpose and scope of the work may dictate at least a partial answer. The who's who data calls for a relatively brief outline or collection of facts. The biographical dictionary may be more discursive. And the essay type of work will approach the same entry in a way peculiar to its own emphasis. Regardless of form, the editor still has to make decisions about balance and length.

Authority   Biography began as an accepted form of praise; e.g., *Ecclesiastes* has the famous line, "Let us now praise famous men"; and this was the purpose of biography until well into the seventeenth century. After a period of relative candor, including the famed Boswell *Life of Johnson* and Johnson's own *Lives of the Poets,* the form returned to uniform panegyric in the Victorian nineteenth century. With the Freudian spirit of the twentieth century, praise once more gave way to reality. Truth now so much guides biographers that many famous people have stipulated that no biography should be written about them.

The development of authoritative biography is necessary to an understanding of the form, particularly when the librarian is confronted with (1) Victorian, i.e., nineteenth and early twentieth century, standard biographical works which took more pride in painting everything with rosy colors than in delivering up the truth or with (2) modern biographical outlines or even essays where the author is so devoted to the subject that the evaluation is not to be trusted.

Today the question about authority must begin with another question: Who wrote the biographical entry—an editor, the subject, an authority in the field, a secretary? In preparing almost any material except statistical information, the person who penned the entry will have had either conscious or subconscious biases. Even in a

[2]Francis X. Cline, "About New York," *The New York Times,* March 11, 1978, p. 21.

straightforward presentation of data, if the biographical subject supplied the information (the usual case with most current biographies), there may be slight understatements or exaggerations concerning age (men more often than women lie about this), education, or experience. Biographical sources relying almost entirely on individual honesty cannot be completely trusted. This leads to the next query: Have sources of information other than the subjects' own questionnaires been cited? The preface should make these two points clear.

When the source is questionable, the information should be verified in one or more other works. If a serious conflict remains which cannot be resolved, what should be done? The only solution is to attempt to trace the information through primary source material: newspapers, contemporary biographies, or articles about the individual or his or her family or friends. This undertaking involves historical research. An excellent example can be found in the recurrent arguments concerning details of Shakespeare's life and times or the famous attempt to straighten out the facts in the life of Sir Thomas Malory, author of the stories of King Arthur and his knights.

How does the librarian know if a work is truly legitimate, i.e., authoritative and based on an accurate, relatively objective selection policy? A rule of thumb will do in most cases: If the title is not listed (or minimally praised) in any of the basic bibliographies, such as Sheehy, Walford, *American Reference Books Annual,* or the current reviewing services, the flag of warning is out. Another test, based on the librarian's knowledge of publishers, is whether or not the publisher is reputable. Even the best, to be sure, make errors in judgment about what constitutes a good biographical source, but they cannot be accused of tyring to build a book on the gullibility of the subjects.

Other Points   Are there photographs? Are there bibliographies containing material both by and about the subject? Is the work adequately indexed or furnished with sufficient cross-references? (This is important when seeking individuals connected with a major figure, but who may be mentioned only as part of a larger biographical sketch.) Is the work arranged logically? The alphabetical approach is usual, although some works may be arranged chronologically by events, birth dates, periods, or areas of subject interest.

In practice, few of these evaluative tests are actually employed. If a person is well known, the problem normally is not one of locating a source but of screening out the many sources for the pertinent details. If the individual is obscure, usually any source is welcome.

SEARCHING BIOGRAPHICAL SOURCES

In determining what biographical source to search, the librarian will work from two basic beginning queries: How much of the history of an individual life does the user require, and what type of data is required? (This query is usually appropriate for a ready-reference question about address, profession, and so on.) At what level of depth and sophistication should the answer be to the essay type of question? This can be determined by the age, education, and needs of the individual user. The quantitative question will require either (1) a silhouette or simple data or (2) an essay form of answer.

This data type of question is by far the most common in the ready-reference situation. Typical queries: "What is the address and phone number of X?" "How does one spell Y's name?" "What is the age of R?" "When did Beethoven die?" Answers will be found in the familiar who's who directory-biographical dictionary sources. Approach varies with each title, but they are consistent in listing names alphabetically and, at a minimum, giving the profession and position (with or without claim-to-fame attributes) of the individual. At a maximum, these sources will give full background on the entry from birth and death dates to publications, names of children, and so on. The information is usually, although not necessarily, in outline form. It is rarely discursive or critical. The data are all.

The second major type of biographical question comes from the person who wants partial or relatively complete information on an individual. The questioner may be writing a paper, preparing a speech, or seeking critical background material. Typical queries: "How can I write a paper on Herman Melville?" "What do you have on [X], a prominent American scientist?" "Is there a book about George Washington and the cherry tree?"

Answers will be found in reference sources with an emphasis on essays (300 words to several pages in length). The reference librarian will turn to such sources as *Current Biography* and the *Dictionary of National Biography*.

INDEXES TO BIOGRAPHY

Indexes to biographical data in directories and dictionaries

> *Biography and Genealogy Master Index.* Detroit: Gale Research Company, 1980–1981, 8 vols. $575 (online, $55 an hour). First published as *Biographical Dictionaries Master Index,* 1975–1976 3 vols. Supplements, 1979, 1980.

Marquis Who's Who Publications/Index to All Books. Chicago: Marquis Who's Who, Inc., 1974, annual to date. $24.95.

Index to the Wilson Author Series. New York: The H. W. Wilson Company, 1976, 72 pp. $4.

There are two types of indexes to biography. The first, represented by *Biography and Genealogy Master Index,* is a key to over 3 million entries found in biographical dictionaries and directories such as *Who's Who in America.* The purpose is to reduce tedious searching of basic, generally current guides.

The second type of index, represented by *Biography Index* (discussed on pages 270–271), includes citations to biographies appearing in books and periodicals. The purpose is to offer a key to biographical information about persons living and dead in a wide variety of general sources.

The first type would be employed for ready reference when the data type of information is required. The second would more likely be used to seek detailed information for a paper, research project, speech, or other presentation.

For example, a user who wished to find the address of John Doe or Mary Doe would turn to the *Master Index* for sources of short data entries in the various biographical dictionaries indexed. The user who wished to write a paper on the achievements of either Doe would need a fuller entry and would turn to biographical information in books and periodicals as indicated in *Biography Index.*

Originally published (1975–1976) as *Biographical Dictionaries Master Index* in three volumes, the revised 8-volume set is an alphabetical listing of over 3 million names, keyed to entries in some 350 biographical works, such as *Who's Who in America, American Men and Women of Science, Who's Who in American Art,* and other basic sources. The majority of entries are living persons, so the work is of limited use for tracing historical figures, i.e., anyone who died before about 1980. The librarian checks for the wanted individual, finds a key to one or more of the biographical dictionaries (some people, of course, are listed several times) and then goes to the dictionary for the reference. The work is updated with annual cumulative paperbound supplements.

The publisher has issued, and will continue to issue, a number of related volumes of this type. The spin-offs draw on the same data as appear in the 8-volume set but, in each case, add just enough unique material to make the additional titles useful—at least in larger libraries.

The spin-offs include (1) *Journalist Biographies Master Index* (1979, 380 pp., $40), which keys 90,000 names from 200 sources. (2) *Theatre, Film and Television Biographies Master Index* (1979, 479 pp.), which includes some 100,000 entries from 40 biographical dictionaries. (3) *Author Biographies Master Index* (1978, 2 vols. plus supplement, 1980), which differs from the others in that it has not a few, but hundreds of both living and dead authors. The 500,000-plus entries (although not individual authors) are taken from 160 biographical works. Only a few of the books analyzed here are in the original master index. Each entry includes the author's name and dates, and a key to where the material is found. Focus is on American and English writers.[3] (4) *Children's Authors and Illustrators* (3d ed. 1980), which includes references from 100 sources and lists about 25,000 names. (5) *Writers for Young Adults* which lists about 9000 writers taken from some 265 biographical dictionaries.

Several other such aids are promised. Each in its way, is of considerable help to the harried librarian, although each, to a lesser or greater extent, duplicates listings found in the basic *Biography and Genealogy Master Index.*

All these works tend to focus on living individuals, but with the publication of *Historical Biographical Dictionaries Master Index* (1980, 1003 pp.) the publisher begins to index biographical sources of people who are dead. The approach is the same as for the other works. Here 35 standard reference titles are analyzed—from the *Dictionary of American Biography* and *Who Was Who in America* to less-known reference works. The publisher claims some 300,000 names are listed.

While some editing is attempted, most of the data in the various sets is taken directly from the biographical dictionaries, i.e., an operator simply keypunches into the computer's memory the listings, line by line, page by page from the hundreds of sources. In the resulting printout, entries are arranged alphabetically, without much attention to pseudonyms, names with prefixes and suffixes, compound surnames, changes of names, spelling variations, and so on. In most cases this is hardly a problem, but for a few names the librarian should double-check. For example, Muhammad Ali is listed also as Ali, Muhammad; Cassius Clay; and Clay, Cassius.

Following the lead of several publishers, Gale now offers the

---

[3] A related work, which includes 13 foreign language biographical sources, but only 68,000 citations from 50 books is: Patricia Havlice, *Index to Literary Biography* (Metuchen, New Jersey: Scarecrow Press, 1975, 2 vols.). It is useful as an addition to the Gale publication.

combined set of master indexes on microfiche. This is called *Bio-Base*. Using a handy reader, the librarian or user has available in alphabetical order close to 3.2 million biographical citations to over 350 biographical dictionaries and works (both published and yet to be published in hard-copy form). The cost for all of this is $600 for the microfiche—plus, of course, the cost of a reader. A supplement is sent out every year or so, at an additional cost of $275. (The 1981–82 supplement adds another 800,000 entries).

This directory is online and can be tapped through the computer terminal. Now a reference librarian need only type in the name of an individual and several sources of material on that person will be shown on a television screen or printed out.

The catch is that few libraries can afford to keep current, or even to own, the hundreds of biographical sources indexed by Gale. It is one thing to find the entry, either online or manually, quite another to tell the individual that the library does not happen to have the indexed work. Just how strongly some librarians feel about this problem is illustrated in a letter published by *American Libraries* (May, 1981, p. 275), where a librarian points out that "a good 250 of these [350] titles would not commonly be found in 90 to 95 percent of the libraries in North America." See, too, the publisher's reply in the same issue. It is an interesting debate in that it will become a more recurrent problem, i.e., more indexes and abstracts are available, but few libraries can keep up with what is indexed or abstracted.

At the other extreme, with 7500 listings for only 7 titles, is the *Index to the Wilson Author Series*. This work includes names of both living and dead writers from not only the United States but around the world. The titles indexed are discussed on pages 286–287.

The *Marquis Who's Who Publications Index* duplicates everything listed in the *Master Index*. It is an index of the 11 *Who's Who* titles discussed later in this chapter. The need for both indexes is questionable for other than libraries which treat the Marquis titles as a unit and want the index on the shelf next to the 11 titles.

Thanks to automated editing and publishing, it will be possible to issue more and more of these indexes to biographical directories and dictionaries. Historically, this type of indexing had to be done laboriously by individuals, which accounts for the lack of many indexes before the 1970s.

Indexes to biographical data in books and serials

Biography Index: A Cumulative Index to Biographical Material in Books and Magazines. New York: The H. W. Wilson Company,

1947 to date, quarterly, annual and three-year cumulations. $50.

The New York Times Obituaries Index, 1858–1968. Sanford: North Carolina: Microfilming Corporation, 1970, 1136 pp. Supplement, 1969–1978, 1980, 240 pp. $85.

The second type of biography index does not analyze short entries in directories and dictionaries but considers fuller information found in books, periodicals, and specialized sources. In this sense it is the familiar index to material in collections or in magazines.

The best-known and most often used is the *Biography Index,* a key to some 2400 periodicals and some 1000 books. The indexed biographical information may run to a paragraph or to hundreds of pages.

The *Biography Index* has some secondary uses: (1) Illustrations and portraits are indicated, and it can be used to find a picture of the subject. (2) An appended index lists the subjects by profession and occupation. The subject classification approach can be of real benefit to the reference librarian. The librarian looking for something on a banker or deep-sea diver, without the faintest idea who might qualify, will be grateful for the subject breakdown. (3) There is a checklist of the composite books—primarily collective biographies—which are analyzed, and it does have some value for the acquisitions librarian. (4) The juvenile biographies are marked in the main index and listed under a separate heading in the appended index. (5) Obituary notices from *The New York Times* are included, but this is less important now that the *Times* has its own obituaries and biographical indexes.

The New York Times Obituaries Index lists in alphabetical order names of persons who rated an obituary in the newspaper between 1858 and 1968, and 1969 to 1978 inclusive. There are a total of over 400,000 names, with reference to the notices, often of essay length, in *The New York Times.* Thanks to the worldwide coverage of the *Times,* the list is not limited to Americans and includes almost every prominent world figure who died during the period covered by the *Index.* Its secondary advantages (primary to many) are: (1) It does include less-known personalities not often found in standard biographical works; (2) the obituary often presents a summation of the reputation of the figure at the time; and (3) as each entry includes not only page and issue number but death date, it can serve as a ready-reference aid. The cutoff date is 1978, but the *Times Biographical Service* (discussed in the next section) fills the gap from 1978 on.

For those who believe, as Bruce Lockhart does, that "the object of biography is to increase self-confidence; the object of obituary notices is to increase caution," much is to be gained from Frank Roberts (comp.), *Obituaries from The Times* (London: Newspaper Archives Developments, 1975, 1979, 1981, 3 vols.). These obituaries do not equal the time span of the American work or the number of entries. About 4000 obituary notices from *The Times* of London are found here, and for only those notables who died between 1951 and 1975. As in *The New York Times,* the obituaries are international in scope, and record deaths of everyone from Stalin and Senator Joe McCarthy to Tyrone Power and Eva Peron.

UNIVERSAL AND CURRENT BIOGRAPHICAL SOURCES

Universal biographical sources include those from all parts of the world, or at least those parts selected by the editors, and normally include both living and dead personalities. The result is a compendium of relatively well known individuals.

Current sources may cover the same geographical area but narrow the scope by concentrating on people who are still active or only recently dead.

Biographical dictionaries

Webster's Biographical Dictionary, rev. ed. Springfield, Massachusetts: G. & C. Merriam Company, 1974, 1697 pp. $15.

Chamber's Biographical Dictionary, rev. ed., ed. by J. O. Thorne, Edinburgh and London: Chambers, Ltd., 1978, 1432 pp. (distributed in the United States by Two Continents). $25. Also available in a two-volume paperback edition (1978, $7.95 each), which is slightly updated to the end of 1977.

The librarian turns to a biographical dictionary when it can be assumed that the person is probably fairly well known and probably dead. The best-known of these numerous sources is *Webster's Biographical Dictionary.* Although it includes 40,000 names, approximately 80 percent of the people listed are deceased. The entries are short sketches which give most of the data found in a who's who approach. American and British subjects receive most space, with appropriate attention given to major international and historical figures. The basic problem with this work is that it has undergone only slight revisions since 1943. While useful for retrospective listings, it is less than trustworthy for current personages.

Chamber's claims only 15,000 names (in contrast with *Webster's* 400,000 entries), but this work is proof that quality will outdo quantity. It gives the same vital information found in *Webster's*, but much of it is updated in a considerably better fashion and puts particular emphasis on British and European biography. The major difference between the two is neither number nor scope, but style. *Chamber's* enjoys a unique position because its editors make a conscious effort to add some human interest and critical observations. The difference between reading *Webster's* and the British work is the difference between reading a telephone book and a book of short, clever essays. As style here is embellished with relative currency and accuracy, there is no comparison between the two.

The librarian will turn to *Chambers's* first, and failing to find the entry, will then go to *Webster's*.[4] If both fail—rather unlikely for average situations—there are other biographical dictionaries. One of the more popular in larger reference collections is *The New Century Cyclopedia of Names*, edited by C. L. Barnhart (New York: Appleton-Century-Crofts, Inc., 1954, 3 vols.). *The New Century* has over 100,000 entries for topics ranging from mythology to place names. Its wide coverage gives it a particularly valuable place in reference work. Here one finds not only standard biographical information, but data on such things as major fictional characters, historical events, opera characters, people from plays and legendary persons. The final volume includes a chronological table of world history, rulers and peoples, and genealogical information.

Essay form: General

> *Current Biography*. New York: The H. W. Wilson Company, 1940 to date, monthly except August. $22; yearbook, $24.
>
> *The New York Times Biographical Service: A Compilation of Current Biographical Information of General Interest*. New York: Arno Press, 1970 to date, monthly, loose-leaf. $85.

Current Biography is the single most popular current essay-length biographical aid in almost all types of libraries. Issued monthly, it is cumulated, often with revised sketches, into annual volumes with excellent cumulative indexing. Annual emphasis is on some 150 international personalities, primarily those in some way influencing the American scene. Articles are long enough to include all vital information about the person and are usually relatively objective. The sketches are prepared by a special staff which draws information from other biographical sources and from the person covered in the article.

---

[4]Actually, it is much faster to begin any biographical search these days with *Biography and Genealogy Master Index* or one of its numerous spin-offs.

Subjects are given the opportunity to check copy before it is published and, presumably, to approve the photograph which accompanies each sketch. Source references are cited. Obituary notices, with due reference to *The New York Times Obituaries Index,* are listed for those who at one time have appeared in the work.

Thanks to the format and rather "catchy" photographs on the cover, *Current Biography* resembles a magazine which, literally, can be read cover to cover.

Each issue includes a cumulative index to past issues of the year, and with the twelfth number, the title is published as a hard-bound yearbook. The yearbook adds a subject index by profession, useful for looking for leaders in various fields. A cumulative index to the yearbooks is issued every 10 years, with paperback cumulative indexes issued between; e.g., as of 1979 there is a hardbound index for 1940–1970 and a paperback for 1971–1979. A hardbound index is planned for 1940–1980. Another feature in the annual is a list of current "biographical references." This serves as a convenient up-to-date checklist for purchases.

The New York Times Biographical Service serves the same purpose, and usually the same audience, as *Current Biography.* The essential difference is that *Current Biography* is staff-written with source references. The *New York Times* biographies are usually written by individuals who do not cite sources. Published each month in loose-leaf form, it is a first choice for any medium-sized or large library. It includes obituaries and the "man in the news," and features stories from the drama, book, sports, and Sunday magazine section. Each sheet is a reprint of biographical material which has appeared in the *Times.* The monthly section has its own index, cumulated every six months and annually. The sketches are often reports on controversial, less-than-leader, individuals. Most of the reporting is objective.

A third aid (the other is the aforementioned *Obituaries Index*) for locating names in *The New York Times* is the *Personal Name Index to the New York Times Index* (Succasunna, New Jersey: Roxbury Data Interface, 1976 to date). This is an index to names in *The New York Times Index* (not taken directly from the newspaper itself); the basic 14-volume set covers the years 1851–1974. The first supplement is from 1975 through 1979, and other supplements are to be published every five years. It is invaluable for locating data on lesser-known figures.

Directory: Who's who form

Who's Who in America. Chicago: Marquis Who's Who, Inc., 1899 to date, biennial, $109.50.

Who's Who. London: Black, 1849 to date, annual (distributed in the United States by St. Martin's Press, Inc.). $95.

International Who's Who. London: Europa Publications Ltd.,1935 to date, annual (distributed in the United States by Gale Research Company). $90.

Other than essay-length material for student papers, the most sought-after current biographical information is of a ready-reference type, or simple data. The questions are familiar enough:How does X spell his name? What degrees does Y hold? What has Z published? Is she married?

Replies to these and similar queries are found in the familiar directory, who's who format. They vary in title, publisher, scope, and often accuracy and timeliness; but their essential purpose is the same: to present objective, usually noncontroversial facts about an individual. The approach and style are monotonously the same; most are arranged alphabetically by the name of the person, with a following paragraph of vital statistics which normally concludes with the person's address and phone number.

The who's who aids may be classified by scope as international, national, local, professional or business, religious or racial, and so on, as is usually indicated by the title.

Information is normally compiled by sending a questionnaire to the candidate, who is then free to provide as much or as little of the requested information as he or she wishes. The better publishers check the returns for flaws or downright lies. Other publishers may be content to rely on the honesty of the individual, who normally has little reason not to tell the truth, although—and this is a large "although"—some candidates for entry may construct life patterns foreign in both detail and general facts to their real lifestyles.

The American *Who's Who in America* has a long history of reliability. The forty-second edition (1982–1983) is a source for about 73,500 names of prominent American men and women, as well as a few foreigners with some influence in the United States. As the nation's current population is about 216 million, how do the editors determine who is, or who is not, to be included? The answer is complex, usually based on some outstanding achievement or excellence.

The inclusion-exclusion process is of more interest when the reputation and fame of a work, such as *Who's Who in America,* is purposefully built upon selectivity of a high order. The natural question is one of legitimacy. Is the selection of Y based on Y's desire to be included (supported by willingness to buy the volume in question or, in a few cases, literally to pay for a place in the volume), or is it based on the editor's notion of eminence, where no amount of persuasion or cash will ensure selection? All works listed here are indeed legitimate; in them, one's way to fame cannot be bought. This is not to say there is no room for argument. No one will entirely agree on all names selected or rejected in, say, *Who's Who in America.*

On balance the selection is adequate, if not brilliant. The data for entrants varies in length but not in style, as each fills out a standard form requesting basic information, from date of birth to education to achievements to address. The form is used to compose the entry, and a proof of the entry is sent to the individual for double-checking.

Beginning in 1978, the editors opened a new avenue with requests that about 1800 people add "Thoughts on My Life" to the mechanical data. Commenting on this new addition, a critic writes:

> *Lives of great men almost invariably remind us of other great men. Altruism is commended, luck is explained as the product of industry, people are alleged to be more important than things, God gets credit for ceaseless wonders and life itself is hard and demanding. . . .* [Some humor creeps in.] *Victor Borge suggested that part of his good fortune stemmed from his faults, of which the greatest is modesty.*[5]

After a subject's death, membership in *Who's Who in America* continues in *Who Was Who in America* (Chicago: Marquis Who's Who, Inc. 1942 to date, irregular). A historical volume covers 1607–1896, then there are volumes for 1897–1942, 1943–1950, 1951–1960, 1961–1968, 1969–1973, and 1974–1978. Now the retrospective volumes appear about every four years. The benefit of this set for reference work is that many people originally listed no longer are famous enough to be listed in the standard biographical dictionaries. *Who Was Who* may be used to trace difficult-to-find individuals who have virtually sunk out of sight.

One work which would be unnecessary if women were not treated as the second sex is *Who's Who of American Women* (Chicago: Marquis Who's Who, Inc., 1959 to date). A biennial dictionary of notable living American females, it follows the same general pattern as all the Marquis works. The ninth edition includes 20,000 women's names. The editor's breakdown of 1000 sketches indicated that, according to occupation, a woman's chances to earn an entry were best if she was a club, civic, or religious leader (9.6 percent of all

---

[5]Israel Shenker, "Who's Who Talks about What's What," *The New York Times,* February 15, 1978, p. C1.

listings) and least if she was a composer (0.4 percent of the entries). Librarians make up a healthy 5.2 percent of the biographies.[6]

Who's Who was first published in Britain on January 15, 1849, some 50 years before there were enough prominent Americans to make a volume possible here. During its first 47 years, *Who's Who* was a slim book of some 250 pages which listed members of the titled and official classes. In 1897, it became a biographical dictionary, and the 1972–1973 edition is close to 4000 pages. Selection is no longer based on nobility but on "personal achievement or prominence." Most entries are English, but it does include some notables from other countries. And in the past decade, it has put more and more emphasis on prominent scholars and professional people as well as political and industrial leaders.

Depending on size and type of audience served, most American public, university, and college libraries will have *Who's Who in America* and possibly *Who's Who*—"possibly" because the better-known figures apt to be objects of inquiry in *Who's Who* are covered in the *International Who's Who*, which opens with a section of names of "reigning royal families," then moves to the alphabetic listing of some 12,000 to 15,000 brief biographies of the outstanding men and women of our time. The range is wide and takes in those who are prominent in international affairs, government, administration, diplomacy, science, medicine, law, finance, business, education, religion, literature, music, art, and entertainment. Also, Marquis issues *Who's Who in the World* (4th ed.; Chicago: Marquis Who's Who, 1978), which lists 20,000 names often duplicated in the *International Who's Who*.

Almost every country in the world has a similar set of "who's who" directories, that is, a basic work for the living famous and a set for the famous who have died. Most of these are published by reputable firms listed in the standard bibliographies such as *Guide to Reference Books* and *Guide to Reference Materials*. For example, there is *Canadian Who's Who* (Toronto: University of Toronto Press, 1910 to date, every three years). While this, as many such works, began as an irregular publication, it is now on a three-year schedule. The last

---

[6]Marquis issues a number of regional who's who works which follow the same arrangement and principles of *Who's Who in America*, differing only in that the coverage is limited to a region and includes many names not found in the basic work. Each biennial volume averages some 20,000 entries, which clearly indicate whether or not they are duplicated in *Who's Who in America*. These supplementary titles include *Who's Who in the Midwest*, 1949 to date; *Who's Who in the South and Southwest*, 1950 to date; *Who's Who in the West*, 1949 to date; and *Who's Who in the East*, 1943 to date. All these are indexed in Marquis's own index and the *Biography and Genealogy Master Index*.

volume, issued in 1979, has approximately 7000 entries. There is another similar Canadian work, as is frequently the case in western countries. This is *Who's Who in Canada* (Toronto: International Press, 1922 to date, biennial) which has considerable overlap with the other title.

RETROSPECTIVE BIOGRAPHICAL SOURCES

Essay form

Dictionary of American Biography. New York: Charles Scribner's Sons, 1974, 11 vols. Supplements, 1977 to date, irregular. The set, $695.

Dictionary of National Biography. Edited by Leslie Stephen and Sidney Lee, 1885 to 1901; reissue, London: Oxford University Press, 1938, 21 vols. and supplement; 2d to 7th supplements, 1912–1971. Base set, $550; Supplements 2–7, $55 each.

National Cyclopaedia of American Biography. New York: James T. White Company, 1892–(in progress).

Notable American Women 1607–1950. A Biographical Dictionary. Edited by Edward T. James. Cambridge, Massachusetts: Harvard University Press, 1971, 3 vols. $75; paper, $35; supplement, 1980, $35.

The proper use of these national, retrospective biographical aids depends on the librarian's or user's recognizing the nationality of the figure in question and the fact that all entrants are deceased. When the nationality is not known, it will save time to first check *Biography and Genealogy Master Index* and its companion for historical figures *Historical Biographical Dictionaries Master Index*. Where neither is available, one might turn first to a biographical dictionary, encyclopedia, or *Biography Index*. The latter may prove particularly productive when the name cannot be found in any of the sources noted.

The *Dictionary of American Biography* (or the *DAB*, as it is usually called), with its supplements, covers some 17,084 figures who have made a major contribution to American life. Almost all are Americans, but there are a few foreigners who significantly contributed to our history. (In this case, they had to have lived in the United States for some considerable length of time.) Furthermore, no British officers "serving in America after the colonies declared their independence" are included. A separate index gives a subject, contributor, birthplace, topic, and occupations entry to the set and its supplements.

Some 3000 scholarly contributors add their distinctive styles and viewpoints to the compilation. As a consequence, most of the entries —which vary from several paragraphs to several pages—can be read as essays rather than as a list of connected, dry facts.[7]

As of 1980 there were six supplements to the main set. Fortunately, there is an index in the sixth volume which covers all the supplements.

The *Dictionary of National Biography* (or *DNB*) is the model for the *DAB;* and having learned one set, the librarian can handle the other without difficulty. The *DNB*, approximately twice the size of the *DAB*, includes entries on over 32,000 deceased "men and women of British or Irish race who have achieved any reasonable measure of distinction in any walk of life." It also includes early settlers in America and "persons of foreign birth who have gained eminence in this country." The original set, edited by Leslie Stephen, Virginia Woolf's father, includes short to long signed articles with bibliographies. Aside from the scope, it can be used in much the same way and for many of the same reasons as the *DAB*.

Supplements are infrequently issued for both sets. The policy is best explained by the publisher of the *DAB:*

> *It is the editorial policy of the Dictionary to allow a sufficient lapse of time between the death of the subject and any attempt to write a just and considered appraisal of his life and contribution to our national history. Therefore, supplements are issued when deemed appropriate.*

An invaluable historical source, the *DAB* (like related titles) can equally be employed for several purposes. In contrasting the intellectual qualities of Boston's founders with the mercantile drive of the Philadelphia Quakers one social commentator made his point by selecting 50 "first families" from each of the two cities, and then examining which individuals are listed in the *DAB*.

> *The Brahmins take the lead with 188 listings to Philadelphia's 146. Even at the outset, Boston has a higher index of accomplishment: an edge of 29 percent, to be precise. A careful count of the 50,129 lines in the entries for both sets of families discloses that the Bostonians average 183 lines each and the Philadelphians 108, raising Boston's margin to 69*

[7]Smaller libraries will find the *Concise Dictionary of American Biography* (3d ed.; New York: Charles Scribner's Sons, 1980) a substitute for the large set. However, it reduces the primary essays to little more than sketches of highlights of a person's life and is more properly suited to ready-reference work than to research. There are some medium-to-long essay entries which are almost the same as in the master set, but the selection is limited to better-known figures who usually can be found in numerous other sources.

percent. Only 54 percent of first family Philadelphians attended college, and most who did went out of town. In contrast, 81 percent of the Boston group matriculated. They, too, went out of town—but only across the Charles River. Professor Baltzell arrays these and other figures with a light, engaging touch. His numbers evoke subtleties and shadings without mathematical gymnastics. Civilized sociology, in short.[8]

There are numerous national versions of the *DNB* and *DAB*. For example: *Dictionary of Canadian Biography*[9] (Toronto: University of Toronto Press, 1966 to date) is an ongoing chronological set with critical essays on major Canadians. People who lived and died between 1000 and 1700 are in the first volume, between 1701 and 1740 in the second, and 1771 to 1800 in a fifth (issued in 1979). Eventually the set will have biographical articles for all major Canadian figures who have died within the past decade or so. It is an interesting venture on several points: (1) It is one of the few sets which is arranged chronologically, not alphabetically by name. Within each time span, of course, the names are alphabetical. (2) It is published out of sequence. After Volume 3 which covers 1741 to 1770, the publisher jumped ahead to publish Volume 9 (death dates 1861 to 1870) in 1976 and Volume 11 (death dates 1881 to 1890) in the early 1980s. The twelfth volume will complete the nineteenth century. The total set is expected to be finished in about 20 years.

Prior to the highly scholarly approach of the *DNB*, *DAB*, and other national works of the twentieth century, there was no dearth of essay-type biographical works. The other biographical essay-type reference titles are now much dated and are used chiefly for hard-to-find retrospective biographies. In the United States, the most famous is *Appleton's Cyclopedia of American Biography* (New York: Appleton-Century-Crofts, Inc., 1887 to 1900, 7 vols., reprinted in 1968 by Gale Research Company). Before the *DAB*, this was favored in many American libraries, and it still has value for biographies not included in the *DAB* and other standard sources. There are some 20,000 short to quite long signed articles dealing with Americans and foreign-born

[8]Andrew Hacker, "Ministers and Merchants," *The New York Times Book Review*, March 9, 1980, p. 7. Hacker is reviewing E. D. Baltzell's *Puritan Boston and Quaker Philadelphia* (New York: The Free Press, 1980).

[9]Not to be confused with *The Macmillan Dictionary of Canadian Biography* (4th ed. Toronto: Macmillan of Canada, 1978) which is frequently updated. This includes about 5000 sketches of Canadians who died before 1976. Most descriptions are short, running from 100 to 600 words. Although there are some factual errors, the coverage is good and the work is used in parallel with the more ambitious *Dictionary* described above.

persons close to the American scene. Except for the bias of the writer, the work is generally quite high in its accuracy. However, "generally" is used advisedly, because *Appleton's* is a literary curiosity and not always very scholarly. There are, for example, some 47 sketches of people invented by the contributors. Authors were paid by space and made the most of it. The nonexistent Bernhard Huhne is credited with the discovery of the California coast; another fictitious character is a French epidemiologist who was supposed to have combated cholera in South America some 50 years before the disease reached that continent. It is indexed in *Historical Biographical Dictionaries Master Index.*

Still another variety of the *DNB* and the *DAB* is the *National Cyclopaedia of American Biography.* The work contains sketches of over 50,000 Americans and is particularly strong on American business-persons and industrialists. (Most of the entrants are deceased.) This work was and continues to be more involved with the subject's ego than with the person's true place in history. The facts are usually correct, but there is a definite bias to make the person look as noteworthy as possible. Hence, except for extremely famous person-ages, the average entry is closer to the type of oration heard at a funeral service than to the entries read in the *DAB*. The articles, which vary in length from one-half column to several pages, are prepared by the publisher's staff. Information is based on questionnaires, inter-views, and data obtained from relatives. The gathering process leaves little latitude for criticism of the subject.

Despite the method of gathering biographical data, the *National Cyclopaedia*—and other members of the genre—is still useful for locating information on less-known Americans. A short sketch of an Ohio banker's life may prove the key to solving a historical problem or, at a more mundane level, serve the curious who are attempting to trace roots of a family tree. Perhaps fitting to the focus, the arrange-ment of the *National Cyclopaedia* is arbitrary and complicated.

None of the material is in alphabetical order, and the more than 60 volumes include several completed sets and sets in progress. The problem is solved by the separate work, *Index: The National Cyclopedia of American Biography* (Clifton, New Jersey: James T. White & Co., 1979). This is updated about every nine years, and the latest indexes the complete set until 1979. Only "current series" volumes issued after that date must be searched individually. Also, the library with *Historical Biographical Dictionaries Master Index* will have access to the *National Cyclopedia* entries to 1979.

Notable American Women includes 1359 biographies of subjects who died prior to 1950, and the supplement adds 442 who died between 1951 and 1975. Inclusion is based on their "lives and careers [having] had significant impact on American life in all fields of thought and action."[10] The long, signed biographies are similar to those in the *DAB* and *DNB,* and the author of each entry has special knowledge of the subject. In explaining who was included or excluded, the editors noted that the usual test of inclusion—being the wife of a famous man—was not considered. (The only exception is the inclusion of the wives of American Presidents.) Once more, the domestic skills of a woman were seldom considered, and no moral judgments as to a female's being a criminal or an adventuress were used to exclude a name. There is an excellent 33-page introduction, which gives a historical survey of the role of women in American life; there is also an index of individuals grouped by occupations.

Several reviewers of the supplement note that the dominant experience for women who died between 1951 and 1975 was to win the vote for women. Close to 40 women are identified as suffragists, more than any other category except writers.

PROFESSIONAL AND SUBJECT BIOGRAPHIES

The importance of biography to almost everyone from the researcher to the layperson has not escaped publishers. Consequently, almost every publisher's list will include biographical works, from individual biographies to collective works to special listings for individuals engaged in a profession. The increase in the number of professions (almost every American claims to be a professional of sorts), coupled with the growth in education, has resulted in a proliferation of specialized biographical sources.

The reliability of some works is questionable, primarily because almost all (and sometimes all) the information is supplied directly to the editor or publisher by the subject. Little or no checking is involved except when there is a definite question or the biographical sketch is evaluative. Entries tend to be brief, normally giving the name, birth date, place of birth, education, particular "claim to fame," and address. There are rare exceptions to this brief form. The H. W. Wilson Company series on authors features rather long, discursive essays. Most biographical works devoted to a subject or profession have mercifully short entries, however.

---

[10]The necessity for the work may be explained by statistical data; e.g., of the 15,000 names in the *DAB*, only 750 are women. For example, there are some 74 librarians listed, but only six are women: Mary Fairchild, Mary Isom, Mary Plummer, Katharine Sharp, and Mary Wood. The compiler evidently had a weakness for Marys.

The primary value of the specialized biographical work is as a

1. Source of address.
2. Source of correct spelling of names and titles.
3. Source of miscellaneous information for those considering the person for employment or as an employer or as a guest speaker, or for a number of other reasons.
4. Valuable aid to the historian or genealogist seeking retrospective information, if maintained for a number of years.

Following are examples of professional and subject sources. The examples touch only the periphery of a truly large field. Again, Slocum's *Biographical Dictionaries* should be consulted for the range of this type of biographical aid. When conducting a search for a specific individual, it is usually faster to begin with *Biography and Genealogy Master Index* or one of its spin-offs.

Art

Who's Who in American Art. New York: R. R. Bowker Company, 1935 to date, biennial. $50. (Publication period varies.)

Limited to living artists of both the United States and Canada, this is the standard *Who's Who* guide in the field. Among the 10,000 entries are not only artists but persons in related areas from executives of museums and foundations to craftspeople and even collectors. Standard biographical information is given for each entry. Useful bibliographies after many of the entries include works by and about the subjects. These are two indexes: a geographical index and an index of specialty.

Selection for entry, according to the Jacques Cattell Press which now edits the volume, is in the hands of a 12-person committee made u¢of directors and members of national art associations. In order to be considered, the artist must have had a local or international exhibit and show signs of a professional approach to art—in this case, often (although not always) the ability to sell work. The volume has the added advantage of being updated with each new edition, and the revision usually is substantial.

The best general place to look for a biography of a famous living or dead artist is the *Master Index* or general encyclopedia or such current essay sources as *Current Biography*. The *Dictionary of American Biography* has numerous long essays on dead American artists. And, once again, a reminder that a standard index to periodicals, such as *Art Index,* is a likely place· to find all the information needed for anyone but the most demanding expert.

The two "classics" in the field are Daniel Mallet's *Index of Artists* . . . (New York: R. R. Bowker Company, 1935, 493 pp.; supplement, 1940, 319 pp.) and Ulrich Thieme's *Allgemeines Lexikon der Bildenden Kunstler* . . . (Leipzig: Seemann, 1907–1950, 37 vols.).

Education

Directory of American Scholars. 7th ed. New York: R. R. Bowker Company, 1978, 4 vols. $175.

Biographical Dictionary of American Educators. Westport, Connecticut: Greenwood Press, 1978, 3 vols. $95.

The *Directory of American Scholars*, a standard work in larger libraries, lists close to 40,000 teachers and research-related individuals in the humanities. The brief, who's who type of entries are arranged alphabetically but divided into various volumes, e.g., history; English, speech and drama; foreign language, linguistics and philology; and philosophy, religion, and law. A breakdown by state or province is provided, which, in turn, is subdivided by city. The final volume has a single alphabetical listing of all names in the previous volumes.

A related work is the two-volume *National Faculty Directory* (Detroit: Gale Research Company, 1970 to date, annual), which lists about 500,000 teachers in junior colleges, colleges, and universities in the United States and Canada. Information is brief: name, department, institution, and address. See, also, *American Men and Women of Science* discussed later in this chapter.

A retrospective, essay-type biographical approach to American educators from the seventeenth to the twentieth century is offered in the *Biographical Dictionary*. Slightly over 1600 people are considered, most of them dead, although anyone over 60 at the time of the edition might be considered for inclusion. While most of these people can be found in other sources, often in more detail, the set has the convenience of having the material in one convenient place. Added features help too, e.g., listings by birth places and dates of all those in the three volumes, listed by states in which the individual worked, fields of specialization, and a chronology of major events in American education.

When seeking both information about an academic's address and recent publications, one might use the *Current Bibliographic Directory of the Arts & Sciences* (Philadelphia: Institute for Scientific Information, 1978 to date, annual). Drawing from entries in its three citation indexes, the publisher lists names and addresses of authors who published during the year covered. Depending as it does on only the three indexes, the work is not complete, although useful at least as a backup for standard directories. Also, when available online the citation indexes may be searched for names.

Government

For a discussion of sources of information on government personnel, see the section "Government Directories" in the previous chapter, and Chapter 11, Government Documents.

Librarianship

> *Who's Who in Library and Information Services.* Chicago: American Library Association, 1982. Appx. $150.
>
> *Dictionary of American Library Biography.* Littleton, Colorado: Libraries Unlimited, Inc., 1978, 596 pp. $65.

Short directory-type biographical entries for American and Canadian librarians (as well as information scientists, trustees, educators, archivists, subject specialists, and so on) will be found in *Who's Who in Library and Information Services.* Due for publication in 1982, this will replace the still useful *Biographical Dictionary of Librarians in the United States and Canada* (5th ed. Chicago: American Library Association, 1970, 1268 pp.). The new title will follow much the same type of entry form, i.e., the typical short directory entry of name, education, previous and current positions, mailing address, and the like. The biographical information was obtained by questionnaires completed by some 18,000 entrants.

Meanwhile, the *American Library Directory* is at least a good way of checking who works where, although it does not give specific biographical information.

Thoroughly researched biographies of over 300 outstanding American librarians and other figures in United States library history are the scope of the *Dictionary of American Library Biography.* The major difference between this and the *American Library Directory* is this: Entrants must be quite dead to be included. Also, it contains essays rather than short directory-type data.

> *Most of the biographies range from approximately 1000 to 6000 words in length, presumably relating to importance. Using this formula, the Big Six are, in descending order, Melvil Dewey, William Frederick Poole, John Shaw Billings, Charles Evans, Charles Ammi Cutter, and John Cotton Dana. Near runners-up include Harry Miller Lydenberg, Ernest*

*Cushing Richardson, Charles Clarence Williamson, Wilberforce Eames,
and Edwin Hatfield Anderson. This ranking will not have universal
endorsement; nor would any other ranking.*[11]

Literature

World Authors, 1950–1970. New York: The H. W. Wilson Company, 1975, 1594 pp. $60. Supplement: *World Authors 1970–1975*,
1979, 900 pp. $40.
Contemporary Authors. Detroit: Gale Research Company, 1962 to
date, annual. $58.

There are biographical essay collections for many subject areas.
One of the most often consulted concerns writers and writing.
Students use the library often for information on specific authors for
class reports. When the author is well known, there is little difficulty.
A good encyclopedia will give information, which can be supple-
mented by literature handbooks and periodical articles.

Another place to check where to find information on a dead or
living author is the aforementioned *Author Biographies Master Index*
which alphabetically lists 400,000 persons, with keys to information
about them in 140 biographical sources. Lacking this, the same
publisher's *Biography and Genealogy Master Index* is almost as useful for
living writers. Most of the basic sources listed here are in one or both
of the indexes.

The best-known series on authors is edited by Stanley J. Kunitz
and issued by the Wilson Company. They are useful because they
include not only the essential biographical information but also
bibliographies of works by and about the author. The source of much
of the material is the author, if living, or careful research if the author
is deceased. Some of the entries are printed almost verbatim as
written by the author and are entertaining reading in their own right.

An example of the series is *World Authors 1950–1970*, edited by
John Wakeman, with Stanley Kunitz as a consultant. International in
scope, the alphabetically arranged volume includes material on 959
authors, most of whom came to prominence between 1950 and 1970
or, for one reason or another, were not included in previous volumes.
Entries run from 800 to 1600 words, with a picture of the writer and a
listing of published works as well as major bio-bibliographies. The

[11]Robert Harlan (review), *Journal of American Librarianship*, January 1979, p. 457.

style is informative, and about half the biographies include autobiographical essays.

Related titles in the H. W. Wilson series are *Twentieth Century Authors,* 1942, and the *Supplement,* 1955. Until publication of *World Authors,* these two titles were the basic sources of "current" information on writers. They now may be used to supplement *World Authors.* For deceased writers, Wilson has five author titles: *Greek and Latin Authors, 800 B.C.–A.D. 1000,* 1980; *American Authors, 1600–1900,* 1938; *European Authors, 1000–1900,* 1967; *British Authors before 1800,* 1952; *British Authors of the Nineteenth Century,* 1936. All these follow the style of *World Authors* and, except for Greek authors, are indexed in the *Index to the Wilson Author Series* mentioned earlier.

In late 1979 *World Authors 1970/1975* was published. Compiled by Wakeman, it consists of biographical sketches of some 350 writers, most new to the series and not found in the former volume. "Nearly one-fifth of the authors have provided autobiographical articles. These have been reproduced without alteration." Critical comments usually written by specialists, are included with articles.

The Wilson series leaves a serious gap, in that the volumes are revised infrequently and do not offer access to newer writers, i.e., of the past five to ten years. Also, the Wilson works disregard authors of more ephemeral titles. Here *Contemporary Authors* is of assistance.

Almost any published American writer is included in the *Contemporary Authors* volumes; the qualifications according to a publicity release by the publisher are:

> *The author must have had at least one book published by a commercial, risk publisher or a university press within the last three or four years. . . . Novelists, poets, dramatists, juvenile writers, writers of nonfiction in the social sciences or the humanities are all covered.*

In fact, just about anyone who has published anything (this side of a vanity or a technical book) is listed. And in late 1977 the publisher went a step further, expanding coverage to include newspaper and television reporters, columnists, editors, syndicated cartoonists, screenwriters, and just about anyone in the media.

The information is gathered from questionnaires sent to the authors and arranged in data form—personal facts; career data; writings; and "sidelights," which includes discursive remarks about the author and his or her work.

As of 1981, the various volumes included about 61,000 contemporary writers. This makes *Contemporary Authors* the most comprehensive biographical source of its type. Each volume has a cumulative index to the whole set. Beginning in 1981, the publisher started to revise the set with publication of *Contemporary Authors . . . New Revision Series*. Essentially a revision of major entries, it requires four pages of prefatory material to explain, and even then the explanation is far from clear. Most libraries will do well to stay with the original set.

Science

> *American Men and Women of Science*. 14th ed. New York: R. R. Bowker Company, 1979, 8 vols. $385.
>
> *Dictionary of Scientific Biography*. New York: Charles Scribner's Sons, 1970–1980, 16 vols. $695.

Approximately 132,000 men and women are listed in an abbreviated who's who fashion in the R. R. Bowker directory. Some 65 scientific disciplines in the physical and biological sciences determine the subject scope. Teachers and scientists and technologists active in government, industry, business, foundations, and so on, in the United States and Canada are included. Entry is alphabetical and there are discipline and geographic location indexes in the final volume. Criteria for inclusion are fairly broad, although something more is required than simply being employed. The committee looks for people with achievement in research, publications, position, and the like.

A related work is *American Men and Women of Science: Social and Behavioral Sciences*. 13th ed. (New York: R. R. Bowker Company, 1978, 1545 pp.). This single volume follows the same pattern as the larger set, listing about 25,000 names.

International in scope, the *Dictionary of Scientific Biography* concentrates on dead, famous scientists from all periods and countries. The work is called monumental by many. It took 17 years to complete, and not only are some 6000 notables covered, but the reader is given a history of science from antiquity to the mid-twentieth century. Most entries are two or three pages, are critical, and highlight the individual's contributions. Several entries (Louis Pasteur, Isaac Newton) run over 50 pages. Fortunately, the material is written with the educated layperson in mind, and most of it is comprehensible to the nonexpert.

The last two volumes are of particular interest to reference librarians. Volume 15 features a series of essays on aspects of the history of science in nonWestern countries. (A criticism of the set is the concentration on western science, and the editors tried to offset this with the fifteenth volume.) The index volume has more than 75,000 topics. Each topic has reference to one or more biographies. The result is a sweeping view of anatomy, blood, fermentation, radiation, and so on as seen through the eyes of the scientists discussed.

SUGGESTED READING

Bernstein, Jeremy, "Essentials," *The New Yorker,* June 16, 1980, pp. 117–121. A loving review of the *Dictionary of Scientific Biography.* The popular writer shows that some reference works are not only useful in the library but fascinating as literary and imaginative contributions. See, too, the detailed review of the same set by A. Rupert Hall in the *Times Literary Supplement,* November 28, 1980, p. 1367. Hall also examines the joys and griefs of the *DNB* and *DAB.*

Gittings, Robert, *The Nature of Biography.* London: Heineman, 1978. A brief description of the history of the biographical form. The author is the biographer of Keats and Hardy, among others.

Lefkowitz, Mary, "The Mythical and the Memorable," *Times Literary Supplement,* August 8, 1980, p. 893. This detailed review of *Greek and Latin Authors* (H. W. Wilson, 1980) points out the problems of trying to write biography when "nothing can be known about the lives of many of the most important ancient authors."

MacShane, Frank, "Writing Biographies," *Columbia Library Columns,* May 1981, pp. 17–27. A skilled author of biography explains why their writing "is a curious occupation." The slim edge between fact and possible fiction is stressed. See, too, a related item: Jo Carr "What Do We Do About Bad Biographies?" *School Library Journal,* May 1981, pp. 19–22.

Olney, James (ed.), *Autobiography.* Princeton, New Jersey: Princeton University Press, 1980. A selection of essays considering the problems that arise in writing and reading an autobiography. Both the practical and theoretical contributions go a long way to explain the difficulty with biographical sources, no matter how limited, which rely on information directly from the subject of the biographical sketch.

Ricker, Ann, "Who's Who in America," *Reference Services Review,* October/December 1980, pp. 7–13. A summary of the history of the service as well as an explanation of how today's volumes are prepared. Note, too, the bibliography which covers the major articles and books on this famous work.

"What's What With 'Who's Whos,'" *The New York Times,* November 11, 1979, pp. E1, E11; the story of the frankly commercial publishers of various high school versions of Who's Who. According to the story, one in four high school students buys a simple listing in one of the books.

CHAPTER NINE

Dictionaries[1]

BAFFLED BY A SPELLING, a definition, or possibly how to use a word correctly, people may turn to a dictionary. Publishers say the number of persons using dictionaries is increasing. Multiplication of printed materials, the coining of new words, a focus on popular culture, a more highly educated public—these are some of the explanations given for the renewed interest in the dictionary.

The reference librarian knows dictionaries are the first place to turn for spelling, meaning, pronunciation and syllabication (word division). A dictionary should also indicate etymology; major place names (with a clear indication of whether the entry represents a river, a mountain, or other geographical feature); major personal names from history, mythology, and the Bible; foreign terms; phrases; synonyms and antonyms; abbreviations; and general slang terms, clearly marked. Some dictionaries include types of information almost encyclopedic, and most have illustrations.

There are other, less apparent, uses. As many dictionaries include quotations to trace either the meaning or the history of a word, one may use the key word of a quotation to trace its source,

---

[1]The term "dictionary" often is used by publishers when a reference work is organized alphabetically. Technically the terminology is correct, but for general use it can be somewhat confusing; e.g., the *Dictionary of National Biography* and the *Dictionary of Scientific Biography* have nothing to do with definitions but everything to do with biographical sketches.

when a book of quotations is not available or all such sources have been exhausted. For example, in *Webster's Dictionary of Synonyms,* a searcher for the source of the quotation "That's the way I've gone through life. Experience has never put a chill upon my warm-heartedness," would look under "warmhearted" and find a mark indicating the reader should turn from "warmhearted" to "tender" for the full reference. There it is found to be by Charles Dickens. A good historical dictionary will also indicate the first time a word was probably employed. Using *The Oxford English Dictionary,* it may be established that the British India Office first mentioned "punch" in 1620.

A dictionary is to be used to define not only words we do not know but words we think we know. The most difficult words to define are not the abstract or the technical, but the words associated with everyday speech or writing. For example, without a dictionary, try to explain the meaning of "door" or "be" or "in."

Keeping up with the automation boom, several companies are busy at work on electronic dictionaries. While not yet totally operational, these dictionaries allow the storage of some 50,000 to 1 million words. When perfected, the word processing systems will display the correct spelling of any needed word, and/or actually correct the spelling as the typist enters material.

Meanwhile, for the decades ahead most libraries will continue to be a source of printed dictionaries.

Scope[2]

The public is apt to think of dictionaries in only one category, but they cover almost every interest. Categorization usually is reduced to (1) general English-language dictionaries, which include unabridged titles (i.e., those with over 265,000 entries) and desk or collegiate dictionaries (from 130,000 to 180,000 entries)—these are for both adults and children; (2) historical or etymological dictionaries, which show the history of a word from date of introduction to the present; (3) foreign-language dictionaries, which are bilingual in that they give the meanings of the words of one language in another language; (4) subject dictionaries which concentrate on the definition of words in a given area, such as science and technology; and (5) "other" dictionaries, including almost everything from abbreviations to slang and

[2]Annie Brewer, *Dictionaries, Encyclopedias, and Other Word Related Books,* 2d ed. (Detroit: Gale, 1979. 2 vols.) includes more than 25,000 titles in a less-than-satisfactory arrangement; but the compilation at least indicates the number of both English and non-English-language dictionaries and related titles. See, too: *International Bibliography of Specialized Dictionaries.* 6th ed. New York: K. G. Saur, 1980.

proper usage. For example, a library not only will have on its shelves the standard *Webster's Third New International* and the usual desk, foreign-language, and subject dictionaries, but also may include such titles as *The Misspeller's Dictionary, Funk & Wagnalls Crossword Puzzle Word Finder,* and *The Poet's Manual and Rhyming Dictionary.* These are only isolated examples of "other" or specialized dictionaries for particular groups and interests.

Compilation

How is a dictionary compiled from the written and spoken words that are its source?

In the beginning, it was basically an individual effort. Dr. Johnson, for example, worked alone, although he did have six assistants for clerical duties. He wrote all the definitions himself, and Boswell explains:

> *The words, partly taken from other dictionaries and partly supplied by himself, having been first written down with spaces left between them, he delivered in writing their etymologies, definitions, and various significations. The authorities were copied from the books themselves.*[3]

Today, the smaller publishers freely copy other dictionaries. They begin by an out-and-out borrowing of words from a dictionary that is no longer copyrighted. More conscientious publishers then hire free-lance lexicographers to make a minimum number of corrections and additions. Others, some of whose handiwork are the dictionaries on display in some supermarkets or low-priced pocket dictionaries, merely borrow without benefit of any editing.

A curious feature of the second edition of *Webster's Unabridged* was the inclusion of a "ghost word." The word "dord" was simply an error on the part of an overzealous clerk, which resulted in its inclusion as a loose synonym for density. After the error was discovered, the publishers decided to keep it in the dictionary for a few years in the hope that another publisher might pick it up and be caught as a plagiarist. The word later was eliminated, and there is no record of whether or not it served its purpose.

---

[3]*Boswell's Life of Johnson,* ed. by G. B. Hill (New York: Bigelow, Brown & Co., n.d.), vol. 1, pp. 217–218. For a detailed description of how Johnson edited and wrote the dictionary, see the extremely well written, and unfortunately last, book by James L. Clifford. *Dictionary Johnson* (New York: McGraw-Hill Book Company, 1979). See, particularly, chapters 4 and 9. The dictionary was reprinted in 1980 by Arno Press: for a review of the reprint (i.e., comments on the original dictionary), see Whitney Balliett's delightful review in *The New Yorker,* July 14, 1980, pp. 92–96.

Plagiarism is not unknown, then, in the dictionary business; but a certain amount of guidance from other dictionaries is legitimate. Dr. Johnson checked previous works to ascertain what might or might not be included in his dictionary, and much the same procedure is used by all compilers today. Smaller versions of "unabridged" works, such as *Webster's New Collegiate Dictionary,* are common.

EVALUATION

For those who seek to evaluate dictionaries, the first rule is not to expect any dictionary to be perfect. Dr. Johnson said, "Dictionaries are like watches: the worst is better than none, and the best cannot be expected to go quite true." There is no perfect dictionary and there never will be until such time as the language of a country has become completely static—an event as unlikely as the discovery of a perpetual-motion mechanism. Language is always evolving because of the addition of new words and the change in meaning of older words. No single dictionary is sufficient. Each has its good points, each its defects.

The second rule should be self-evident, but rarely is is followed: Consult the preface and explanatory notes at the beginning of a dictionary. The art of successfully using a dictionary, or any other reference book, requires an understanding of how it is put together. This is important because of the dictionary's constant use of shortcuts in the form of abbreviations, various methods of indicating pronunciation, and grammatical approaches.

The best single source of evaluation of dictionaries is Kenneth Kister's *Dictionary Buying Guide* (New York: R. R. Bowker Company, 1977. 358 pp.). Following the same general style as his *Encyclopedia Buying Guide,* it gives data on some 58 general English-language dictionaries; evaluates 60 children's works; and has briefer notes on 225 special-purpose titles, such as rhyming and slang dictionaries. The work begins with an intelligent and lucid guide to evaluation, i.e., an essay on "Choosing the Right Dictionary." This seven-page summary is followed by comparative charts of the primary dictionaries. Kister not only points out the good and bad points of a title but frequently compares works of a similar type. A required guide for libraries, it may be used by both librarians and the general public, and will help anyone looking for objective advice.[4]

---

[4]See Kister's detailed and helpful article: "Cheap Words: A Paperback Dictionary Roundup," *Library Journal,* November 15, 1979, pp. 2417–2421.

Ongoing reviews of popular dictionaries are found in the general review media, from *The New York Times Book Review* to *Choice, Library Journal, RQ,* and the *Wilson Library Bulletin.* For detailed notices, the "reference and Subscription Books Reviews" in *Booklist* remain the best source. Dictionaries are frequently considered, and from time to time there is a summary, e.g., "Purchasing a Desk Dictionary" (July 1, 1979, pp. 1591–1594) where the reviewers compare eight basic titles. A somewhat more sprightly, opinionated review of dictionaries of various types and kinds is the personalized summary of Elsie M. Stainton ("The Use of Dictionaries," *Scholarly Publishing,* April 1980, pp. 229–241.) Each entry is annotated, and this is a fine overview of the field.

Authority   In order to discuss with any meaning how to evaluate a general English-language dictionary, it should be first understood that, as in the case of encyclopedias, there are only a limited number of publishers whose general unabridged adult works have been accepted as satisfactory by any reliable authority.

1. G. & C. Merriam Company (Encyclopaedia Britannica, Inc.), which publishes *Webster's Third New International Dictionary.*
2. Random House, Inc., which publishes *The Random House Dictionary of the English Language.*

The same publishers issue abridged, college, or desk dictionaries, but a number of other reputable firms are also in this more limited field. More particularly, Houghton Mifflin (*American Heritage*), Collins and World Publishing Company (*Webster's New World*), and Oxford University Press are longtime publishers of quite acceptable abridged dictionaries.

In specialized fields and other areas where dictionaries are employed, there are almost as many reputable publishers as there are works. No particular monopoly of either quality or quantity exists outside the standard unabridged and desk dictionary fields.

Often, the name "Webster" is the sign of reassurance, and it frequently is found as the principal name of a number of dictionaries. The original claim to use the name is held by G. & C. Merriam Company, which bought out the unsold copies of Noah Webster's dictionary at the time of his death. For years, the use of Webster's name was the subject of litigation. G. & C. Merriam finally lost its case when the copyright on the name lapsed. It is now common property and may be used by any publisher. Hence the name "Webster's" in the title may or may not have something to do with the original work which bore the name. Unless the publisher's name is recognized, "Webster" per se means nothing.

Vocabulary   Vocabulary can be considered in terms of the period of the language covered and the number of words or entries. These terms may be extended to include special features such as slang, dialect, obsolete forms, and scientific or technical terms. Still, the primary consideration comes down to the question of how many words or definitions will be found.

In the United States the problem is divided between the "unabridged" (over 265,000 words) and the "abridged" (from 130,000 to 265,000 words) type of dictionary. Most dictionaries are abridged or limited to a given subject or topic. The two unabridged vary from about 460,000 entries for *Webster's* to 260,000 for *Random House.* The *Oxford English Dictionary* has some 500,000 words but is not considered a general dictionary.

Most desk dictionaries, such as the much-used *Webster's New Collegiate* or the *American Heritage,* have about 150,000 to 155,000 words, considered more than sufficient for average use. How important is it to have a title of more than 100,000 words? There are many paperback dictionaries of from 50,000 to 55,000 words which serve the purpose of millions of people. Let us take an extreme case to answer the question of how much is enough.

The *Longman Dictionary of Contemporary English* (London: Longman, 1978), a dictionary for foreigners learning English, is limited to 2000 words. The number is based on several studies, but thought to be sufficient to make most foreigners comfortable in the language. Mastery of other languages shows about the same ratio, i.e., a knowledge of about 2000 French, German, Spanish, or Italian words will suffice for the English-speaking individual who wants to converse or read in one of those languages.

There are countless studies of how many and what type of words are used most, but there seems to be a consensus that in the books read by the average person, about 135 words appear over 50 percent of the time. Tallentire found, too, that about 10 percent of the vocabulary of English covers 90 percent of all the text of all the volumes of literature in our libraries.[5]

Why then bother with a dictionary of more than 2000 words? The answer is that the dictionary is not for users of limited vocabu-

[5]D. R. Tallentire, "The Mathematics of Style," *The Times Literary Supplement,* August 13, 1971, p. 973.

lary. It is for the uncommon words, and that is why a 2000-word listing simply is not enough, nor is even 50,000. Another way of putting this is that the average desk or unabridged dictionary is not for the common reader but for the uncommon one who reads carefully, reads more than simplified material, and has a curiosity about words. It is assumed that the library is for both types of readers, and will have as many varieties of dictionaries as is necessary to meet needs of both the common and the uncommon reader.

Currency   A dictionary must be kept current, and this may be illustrated by the user looking for a definition of relatively new words or expressions, such as: punk, Ac/Dc in the bisexual sense, word processing, or greenhouse effect. For example, in many dictionaries the definition of "punk," as in "punk rock" is nonexistent; *Webster's New Collegiate Dictionary* has several definitions, from "being in poor health" to "a petty gangster, hoodlum, or ruffian,"[6] but none relating punk to modern music.

Also, subtle changes in meaning should be indicated but often are not. "Rogue," depending on who is using the term and in what set of circumstances, may mean a scoundrel or worthless individual. If it is employed in a romantic situation, it may well mean a person with a high degree of individualistic talents, not always considered bad. The term, then, may be one of approbation or a less than favorable description of a person.

Neologisms, in the sense of the use of an established word for a new meaning, often baffle the best dictionary editor.

> *Sometimes the dictionary is hopelessly inadequate. It's a fact that not every word we know is there. All of us create new words without thinking about the process, and those around us understand what is meant with equal ease. If you can take a four-wheel drive vehicle across rugged terrain, isn't that land "Jeepable"? Sure it is, but don't bother looking for verification. Webster never head the word. . . . Not only do we create new words, but we also give them flavor, color, a palpable edge that changes from time to time and even from person to person. We sense facets to words, nuances, which dictionaries can only barely apprehend. What does "home" mean? To a real estate broker, it's a marketable house. To most of us, it's mom and dad, children, inner warmth against the*

---

[6]The Reference and Subscription Book Review Committee (*Booklist,* July 1, 1979, p. 1591) checks currency by looking for examples of contemporary English such as *CB, acupuncture, jet lag, maven, videodisc.* (*Maven* is questionable, as many New Yorkers can tell you, but the other words indicate the approach). See, also, Kister's imaginative use of checkwords in his evaluation of dictionaries.

coldness of nature and our own loneliness. To a battered child, home is hell. In every case, home represents far more than just a building or rooms of residence. Home carries all the emotions we share approximately in common with those around us. Other feelings belong uniquely to each individual. Dictionaries only sketchily reproduce the quality of emotion surrounding words.[7]

Publishers estimate that the average household has a dictionary at least 15 to 20 years out of date. The definitions are less than timely. The purchase of a new dictionary is, however, no guarantee it will be current.

Each year, a new work or a new edition comes along; but, on the whole, the original copyright date signifies the time when most of the words in the dictionary were entered. (Possibly, although not necessarily, revision is indicated, as in encyclopedias, by the new copyright date; on the verso of most title pages will be found, for example, "Copyright 1966, 1970, 1980." The first date indicates the initial work.)

Somewhat like encyclopedia publishers, the major dictionary firms employ a type of continuous revision. With each new printing, they may add or delete a given number of words. This is particularly true of the desk dictionaries which are most used by young people and must reflect current usage and new words introduced into the language through radio, television, music, technology, and the like. On the whole, the system works rather well.

Format A major aspect of format is binding. Both individuals and libraries should purchase hardcover editions. Not only are paperbacks more likely to come apart after long wear, but more important, this format normally indicates an abridged version, usually some 45,000 to 55,000 words.[8]

Another noticeable factor is the print size and how its readability is affected by spacing between words, the use of boldface type, and

---

[7]Leigh Lerner, "Don't Follow Webster Out of the Window," *The Minneapolis Star,* January 16, 1980, p. 9A. Sanford Berman, who sent this quotation along to the author, points out there are at least two useful sources for identifying neologisms, each defining recently coined words and phrases and also illustrating how they have actually been used. One is *The Barnhart Dictionary of New English Since 1963* (New York: Harper & Row, 1973); and *The Second Barnhart Dictionary of New English* (New York: Harper & Row, 1980); and the other *6,000 Words: A Supplement to Webster's Third New International Dictionary* (Springfield, Massachusetts: Merriam-Webster, 1976). There are several others, as well.

[8]For a detailed discussion of paperback dictionaries, see Kister, op. cit.

the differences in type families. Individual tastes will play an important part in evaluating this, but from the viewpoint of many users, *The American Heritage Dictionary* is the best for its typography. It is instructive to compare the typography of this dictionary with that in other works.

With the exception of some colored plates, most dictionary illustrations are black-and-white line drawings. Where appropriate, the actual size of the object illustrated should be indicated, for example, in the case of an animal or a plant. The average desk dictionary has from 600 to 1500 illustrations, the unabridged from 7000 to 12,000.

Usage Although traditional titles have regularly prescribed rules for correct usage by most Americans, the ultimate authority is the dictionary. But which dictionary? Up until the publication of *Webster's Third,* it was *Webster's Second.* With the advent of the latter title, the editors broke with tradition. The third made little or no effort to prescribe correct usage. Critics contend that it opened the floodgate of permissiveness, providing no rule other than popularity. This laxity, it is argued, not only removes *Webster's* as a source of proper usage, but in so doing, clears the road for progressive deterioration of the language.

The editors abolished such labels as "colloquial" and "slang" and replaced them with general prescriptive terms such as "standard" and "substandard." Furthermore, many words labeled slang in the earlier edition are now left unlabeled. Today it is safe to generalize that almost all modern dictionaries are descriptive rather than prescriptive. However—and this is a major "however"—while most dictionaries are descriptive in giving current usage, they may become prescriptive when they use labels to reflect what is poor, best, or better usage. For example, *The American Heritage Dictionary* gives the same definition of a word, at least in essence, as *Webster's Third,* but makes a point of advertising its extensive proper-usage labels. Conversely, the *American College Dictionary* is less rigorous in labeling, because the editors do not believe it is the function of a dictionary to be a guide to usage.

Prescriptive versus Descriptive Approach Arguments for the descriptive and the prescriptive schools can be summarized briefly.

Advocates of the *descriptive* approach, who now govern the compilation of almost every major dictionary, claim:

(1) The people dictate the proper usage of the language. Language is in a natural process of change. In time, the new word, the

altered definition or pronunciation becomes the standard. Anyone who wishes to return to the original meaning stands in the way of understanding.

(2) The prescriptors or guardians are guarding a myth, in that language has never been stable, is always changing; e.g., try reading any middle-English text without a dictionary or, conversely, attempt to use Dr. Johnson's dictionary to decipher a government memorandum. As Guralnik points out, "Johnson's work covered about 40,000 items. Noah Webster's 1828 dictionary contained 70,000 entries."[9] A passable desk dictionary today should have between 130,000 and 175,000 words.

(3) The language reflects the common culture in which it is used. To tamper with the language is to deny the culture. For example:

> *A reader chides me for using the term "prerecorded tape," pointing out that tape can be either recorded or blank, which leaves the meaning of "prerecorded" hanging firmly in mid-absurdity. I follow his logic but won't bow to it. "Prerecorded" is indeed nonsensical if you insist on picking linguistic nits. But it is firmly and clearly established as denoting cassettes on which some program has been recorded before purchase—as contrasted to blank tapes. And because, in language as elsewhere, usage rather than logic carries the day, we're stuck with the irrational word and I'll stick with it.[10]*

Advocates of the *prescriptive* approach assert that the major role of a dictionary is to set standards.

(1) Word definitions and approved usage should adhere to tradition and authority based on correct historic usage.

(2) Support of this philosophy is essential to prevent the contamination of the pure language by slang, lingo, and fashionable jargon. Here scores of examples are given, from the refusal of *Webster's* to categorically outlaw "ain't" to creeping misuses of the language, from "hopefully" used as a synonym for "it is to be hoped" to "due to" for "because of" to the use of buzzwords to hide real meaning, e.g., "pacification" for "killing."

(3) Failure to maintain these principles is virtually an agreement to debase the language.[11]

---

[9]David Guralnik, "Coinage and Change," *The New York Times Magazine,* August 26, 1979, p. 6. Guralnik is editor of *Webster's New World Dictionary of the American Language.*

[10]Hans Fantel, "Sound," *The New York Times,* February 7, 1980, p. C9.

[11]William Borders, "BBC Turns Keen Ear to Its Own Speech," *The New York Times,* November 11, 1979, p. 15. Here it is reported that the British Broadcasting Corporation considers itself an arbiter of the English language.

Guralnik believes that the prescriptive advocates are really concerned about style and taste, subjective matters that are not always teachable.[12]

An English title, the *Oxford Paperback Dictionary* (Oxford: Oxford University Press, 1979) is one of the first modern dictionaries to be firm about proper usage. It is recommended for all libraries. According to its editor:

> We feel the time has come to lay down the law on what is right and wrong. This is something which people both need and want very badly. The public in general is much more conscious than it used to be about what is right and wrong. We rather think things are changing away from permissiveness.[13]

There are several American dictionaries which tend to be more prescriptive than descriptive. The two most commonly found in a library are *The American Heritage Dictionary* and *Webster's New World Dictionary* (published by Collins-World, *not* G. & C. Merriam Company). The latter is the choice of *The New York Times* as its primary guide. More specific titles devoted to usage are considered later in the chapter.

Even when indication of proper usage is the most debated aspect of word treatment in a dictionary, other elements are of equal concern.

Spelling Where there are several forms of spelling, they should be clearly indicated. *Webster's* identifies the English spelling by the label *"Brit."*; other dictionaries normally indicate this variant by simply giving the American spelling first, e.g., "analyze, analyse" or "theater, theatre." Frequently two different spellings are given, either of which is acceptable. The user must determine the form to use. For example, "addable" or "addible," "lollipop" or "lollypop."

Etymologies All dictionaries indicate the etymology of a word by a shorthand system in brackets. The normal procedure is to show the root word in Latin, Greek, French, German, Old English, or some other language. Useful as this feature is, the student of etymology will be satisfied only with historical dictionaries, such as Mencken's *The American Language,* to trace properly the history of a word and how it developed.

[12]Guralnik, op. cit.

[13]John Ezard, "Definitively, It Is To Be Hoped," *The Weekly Guardian,* March 18, 1979, p. 22. The same title is published in the United States by Avon and has been revised for American audiences.

Definitions Dictionaries usually give the modern meaning of words first. Exceptions include most older English-based dictionaries as well as the G. & C. Merriam-Webster publications and *Webster's New World*. Without understanding the definition ladder, an unsuspecting reader will leave the dictionary with an antiquated meaning. For example, *Webster's New Collegiate Dictionary* (definition in historical order) explains that the noun "sock" means "a low shoe or slipper." To be sure, this is preceded by the warning "archaic," but few people read carefully and the modern meaning is buried. It is a fascinating exercise to check at random definitions in *Webster's* imagining yourself believing the first definition is the modern meaning. The results are as startling as they are illustrative of the changes in language.

The wording of the definition is of equal importance. How would you define "dog"? Again, *Webster's* gives the simple explanation: "a highly variable carnivorous domesticated mammal." Now this is all very well for anyone who can tell a dog from a cat or is a native American, but what of the stranger from Mars or the person who does not know English? Will the definition suffice? As one critic puts it, the unhappy student of English as a foreign language "has to look up four other words to understand the definition, and may well find his paper chase is circular, leading back to the word he started from. What he wants for dog is something simple and snappy like a common four-legged hairy animal that barks and eats meat."[14] "Simple" and "snappy" are useful for any dictionary definition.

In his review of the *Longman Dictionary of Contemporary English*, Anthony Burgess gives an example of the complex versus the direct definition. "What is an angel?"

> *I reply "a kind of man like a bird that comes from God." "Longman" gives us: "a messenger and servant of God, usu. represented as a person with large wings and dressed in white clothes." Join the A-train of the "American Heritage" and you will arrive at "an immortal, spiritual being attendant upon God. In medieval angelology, one of nine orders of spiritual beings (listed from the highest to the lowest in rank): seraphim, cherubin, thrones, dominations or dominions, virtues, towers, principalities, archangels, and angels." No wings, no white garments.[15]*

Many have had the experience of being forced to follow a definition in a circle throughout the dictionary, only to arrive at a confusing roundabout definition; e.g., *The American Heritage* defines "entropy" as "A measure of the capacity of a system to undergo spontaneous change, thermodynamically specified by the relationship

---

[14]Philip Howard, "A Simple Guide for Word Groupies," *The Times,* June 26, 1978, p. 14.

[15]Anthony Burgess, "English in the Nude," *The Observer,* July 16, 1978, p. 26.

dS=dQT, where dS is an infinitesimal quantity of heat dQ at absolute temperature T."[16] Even a simple definition of a simple term can be confusing, e.g., defining "cornhusking" as the "husking of corn."

Ken Kister informs the author that he has counted the words in definitions in several dictionaries. The method is instructive. For example, *Webster's New International* averages 23 words in a definition, as does the children's *World Book Dictionary*. When one gets to the less than satisfactory *Webster's New Twentieth* Century Dictionary, the count drops to 11.

Pronunciation   There are different methods of indicating pronunciation, but the most common is the diacritical one. Usually, a handy key to the system is given at the bottom of every other page. Acceptable pronunciation is usually indicated, not only in general, but for specific regions.

Synonyms   The average user does not turn to a general dictionary for synonyms, but their inclusion helps to differentiate between similar words. Some desk dictionaries indicate the differentiation and shades of meaning by short essays at the conclusion of many definitions.

Syllabication   All dictionaries indicate usually by a centered period or hyphen, how a word is to be divided into syllables. The information is mainly to help writers and editors, not to mention secretaries, divide words at the ends of lines. There are special short desk dictionaries which simply indicate syllabication of more common words without benefit of definition or pronunciation.

Grammatical Information   The most generally useful grammatical help a dictionary renders is to indicate parts of speech. All single entries are classified as nouns, adjectives, verbs, and so on. Aside from this major division, dictionaries vary in method of showing adverbs, adjectives, plurals, and principal parts of a verb, particularly the past tenses of irregular verbs. Usually the method is clearly ascertainable; but, again, the prefatory remarks should be studied in order to understand any particular presentation.

Bias   Most dictionaries are quick to point out that certain terms or words are not socially acceptable because they are vulgar or have

---

[16]In the *Longman Dictionary of Contemporary English* (London: Longman, 1978), a dictionary for foreign students, the definition is understandable: "The state which the universe will reach when all the heat is spread out evenly."

insulting ethnic overtones. This type of label is found even in the most descriptive work. The interesting point is when the editor and the editorial board come to recognize what is or is not acceptable. Cultural prejudices against women in such words as "girl" for a grown woman took many years to overcome in dictionaries. No one seemed to question sexist attitudes. Although this has changed, at least in part, dictionaries continue to err.

The alert reviewers for the American Library Association's Reference and Subscription Books Committee are quick to point out elements of racial or sexist tendencies. In considering the *Funk & Wagnalls Standard College Dictionary* (New York: Funk & Wagnalls, 1977), the committee observed

> *The treatment of terms of dubious social acceptability is uneven, in that the ethnic epithets frog, kraut, and wop are called "offensive," kike and nigger both "vulgar" and "offensive," and bogtrotter "contemptuous"— but certain uses of broad, dike, dish, fairy, and fruit (surely experienced as contemptuous, etc., by those to whom applied) are labeled merely "slang."*[17]

UNABRIDGED DICTIONARIES[18]

Webster's New International Dictionary of the English Language. Springfield, Massachusetts: G. & C. Merriam Company, 2d ed., 1934, 3195 pp. (600,000 entries), o.p.

Webster's Third New International Dictionary. Springfield Massachusetts: G. & C. Merriam Company, 1961, 2736 pp. (450,000 entries). $59.95. *6,000 Words, A Supplement to Webster's Third New International Dictionary,* 1976, 220 pp. $8.50.

Encyclopedia type

The Random House Dictionary of the English Language. New York: Random House, 1966, 2059 pp. (260,000 entries). $39.95.

Webster's

The single unabridged dictionary found in the majority of libraries

---

[17]*The Booklist,* September 15, 1979, p. 147.

[18]As of this writing the traditional unabridged competitor to Webster's was out of print; i.e., *Funk & Wagnalls New Standard Dictionary of the English Language,* which has not been totally revised since 1913. The dictionary may be revived, revised, and reissued, but there was no announcement regarding its fate as of late 1981.

and government agencies, *Webster's,* was published first in 1909. (Actually, Noah Webster had been involved with publishing dictionaries through the early nineteenth century, so it is important to stress 1909 is the date of the first *unabridged* title.) A second edition came out in 1934 and a third in 1961. A 1980 dictionary has several copyright dates: 1961, the date of the original revision, and later dates—usually every five years—which imply some revisions since 1961. However, the work is primarily the original 1961 edition. While the 1909 edition is rarely found in libraries, the second and third editions are commonly stocked. The two vary so radically from one another that many consider them to be almost two different works.

The differences may be summarized as follows:

Vocabulary The 1934 edition contains 600,000 entries; the 1961 edition, 450,000. The Third was cut by eliminating some 250,000 words from the earlier work and then adding 100,000 words which have come into the language between 1934 and 1961. Because many obsolete and rare words have been deleted, the older work is absolutely necessary for historical purposes.

Special Features The 1934 edition had an appendix with abbreviations, arbitrary signs and symbols, forms of address, pronouncing gazetteer, and biographical dictionary. A reference-history edition included a supplement, "Reference History of the World," which was a basic handbook on world history. The 1961 edition deleted all these features, but major abbreviations are included in the main alphabet. However, there are few proper names or geographical entries. This means that a library must either retain the earlier edition or puchase separate volumes for biographical and gazetteer information.

Format The format is basically the same in the 1934 and 1961 works. An important typographical exception is that in the third edition, all proper names and adjectives are in lower case. For example, "Christmas," "French," and "English" are noted in lower-case but marked "usu cap" or "often cap." The only words capitalized in the dictionary are "God" and trade names such as Kodak, Kleenex, and Frisbee. The rigid noncapitalization is not followed in the other versions of *Webster's.* See, for example, the explanatory notes in any *Webster's* desk dictionary.

Word Treatment The treatment of words was the single most controversial point regarding the 1961 edition. Following the descriptive school, the third edition included many words not qualified by certain terms found in the earlier editions. The label "colloquial" was completely dropped, being replaced by "substandard" or "nonstandard." Labeling with these terms, and others such as "slang," is used cautiously. Many items were left unlabeled, e.g., "ain't" ("though disapproved by many . . . used orally by many cultivated speakers"). The new concept of acceptability is reason enough for all libraries to have the second edition on hand to double-check the proper use of a given word. The earlier work definitely was under the control of the prescriptive advocates.

Quotations The Second tended to use classical and standard quotations; the Third's 200,000 or so quotations are largely drawn from contemporary sources, i.e., newspapers, magazines, speeches of politicians, and writers such as P. G. Wodehouse and Mickey Spillane.

Other Elements In both works, the historical meaning is given first; pronunciations are indicated by methods unique to *Webster's*, and the third edition represents a radical change in procedure from the Second. There are other differences, many of them controversial, but suffice it to say that both editions will be essential in any library. The Second may be difficult to obtain. Booksellers report a constant demand for the earlier work.

Encyclopedia dictionaries

Chiefly because of bulky size and added material, the "encyclopedic" dictionary stands between the unabridged and the standard desk dictionary. Most encyclopedic dictionaries add to their price by including extraneous materials, usually at the end of the dictionary proper. Many "supermarket" dictionaries are of this variety, particularly the ubiquitous *"Webster's,"* which may be made to look as large as the unabridged versions simply by padding with usually dated, unorganized information. *Webster's Third New International* has some encyclopedic materials, but it is extremely limited and hardly a consideration. See Kister's guide for specifics on what is included.

Random House

Libraries are likely to bypass the usual rule against encyclopedic dictionaries in the case of *The Random House Dictionary.* The reason is that this title includes 260,000 words, or about 100,000 more than contained in the usual desk or encyclopedic dictionary. While still not up to the 450,000 words in *Webster's Third*, the *Random House* is impressive in the number of words included, and it more than meets the needs of smaller libraries where an unabridged dictionary may not be necessary.

Aside from the rather pointless (at least from a library point of view) added material at the end of the volume, many critics were disenchanted with *The Random House Dictionary* because it is divided between the descriptive and prescriptive philosophy. The editor calls the dictionary purely descriptive, but it does include definite indications of how the average person (if not the expert) is likely to react to the use of certain words and expressions. This is done by the liberal employment of usage labels ("nonstandard," "informal," "slang," and so on) to guide readers to appropriate speech.

Definitions are concise (some believe too concise) but generally clear, and supported by quotations—the majority composed by the editors, not taken from literature and current magazines and newspapers as is the custom with other dictionaries. The editors claim the made-up quotations better illustrate meaning than those taken from actual works. That is questionable. For example, nearly a full column is devoted to variations of "lay" among the quotations: "They laid themselves out to see the reception would be a success," to illustrate the meaning of "lay out" as "to try one's best." One wonders how a foreign language student would take it. Or what a nonbricklayer would make of this: "The masons laid the outer walls up in Flemish bond." And then, what is one to say about confusing English construction?—"She was glad to be told what a fine cook she was, but they didn't have to lay it on so much." (This, by the way, is labeled "informal" English.)

Somewhat similar to the *Random House Dictionary*, but much more current, is the *Collins English Dictionary* (London: William Collins, 1979), which lists more than 200,000 words, and is the first major dictionary of more than desk type to originate from England since the *Shorter Oxford Dictionary* of about 50 years ago.

The publisher claims that it took more than 100 people 10 years to prepare the completely new work, and at a cost of over $2 million dollars. First published in late 1979, it is aimed directly at an English audience but will be of value in American libraries. It is a nice combination of the permissive and descriptive, in that proper usage is indicated but a liberal attitude is evident on what is proper or improper.

Published by the same firm which issues the excellent desk dictionary, *Webster's New World Dictionary of the American Language*, the encyclopedic *Webster's New Twentieth Century Dictionary of the English Language* (New York: Collins-World, 1975, 2345 pp. 320,000 entries, $59.95) is another matter. The dictionary claims to have 320,000 entries, but many of these are proper names. The actual number of definitions would put this out of the unabridged classification.

The definitions are neither clear nor up-to-date, nor are they listed in any logical order. Also, most are so short as to be of little value for other than simple words or expressions. The current work appeared in 1955 and while continuous revision is claimed, it is not evident. It is overpriced, almost twice as much as the much better *Random House* entry; and includes close to 200 pages of extraneous, little-needed material. The encyclopedic data (from biographical material to lists of foreign words) is much more up-to-date than the dictionary itself.

It is mentioned here because it is often advertised, usually at a cut price, on television, in supermarkets, and as a bonus book. While any dictionary is of some use, the average person is better off spending less and getting more with the same firm's excellent desk dictionary.

DESK (COLLEGIATE) DICTIONARIES

> *The American Heritage Dictionary of the English Language, New College Edition.* Boston: Houghton Mifflin Company, rev. ed., 1978, 1550 pp. (150,000 entries). $11.95.
>
> *Webster's New World Dictionary of the American Language.* 2d ed. New York: William Collins Pubs. Inc., 1980, 1928 pp. (150,000 entries). $11.95.
>
> *Webster's New Collegiate Dictionary,* 8th ed. Springfield, Massachusetts: G. & C. Merriam Company, 1980, 1568 pp. (150,000 entries). $11.95.
>
> Note: All prices are for thumb-indexed versions. Prices are usually about $1 less for the non-thumb-indexed work.

These are the three desk dictionaries found in most libraries and millions of homes.

The standard publishers' dictionaries are periodically revised and all are authoritative. Differences are essentially of format, arrangement, systems of indicating pronunciation, and length of definitions. All include synonyms, antonyms, etymologies, and limited biographical and gazetteer information. Price variations are minimal.

The natural question is which is best, and the answer depends primarily on personal need. All have about the same number of words, and all meet the evaluative tests for excellence. Still, there are differences, from usage notes to order of definitions to focus on illustrations.

The author votes for *American Heritage,* possibly because it is used constantly. On the other hand, in his excellent evaluation of dictionaries Ken Kister ranks *"Webster's New Collegiate Dictionary* and *Webster's New World Dictionary* [as] the best buys. Both are superior . . . with *Webster's New Collegiate* perhaps having the edge when it comes to treatment of scientific and literary terms and *Webster's New World* out front in coverage of Americanisms and etymological depth."[19] Actually, all are good, and final decision depends on personal need and preference. The wise librarian will have all three about.

Houghton Mifflin

The American Heritage Dictionary is the "best buy" in dictionaries of the desk and college type. First published in 1969, it is continuously revised, and a new edition appears about every four or five years. It has two major claims for attention. (1) Illustrations: the publisher claims there are 4000 illustrations and more than 200 maps which are placed at irregular intervals down the broad and otherwise blank outer margins of the pages. Most are halftones based upon great paintings and drawings and are far better than those in any other dictionary, regardless of size. Furthermore, the typography, spacing, and so on, are excellent. These features all add up to ease of reading and explanation through illustrations. (2) Prescriptive entries: One of the major selling points of this dictionary is that it provides definite guidance on acceptable usage. This is done by a panel, and while the individual members may argue, the result is a valuable guide for laypersons. The *Random House* does the same but tends to be more temperate; the *Heritage* is more forthright.

Another valuable feature is the appendix, which includes a lengthy list of the Indo-European roots and the English words that embody them. This etymology feature complements rather extensive etymologies in the body of the dictionary.

Many dictionary publishers have just as many versions of the standard desk dictionary. A good example is Houghton Mifflin and its American Heritage series, which not only includes *The American Heritage Dictionary* listed here, but also a "larger format" edition, *The American Heritage Dictionary of the English Language* ($12.95); *The*

[19]Ken Kister, *Dictionary Buying Guide* (New York: R. R. Bowker, 1977), p. 98.

American Heritage School Dictionary ($8.95) with 55,000 entries for grades 5 through 11; *The Concise Heritage Dictionary* ($5.95) with 55,000 entries for middle schools; and *The Word Book* ($2.95), which cuts the number of entries to the 40,000 most often used words. Furthermore, there is an encyclopedic version, *The Illustrated Heritage Dictionary and Information Book* ($29.95), which is the basic dictionary plus added sections on American history, quotations, and a five-language dictionary. Each of these publications fulfills some need, but not for the library. In the library, the best bet is the "new college edition," which has the basic vocabulary less all the frills, or with more words than are provided in the cut-down versions. Other publishers tend to follow the same approach, and in every case this side of the unabridged dictionaries, the library is better off with the standard "college" editions, no matter what they may be called. Another possible exception might be the special dictionaries, such as *The Concise Heritage Dictionary*, which can be used in junior high schools and even high schools as a bridge between the children's dictionary and the college dictionary.

Collins

Webster's New World Dictionary of the American Language is not a G. & C. Merriam *"Webster's,"* but unlike any supermarket dictionaries that boast the same name, it is a quite legitimate desk dictionary. First published in 1953, it was totally revised in 1970, and through continuous revision new editions are issued about every four years. It is, like *The American Heritage*, a new work not based on a larger dictionary. It includes some 158,000 entries in a single alphabet, but definitions are given in chronological order rather than by frequency of modern usage.

It is particularly strong on contemporary American vocabulary and the latest technological terms. Another feature is the inclusion of a considerable number of colloquialisms, slang expressions, and idiomatic expressions, all clearly labeled. In fact, a point for the *World* entry, and one that recommended it for use by *The New York Times* editorial staff, is this emphasis on identifying and showing the roots of Americanisms. It follows the descriptive school although it has a liberal number of usage labels.

Webster's

Now in its eighth edition, *Webster's New Collegiate Dictionary* is based on the unabridged Third. It reflects the philosophy of the larger work and places considerable emphasis on contemporary pronunciation and definitions. As in the larger work, the philosophy is descriptive rather than prescriptive and usage labels are kept to a minimum—so much so that slang terms are rarely isolated from normal English. In fact, some critics believe the *Collegiate* version is more relaxed about correct use than the unabridged work.

The pronunciation system is difficult to follow; and, as in all Webster's dictionaries, the definitions are in chronological order with the modern meaning coming last. Unlike most desk dictionaries, geographical and personal names are not included in the main alphabet but are in the back. Added features include appendixes which cover forms of address, colleges and universities in the United States, vocabulary rhymes, and the like.

Currency is a major problem with the best of dictionaries. For that reason it is wise for the library to (1) annually acquire the new editions of standard publishers' desk dictionaries (there are not many, particularly if the librarian is quick to notice whether the entry is a new edition or merely an annual revision) and (2) have on hand the three basics listed here, namely, the *American Heritage*, the *New World Dictionary*, and *Webster's New Collegiate*.

There are numerous other acceptable desk dictionaries, although for most libraries the above three would be sufficient. Among the others recommended by the Reference and Subscription Books Reviews committee: *Funk & Wagnalls Standard College Dictionary* and the *Random House College Dictionary*.

Children's Dictionaries

World Book Dictionary. Chicago: Field Enterprises Educational Corporation, 1980, 2 vols. (revised annually). $59.

Scott, Foresman Intermediate Dictionary. Glenview, Illinois: Scott, Foresman and Company, 1979. 1104 pp. $12.95.

Children's dictionaries are composed of words based on frequency of occurrence in speech and reading encountered in school. Definitions are written in simple language, the type is usually large, there are many illustrations, and the format is generally pleasing.

The most ambitious is the two-volume *World Book Dictionary*, edited by the expert in the field, Clarence L. Barnhart. It contains 225,000 words. All entries are in a single alphabet, pronunciation is simple to follow, and there are more than 3000 pictures. The work, which may be used by adults, is considered by experts to be excellent, and it is recommended for all school libraries.

The *Scott, Foresman* dictionary is one of a series which includes beginning through high school dictionaries. The intermediate version for upper elementary and junior high has 69,000 entries and 1600 illustrations. Among other reputable publishers of children's dictionaries are Macmillan, Doubleday, Collins-World, and G. & C. Merriam.

The problem with children's dictionaries is whether the format and general editorial policy should (1) stress material for the beginning reader or (2) balance beginning material with enough adult matter to offer the reader the best of two worlds. Larger firms solve the problem by offering a family of dictionaries for every level; for example, G. & C. Merriam starts the child off with the *New Elementary Dictionary,* moves to the *Intermediate Dictionary,* and from there goes to the *New Students' Dictionary* and the *New Collegiate Dictionary.* Other reputable publishers follow much the same procedure.

HISTORICAL DICTIONARIES

Murray, James. et al. *New English Dictionary on Historical Principles.* Oxford: Clarendon Press, 1888 to 1933, 10 vols. and supplement; reissued in 1933 as 13 vols. under the title *The Oxford English Dictionary.* $595.

————. *A Supplement to The Oxford English Dictionary.* Edited by R. W. Burchfield. New York: Oxford University Press, 1972, 1977, 2 vols. $60 each.

The Compact Edition of The Oxford English Dictionary. New York: Oxford University Press, 1971, 2 vols. $90.

Of all the dictionaries of the English language, the *Oxford English Dictionary* (begun as the *New English Dictionary on Historical Principles*) is the most magnificent, and it is with some justification that H. L. Mencken called it "the emperor of dictionaries." The purpose of the dictionary is to trace the history of the English language. This is done through definitions and quotations which illustrate the variations in meaning and use.

James Murray, the principal editor of the original 10-volume set began the project in 1878. The last volume was issued in 1928. Murray had in mind

> *a lexicon that would literally encompass the entire formal and substantive history of the English language, from its Anglo-Saxon, Latin, and Anglo-Norman roots to the latest ideological, literary, journalisitc, and*

scientific coinage. Illustrations of usage would be drawn not only, as they had been in Dr. Johnson, from eminent and approved authors but from that almost incommensurable spectrum of printed material—literary, technical, ephemeral, colloquial—which articulates the organic existence and echo chamber of a civilization. Moreover, the etymology and, where applicable, the dialectological genesis of every word were to be traced and set down according to the most rigorous standards of modern scholarship.[20]

The final result, which Murray did not live to see, is a dictionary that defines over 500,000 words and supports the definitions and usage with some 2 million quotations. In *Webster's New World Dictionary* the etymology of "black" takes 5 lines, whereas in the OED it takes 23 lines. The word "point" in the OED consumes 18 columns; "put," 30.

There is no completion for such a dictionary, and the first of four supplements was issued in the 1970s.[21] The final volume, which will incorporate the last of the estimated 60,000 new words and variations, is to be published in the mid-1980s. There is discussion of totally revising the whole set. The editor believes the work will continue to be useful for another century. "By that date, computerized stores of information will probably have replaced dictionaries of this kind altogether, when private terminals to information centers have become as ubiquitous as telephones."[22]

Technology of another sort is responsible for the *Compact Edition* published in 1971, in which the text was reproduced micrographically and the 13 volumes (the original 10 plus the supplement was reissued in 1933 as 13 volumes) reduced to two. The miniaturization of the typeface requires the use of a magnifier. The edition is well known to readers of book clubs because it is often a "gift" for new members at a considerably reduced price. Most libraries should have the full printed set, but the Compact Edition is a good buy for individuals. It does not include the 1970s and 1980s supplements.

A more familiar version of the OED for many Americans is *The Shorter Oxford English Dictionary on Historical Principles* (New York: Oxford University Press, 1973, 2672 pp.). Since the first publication of this third edition in 1944 (there were two other editions, 1933 and

[20]George Steiner, "Give the Word," *The New Yorker,* November 21, 1977, pp. 224–227.

[21]Actually the first supplement to the basic set came out in 1933, but after that nothing happened until 1972, when the first really new supplement (covering A–G) was issued. Consequently, most librarians consider the 1933 supplement part of the basic set.

[22]Anthony Storr, "A Man of Many Words," *The New York Times Book Review,* April 16, 1978, p. 36.

1936), it has undergone three revisions, the most complete in 1973 when most of the etymologies were updated. Also, there is a 74-page addendum which includes a number of. words from the *OED Supplements.* As with earlier versions, the emphasis is almost entirely on definitions, with names of people and places eliminated and quotations cut back. The net result is that the abridgement includes about two-thirds the original number of words.

The OED is not a dictionary for ready reference, but it is encyclopedic in its treatment of individual words. Under every word, anything that could be found about the historical development of the word is traced in chronological order. Meaning, origin, relationship to similar words, various dialects, fashions in speaking, pronunciation, compounds, derivatives, and even more are treated in full. Every change is illustrated by an example, and each quotation is dated and the source clearly indicated.

As a source of information about words, the OED is miraculously accurate and complete. It is weak in only one area, that of American words. However, these are treated quite fully by Craigie and Mathews in two other works to be discussed in the following subsection. The library will find many uses for the OED; and, as indicated, it is an oblique source for quotations or for "first" facts when other, more conventional, books of quotations and ready-reference tools fail to produce results.

The OED abstains from any critical judgments, and there are no usage labels. The validity of some of the forms is open to question, but the editors saw their duty as recorders.

It is difficult to imagine any librarian who is not familiar with the OED, and while it may not be found in every library, its spirit is there, as is the spirit of its first editor. It is a matchless work which scholar George Steiner praises with good reason as

> . . . the living history of the English tongue and the dynamic embodiment of its spread over the earth. The master wordsmiths in modern letters—Joyce, Nabokov, Anthony Burgess, John Updike—are Murray's debtors. Where speech is vital and exact, it springs from the O.E.D. and enriches it in turn. To anyone who knows and loves English, the old quiz question "What single work would you take to read on a desert island?" does not require even an instant's thought. The O.E.D. carries within its dark-blue boards the libraries of fact and of feeling. Dip into it anywhere and life itself crowds at you.[23]

[23]Steiner, op. cit., p. 230.

American regional dictionaries

> Craigie, William, and James R. Hulbert. A *Dictionary of American English on Historical Principles*. Chicago: The University of Chicago Press, 1936 to 1944, 4 vols. $160.

> Mathews, Milford. A *Dictionary of Americanisms on Historical Principles*. Chicago: The University of Chicago Press, 1951, 2 vols., 1946 pp. o.p.

> *Dictionary of American Regional English* (DARE). Cambridge, Massachusetts: Harvard University Press, 4 vols. (Date of publication to be announced.)

While the *OED* remains the "bible" of the linguist, or the layperson tracing the history and various meanings of a word, it is not the best place to go for correct usage, at least for Americans. In fact, according to its current editor, Robert Burchfield, English-speaking Americans and English-speaking Britons actually come close to using two different languages, the latter, of course, being recorded in the OED. Mr. Burchfield believes that within the next 200 years the two nations will no longer be able to understand each other.

> *His staff cited some dissimilar words used about the same object in British and American: braces and suspenders; bumper and fender; car bonnet and car hood. "In America," added an editor, "the first floor is always called the ground floor."*
>
> *At the US embassy, Helen McCain Smith said: "I really believe he's right. I'm half-English and half-American and its terribly hard switching from saying 'I'll ring you' to 'I'll call you,' from 'Sorry' to 'Excuse me' and from 'Thank you' to 'it's been a pleasure.' Americans like to put their own stamp on the language. But they don't always improve it." [24]*

W. A. Craigie (who was one of the editors of the *OED*) developed *A Dictionary of American English on Historical Principles*. Craigie supplements the *OED* by demonstrating changes in English words (many included in the *OED*) which took place in the American colonies and the United States. In order to trace a word used in both the United States and the British Isles, it is necessary to use both Craigie and the *OED*.

Craigie includes words which originated on the American

---

[24]John Ezard, "Worrying Ongoing Language Rift Situation," *The Guardian*, June 28, 1978, p. 1. The debate began when the editor spoke at the annual American Library Convention in 1978.

continent, giving a complete history and showing the development, as in the *OED*, by use of quotations. This feature makes it valuable as an aid to tracing quotations and early facts about American folklore, habits, and customs.

Mathews's work is confined to words peculiar to America and augments Craigie nicely. It also includes over 400 useful pen-and-ink drawings. There are approximately 50,000 words, including many terms that were adopted from other languages. Many place names and names of plants and animals were drawn from American Indian words, whereas the Dutch and Germans furnished us with many domestic words.

Despite the name, the *Oxford American Dictionary* (New York: Oxford University Press, 1980) is little more than an abbreviated desk dictionary. It has only 35,000 definitions. The claims to fame, aside from having among its editors one from the *OED*, are (1) simple, direct definitions, (2) precise usage notes, and (3) a clear system of pronunciation. As a desk dictionary it is excellent, but it is unfortunate that the publisher had to confuse matters by borrowing the title from the *OED*.

In any discussion of the history of the American language, there is one outstanding work which many have enjoyed reading, literally from cover to cover. This is Henry Mencken's *The American Language* (New York: Alfred A. Knopf, Inc., 1936 to 1948). In three volumes, the sage of Baltimore examines a very large proportion of all American words in a style and manner that are extremely pleasing, always entertaining, and informative. The initial one-volume work of 1936 was supplemented with two volumes. All are easy to use as each volume has a detailed index.

Planned for publication in the mid-1980s, the *Dictionary of American Regional English* will assemble colloquial expressions and their meanings from all 50 states.[25] The monumental project began in 1965, and specially trained workers spent five years interviewing nearly 3000 native Americans in over 1000 communities. In addition to the interviews, material for the *Dictionary of American Regional English,* often referred to as DARE, has been gathered from countless printed sources including regional novels, folklore journals, newspapers and diaries.

There are practical aspects to DARE, as William Safire constantly reminds readers of his column on language. For example, anyone who has traveled in the United States has a problem ordering a

[25]Joy Schaleben Lewis, "A Dictionary of How Just Plain Folks Talk," *The New York Times,* September 5, 1979, p. C10. See also, William Safire, "Taking a Dare," *The New York Times Magazine,* November 11, 1979, p. 14.

breakfast roll, which may be called many things depending on the region. DARE solves the difficulty:

> *What's the difference between a Danish and a sweet roll? A doughball and a huffle-duffle? a jelly doughnut and a jelly roll, a turnover and a pocketbook, a Bismarck and a bear claw?*
>
> *These and other dialectical variations were put to the man from DARE: Dr. Fredric Cassidy, editor of the Dictionary of American Regional English, the great linguistic project cooking at the University of Wisconsin. It turns out that one of DARE's national interviewing questions has been "What names are used around here for fancy rolls and pastries?"*[26]

The expression "bear claws" is used in the West, a "fantan" is Middlewest, and in the South "jelly roll" is favored, although this is tricky as the phrase is "often a code word for copulation: 'Jelly Roll Blues' is a far cry from a passion for prune Danish."[27]

SPECIALIZED DICTIONARIES

There are numerous forms and types of dictionaries. Among the most common found in libraries: slang, synonyms and antonyms, usage, abbreviations, subject, and foreign language.

Slang

> Wentworth, Harold, and Stuart Flexner. *Dictionary of American Slang,* 2d supplemented ed. New York: Thomas Y. Crowell Company, 1975, 766 pp. $12.95.

Freedom of expression in films, television, books, magazines, and conservation has resulted in use of many slang, four-letter words which several decades ago would have not been recognized as even existing. Of course they did exist, but were not given a place in dictionaries. The attitude was that if one waited long enough they would disappear. They did not, and as a result of this and a relaxed attitude toward censorship, dictionary editors now include the forbidden words of a generation or so ago. The *Oxford English Dictionary* supplements, as well as most desk dictionaries, define the so-called sexually slanted vulgarisms as well as words and terms used to refer to ethnic minorities in a less-than-favorable way.

[26]William Safire, "Good Night, Sweet Roll!" *The New York Times Magazine,* April 13, 1980, p. 16.
[27]Ibid.

Today the committee of the Reference and Subscription Books Reviews considers a dictionary lacking if it refuses to include such terms—carefully labeled, to be sure, as vulgarisms or unacceptable.[28] Other reviewers, aside from those evaluating children's works, take much the same attitude.

Nevertheless, the library needs dictionaries of slang. Why? There are several answers: (1) Most dictionaries do not indicate the variations of meaning of given slang terms or words, and few trace their history, which is as much a part of the history of a nation's popular culture as are its primary figures and events. (2) Readers often come across expressions which are not well-defined in an ordinary dictionary. (3) Authors often look for words which will convey the background, class, or occupation of a given character, and the slang dictionary is a fine place to double-check such words. (4) Finally, just plain curiosity and interest in the language will lead anyone to pause and enjoy the wild imagination of people able to conceive of the 22,000 different slang words in Wentworth and Flexner.

General in scope, Wentworth and Flexner's *Dictionary of American Slang* gives definitions each of which is supplemented by a source and one or more illustrative quotations. It is accepted in libraries, and certainly by all scholars. The particular merit of the work is its broad general approach to all aspects of the culture, from the slang of space scientists and FBI men to the jargon of stripteasers and Madison Avenue advertising tycoons. Where possible, the history of the term is given, with the approximate date when the slang entered the written (not the oral) language. And there is an excellent preface which anyone who questions the merit of such dictionaries would do well to read. Unfortunately, the arrangement is wanting, in that the additional words in the 1967 first supplement and the 1975 second supplement are incorporated into appendixes in the revised edition.

The name in this field remains Eric Partridge. He was a one-man operation who during a long lifetime prepared numerous dictionaries. Probably his most famous is *A Dictionary of Slang and Unconventional English* (7th ed.; New York: The Macmillan Company, 1970, 1528 pp.). As William Safire has said in discussing Partridge's lifework, he taught the English-speaking world to treat slang with respect. Many consider him to be the modern Samuel Johnson, and his is a name every self-respecting librarian should know.

Finally, there is a journal devoted completely to what the editor

[28]*Booklist*, July 1, 1979, p. 1592.

terms "verbal aggression." This is *Maledicta* (1976 to date, semiannual). The 160 to 200 pages contain scholarly articles on slang.

Synonyms and antonyms

Webster's New Dictionary of Synonyms. Springfield, Massachusetts: G. & C. Merriam Company, rev. ed., 1980, 909 pp. $10.95.

Roget's International Thesaurus, 3d ed. New York: Thomas Y Crowell Company, 4th ed., 1977, 1455 pp. $10.50.

Webster's Collegiate Thesaurus. Springfield, Massachusetts: G. & C. Merriam Company, 1976, 944 pp. $9.95.

A book of synonyms often is among the most popular books in the private or public library. It offers a key to crossword puzzles, and it serves almost everyone who wishes to increase his or her command of English. There are several dictionaries giving both synonyms and antonyms in English, but the titles listed above appear more often in libraries. Certainly, the most popular and best known is the work of Peter Mark Roget (1779–1869), inventor of the slide rule and a doctor in an English mental asylum. He began the work at age seventy-one and by his ninetieth birthday had seen it through 20 editions. (The term "thesaurus" means a treasury, a store, a hoard; and Roget's is precisely that.) His optimistic aim was to classify all human thought under a series of verbal categories, and his book is so arranged. There are approximately 1000 classifications; and within each section, headed by a key word, there are listed by parts of speech the words and phrases from which the reader may select the proper synonym. Antonyms are usually placed immediately after the main listing. Thus: "possibility/impossibility"; "pride/humility."

The advantage of grouping is that like ideas are placed together. The distinct disadvantage is that *Roget* offers no guidance or annotations; and an overzealous user may select a synonym or an antonym which looks and sounds better but is far from expressing what is meant. Sean O'Faolain, the Irish short story writer, recalls giving a copy of Roget's to a Dutch-born journalist to improve his English, but the effect was appalling. For example, the journalist might wish to know the synonym for "sad." He would consult the index and find four or five alternatives, such as "painful"; "gray"; "bad"; "dejected"; and, surprisingly, "great." When he turned to the proper section, he would find two or three hundred synonyms. Unless the user has a clear understanding of the language, *Roget's* can be a difficult work. One method of overcoming the problem is to provide definitions and then offer the synonyms, e.g., *Roget's II: The New Thesaurus* (Boston: Houghton Mifflin Company, 1980).

There are at least a dozen titles which freely use Roget's name. (Like "Webster," the name "Roget" cannot be copyrighted and is free to any publisher. Many of the dozen titles are little more than poor, dated copies of the master's original work.) Of this group, the Crowell is the best, certainly the most frequently updated, and maintained in the spirit of Peter Mark Roget. The 1977 editions, for example, added synonyms and antonyms from the 1960s and 1970s. Crowell, which brings out an edition about every 10 years, files away candidates for inclusion in the next edition. Some of the words may fall away from disuse; most will probably stay, such as these words:

upscale, an advertising derivative for people with money; *double-dipper,* a person on a pension who then goes on salary; *no-frills,* stripped to bare essentials, as in no meals on a flight; *jigglies,* television programs where female stars shake their bosoms and behinds; *kneecapping,* shooting in the knees, an Italian terrorist method; *pop,* a transaction or sale, as in $10 a pop; *swagging,* appropriating government property for personal use; *push-in's,* muggings at the door; *android,* an automaton, a not-quite-human fellow. All of which means that Roget's has a future (hereafter, by and by, aftertime, imminent, in the fullness of time, eventually, sooner or later).[29]

The difference between Roget's and other word-finding devices is that Roget's retains the original scheme of grouping like ideas together. The arrangement of words and phrases in clusters by a single thought or concept differs from the average book of synonyms, where the arrangement is alphabetical. For example, aside from *Roget's International,* the most popular book of synonyms is *Webster's Collegiate Thesaurus.* Here the 100,000 entries (as contrasted with about 250,000 in the *International*) are arranged alphabetically. After each main entry there is a definition (a useful device) and then a list of synonyms. This is followed by related words and, finally, a list of antonyms. Sometimes quotations are employed to make it clear how words should be used.

Webster's New Dictionary of Synonyms is a more comprehensive approach. Almost each of the synonyms is carefully illustrated by discriminating quotations. The quotations help the reader to distinguish shades of differences between the same type of words. Often revised and updated, the dictionary includes antonyms and lists of

---

[29]Herbert Mitang, "Thesaurus, at 200, Still Looks for (Seeks) Words." *The New York Times,* January 18, 1979, p. C15.

analogous words and their opposites. The work is certainly more useful for the careful writer than the *Collegiate.*

There are dozens of other books of synonyms, antonyms, and homonyms, listed and briefly described in Kister's *Dictionary Buying Guide.* Several are excellent. Among these is Laurence Urdang, *A Basic Dictionary of Synonyms and Antonyms* (New York: Elsevier/Nelson Books, 1979, 373 pp.), which is notable for its currency and careful discrimination in the use of synonyms. Another is J. I. Rodale *The Synonym Finder* (2d ed. Emmaus, Pennsylvania: Rodale Press, 1979, 1361 pp.). The strength of this is the alphabetical arrangement and the publisher's claims that there are 1 million synonyms for the 17,000 entries. An added feature is usage labels such as "slang" or "informal." The problem is that the compilation does not differentiate between meanings, and the user must be careful that the "synonym" is really close in meaning.

Usage and manuscript style

Fowler, Henry Watson. *Dictionary of Modern English Usage,* 2d ed., rev. by Sir Ernest Gowers. New York: Oxford University Press,1965, 725 pp. $14.50.

Turabian, Kate L. *A Manual of Style,* 13th ed. Chicago: The University of Chicago Press, 1980. $15.

The library is the place where people expect to find suitable manuals to guide them in speech and writing.[30] One of the classics in the field is Fowler, who deals extensively with grammar and syntax, analyzes how words should be used, distinguishes clichés and common errors, and settles almost any question that might arise concerning the English language. The dictionary, and the revision by Sir Ernest Gowers, has a special flavor treasured by all readers. Fowler commented on practically anything that interested him, and the hundreds of general articles can be savored for their literary quality, aside from their instructional value.

Another version of this, although now dated, is Margaret Nicholson, *A Dictionary of American-English Usage* (New York: New American Library, 1957, 671 pp.), which is based on Fowler but revised for American use.

Fowler presupposes an intense interest in language, but how is one to answer the average question about proper usage. Here there

---

[30]William Safire, "The Wiseguy Problem," *The New York Times Magazine,* March 25, 1979, p. 12.

are several useful titles, all of which are written for the layperson seeking a quick, uncomplicated guide. Among acceptable works: William and Mary Morris, *Harper Dictionary of Contemporary Usage* (New York: Harper & Row, 1975, 648 pp.) The editors follow the conservative, prescriptive line, which some find difficult to appreciate. At the other extreme, where almost anything goes as long as enough people use it, is the descriptive attitude of Bergen and Cornelia Evans, and their *A Dictionary of Contemporary American Usage* (New York: Random House, 1957, 567 pp.). Despite the green light for usage, the book is one of the best for clear explanations of grammar, punctuation and style. Compromise is suggested by *The Britannica Book of English Usage* (New York: Doubleday, 1980), which offers flexible guidelines on everything from grammar and spelling to diction and letter writing. Another first choice, with a self-explanatory title: John B. Bremner's *Words on Words: A Dictionary for Writers and Others Who Care About Words* (Columbia University Press, 1980, 405 pp.). This is available in both hardback and paperback.

A Manual of Style, or "Turabian" as many librarians call it, is the bible of both trade and scholarly book editors as well as writers. It is not a book on word usage, although many of the rules and examples are useful in determining which word or style to employ. It does answer questions on how to prepare footnotes; how to edit a manuscript; and rules concerning punctuation, spacing, and indexing. There are explanations of how to cite nonprint materials, the meaning of cataloging in publication, and even how an author should phrase a letter when sending a publisher a manuscript.[31]

A shorter version of the manual is: *A Manual for Writers of Term Papers, Theses and Dissertations* (Chicago: University of Chicago Press, 5th ed. 1980), which simply extracts rules of use to students from the primary work. It is particularly helpful for abbreviations, footnotes, and general preparation of term papers and theses.

Abbreviations and acronyms

DeSola, Ralph. *Abbreviations Dictionary,* 5th ed. New York: American Elsevier Publishing Company, 1977, 640 pp. $28.

Acronyms, Initialisms, and Abbreviations Dictionary, 6th ed. Detroit: Gale Research Company, 1978, 1103 pp. $62. *New Acronyms, Initialisms, and Abbreviations,* 1979 to date, annual. Paper, $56.

Most general dictionaries include basic abbreviations as part of

[31]Donna Martin, "The New Chicago Manual of Style," *Publishers Weekly,* September 25, 1978, pp. 113, 114. A brief history of the work and how it has developed over the years.

the main work or as an appendix. Many acronyms (i.e., words formed from the initial letters of words of the successive parts of a compound term such as CARE, WAVE, NATO) are included, too. Also, encyclopedias, almanacs, and numerous handbooks include sections for general or specific abbreviations and acronyms. Still, for ready reference, it is desirable to have at least one good, up-to-date source at hand.

One of the best is Gale's *Acronyms,. . . .* Terms are in alphabetical order, by abbreviation, acronym, or initial, and various meanings are given. There are over 180,000 entries, and each of the supplements adds some 12,000 more from all fields. (What this may be doing to the language, not to mention the sanity of the average reader, is not considered by the compilers.) If one considers that there are at least 12,000 new acronyms, abbreviations, and initials added each year, the need for a current source is obvious. A companion volume to *Acronyms, . . . ,* is *Reverse Acronyms, Initialisms, and Abbreviations Dictionary* (Detroit: Gale Research Company, 1978), gives the term first and then the acronym.

The basic guide to abbreviations, DeSola's *Abbreviations Dictionary* is often revised—usually every four or five years. Entries are arranged alphabetically, letter by letter. Some notion as to possibilities can be gained by looking at the first entry for the lower case "a," which has over 25 possible meanings. The capital "A" lists over 30 meanings. DeSola differs from the Gale work in that the Gale entry is longer and extremely strong on those words which are composed of initialisms. But DeSola includes items not found in Gale, e.g., slang, nicknames, contractions, signs and symbols, and anonyms. There is just enough difference between the two that both should be found in larger collections.

Subject dictionaries[32]

Dictionaries devoted to specialized subject fields, occupations, or professions make up an important part of any reference collection. This is especially true in the sciences. General dictionaries tend to be stronger in the humanities, weaker in the fast-changing scientific fields. Consequently, there are a vast number of scientific dictionaries, but relatively few in the humanities.

[32]Reproducing Library of Congress cards under a large number of subject headings, the editor of *Dictionaries, Encyclopedias and Other Word-Related Books* (Detroit: Gale Research Company, 2d ed., 1979, 2 vols.) offers some 25,000 subject dictionaries. While limited to Library of Congress cataloged titles between 1966 and 1978, the listing is impressive.

The major question to ask when determining selection is: Does this dictionary offer anything that cannot be found in a standard work now in the library? A careful answer may result in bypassing a special dictionary. It is surprising, particularly in the humanities and social sciences, how much of the information is readily available in a general English dictionary.

While all evaluative checks for other dictionaries apply, there are also some special points to watch:

1. Are the illustrations pertinent and helpful to either the specialist or the layperson? Where a technical work is directed to a lay audience, there should be a number of diagrams, photographs, or other forms of graphic art, which frequently make it easier for the uninitiated to understand the terms.

2. Are the definitions simply brief word equivalents, or is some effort made to give a real explanation of the word in context with the subject?

3. Is the dictionary international in scope or limited chiefly to an American audience? This is a particularly valuable question when the sciences are being considered. Several publishers have met the need by offering bilingual scientific dictionaries.

4. Are the terms up to date? Again, this is a necessity in a scientific work, somewhat less so in a social science dictionary, and perhaps of relatively little importance in a humanistic study.

Many of the subject dictionaries are virtually encyclopedic in terms of information and presentation. They use the specific-entry form, but the entry may run to considerably more than a simple definition.

Foreign-language dictionaries (bilingual)[33]

The Cassell's series, all published by The Macmillan Company, different editions and dates, various pagination, e.g., *Cassell's French Dictionary; Cassell's German Dictionary; Cassell's Italian-English, English-Italian Dictionary;* etc. Price range $13.50 to $14.95.

---

[33]John Alvey, "Dictionaries and Reference Books for the Translator," *Aslib Proceedings,* November 1979, pp. 521–524. A useful discussion of various dictionaries and other sources, many of which should be found in libraries.

Mawson, C. O. Sylvester. *Dictionary of Foreign Terms.* 2d ed. rev. and updated by Charles Berlitz. New York: Thomas Y. Crowell, 1975, 368 pp., $9.95.

Sheehy's *Guide to Reference Books* lists and annotates 641 various types of foreign-language dictionaries under headings from Afrikaans to Zulu. There are only 129 English-language titles. The compiler rightly notes that "foreign language dictionaries are important in any library."

Most readers are familiar with the typical bilingual dictionary which offers the foreign word and the equivalent English word. The process is then reversed with the English word first, followed by the equivalent foreign word. For other than large public, academic, and special libraries, the bilingual dictionary is usually quite enough, particularly as the number is limited to European languages. For that purpose the Cassell's entries are standard, familiar desk dictionaries (issued in England under the Cassell imprint, here by Macmillan). Most have gone through numerous editions and revisions by just as many editors. Pronunciation is given clearly enough for even the amateur to follow, and the equivalent words are accurate. Definitions, of course, are not given. All the dictionaries usually include slang words, colloquialisms, idioms, and more common terms from various subject areas. The number of main entries varies from 120,000 to 130,000.

Scribner's Sons publishes a similar variety of bilingual dictionaries, equally good. The library wishing the most up-to-date version should check *Publishers Trade List Annual* under the two publishers and find the most current dictionaries required. In other words, over the years Macmillan and Scribner's have established themselves as reliable sources of standard college-type bilingual dictionaries, and the library can rarely go wrong ordering from either one. The editors of *American Reference Books Annual* have a particular interest in foreign dictionaries, and these are reviewed in each volume. The reviews are controversial. In the majority of libraries the two basic series by the two publishers are enough.

Harrap's New Standard French and English Dictionary (London: Harrap, 1972–1980, 4 vols.) is the basic bilingual set found in most libraries. As one reviewer puts it: "Harrap has passed into the language as an eponym. It has been called "La Bible des dictionnaires bilingues."[34]

When the librarian moves toward less or more specialization, there are two avenues open. The Mawson title is a good example of the less-specialized aid for ready-reference work. It contains about

15,000 words and phrases from some 50 languages, listed in alphabetical order by the word or phrase with an English equivalent. Words from both classical and modern technical literature are included. Actually, it is a good dictionary for the avid reader to have when reading authors likely to employ foreign terms. It is true that many of the standard English-language dictionaries include at least major foreign words and expressions, but they hardly touch the surface. For both ready reference and as an adjunct to general reading at home, a dictionary with a wide variety of foreign terms is of considerable help.

At the other extreme is the standard monolingual dictionary which may range in size from the equivalent English-language desk dictionary to the unabridged version. The flaw for reference work is that the dictionary is completely in the language of origin and presupposes a fairly solid command of the language. This is particularly true of the historical and the unabridged current dictionaries, such as the classic Littre *Dictionnaire de la Langue Francaise,* issued in the late nineteenth century, which contains numerous supporting quotations and thus is on the order of *The Oxford English Dictionary.*

One is inclined to agree that monolingual dictionaries are important for large libraries, certainly for those serving a foreign population of any size, but of only passing interest for reference work. This is not entirely true, especially if the reference librarian is thorough and possibly frustrated in seeking a bit of information about a quotation (which can be checked in the larger, historical type of foreign dictionaries) or a point of local history (again, often tracked down through the dictionary). Even facts on folklore, technical developments in industry, and so on, are possible to find in a large dictionary.

SUGGESTED READING

Adams, Robert, *Bad Mouth.* Berkeley: University of California Press, 1978. A scholarly study of the "dark side" of language, including slang, swearing, and just plain insults. As one critic observed, Adams has an "elegant and sinuous prose" style.

Maleska, Eugene T., "Confessions of a Crossword Editor," *The New York Times Magazine,* October 28, 1979, pp. 96–98. The editor of the paper's crossword section explains how a puzzle is put together and the use of the dictionary in such a situation.

Michaels, Leonard and Christopher Ricks (eds.), *The State of the Language.* Berkeley,

---

[34]Philip Howard, "Breaking Through the Language Barrier," *The (London) Times,* June 9, 1980, p. 7. The review traces the history of the set.

California: University of California Press, 1979. A series of essays on the state of the English language, with 63 contributors considering various aspects, from permissive versus descriptive dictionary practices to slang.

Murray, Elizabeth, *Caught in the Web of Words: James A. H. Murray and the Oxford English Dictionary*. New Haven, Connecticut: Yale University Press, 1977. A lively, informative biography of the genius behind the OED, who died 13 years before the last of the dictionary appeared. According to Murray's granddaughter (author of this work), he worked himself to death.

Smith, Alice, "Current Survey of Reference Sources for Children and Youth," *Reference Services Review,* January/March 1980, pp. 5–13. The first part of this historical article concerns children's dictionaries, and there is a useful annotated listing of landmarks in the field.

Urdang, Laurence, "Perennial Plagues," *The New York Times Magazine,* September 2, 1979, pp. 8, 9. A brief discussion of the development of dictionaries of usage in America.

CHAPTER TEN

Geographical Sources

T HE VALUE OF GEOGRAPHICAL AIDS to everyone from the Sunday driver and the military commander to the economist and the high school student is too well known to belabor here. Still, the map is sometimes underestimated, and one expert would go so far as to say that "the need for maps is closely linked to a country's economic development. Cost-benefit analyses have shown the value of maps for developing and maintaining the economic level of a country."[1]

On the purely imaginative level, geographical sources have the ability to transport the viewer to any part of the world and, in this day, to the universe. The difference between geographical sources and other works is that they are primarily graphic representations which allow the imagination full reign. Indeed, many of them are works of art, and they provide a type of satisfaction rarely found in the purely textual approach to knowledge. A map, then, "is a representation of the environment. It is an abstraction, a simplification, and often

---

[1]Donald A. Wise, "Cartographic Sources and Acquisitions Techniques," *Western Association of Map Libraries. Information Bulletin,* March 1979, p. 176. Despite the known value of maps, not all countries are well mapped. According to early 1980s United Nations figures, only about 25 percent of Asia's land mass is to be found in topographic mapping. "The Americans have discovered that all the detailed maps of the Gulf area are British ones 20 to 30 years old and inadequate for attempting to land marines on beaches or for dropping parachutes." *The (London) Observer,* August 3, 1980, p. 8.

styled. . . . We see a clear tradition of art and information, intimately connected, the form and the presentation being at once appealing and enhancing the usefulness of the map."[2]

There are as many reasons for consulting these sources as there are patrons, and most are self-evident—the location of a small town in some country, the nearest railroad or airline serving a village, the condition of roads in a state, the number of hotels in a city, and so on. More specialized or thematic sources will serve to answer almost every geographical question from the location of a specific archaeological site to the name and size of a canyon on the moon.

The variety of the sources requires a basic understanding of general features shared by all. Beyond that, the reference librarian must become familiar with the specific qualities of the individual works. Answers to geographical questions are not necessarily limited to specialized books. Geography is a component part of many other reference tools. Encyclopedias usually have individual maps or separate atlas volumes. Information about cities, towns, states, and countries frequently will be found in greater detail in an encyclopedia, a yearbook, or an almanac than in many of the geographical sources cited here. The distinct advantage of geographical works over more generalized reference books is that (1) they give information for smaller units not found in general works; (2) the information given often will be more precise; and (3) since they are limited to one area, they are usually easier to use. More in-depth indexing is another major advantage.

Definition and scope

Geographical sources used in reference work may be subdivided into three large categories: maps and atlases, gazetteers, and guidebooks.

Maps and Atlases Everyone understands that a map is, among other things, a representation of certain boundaries of the earth on a flat surface. (It may include the representation of the moon and planets as well.) The Library of Congress defines maps in a broad way; i.e., "all forms of cartographic materials normally added to the collections of the Library, including flat maps and charts, collections of maps in atlas form, terrain models, globes, etc."[3]

[2]Nancy Green and Michael Donovan, "Maps: One Kind and Another," *Print,* March/April 1979, p. 37. This short article includes after the text numerous illustrations showing different types of maps and problems concerned with mapmaking.

[3]Donald A. Wise, "Cartographic Acquisitions at the Library of Congress," *Special Libraries,* December 1978, p. 486.

A physical map traces the various features of the land, from the rivers and valleys to the mountains and hills. A route map shows roads, railroads, bridges, and the like. A political map normally limits itself to political boundaries (e.g., towns, cities, counties, states) but may include topographical and route features. Either separately or as one, these three types make up a large number of maps found in general atlases.

> *More than four hundred years have passed since Mercator first coined the term "atlas" to describe a collection of maps bound up in a volume. The popularity of the atlas was rapidly established with sixteenth-century armchair geographers who could now travel at will over a paper landscape which encompassed the world within the pages of an albeit weighty tome. When the art of chromolithographic printing for maps was mastered at the turn of the nineteenth century the scope of atlas production was widened considerably. Now, by varying the combinations of content and style even slightly, a publisher can produce almost a dozen different general atlases for different sectors of the market.*[4]

Cartography is the art of mapmaking, and a major headache of cartographers has been the accurate representation of the features of the earth on maps. This task has resulted in various projections, i.e., the effort to display the surface of a sphere upon a plane without undue distortion. Mercator or his forerunners devised a system, still the best known today, which is based on parallel lines, that is, latitude (the lines measuring the "width" of the globe, i.e., the angular distance north or south from the equator) and longitude (the lines measuring the "length" of the globe, i.e., the angular distance east or west on the earth's surface). This system works well enough except at the polar regions, where it distorts the facts. Hence on any Mercator projection, Greenland is completely out of proportion to the United States. Since Mercator, hundreds of projections have been designed; but distortion is always evident—if not in one section, in another. For example, the much-praised azimuthal equidistant projection, with the North Pole at the center of the map, indicates directions and distances more accurately, but in other respects it gives a peculiar stretched and pulled appearance to much of the globe.

The only relatively accurate representation of the earth is a globe. The need for a globe in a reference situation is probably questionable. It is certainly desirable to have one; however, the reference librarian who has had occasion to use a globe instead of a map to answer particular reference questions is rare indeed.

[4]Y. O'Donoghue, "Some Recent British Atlases," *British Book News,* August 1977, p. 584.

While maps and charts represent features of the earth's surfaces, there are now many which focus on points in space. Increasing data becomes readily available as computers and space cameras operate to map the universe. A set of procedures which uses electronics, computers, and sophisticated lenses also makes it possible to photograph almost any point on the earth for detailed study. Mapping techniques for both the earth and the universe are expanding—closely tied together.

Thanks to such technology, it is now possible to have an accurate picture of at least part of the universe; e.g., the *Rand McNally New Concise Atlas of the Universe* (Chicago: Rand McNally, 1978, 190 pp.) is an example of several good-to-excellent atlases of this type. Here the four parts show the earth from space and the universe as seen from the earth—as well as from cameras launched into space. This particular work includes not only clear and detailed maps, but a well-written text, pictures, diagrams, and other features to help the layperson appreciate what is beyond the earth. There is a less-than-satisfactory index, but it is good enough for most ready-reference purposes.

EVALUATION

Maps and atlases are a mysterious area for the average librarian or patron. They depend primarily on the graphic arts and mathematics for presentation and compilation. Skill in determining the best map or atlas draws upon a type of knowledge not normally employed in evaluating a book.

Map printing is a specialized department of the graphic arts; and while simple maps can be prepared by an artist or draftsperson, more complicated works require a high degree of skill. More important, their proper reproduction necessitates expensive processes which the average printer of reference works is not equipped to handle. As with dictionaries and encyclopedias, the inherent expenses and skills of the field narrow the competent cartographic firms down to a half-dozen or so. In the United States, the leading publishers are Rand McNally & Company, C. S. Hammond & Company, and the National Geographic Society. In Great Britain, the leaders are John G. Bartholomew (Edinburgh)[5] and the cartographic department of the Oxford University Press.

[5] James Sage, "Bartholomew's Maps," *Print*, March/April 1979, pp. 50–51+. The 150th anniversary of the Edinburgh mapmaking firm is the focus of this short history.

When the cartographic firm is not known, it is advisable to check on its reputation and integrity through other works it may have issued. The mapmaker may differ from the publisher and, in the case of an atlas, both should be checked.

Currency

Names on the face of the earth change often, and the result is that no map can be completely current. Few cartographers, for example, can keep up with rapid place-name conversions in newly independent countries, or where rulers refashion names to suit.

Then, too, mapmakers may be fighting secrecy. Here, they usually win. For example, Soviet censors have tried to keep the name of a highly secret space-city out of print. The city, Leninsk, is well known and is even included in the National Geographic map of the Soviet Union. No matter:

> *The Soviet authorities prefer to make believe that it does not exist. As part of a traditional policy of secrecy in anything relating to military, aerospace and nuclear activities, they are making an effort, not always successfully, to conceal the presence of some entire towns.*
>
> *When Soviet reporters file on space launchings from the so-called Baikonus Cosmodrome outside Leninsk, they do not mention the city. They use the dateline "Baikonur," a code name borrowed from a sheep ranch 200 miles away.*
>
> *The name of Leninsk is being assiduously kept out of official Soviet reference books and off Soviet maps. It is so sensitive that its population, estimated by the American astronauts at 50,000, is not included in census reports even within the nation's overall population figures.*[6]

Reputable mapmakers follow a policy similar to that of encyclopedia firms: continuous revising and reprinting. This practice normally is clearly indicated by: (1) copyright date on the verso of the title page; and (2) revision date, with some indication in revision.

As of this writing (early 1981) the mapmakers were preparing new editions of all their standard works. The reason is the completion or near completion of the 1980 U.S. census which, if it does not change names on the land, does date much of the statistical data for population and eventually results in new congressional alignments which many of the mapmakers indicate.

[6]Theodore Shabad, "Soviet Censors in Losing Battle," *The New York Times,* October 22, 1979, p. 10.

Scale

Maps often are classed according to scale. The detailed map will have a larger scale. The scale is indicated, usually at the bottom of the map, by a line or bar which shows distances in kilometers or miles or both.

Geographers use map scale to refer to the size of the representation on the map. A scale of 1:63,360 is one inch to the mile (63,360 inches). The larger the second figure (scale denominator), the smaller the scale of the map. For example, on a map which shows the whole United States, the scale may be 1:16,000,000 (one inch is equal to about 250 miles). This is a small-scale map. A large-scale map of a section of the United States, say the Northwest, would have a scale of 1:4,000,000. In the same atlas, the scale for Europe (and part of Russia) is 1:16,000,000; but for France (and the Alps) it is 1:4,000,000.

Within an atlas the scale from map to map may vary considerably, although better atlases attempt to standardize. The standardization is based as much on the size of the page on which the map appears as on any effort of the publisher to use the same basic scales throughout.

American atlases are often faulted for failure to maintain the same relative scales throughout their works. This is true when the United States and Canada are given emphasis and the remainder of the world is pushed into a small section of the atlas. For example, in the basic *Rand McNally Cosmopolitan World Atlas,* the scale for the United States and Europe is larger than for the rest of the world. In the same company's *Pictorial World Atlas* (published in 1980), scales vary so that a map of Australia is at 1:13,200,000 while the New Zealand map is at 1:3,300,000. The difference would make some believe the two countries are approximately the same size.

One way out of the problem is to show regional maps in the same scale; the *Cosmopolitan,* for example, does have double-page, full-color global sections which use the same scale. Thus the innocent viewer gets a fair comparison of sizes and distances between different parts of the world.

It may be argued, and justifiably in some cases, that the atlas is primarily for nationals who are more interested in particulars of North America than in the remainder of the world. European atlases frequently are guilty of the same fault, with emphasis on Europe at the expense of the remainder of the world.

The page size, or the size of an individual sheet map, will be a rapid indicator of the probable scale. Normally, the larger the page, the larger the scale. Hence, the *Rand McNally Commercial Atlas,* which concentrates on large-scale reproductions of states and cities, has a map-page size of 21 by 15 inches. Other large atlases vary from 16 by 13 to 19 by 12 inches. Smaller works range from 10 by 7 inches to 12 by 9 inches.

Page size is not always indicative of scale. For example, an atlas may concentrate on showing only major countries and not divisions of those countries. It will have a large format, but small-scale maps. Another atlas may emphasize thematic maps of a small area and have a relatively large scale for its maps, yet may have a small or medium-sized format. Also, the page may include other material besides the map. This will increase the page size without increasing the scale of the map. Conversely, another publisher will use the full page for the map. The format, then is a poor guide; in every case, the librarian needs to check the scale employed.

Wise furnishes a fascinating footnote to the discussion of scale:

Another problem for the map librarian is the security classification or caveats which are applied to current large-scale topographic map coverage in some countries. In the free world, long-standing tradition has made maps both numerous and relatively easy to acquire. The Soviet Union, the People's Republic of China, Eastern European countries, some Arab countries, Pakistan, India, and Burma are countries which consider all maps 1:250,000 scale or larger as classified documents. Their major mapping agencies are under military control and basic policies are restrictive concerning public use or purchase of such items.[7]

Color Color's chief value is to enable different classes of data to be related to one another and to show distinctions among details. On physical maps, color clarifies approximate height by hatch lines, hill shading, and special cross sections.

The success or failure of color depends on careful consideration in printing. Most multicolor maps are printed on two- or three-color lithographic offset presses, the latter allowing six-color reproduction. This is delicate work, and where it is not successful, there is a lack of perfect registration. In a word, where colors slop over, where the color for a town does not correspond with the outline of the town, the librarian can be sure that the map was poorly printed. The secret is to have colors which make the printing legible. Contrasts are sometimes so severe as to make it nearly impossible to read the maps. A poorly printed work is indicative of the publisher's whole attitude toward the map.

[7]Wise, op. cit. p. 181.

Symbols As important as the choice of colors is the selection of symbols. A standard set of symbols for roads, streams, villages, cities, airports, historical sites, parks, and the like is shown on most maps. While these legends are fairly well standardized in American maps, they vary in European maps. Consequently, the symbols should be clearly explained on individual maps, or in an atlas at some convenient place in the preface or introductory remarks.

Thematic mapmakers have a considerable problem with symbols, and here the variation from map to map and country to country will be significant. The problem becomes complicated when a number of different subjects are to be displayed on a single map. Frequently, the task is so complex that the map becomes illegible. Hence, in the case of thematic maps, it is best to have different maps indicating different items, such as population, rainfall, or industry, rather than a single map.

Projections All maps are distorted, and with any single method employed to indicate surface, numerous distortions are possible. Normally, an atlas will use a number of projections to overcome distortions and to indicate the degree of distortion in a map. These may range from global views of continents as seen from space to the world as seen from an airplane crossing the North Pole. The projections should be clearly indicated, although the technique may be of more interest to the professional cartographer than to the casual reader.

The maps may be distorted on purpose; e.g., in *The Times Atlas of World History* some maps are three-dimensional, as when the Alps tower over Europe; others curve to show the vast extent of the Mongol empire as contrasted with Europe; and "a tilted map of Europe gives actuality to the inundation of the civilized world"; e.g., Europe assumes a graphically minor position in contrast with the Mongol empire. In discussing the *Times Atlas,* critic J. H. Elliott considers projection and distortion:

> *Behind the deliberate distortions lies an exercise in relativism. Professor Barraclough wants to help us see the world through eyes other than our own. The Islamic world is therefore depicted from the standpoint of Mecca. We get an idea of how the policy of containment must look to the Soviet Union. Where normally we look up the Adriatic toward Venice, here Venice itself gazes down upon its Adriatic lifeline.*
>
> *On the other hand, there are bound to be occasions when cartography—even with all the technical resources available to it here—is simply incapable of depicting the angle of vision which the*

editor and compilers are anxious to present. How, for instance, can one depict on a map the contracting spaces of North America as seen by the Indians? The intention is clearly there, but we are left with a map which looks very much like any other map on this subject.[8]

Grid Systems   Latitude and longitude are the essentials of any map, and are particularly helpful for locating a special place on the map. These are further subdivided by degrees, minutes, and seconds —45°12′18″N, 1°15′E, for example, is the location of a certain French town. The advantage of this system is its ultimate accuracy, but it has the distinct disadvantage of being a number of such length as to be difficult to remember from index to map. Consequently, most maps also are divided into grids, or key reference squares. Index references are then made to these squares, usually by letter and number—E5, D6, and so on, with the page number of the map.

The usefulness of a map may be evaluated by the size of the grid system. Obviously, the larger the squares, the more difficult it is to pinpoint a place.

Type   There is clearly scope for considerable improvement in the design of lettering on most maps. Even the best of them often use typefaces developed for display or book texts, and not specifically for maps. Sans serif is used as the basic face for many maps, variation being shown more in the size of the type than in the different kinds of faces. The normal procedure is to use a scale whereby large places are indicated by large type, medium ones by medium-sized type, and so on.

Binding   The need for a sturdy binding is evident, but in addition to strength it must allow the atlas to be opened easily. When the book is lying flat, the entire map should be visible and not hidden in part of the binding. Oddly enough, this latter fault is more frequent than the relatively high prices of some atlases would indicate.

Marginal Information   Each map should give certain basic information, usually in the margin. A quick way of ascertaining the worth of a map is to check for this type of information. It should include, at minimum, the scale (inclusion of both a bar and natural scale is desirable), the type of projection, and where thematic maps are employed, the symbols and significance of the colors. In an atlas, the

[8]J. H. Elliott, "Global Vision," *The New York Review of Books,* December 7, 1978, p. 14.

meaning of the general symbols may be given in the preface or introduction, as well as the date of printing, the dates of revision, and other such data. Normally the directions are not given in an atlas, it being understood that north is at the top of the map. On single sheets, there should be a compass rose indicating direction.

The index

A comprehensive index is as important in reference work as the maps. A good index is in alphabetical sequence and clearly lists all place names which appear on the map. In addition, there should be reference to the exact page; the exact map; and latitude, longitude, and grid information. A page number alone is never enough, as anyone will testify who has sought an elusive town or city on a map lacking such information.

The index in many atlases is really an excellent gazetteer; that is, in addition to basic information, each entry includes data on population and country. When an index becomes a gazetteer, it should include not only place names shown on the map, but places so small or inconsequential as not to be located on the maps. The difference may be indicated by some type of marking or special column. But the difference must be apparent or the user may be searching in vain for something not in the atlas proper.

Other useful index information will include pronunciation, standard transliteration of non-Romanized place names, and sufficient cross-references from spellings used in a foreign country to those employed by the country issuing the atlas or map; e.g., Wien, Austria, should be cross-referenced to Vienna, as well as an entry from Vienna to "*see* Wien."

A check: Try to find four or five names listed in the index on the maps. How long did it take, and how difficult was the task? Reverse this test by finding names on the maps and trying to locate them in the index. Failure of either test spells trouble.

Guides and bibliographies

Larsgaard, Mary. *Map Librarianship*. Littleton, Colorado: Libraries Unlimited, 1978, 330 pp. $18.50.

Winch, Kenneth. *International Maps and Atlases in Print*, 2d ed., New York: R. R. Bowker Company, 1976, 866 pp., $47.50.

The best general guide for map librarians and those who just want to know something about how to manage a collection in a small or medium-sized library is the Larsgaard title. The author offers specific advice on acquisitions; evaluating a collection; and, most important, how to develop a reference policy around the daily use of the map section. The work concludes with samples of map acquisition policies. It is by far the best text of its type now available and should be a beginning point for any librarian interested in the subject. Note, too, that the author is the editor for the special issue of *Library Trends* on maps. (See Suggested Reading at the end of the chpter.)

More a history than a guide, Walter Ristow, *The Emergence of Maps in Libraries* (Hamden, Connecticut: Shoe String Press, 1980) gives a good overflow of the subject. The collection of articles from 1939 to 1979 touches on most aspects of maps and will give both the beginner and the expert a handy overview of the subject.

The basic bibliography in the field is the *International* work which lists all maps and atlases known to be available for purchase as of the publication of the bibliography. There are approximately 8000 entries by 700 publishers, and the whole is arranged by country, with subdivisions for various types of maps.

The Library of Congress includes maps and atlases in the *National Union Catalog,* and for larger libraries the Geography and Map Division offers as its contribution to the MARC tapes of the NUC a section called "MARC Map." This is some 60,000 titles of single-sheet maps acquired by the Library of Congress. Librarians, as with other sections of the NUC/MARC tape, may subscribe to the "MARC Map" series. About 400 new titles are added each month.

The Bibliographic Guide to Maps and Atlases (Boston: G. K. Hall Company, 1980) includes both the Library of Congress and the New York Public Library Map Division entries. It is a supplement to the New York Public Library *Dictionary Catalog of the Map Division,* published in 1971. G. K. Hall apparently plans to continue the series on an annual basis and, within a few years, to publish the volumes between 1971 and 1980.

For the average library, the listing of maps and atlases in *Subject Guide to Books in Print* is sufficient. Librarians seeking evaluations of geographical publications other than those in standard reviews should consult the *Bulletin, Special Libraries Association, Geography and Map Division.* A related item, with equally useful reviews: *Western Association of Map Libraries, Information Bulletin.* Also reliable are the reviews in *Geographical Review* and "Reference and Subscription Book Reviews" in *The Booklist.*

Ken Kister, who has a buying guide for dictionaries and one for encyclopedias, has another guide scheduled for 1982, i.e., *Atlas Buying Guide* (Phoenix, Arizona: Oryx Press). This is an objective analysis of about 350 atlases, from the Rand McNally and Hammond standard titles to such specialized items as Peter Young's *Atlas of the Second World War* (New York: G. P. Putnams Sons, 1973). After a general introduction, the reviews are divided by general world atlases and thematic atlases. As in his other evaluative guides, Kister offers tips on how to select an atlas and has an invaluable comparative chart of the different atlases. This is by far the best retrospective aid for librarians, and the author promises to update it every three or four years.

WORLD ATLASES

The Times Atlas of the World: Comprehensive 6th Edition. London: Times Newspapers Limited, 1980, 125 map plates, 268 pp. $125 (distributed in the United States by The New York Times Book Company).

Hammond Medallion World Atlas. Maplewood; New Jersey: Hammond, Incorporated, 1978, various paging, $50.

Rand McNally Cosmopolitan World Atlas. Chicago: Rand McNally & Company, 1981, various paging. $45. *The New International Atlas.* Chicago: Rand McNally & Company, 1980, 562 pp. $60. *Goode's World Atlas.* Chicago: Rand McNally & Company, 1981, 372 pp. $16.95.

At least one, and probably all, of these American-published atlases will be found in libraries. They are compiled by the leaders in the field and are frequently updated and totally revised. The list represents two extremes. The best atlas is the *Times* entry; but probably the most used, certainly the best known to Americans, is the traditional school-based *Goode's World Atlas*.

By any judgment, *The Times Atlas* is the best world atlas in the English language, or for that matter in any language. That it happens to be the most expensive is chiefly because such meticulous care has been taken, with emphasis on large-scale, multiple maps for several countries and an attention to detail and color rarely rivaled by other American atlases.

The volume consists of three basic parts. The first 40-page section is a conspectus of world minerals, sources of energy and food, and a variety of diagrams and star charts. The atlas proper comprises 124 double-page eight-color maps, the work of the Edinburgh house of Bartholomew. This is the vital part, and it is perfect in both typography and color. The clear typeface enables the reader to make out each of the enormous number of names. A variety of colors are used with skill and taste to show physical features, railways, rivers, political boundaries, and so on. A remarkable thing about this atlas is that it shows almost every noteworthy geographical feature from lighthouses and tunnels to mangrove swamps—all by symbols which are carefully explained.

The Times Atlas is suited for American libraries because, unlike many other atlases, it gives a large amount of space to non-European countries. No other atlas matches it for the detailed coverage of the Soviet Union, China, Africa, and Southeast Asia—lands hardly overlooked in other atlases, but usually covered in considerably less detail. A uniform scale of 1:2,500,000 is employed for most maps, but is changed to 1:850,000 for the United Kingdom. Maps of the larger land masses are supplemented with smaller, detailed maps which range from maps of urban centers to maps of the environs of Mt. Everest.

The final section is a 210,000-name index, which, for most purposes, serves as an excellent gazetteer. After each name, the country is given with an exact reference to a map.

The Times Atlas is frequently updated. The 1980 edition includes new countries and name changes, particularly those in Africa; plans of more cities than previously; and completely revised prefatory material on physiography, oceanography, and detailed up-to-date thematic maps.

In the new edition more attention is given to mainland China than in previous works; and while the reason for this is obvious, it may not be so obvious that the cartographers had a spelling problem to solve. China has introduced what is known as the Pinyin system of rendering its language in the Roman alphabet, as opposed to the previous Wade-Giles method based on English rendition of the phonetically representative Chinese ideograms. The American press has adopted the Pinyin approach as have the cartographers for the *Times* atlas—not an easy decision, as the new approach is opposed by many librarians who have cataloged holdings by the old method and now must change over to the Pinyin system. (Incidentally, the Library of Congress now uses the Pinyin, but is opposed in this by several university experts and libraries.)

The Times Atlas comes in a shorter version: *The New York Times Atlas of the World* (New York: Times Books, 1981, various paging, $60). This is revised frequently and has many of the same features, certainly the same maps, as the more expensive, larger edition. However, it is a smaller work and instead of 200,000 names in the index, it has half as many, about 90,000. It weighs only 5 pounds, compared with 10 pounds for the English version. *The New York Times* edition has maps on a single 11- by 15-inch page, compared with two facing pages of 12 by 18 inches for *The Times Atlas*. For many libraries, the *New York Times* edition will be suitable, as it is for homes.

Rand McNally offers a number of atlases and services. The basic atlas, upon which several others are based, is the frequently revised *Cosmopolitan World Atlas,* usually known simply as the *Cosmopolitan.* Rand McNally, like most major publishers, updates the maps each time the atlas is printed. However, a complete revision of the *Cosmopolitan* (including prefatory material) is usually limited to every six or seven years.

The *Cosmopolitan* 1981 edition is an entirely new effort, the last edition appearing in 1971. There are approximately 300 maps on a scale of from 1:300,000 (1 inch equals about 4.75 miles) to 1:16,000,000 (1 inch equals about 250 miles). For the 12 largest metropolitan areas in the United States, the scale is jumped to 1:300,000. Heaviest emphasis, as might be expected, is on American maps (84 pages, with separate maps for each of the states). Europe is assigned 25 pages, and the rest of the world shares 30, which represents a 2-page increase from the 1971 edition—some indication of the primary focus of Rand McNally.

There are two separate indexes. About 85,000 entries are in the general index, and these help to locate political names and physical features. The facts and text material found in the nonmap sections are in another index. Most of these sections are given over to descriptions of the United States, including many travel maps.

The *Hammond Medallion World Atlas* has some 600 maps, including one for each of the 500 states. Among other basic features: a world index of over 100,000 place names (some 100,000 less, let it be noted, than *The Times Atlas*); numerous subindexes interleaved with the maps; zip codes; sections on ecology and the Bible, as well as history; numerous diagrams and photographs; and so on. The maps are passable and the index is excellent. One way to avoid the frills and save money is to purchase Hammond's *Ambassador* edition, which sells for $18.95 and is the same as the *Medallion* except for its omission of the extra materials.

A higher-priced, larger Rand McNally atlas found in many libraries is *The New International Atlas*. First published in 1969, it was revised for the second time in 1980. Many consider it, next to *The Times Atlas,* one of the best single-volume works now available. The oversized atlas includes an index of close to 200,000 names and features large-scale map coverage of Europe. In fact, the editors make a point of stressing how well the scale shows the entire world in some kind of reasonable balance.

The relatively accurate balance is achieved by employing six map series or scales, which range from portrait maps with 1 inch equal to 380 miles to urban-area maps of 1 inch to 4.7 miles. In addition there are numerous charts and diagrams and thematic maps which are nicely arranged and easy to use.

Used extensively in American shcools, the *Goode's World Atlas* is as familiar as any in the United States. By 1981, it was in its sixteenth edition and is updated frequently to meet the needs of schools. Both the maps and the text are clear, easy to understand, and carefully prepared. The maps are arranged by continent and within each section by region, and usually by country for Europe and North America. In later editions, more attention has been given to Africa and Third World countries, but emphasis remains on the Western nations. The standard maps are supplemented by a section on urbanized areas of the world. Thematic maps include a cartogram to show each country at a size in proportion to population. A final section has the geographic tables, glossary, and a main index of about 32,000 entries.

NATIONAL MAPS

U.S. Geological Survey, *The National Atlas of the United States of America*. Washington: Government Printing Office, 1970, 417 pp. $150.

The United States has its own national atlas, a 14-pound oversized volume with 335 pages of maps and a 41,000-entry index. The volume is in two sections: "General Reference Maps" and "Special Subject Maps." The short first part consists of a general United States atlas. Most of the maps are at the scale of 1:200,000,000. with urban areas at 1:500,000 and certain other areas at 1:1,000,000. These are the basic maps familiar to the general atlas user. They show every geographical feature from national parks and wildlife refuges to 13 different varieties of water features. There are only a limited number of physical maps.

The U.S. Geological Survey has a continuing publishing program, and many libraries regularly receive new maps as issued. These are detailed, covering elevation, vegetation, and cultural features and, as the University of Idaho map librarian points out, are ideal "sources of information for fishing, hiking and hunting.[9]

In addition to the U.S. Geological Survey, the three agencies

---

[9]Dennis Baird. "The University Library Map Collection," *The Bookmark,* December 1978, p. 31.

most likely to generate maps for general use are the Department of Housing and Urban Development, the Defense Mapping Agency (DMA), and the Bureau of the Census.

The DMA maps have their own cataloging system, and many librarians keep near the file the *DMA Depository Catalog Index.* The index makes it relatively easy to find maps covering a particular geographic area. The same agency supplies foreign hydrographic and aeronautical charts.

The government LANDSAT satellites have photographed almost every area, and larger libraries have various photos from the satellite sources. These, along with other sources of aerial photos, often are part of the map collection.

Sources of government maps

This side of the large or specialized library, the three best sources of government maps remain (1) *The Monthly Catalog of United States Government Publications,* which lists some, but certainly not all, government maps; (2) *Selected U.S. Government Publications* which, as the title suggests, is more selective and useful for smaller libraries; and (3) *Subject Bibliography* 102 (the subject bibliographies which took the place of the familiar *Price Lists*), which lists maps. (All of these are discussed in the chapter on government documents.) See, too, the bibliographies mentioned previously; for example, Larsgaard's text has a section on "U.S. Government Produced Maps," as does Joe Morehead's text on *United States Public Documents* to be considered later.

A useful overview for both beginners and experienced map librarians will be found in Jane Low's "The Acquisition of Maps and Charts Published by the United States Government," *Occasional Papers No. 125* (Urbana: University of Illinois Graduate School of Library Science, November 1976). This includes about 30 pages of text and 6 pages of references.

Local and regional maps

> *Rand McNally Road Atlas: United States, Canada, Mexico.* Chicago: Rand McNally, 1970 to date, various updates and pages. $4.95, paperback. (Note: Title varies slightly from year to year.)

Every library will have a suitable map of its own state and city or town—preferably in clear view—plus maps of the county and surrounding states. As noted, these maps are easily obtained. A problem arises when someone wants to locate a particular street in a distant city. Lacking a specific map such as those in the Rand McNally *International Atlas,* the next best thing is one of the larger atlases, an encyclopedia, or a guidebook. Guidebooks frequently include maps of many smaller cities not found in the standard works. Companies often issue detailed block maps, particularly if they have interests in real estate. Also, the telephone company often will give the library a copy of its local map which shows areas where tolls are not charged. Usually, this map is quite large and extremely detailed and it often shows considerably more than is found on most standard local maps.

The familiar road map (at one time free from many gasoline service stations, now usually available only for 75 cents, is a familiar part of many library collections. The maps are maintained in an effort to give current tourist information, to assist students in geography classes, and for the general edification of the layperson. Note: As of late 1981, apparently Exxon is the only major oil company which still gives away maps.

The road or local map is available from other sources: (1) the American Automobile Association issues such maps, along with tourist aids, to its members and often will cooperate with the local library in suggesting sources for maps; (2) state and provincial offices issue maps, usually to encourage tourists; and[10] (3) local Chambers of Commerce usually have detailed city maps as well as detailed information on the city itself. The easiest way for a library to get such material is to send a request to the Chamber of Commerce in the city or town needed. If an exact address is required, see: *World Wide Chamber of Commerce Directory* (Loveland, Colorado: Johnson Publishing Co., 1976 to date). This is frequently updated.

Libraries, as well as the average traveler, will buy a commercial road atlas to supplement what is available elsewhere. There are numerous such atlases, among the most familiar being those issued by Rand McNally. Their *Road Atlas* includes detailed maps of the states, the Canadian provinces, Mexico, and some larger cities. In addition to clear indication of highways, roads, and minor routes, the 130-page-or-so guide shows such things as national parks as well as listing amusement parks. In reviewing the 1977 edition, the Reference and

---

[10] For a detailed list of state offices, arranged by state, with exact addresses, see James Retting, "Road Maps and Tourist Information for the States and Canada: A List of Correct Addresses," *RQ,* Winter 1977, pp. 129–135. This is updated by results of a questionnaire sent to states asking for maps (and other information) for tourists. The list of agencies, along with a running account of what to expect, is found in Paul Grimes's "Still a Bargain: Maps and Data From 50 States," *The New York Times,* April 13, 1980, pp. XX1, XX35.

Subscription Books Review Committee makes an important point about all such maps—format. "The [atlas is] in a convenient size that will fit easily into the glove compartment of most cars."[11] And, one might add, the vertical file of most libraries.

Some idea of how many maps are produced locally is indicated by Library of Congress acquisitions. During 1977, the Library acquired "over 2900 atlases and maps from state and local organizations," i.e., "city managers or engineering offices, Chambers of Commerce, planning, transportation and educational organizations and other official agencies which produce maps, atlases and city plans."[12]

THEMATIC MAPS AND ATLASES

> *The Times Atlas of World History*. Maplewood, New Jersey: Hammond Incorporated, 1978, 360 pp., $70.
>
> *Rand McNally Commercial Atlas and Marketing Guide*. Chicago: Rand McNally & Company, 1976 to date, annual. $125.
>
> Shepherd, William. *Historical Atlas*, 9th ed. New York: Barnes & Noble, Inc., 1964, 226 maps. $28.50.

A primary method of classification of maps is by content and purpose. There are two basic types of maps other than those which are used for standard charting of the earth's surface. *Topographic* maps usually give details on geologic, soil, forest, and other basic features of the earth. *Thematic* maps, of which technically topographic titles are a part, usually refer to historical, economic, political, or other types of development. The thematic map may be used to show land use, land ownership, various methods of communication and transportation, transportation, and the like.

The thematic map requires constant updating. The exception may be the historical map which charts the flow of a given battle on a given day, although, in a broader context, historical opinions change and even this type of map may need revision.

Among the long line of atlases which have tried to give visual comprehensibility to history, the most familiar to American students

---

[11]*Booklist*, April 15, 1978, p. 1384.

[12]Donald J. Wise, op.cit., p. 486. Comparatively, for the same year the Library acquired 2083 maps, 380 atlases and 4 globes from copyright; 154 atlases and 18,955 maps from foreign exchange; 31,000 cartographic pieces from various federal agencies; 508 atlases and 13,685 maps by outright purchase; and 98 atlases and 2500 maps from donations. Accessions average over 60,000 items a year.

is Shepherd's *Historical Atlas.* The last edition covers world history from about 2000 B.C. to A.D. 1955. Outline maps prepared by Hammond indicate developments of commerce, war campaigns, adjustments of boundaries after various wars, and countless other useful approaches to history. There is a full index of names. Despite its usefulness, the volume is relatively poor typographically and the colored maps tend to be somewhat out of register.

Edited by the historian Geoffrey Barraclough, *The Times Atlas of World History* follows in the tradition of *The Times Atlas of the World,* that is to say, it is the best of its kind now available.[13] Here the focus is not on shifting borders brought about by battles and political maneuvering but on maps which clearly indicate the more important economic and social changes. Each map presents a given piece of information, and is accompanied by a text which clearly explains the situation. The maps include such topics as: Man in the Ice Age; African Peoples and Cultures to A.D. 1000; the Conflict of Church and State in Europe 1056 to 1314; The Americas on the Eve of European Conquest; The Ascendancy of France 1647 to 1715; The Chinese Revolution 1912 to 1949; and, finally, The World in 1975: Rich Nations and Poor Nations.

There are some 600 maps, of which close to 150 are double-page within the 15 by 11½ inch format. In addition, there is a 100,000-word glossary of individuals, events, and so on, which are shown on the maps, mentioned in the text, or both; a chronology of events, including cultural activities; and a separate index of geographical names. Another innovation is the focus. Most atlases concentrate on Western countries. Here, the editor, with the help of scholars throughout the world, pays considerable attention to the history of Africa and Asia.

The price of the atlas seems low for a work of such high quality—a quality obtained only after six years of work by the editor and some 125 historians, cartographers, designers, and so on. The total cost of producing the volume is reported to be over $1 million.[14]

The value of the *Rand McNally Commercial Atlas* is that it is revised every year, and for the library which can afford to rent it (it is rented, not purchased), the *Atlas* not only solves the problem of adequate United States and Canadian coverage, but solves it in the best form possible.

---

[13]Thomas Hodgkin, "The Global Picture," *The Times Literary Supplement,* February 29, 1980, p. 245. Here the critic points out a few flaws in the work.

[14]For a short summary of the development of the work, see the "Trade News" section of *Publishers Weekly,* July 31, 1978, p. 67.

The *Commercial Atlas* accurately records changes on a year-by-year basis. All information is the most up to date of any single atlas or, for that matter, any reference work of this type. It is an excellent source for current statistical data, and the first 95 or so pages offer general information on business facts ranging from U.S. agriculture and communications to retail trade and transportation. The maps give basic, demographic, and business data for some 116,000 places in the United States.

Technically, the *Commercial Atlas* is not devoted entirely to the United States and Canada; but aside from a small number of world and foreign maps, the concentration is on the individual states and provinces. Each of the maps, usually a double-page spread, places emphasis on the political-commercial aspects of the state or province. The maps are especially useful for indicating city and county boundaries. There is a wealth of statistical information (retail sales maps and analyses of businesses, manufacturers, and principal business centers) in each of the sections. By far the finest atlas for detailed treatment of the individual states and provinces, the whole is tied together with a superb index.

The index serves as a fine ready-reference source for (1) location of cities and towns by state and county; (2) the number and names of railroads and airlines serving the community; (3) estimated current population, including a separate figure for college and university students; and (4) zip codes. (In fact, the publisher claims there are more than 60,000 zips not listed in the official post office *Zip Code Directory*.)

As both an atlas and a handy compilation of up-to-date statistics, the *Rand McNally Commercial Atlas* is unrivaled. Limited for the most part to the United States and Canada, the encyclopedic information not only seems legitimate but also is a blessing.

Quick data on American cities can be found in hundreds of reference works, from the geographical sources discussed here to the almanac and encyclopedia to the yearbooks and statistical titles. One often used title is *Editor & Publisher Market Guide* (New York: Editor & Publisher, 1924 to date, annual). By state (and province) it lists alphabetically some 1500 communities. Standard pieces of information are given for each entry, from the names of newspapers to the more difficult-to-find data on average household income, number of households, kinds of businesses, number of passenger cars, and so on.

Similar information is available on the census maps issued by the U.S. Bureau of the Census, but these are likely to be more detailed. The maps take many forms, although a favored one is the SMSA

(Standard Metropolitan Statistical Area) which indicates geographical distributions of economic, social, and other types of data. These maps often are used by librarians attempting to chart a current profile of patrons and potential patrons in the library area. The Bureau of the Census will provide a list of maps or answer specific requests—say for thematic maps of central urban business districts—submitted by libraries.

GAZETTEERS

Columbia Lippincott Gazetteer of the World. New York: Columbia University Press, 1952 (supplement, 1962), 2148 pp. + 22 pp. $135.

Webster's New Geographical Dictionary, rev. ed. Springfield, Massachusetts: G. & C. Merriam Company, 1972, 1370 pp. $14.95.

U.S. Board of Geographic Names. *Gazetteer.* Washington: U.S. Government Printing Office, 1953 to date. Irregular.

In one sense, the index in any atlas is a gazetteer—that is, it is a geographical dictionary or finding list of cities, mountains, rivers, population, and the features in the atlas. A separate gazetteer is precisely the same, usually without maps. Why, then, bother with a separate volume? There are three reasons: (1) The gazetteers tend to list more names; (2) the information is usually detailed; and (3) a single, easily-managed volume is often welcomed. Having made these points, one can argue, and with some justification, that many atlas indexes have more entries, are more up to date, and contain a larger amount of information than one finds in a gazetteer. The wise librarian will first consider what is to be found in atlases before purchasing any gazetteer.

The number of gazetteers and the indexes found in good atlases, the expense of preparation, and the limited sales probably account for the lack of interest by many publishers in gazetteers as a separate group. The fact that most information sought by the layperson can be found in even greater detail in a general or geographical encyclopedia does not increase the use of gazetteers. Their primary value is as a source for locating places possibly overlooked by a standard atlas and as informal indexes.

The two American gazetteers found in almost every reference department differ in two important respects. The *Columbia* work has some 130,000 entries compared with about 48,000 in *Webster's,* although its price is about 7 times that of the *Webster's.* A minor difference which makes the *Webster's* more attractive for casual use is its comparatively compact size. Also, it has the advantage of being more up-to-date than the *Columbia*.

Aside from sheer volume, the *Columbia Gazetteer* tends to give considerably more information about each place. For example, it devotes one and one-half long columns to Berlin, while *Webster's* dismisses the former West German capital in a few short paragraphs. Entries in both include pronunciation, location, population, geographical and physical descriptions, and economic and some historical data.

The U.S. Board of Geographic Names issues its gazetteer in parts. These come out frequently, and each number covers a particular country, for example, the series includes the seven-volume *U.S.S.R. and Certain Neighboring Areas* as well as the more modest gazetteer on Greece, Algeria, Australia, and so on. Approved names and cross-references from variant names are given, as is the latitude and longitude on specified official maps. Of primary value to the large, specialized collection, this series offers an alternative when the librarian cannot find a name in other sources.

TRAVEL GUIDES

American Automobile Association. *Tour Book.* Washington: American Automobile Association, various dates, titles. Free to members.

American Guide Series. Prepared by Works Progress Administration, Federal Writers' Project. Various publishers, 1937 to 1950; frequently reprinted and reissued by numerous publishers.

Hotel and Motel Red Book. New York: American Hotel and Motel Association Directory Corp., 1886 to date, annual. $16.50.

Heise, Jon O., with Dennis O'Reilly. *The Travel Book: Guide to the Travel Guides.* New York: R. R. Bowker Company, 1981, 419 pp., $26.95.

The purpose of the general guidebook is to inform the traveler about what to see, where to stay, where to dine, and the best way of getting there. It is the type of book best carried in the car or in one's pocket. Librarians frequently find these works useful for the vast amount of details about specific places. Atlases and gazetteers are specific enough about pinpointing location, yet rarely deal with the down-to-earth facts travelers require.

Of all the guides, the single most useful work for reference is unquestionably the *American Guide Series*. Originally produced during the Depression by writers for the Federal Writers' Project of the Works Progress Administration, the series includes over 150 volumes.[15] Either private publishers or historical groups working within the various states have managed to update many of these works and to keep them in print. The guides include basic, usually accurate, historical, social, and economic information for almost every place in the state from the smallest unmarked hamlet to the largest cities. Maps, illustrations, and highway distances add to their usefulness, and most also have excellent indexes. For the reference desk, they are particularly helpful for locating information on communities, either entirely overlooked or only mentioned in standard reference books.

Putting more emphasis on comfort than on courage, the *Mobil Travel Guides* (Chicago: Rand McNally & Company, 1958 to date, annual) are a typical example of annual guides organized to inform the traveler about the best motels, hotels, restaurants, and resorts. The work is divided into seven regional volumes, each divided by state and town. There are a number of city maps, and the usual data on each place are covered. Some 21,000 different spots are graded with the star system—one for good, five for the best.

If the more adventuresome American traveler wants a simple listing of hotels and motels without ratings but including prices, the old standby is the *Hotel and Motel Red Book*. Revised annually, it is arranged by state and city and gives basic information about each accommodation. Since it lists only association members, facilities in small towns are often not included. There are advertisements that further indicate features.

Beyond these basic guides, the library will have a number of series. Among the standards are *Fielding's Travel Guide to Europe* (New York: Sloane, 1948 to date, annual) and the *Fodor's* modern guides (New York: McKay, 1953 to date, annual), which cover much the same material as found in *Fielding's*, although in a different fashion.

With close to 60 different published guides, the Fodor series is one of the more popular, certainly among people over 40 years of age.[16] Material is collected and written by couples who are natives of the country being examined and is annually updated. The guides

[15]Those in print are listed in *Subject Guide to Books in Print* under the state name. The whole series is in E. A. Baer's *Titles in Series* (Metuchen, New Jersey: Scarecrow Press, 1954, vol. 1, nos. 492 to 660, 2 vols., 1964).

[16]Sarah Ferrell. "New Fodor Pilot. . . ." *The New York Times*, March 19, 1979, Travel section, p. 17. A survey of readers of Fodor guides shows "the average reader to be 40 years old"; so it is not unusual that a guide of this type is directed to the individuals with better-than-average income, not to teen-agers.

serve the double purpose of giving information on daily needs (from hotels and restaurants to shopping) and instruction on the history and culture of the country. As might be expected in any series, some of the books are better than others, and in the Fodor collection the best, at least in terms of sales, is the general European guide.

While travel guidebooks are reviewed in all the standard reviewing services, the Heise title is a useful compendium of opinion. The editor picks 700 of the best series and titles. The guides are arranged geographically, and there is a title and subject index. The annotations for each guide are both evaluative and descriptive.

For an annual review of what has been published in this area, the best single source is *American Reference Books Annual.* Each volume devotes a section to travel guides. The reviews by various experts are excellent.

SUGGESTED READING

Coombs, James, "Globes: A Librarian's Guide to Selection and Purchase," *Wilson Library Bulletin,* March 1981, pp. 503–508. One of the few thorough discussions of how to evaluate modern globes. The author includes a section on special and extraterrestrial globes.

Kidd, Betty, "Preventive Conservation for Map Collections," *Special Libraries,* December 1980, pp. 529–538. A detailed review of the physical care of maps with practical tips on conservation methods.

Larsgaard, Mary (ed.), "Trends in Map Librarianship and Collections," *Library Trends,* Winter 1981. The total issue is given over to modern approaches to the subject, and it serves as a good introduction to map collecting and map librarianship.

Ristow, Walter W., "Aborted American Atlases," *The Quarterly Journal of the Library of Congress,* Summer 1979, pp. 320–345. An exciting historical account by the former chief of the Geography and Map Division of the Library of Congress, concerning the development, or lack of development of American atlases.

Robinson, Arthur and Barbara Petchenik, *The Nature of Maps: Essays Toward Understanding Maps and Mapping.* Chicago: University of Chicago Press, 1976. A discussion of the problems of making maps and the role distortion plays in the mapping process. Intended for professional cartographers, it is not easy going but is well worth the effort.

Wilford, John, *The Mapmakers.* New York: Alfred A. Knopf, 1981. A lively history of the men and women who have mapped the earth, including the oceans and, later, territory in space. The work begins in 200 B.C., and ends with modern passes at the universe.

CHAPTER ELEVEN

Government Documents[1]

THE BASIC MYSTERY for many beginning reference librarians is the government document. For some peculiar reason, the very term seems to frighten and confuse. Most of the cause may be attributed to a simple fact: Too many libraries tend to forget that the purpose of a government publication is to inform, to answer questions, and not to be an ignoble excuse for setting off hot discussion on organizational cataloging and administration.

Definition

A government document is any publication that is printed at government expense or published by authority of a governmental body. Documents may be considered in terms of issuing agencies: the congressional, judiciary, and executive branches, which include many departments and agencies. In terms of use, the documents may be classified as (1) records of government administration; (2) research documents for specialists, including a considerable number of statis-

---

[1]In view of the nature of government publications, most accredited library schools offer one or more special documents courses. It is as complicated and as rewarding a study as any of the specialized subject areas. Throughout this text, various government publications are noted as parts of units. This approach stems from a conviction that they should be an integral part of a reference collection rather than treated as separate items.

tics and data of value to science and business; and (3) popular sources of information. The physical form may be a book, pamphlet, magazine, report monograph, or microform.

While this discussion mainly concerns federal documents, state, county, and municipal publications are also a major concern of any library.

Some of the mystery surrounding government documents will be dispelled if one likens the government to the average private publisher. The latter may well issue a record of government action, although normally the commercial publication will be in somewhat more felicitous prose and with editorial comments. The transcendent purpose is to publish documents that may be considered useful for research, while the substantial returns are realized by popular works.

What, then, is the difference between using the government document and the average work issued by one of the publishers whose items appear in *Books in Print?* The source, the retrieval, and the organization puzzle most people.

One may freely admit that the bibliographical control and daily use of documents in reference work often are difficult and require expertise beyond the average experience of the reference librarian. Nevertheless, there are certain basic guides and approaches to government documents which should be familiar to all librarians.

GUIDES

Morehead, Joe. *Introduction to United States Public Documents*, 2d ed. Littleton, Colorado: Libraries Unlimited, Inc., 1978, 377 pp.. $17.50; paper, $11.50.

Schorr, Alan. *Government Reference Books*, Littleton, Colorado: Libraries Unlimited, Inc., 1972 to date, biennial. $18.50.

The basic textbook in the field is the Morehead volume, which is revised about every four years. It is a nice combination of facts about individual reference works and a clear, concise explanation of how the government manages to publish documents. Thanks to the superior organization and the fine writing style, the textbook is easy to read. Both the beginner and the expert will find considerable assistance here, and it is a first place to turn when puzzled about some mysterious aspect of the acquisition, organization, and selection of government documents. It should be noted that the author is a frequent contributor to periodicals and for a number of years has been the editor of the government documents column in *The Serials Librarian.*

Another useful guide is Nakata Yuri's *From Press to People: Collecting and Using U.S. Government Publications* (Chicago: American Library Association, 1979, 212 pp.). Here is a basic aid for librarians organizing a collection. In fact, its primary strength is the "how-to-do-it," aspect, contrasted with Morehead's much more decisive and detailed explanation of government documents and how they are produced, classified, and distributed. Various aspects of reference work are well handled.

Frederick O'Hara, who frequently writes about government documents, offers the librarian help with his *A Guide to Publications of the Executive Branch* (Ann Arbor, Michigan: Pierian Press, 1979, 288 pp.). A brief description is given of each agency which issues documents, and the work is of benefit to the nonspecialist seeking basic information for acquisitions. It is of somewhat less assistance for daily reference work.

Larger, usually depository libraries, rely on John Andriot, *Guide to U.S. Government Publications* (McLean, Virginia: Documents Index, 1959 to date, irregular).[2] Here basic data is given on over 2000 agencies and what they publish. The multivolume set lists a vast number of periodicals and series. The *Guide* is a valuable retrieval tool in reference work. It is arranged by Superintendent of Documents class numbers and has an agency and a title index. For most entries, there is an annotation indicating the content and use of the serial or periodical issued by the agency. While too detailed for many libraries, it is an aid for reference service when the normal guides fail to turn up an agency or its publications and has a method of discovering even the most elusive bureaucratic organization for listing in the work.[3]

Government Reference Books is a two-year roundup of basic reference books, many of which are not familiar to either the layperson or the expert. Here they are arranged by broad subject, i.e., general, social sciences, science and technology, and humanities. The documents are then indexed by author, title, and subject. Each is fully described. About 1500 to 2000 titles are annotated every two years, and it has become a habit to star those which the editor believes of

---

[2] Originally this was called *Guide to U.S. Government Serials and Periodicals* and was loose-leaf. It is now hardbound in three to five volumes, depending on the year it is updated. The 1979 edition is 3 volumes at $250.

[3] The *CIS/Index* lists serials and periodicals, and there are other sources such as the frequently revised *Government Periodicals and Subscription Services* from the Government Printing Office.

particular importance to smaller and medium-sized libraries. Carefully edited and easy to use, the Schorr bibliography augments the
standard sources and now stands as the Sheehy-Walford of the
government documents field.

The basic retrospective bibliography is *Government Publications: A
Guide to Bibliographic Tools* 4th ed. (Washington: Government Printing
Office, 1975.). First issued in 1927, this work lists about 3000 catalogs,
indexes, abstracts, guides, and so on, and is used for work with not
only federal documents but those of individual states, the United
Nations, and other countries. Most of the entries, arranged by
geographical area, have brief annotations. In addition, there is a short
history of each of the U.S. agencies and an excellent index.

CATALOGS

> U.S. Superintendent of Documents. *Monthly Catalog of United
> States Government Publications.* Washington: U.S. Government
> Printing Office. 1895 to date, monthly, $45. (Online, $35 an
> hour).[4]
>
> ———. *Selected U.S. Government Publications.* 1928 to date,
> monthly. Free.
>
> ———. *Subject Bibliographies.* 1975 to date, irregular. Free.
>
> Leidy, W. Philip. *A Popular Guide to Government Publications.* 4th
> ed. New York: Columbia University Press, 1976.

Government documents take numerous forms, from reports on
arms to studies of tulip growing, but they do have one thing in
common, and that is numbers. In 1980, the Superintendent of
Documents sold over 75 million publications.

Government documents are not all legal, technical, or how-to-
do-it approaches to existence. They touch on almost every human
activity, and some, according to how they are used, can be termed
dangerous. A librarian, for example, might be asked for what is
virtually an outline of how to break into nuclear power plants.

The Nuclear Regulatory Commission has distributed to deposit-

---

[4]Another catalog of interest to larger libraries is the *Publications Reference File,*
(Washington: U.S. Government Printing Office, 1977 to date, bimonthly). A type of
Books in Print for government documents, it consists of about 30,000 titles available or
about to become available. The PRF is issued in microfiche and updated in alternate
months with *GPO Sales Publications Reference File-Update* (1978 to date, bimonthly),
which includes new titles of microform: "Reference Material in Microformat . . ."
Microform Review, Fall 1979, pp. 259–262 by Sharon Anderson.

ory libraries. *Barrier Penetration Database.* The booklet, "revised in November 1978 to include technological advances, provides detailed information on how one can break through 32 different fences and barriers. The booklet explains what type of tools or explosives to use, tells how much some of the instruments weigh, and gives estimated penetration times."[5]

Then there is the drug formula developed by the U.S. Army for chemical warfare which may be found at the British Library. According to one story, the nerve gas can be manufactured with the help of less than $250 worth of readily available equipment. The formula has since "the 1960s been publicly available at the British Patents Office," as well as the British Library.[6]

This is not to suggest that even a small number of government documents are dangerous or controversial but only to indicate the possibilities, which range from nuclear power and chemical warfare to such pamphlets as "Now a Word About Your Shampoo" to a title for children on ecology, "Once There Lives a Wicked Dragon." Government documents are almost as varied as the people who prepare and read them.

There are three basic bibliographies of government documents used in almost all libraries, either singly or in total. The first is the *Monthly Catalog of United States Government Publications.* The second, which is little more than someone going through the *Monthly Catalog* and selecting out popular titles for the month, is the related *Selected U.S. Government Publications.* The latter is found in smaller libraries, but can be used equally in larger institutions, as can the third, *The Subject Bibliographies,* select lists of government documents by subject.

Arrangement in the *Monthly Catalog* is by Superintendent of Documents classification number which amounts to an index by issuing agency; that is, most documents issued by the Library of Congress will be listed under that agency name—most, but not all. Special classification situations arise when documents are arranged under a main entry other than by the organization that issued the document. Hence, it is always wise to check the indexes and not to rely

---

[5]"U.S. Sells Booklets on A-Plant Security," *The New York Times,* November 29, 1979, p. B16. The booklet is available through the National Technical Information Service. See, too, Richard Lyons, "Living Underground Presents No Identity Crisis," *The New York Times,* December 14 1980, p. E8. Here the author points out that the GPO will furnish for $1.25 "Where to Write For Birth and Death Records . . ." which can be the first step in someone assuming a new identity by obtaining the certificate of a dead person and assuming that person's records.

[6]David Beresford, "Chemical Warfare Drug an Open Secret," *The (London) Guardian,* August 22, 1979, p. 2.

on the document being under the likely agency, department, and so on.

Full cataloging information is given for each entry, so the user can generally tell much of the contents from the descriptors.[7] There are four major indexes: author, title, subject, and by series and reports. For reference, the subject and title indexes are the most useful. The subject and author indexes list the documents by their full title.

In many library situations where government documents are either a major or a minor consideration, the basic method of retrieval is to use the *Monthly Catalog* as a type of index to what is needed. More sophisticated approaches are also necessary, but recourse to the *Catalog* is usually the beginning step. If documents are kept in a separate collection, the tendency is to follow the Superintendent of Documents classification system. This consists of a combination of letters and numbers assigned to documents. Unlike the more common systems known to librarians, the classification has no visible relationship to subject matter. It is related to the issuing agency.

The Superintendent of Documents classification system is used as a method of identification in all current Superintendent of Documents bibliographies and lists—of which the *Monthly Catalog* is basic—as well as lists issued by various departments and agencies. Consequently, the lists serve most libraries as a catalog, and the documents are organized and arranged on the shelves according to this system.

In smaller libraries, the documents and periodicals are integrated into the general collection or are variously classified like other ephemera in the vertical file. Little or no effort is made to consider them as unique.

Most government documents are listed under a corporate entry in the card catalog, rarely by title or by subject. A corporate entry is a listing under the name of the author, that is, the government body responsible for its issue. For example, a corporate government entry will be under the country (United States), state (Minnesota), city (St.

---

[7]Until July 1976, the *Monthly Catalog* had different types of entries. With the July issue, the system was shifted to entries in keeping with the Anglo-American Cataloging Rules and the Library of Congress subject headings. The shift came to make it possible to put the *Monthly Catalog* online and make it part of the OCLC system of instant cataloging, i.e., via MARC tapes. The reference librarian should be aware of the change, as the arrangement influences searching. One can note the difference in the series by the size of the *Monthly Catalog*. The provision for full cataloging meant more pages; e.g., the 1980 series used three times as much paper as that of 1975 to list 15 percent fewer entries.

Paul), or other official unit that sponsored publication. Thus someone requesting a publication about foreign affairs would probably first look under the U.S. Department of State. Since there are a vast number of government agencies, it is frequently difficult to remember the proper point of entry.

Another problem is that usually people ask for a government document by its popular name, not by the Superintendent of Documents classification or its official title. For example, The Senate Nutrition Subcommittee released a report, "Dietary Goals for the United States." How does the librarian locate it by its popular name or, for that matter, the follow-up 1979 report on the same subject by the Surgeon General's Office?

Popular names are now used in the title index of the *Monthly Catalog*, with cross-references or by themselves. However, there never seem to be enough, so when this fails, *Popular Names of U.S. Government Reports* (Washington: The Library of Congress, various dates) should be tried. This is frequently updated and contains reports listed alphabetically by popular name. There is a valuable subject index. Despite the popular-name approach, there still is no single all-inclusive source which will give entry in this fashion. The *CIS/Index* does have a good listing of such documents by popular name, as do several other of the more detailed commercial services.

Although a basic finding tool for government documents, the *Monthly Catalog* does not index the majority of such documents. Estimates vary, but only about two or three out of every 10 documents come from the Government Printing Office. The remainder, therefore, are not in the *Catalog*. Neither does it index periodicals and the material therein. A special supplement lists some 2000, but if one wants to find out what was in any particular issue, it is necessary to turn to other indexes. The index to the *Monthly Catalog* is cumulated every six months and once a year.

The lack of total coverage must be stressed. For many small and medium-sized libraries, the indexing is more than adequate, but when one turns to research, to current topics, to statistical data, it is important to have much more complete listings than offered by the *Monthly Catalog*. Experienced librarians know the limitations of the work, but probably not many laypeople are so aware; hence the added need for assistance from an experienced librarian when it comes to working with documents.

A private publisher has published the *Cumulative Subject Index to the Monthly Catalog . . . 1900–1971* (Washington: Carrollton Press, 1973–1976, 15 vols. plus annual supplements), which eliminates the need to search each and every annual index. The set provides a subject approach to over 800,000 documents issued over a 72-year period. The citation is to the appropriate year of the *Monthly Catalog* and the page number. This is a two-step index. The user must look up the subject, locate the year and page in the *Monthly Catalog,* and then turn to the *Catalog* to find the Superintendent of Documents classification number to locate the document on the shelves.[8]

The free *Selected U.S. Government Publications* is a pamphlet which annotates about 150 to 200 popular government publications each month. Most of these, as is clearly indicated in the list, are to be ordered from the documents center in Pueblo, Colorado. Arranged under broad subject categories, the publications are those most likely to appeal to a wide audience; that is, they will cover everything from gardening and health to swimming instructions. Some titles are quite technical and esoteric, but the majority are directed to a wide audience. Often maps and even photographs and prints are included. Some 1.5 million institutions and individuals receive the list, and it is by far the best known of all government publications. It is essential for small and medium-sized libraries, particularly as a selection source of materials which are relatively current and often hard to find in other places.

A related free government document selection aid: *Consumer Information Catalog* (Pueblo, Colorado: Consumer Information Center, 1970 to date. Irregular. Free). As the title suggests, this lists and annotates pamphlets and booklets concerned with everything from purchase and maintenance of automobiles to diet and health. It has much, too, on family and children.

The *Selected List* is not cumulated or indexed. It is only a method of indicating to librarians and laypersons what is available among both new and older government publications. Therefore, many libraries with small government documents collections may take the *Monthly Catalog,* as they would extra indexes, to assist as a finding device for documents to be borrowed on interlibrary loan.

First issued in 1975, the *Subject Bibliographies* replaced the familiar *Price List.*[9] No matter what it is called, the 2- to 15-page listing remains the same: bibliographies of government documents relating to a specific subject. For example, "Home Gardening of Fruits and Vegetables" lists publications in print and likely to be of value to

---

[8]*The Decennial Cumulative Index* (Washington: Government Printing Office, various dates) covers a much shorter period, i.e., it is a cumulative index to the *Monthly Catalog* for 1941–1950, 1951–1960, 1961–1965 but is suitable for smaller libraries without extensive collections.

[9]One *Price List* (No. 36) is still issued: *Government Periodicals and Subscription Services.*

someone involved with such matters at the domestic level. There are now 300 or more of the subject bibliographies available.

The arrangement, length, and even quality of the *SB* (subject bibliography) series varies. For example, some titles may be annotated, others not. Still, basic bibliographic information is included, and all the lists have a form for ordering the items from the Superintendent of Documents.

The most exhaustive of several nongovernmental guides to publications is the annual *Bibliographic Guide to Government Publications —U.S.* (Boston, Massachusetts, G. K. Hall & Company. 1972 to date). Entries are from the New York Public Research Libraries and the Library of Congress. The two-volume work lists documents by the standard author main entry but it is most useful for the subject approach. Access in the single alphabet includes a number of other channels from added entries to titles and series titles. Full bibliographic information is given. There are several shortcomings in this work, but for the average library it is useful because of the annual coverage and the single alphabetical arrangement. One test is to look up "Libraries," with the numerous subheadings, here and in the *Monthly Catalog* and in the works to be described next. Generally, the *Bibliographic Guide* offers more, including some foreign, state, and regional entries.

Often updated, Leidy's *Popular Guide to Government Publications* lists about 3000 different titles under broad subject headings. Most of the documents are still available, often spanning many years. Short annotations help the librarian to decide what might be useful. There is also a detailed subject index.

Equally valuable, and some would say even better than Leidy, is Walter Newsome's *New Guide to Popular Government Publications: for Libraries and Home Reference.* (Littleton, Colorado: Libraries Unlimited, 1978, 370 pp.) This has the advantage of being more up-to-date than Leidy, listing and annotating about 2500 titles. Newsome also furnishes a first-rate subject and title index as well as clear sections on how to order the various documents, a guide to audiovisual aids, and a list of agency catalogs. Leidy cites somewhat more documents, but Newsome confines himself to the really popular items and his annotations tend to be clearer. Actually, the two works can be used together as there is not much overlap. Both are good ways of offering the layperson a subject approach to a topic of interest.

Historical Documents of 198– (Washington: Congressional Quarterly, 1972 to date, annual) is a collection of the basic government documents of the previous year. Each entry is prefaced by an introduction, with background materials and usually an abstract of the document. The documents cover everything from arms and peace to economics and court decisions. Basic presidential statements, committee reports, special studies, and the like are included if not all in full text, at least in major excerpts. Material is arranged chronologically by month, and the table of contents gives a brief summary of each document. There is a subject index which is cumulated every five years.

ORGANIZATION AND SELECTION

The organization and selection of government documents in all but the largest of libraries are relatively simple. Librarians purchase a limited number of documents, usually in terms of subjects of interest to users or standard titles, such as the *Statistical Abstract of the United States*. If pamphlets, they are usually deposited by subject in a vertical file. If books, they are cataloged and shelved as such.

The reference librarian normally will be responsible for the acquisition of documents, although in many libraries the *Selected List*, like the book and nonbook reviews, is regularly routed to all in the library. At any rate, confusion is minimal at this level because government documents are rightly treated like any other information source and shelved, filed, or clipped like other media.

When one moves to the large or specialized libraries, the organizational pattern is either a separate government documents collection or an integration of the documents into the general collection. Even the large libraries tend to partially integrate government documents with the collection, although complete integration is rare. About one-third of the large libraries have totally separate collections.

Where there is a major collection, an average of two or three people are in charge. Almost 60 percent of the libraries organize the material by the standard Superintendent of Documents classification.[10]

The justification for separate collections is that the volume of publications swamps the library and necessitates special considerations of organization and classification. There are other reasons; but on the whole, it is a matter of the librarian's seeking to find the simplest and best method of making the documents available. Some

---

[10]George W. Whitbeck et al., "The Federal Depository Library System: A Descriptive Analysis," *Government Publications Review*, no. 3, 1978. The figures are from this study and apply only to the depository libraries.

argue that separation tends to limit use, and they try to compromise by separating the administrative and official works while integrating the more popular and highly specialized subject documents into the general collection.

A distinct disadvantage of a separate documents collection is that it isolates the materials from the main reference collection. The reference librarians are inclined to think of it as a thing apart and may answer questions with materials at hand rather than attempt to fathom the holdings of the documents department. If patrons are referred to the documents section, the librarian there may attempt to answer questions that might be better handled by the reference librarian.

For most librarians, the matter of organization is not a problem, chiefly because they are coming to rely more and more on the large research and depository libraries for help in answering questions which call for specialized documents. The two major factors determining the selection and use of government documents are similar to those governing the selection and use of all forms of communication: the size of the library and its purpose.

The majority of large libraries are depository libraries for government documents. Since the Printing Act of 1895, modified by the Depository Act of 1962, approximately 1313 libraries have been designated as depositories for government documents. The law was modified in 1972 and 1978 to include law school libraries and court libraries. They are entitled to receive publications free of charge from the Superintendent of Documents. While few of them take all the government documents (the average is about 54 percent of what is published), they at least have a larger-than-average collection. The purpose is to have centers with relatively complete runs of government documents located throughout the country. These are likely to be state, regional, and large-city public libraries and the major college and university libraries.[11]

A handy guide to depository libraries and other information on who handles what is Nancy Cline and Jaia Heymann (eds.), *Directory of Government Document Collections and Librarians,* 2d ed.(Washington: Congressional Information Service, 1978. 544 pp.).The main entries are by state and library name, with complete information given on the type and size of the documents collection.There are several indexes,

---

[11]The depository system is more complex than indicated here, and is the topic of a complete chapter in Morehead's *Introduction to United States Public Documents,* op. cit., pp. 76–95. For a lengthy discussion of developments in depository libraries, see Whitbeck op. cit. For a short overview: William J. Barrett, "The Depository Library Program," *Wilson Library Bulletin,* September 1979, pp. 31–35.

one of which allows the user to trace libraries with special collection strengths.

Evaluation

Government publications, for the most part, can be evaluated from the following standpoints:

Cost The relatively low cost of popular government documents remains a selection factor. Documents have increased in price, although still less expensive than many commercial titles. Some examples of the price changes from 1966 to 1976: "Your Federal Income Tax" went from $.50 to $1.25; "Infant Care," from $.20 to $1; and "Your Child from One to Six," from $.20 to $1.20. Many would argue that Congress "should establish a policy on the subsidization of government publications . . . and should adopt a national policy which recognizes the importance of information."[12]

Scrutiny of the *Selected List* and the *Subject Bibliographies* series will show that it is possible to purchase numerous works at low prices. For example:

> *Among other interesting subjects, an identification guide (copiously illustrated) of whales and dolphins ($2.45); a $14 item from NASA containing over 400 satellite photos of earth (that would cost $35–$50 anywhere else); a 17-page pamphlet on indoor gardening ($1.50) and a teacher's guide to toy safety featuring a marvelous green critter named Leon the Lizard (70¢). A recent order [1979] of 56 items garnered from the* Selected List *. . . totaled $147.90—an average cost of $2.64 per item.[13]*

As the majority of government publications are not copyrighted, a publisher may reissue the original document under a different name and, usually, at a higher price. For example, *Drug Abuse Emergencies* (New York: Academic Press, 1976) includes 25 chapters which are identical to the government document *A Treatment Manual for Acute Drug Abuse* (Washington: U.S. Department of Health Education and Welfare, 1975). The Academic Press did add three additional chapters and revised the index but charged $16.50 for the hardcover

[12]Arthur D. Larson, "The Pricing of Documents . . .," *Government Publications Review*, no. 4, 1977, p. 277+. A detailed study which explains the price rises of documents. The author believes the time has long passed when the government should try to make a profit, or even break even in the sale of its publications.

[13]Charles A. Seavey, "GovPubs are Budget Stretchers," *School Library Journal*, January 1979, p. 34. It should be stressed that the prices are for popular documents.

edition (or $7.95 paper). The government paperback work may be purchased for $2.25 and is *free* from the National Clearinghouse for Drug Abuse Information.[14]

Currency   Currency is another valuable feature, particularly in the statistical reports and with the present methods of keeping up with scientific and technological advancement. Many publications are issued daily or weekly. Still the problem remains of frequency of indexing or abstracting; e.g., the *Monthly Catalog* has been almost five months behind the material published.

Range of Interest   The range of interest is all-encompassing. No publisher except the government has such a varied list.

Indexes and Bibliographies   Indexes and bibliographies are improving, not only in the documents themselves, but in works intended as finding devices for those documents.

Other aspects, such as arrangement, treatment, and format, may not be perfect, but the reference librarian hardly has any choice. There is, after all, only one *Congressional Record;* it is judged not for its intrinsic value, but in terms of whether it can be used in a particular library.

Selection/Reviews

For depository libraries, the selection of government documents is effectively accomplished by the government's automatically sending much of what is published to the library. Other libraries depend on more traditional methods of selection.

The basic buying guides for most libraries are the *Selected List* and the *Subject Bibliographies.* As the library needs increase, or a special document is required, the library turns to the *Monthly Catalog.* Beyond that, the larger libraries rely on indexes and often the publisher's microfiche copies of documents which come with the index.

Several of the book and media reviews carry information on government documents. *Booklist,* for example, has a regular annotated selection as does *School Media Quarterly.* For the librarian wishing to keep up with not only documents but developments in the field, the

---

[14]Documented by Kenneth L. Firestein in a letter to *Library Journal,* October 1, 1977, p. 1975, "Republished GPO Book." See, too, the letters from the author of the book and the publisher which follow.

best single periodical is *Government Publications Review* (1973. Quarterly. New York: Pergamon Press),which considers not only federal but state and local materials. In addition to scholarly, well-researched articles, it has a major section on the review of government publications and works about documents. Of particular interest for selection and acquisition: nos. 1 and 2 (combined issue), 1981. The 150-plus pages are devoted exclusively to collection development for government publications.

A running account of documents is found in the bimonthly *Documents to the People (DTTP)*[15] (Chicago: American Library Association, 1972 to date, bimonthly). The 30- to 60-page newsletter is a watchdog for the Freedom of Information Act and includes news on government documents, abstracts of ERIC titles, notices of new commercial indexes, and so on.

While *DTTP* is the official voice of the ALA Government Documents Round Table (Godort), the American Association of Law Libraries have their own publication in *Jurisdocs* (New York: American Association of Law Libraries, 1978 to date, bimonthly). This is a well-written, informative journal, of interest to anyone involved with documents, not just law librarians.

Joe Moorehead follows documents in a regular column in *Serials Librarian,* and there are many other columns in the library press from *Serials Review* to its companion publication *Reference Services Review* to *RQ* to the *Wilson Library Bulletin.*[16] For those with only a limited budget or need, a good method of keeping up with a few government documents is through the *Vertical File Index,* which has a scattering of titles in each issue.

A useful summary will be found in a special section of *American Reference Books Annual.* Here the major government documents reference aids are critically annotated. Unless a reference work in itself, a government document per se is not included.

Acquisition

Once a document has been selected for purchase, its acquisition is no more difficult—indeed, often somewhat easier—than acquiring a

---

[15] Paul Fisher and Aurora Davis, "Access to Information," *Documents to the People,* May 1979, p. 104 + discusses the need for access to public records and the role librarians should play.

[16] In a 1976 survey of 157 libraries, it was found that (in order of preference) librarians consulted the following for documents: *Booklist, Selected U.S. Government Publications, Reference Services Review, Choice, Monthly Catalog,* and *RQ.* George Whitbeck and Peter Hernon, "The Attitude of Librarians . . ." *Government Publications Review,* no. 3, 1977, p. 185.

book or periodical. Depository libraries have a peculiar set of problems, but for the average library, the process may be as follows:

1. Full information is given in the *Monthly Catalog* on methods of purchase from the Superintendent of Documents. Payment may be made in advance by purchase of coupons from the Superintendent of Documents. In case of extensive purchases, deposit accounts may be established.

2. Some documents may be obtained free from members of Congress. However, as the supply of some documents is limited, the specific member should be warned in advance. It is particularly advisable to get on the regular mailing list of one's representative or senator to receive such publications as the *Yearbook of Agriculture*.

   Issuing agencies often have a stock of publications which must be ordered directly from the agency. These are noted by a plus sign in the *Monthly Catalog* and frequently include valuable specialized materials, from ERIC documents to scientific reports.

3. A growing number of private firms now publish government documents; for example, the *CIS/Index* offers a complete collection of the working papers of Congress on microfiche. Most of the publications are highly specialized, expensive, and reviewed in a number of the reviewing services mentioned earlier.

There is, too, a definite move by the Government Printing Office to provide more documents on microform for libraries. This promises to develop considerably in the 1980s.[17]

INDEXES

(CIS/Index) Congressional Information Service. *Index to Publications of the United States Congress.* Washington: Congressional Information Service, 1970 to date, monthly. Service basis (Online, $90 an hour).

CQ Weekly Report. Washington: Congressional Quarterly, 1945 to date, weekly. Libraries: $171 to $264.

[17]Nancy M. Cline, "A Librarian's Perspective of the GPO and Micro-publishing," *Microform Review,* Winter 1979, pp. 23–28; a good overview of the progress being made by the GPO in this important area. A representative of the GPO reported by midsummer 1980 that "GPO publications on fiche distributed to depository libraries outnumbered hard copy publications for the first time." *Library Journal,* Auguat 1980, p. 1601.

Beyond the *Monthly Catalog* is a wide variety of bibliographies, indexes, and retrieval aids. The ones listed here are considered basic for medium and large libraries, and, if nothing else, should be known to the librarian who is to even casually use documents in reference work.

A unique feature about the form of many government documents is their ready availability on microform.[18] This can be microform issued by the Government Printing Office or by private firms. In the former case, an effort has been made since the early 1970s to convert more documents to microform, but it was not until late 1973 that a pilot project was launched to put some documents on microfiche. The project was a success, and in 1977 the Printing Office agreed to make more documents available in this form.[19]

Librarians prefer to maintain much-used government documents in hard-copy form, but few object to the less-called-for pieces (from current bills to annual reports) being converted. Private publishers have contributed to the conversion. Part of the attraction is that there is no copyright on government documents, no royalties to pay. The result is clear profit once the document is converted to microform.

Most of the major commercial indexes are backed up by microfiche copies of all or most of the documents analyzed. In addition, the users of the *Monthly Catalog* are now advised what is available on microfiche. In time, it is expected, because the *Monthly Catalog* is available through a computer search, that it will be possible to order the microfiche as well as other documents at the computer terminal.

Turning to the indexes, one of the most frequently used is the *Index to Publications of the United States Congress,* usually called the *CIS/Index.* The *Monthly Catalog* lists only complete congressional documents; the *CIS/Index* analyzes what is *in* those documents, covering nearly 875,000 pages of special studies, bills, hearings, and so on each year.

Published by a private concern the *Index* averages between 100 and 200 pages a month in loose-leaf form. It is in two parts: (1) The index section offers access by subject, author, and title. This section is cumulated quarterly and there is an annual. (2) The summary section gives the full title of the document and includes an abstract of most of the items indexed.

---

[18] Joan Chambers, "Federal Documents in Microform," *Microform Review,* September/October 1978, pp. 262–267; a summary of what is available on microform with a directory and brief discussion of commercial publishers.

[19] See Morehead, op. cit., pp. 32–34 and pp. 88–90 for a discussion of micropublishing.

There is a complete system for the library that can afford to purchase all the indexed materials. These are made available by Congressional Information Service (CIS) on microfiche. The user locates the desired item in the index and through a simple key system finds the microfiche copy.

As one of the most comprehensive of document indexes, although limited to the activities of Congress, the *CIS/Index* is a blessing for the reference librarian seeking information on the progress of a bill through Congress. Popular names of bills, laws, and reports are given, as well as the subject matter of those materials. In addition, an index covers the same material by bill number, report number, and so on. Hearings are covered as well as the names of witnesses, committees, and the like, so the librarian can easily keep up with the development of legislation.

The comprehensive quality of the *CIS/Index* is such that, with a little practice, the reference librarian will feel fully capable of tracking down even the most elusive material. It is an exemplary index and abstracting service for current materials. (In time, of course, it will be equally useful for retrospective searching.)

The *American Statistics Index* (Washington: Congressional Information Service, 1973 to date, annual, monthly, and quarterly supplements) discussed in the subsection "Statistical Data," in Chapter 7, the *Index* is worth listing again, because it is as comprehensive for government statistics as the *CIS/Index* is for congressional documents. Again, this work is in two parts, with a separate exhaustive index section and a separate abstract section with the same detailed data as found in abstracts for the *CIS/Index*.

The *CQ Weekly Report,* a much-used reference aid similar in some ways to a congressional version of *Facts on File,* was mentioned earlier in the text. It is *not* an index but a summary of the week's past events—a summary which is often sufficient either to identify a government document to be later found in a specialized work or to answer in one step a reference query.

Each issue analyzes in detail both congressional and general political activity of the week. The major bills are followed from the time they are introduced until they are passed and enacted into law (or killed along the way). A handy table of legislation shows at a glance where bills are in the Congress. Cross-references to previous weekly reports allow easy access to material until the quarterly index is issued and cumulated throughout the year.The service is also indexed in the *Public Affairs Information Service PAIS Bulletin.*

A somewhat similar service is the *National Journal* (Washington: Government Research Corporation, 1969 to date, weekly). Critics claim the 10 to 12 stories differ from the *CQ Weekly Report* in that they reflect opinion of the executive branch while *CQ* is more involved with Congressional attitudes. Weekly reports are supported by charts and statistical data, and the good indexes cumulate regularly. While some duplication is found between this and *CQ,* there is enough difference to warrant purchase of both by large research libraries.[20]

Periodical indexes

> *Index to U.S. Government Periodicals.* Chicago: Infordata International, 1974 to date, quarterly. $200. (Cumulations back to and including 1970, 1971, 1973 available at $150 each.)

There are a number of practical indexes which make some effort to index government periodicals and documents selectively. The best known, most often used is the *Public Affairs Information Service Bulletin,* followed by *Resources in Education,* published by the U.S. Educational Resources Information Center (ERIC). Beyond that, librarians will approach documents in terms of subjects as focused in more specialized indexes such as *Science Research Abstracts, Nuclear Science Abstracts,* and other technical and scientific services which usually include government documents and reports. With the exception of ERIC and *PAIS* (both discussed in Chapter 4), few of the more general subject indexes in the humanities and the social sciences include government titles.[21]

Much the same situation exists for other government documents; i.e., even when they are located by citation the user has difficulty finding the document itself. Here McLure makes the practical suggestion that signs and markers be displayed clearly, pointing out that certain periodicals, books, documents, and so on, are available in another part of the library. He even suggests, wisely, that a notice should be placed in the inside cover of PAIS to the effect that documents are not in with the regular periodicals.

Given this situation, the librarian looking for current material should turn to one or both of the specialized indexes. The most generally useful is the *Index to U.S. Government Periodicals,* which

---

[20]"Capital Reading, National Journal Tells All," *Time,* August 27, 1979, pp. 66–67. A short history of the Journal and its influence.

[21]Charles R. McClure, "Indexing U.S. Government Periodicals . . .," *Government Publications Review,* no. 4, 1978, pp. 409–421. The author found that except for *ASI* and *Index to U.S. Government Periodicals* few indexes bother with the genre. PAIS had the most (37), followed by *Science Citation Index* (13). *The Readers' Guide* indexes 4 government periodicals.

indexes between 160 and 200 titles. Comparatively, there are about 2000 periodicals and serials currently available from the federal government and probably several times that number from agencies and sections not found in Washington, D.C.[22]

The limitation of numbers imposed by the index is a blessing, in that many of the 2000-plus government periodicals and serials are so specialized as to be of little use to more than a few people and, except in a depository library, not likely to be readily available. While primarily used by subject, the index does provide an author index which is useful to check what has been published by an agency, bureau, or department. The index has proved particularly useful for searches involved with the sciences and social sciences.

There are several reference selection aids, primarily for more specialized areas. *Selected U.S. Government Series* (Chicago: American Library Association, 1978, 184 pp.) is an annotated guide to about 600 commonly used series found in libraries. *Business Serial Publications of the U.S. Government* (Chicago: American Library Association, 1978, 46 pp.) lists and annotates basic titles in business and commerce. The author's *Magazines for Libraries* (4th ed. New York: R. R. Bowker, 1982) includes many government periodicals and serials under various subject headings, although there is no separate listing as in previous editions.

TYPES OF PUBLICATIONS

Too much emphasis can be placed on categorizing the various forms or types of government publications. The user, after all, is interested only in information, not in whether this or that document happens to be executive or congressional. The categorization is useful primarily as a mnemonic device for the librarian or an organizational device for teachers of documents courses. For example, a question about current legislation will require one type of document; a statistical question, quite another. Recognizing the likely branch of the government dealing with the subject of the request helps to narrow the search.

Executive Publications This category does not mean simply papers of the president; all papers issued by the 10 departments and

[22]The source of information on government periodicals: *(a) Serials Supplement to the Monthly Catalog* (Washington: U.S. Government Printing Office, 1977 to date, annual), which lists 2000 titles, and *(b) Price List* 36 from the Government Printing Office, which lists about 340 more popular titles, as well as serials such as indexes.

the various agencies of the government are likewise called executive documents. Agencies related to the main departments also publish a variety of documents.

From a reference viewpoint, these documents are of interest mainly for the information given on subject material. Anyone doing research in such fields as economics, labor, industry, or education will inevitably need a number of executive publications.

They may be located through the various catalogs and indexes, particularly the *Monthly Catalog*. If the document is known to be the publication of a particular department or agency, a number of department lists and indexes will give fuller information than any of the general catalogs and indexes. Most of the departments issue current lists, and they are discussed in Morehead's text. A number of the documents of more general interest may be located through standard periodical indexes.

Congressional (Legislative) Publications Congressional publications are basically a record of congressional activities, from debates in Congress to committee hearings and reports. There are a number of aids, discussed in the section "Catalogs and Indexes," to help the librarian locate ongoing activities and publications of Congress. The legislative history, though, may be traced through a number of publications.

(1) *The Congressional Record.* This serial is the daily record of the proceedings of Congress. There is an index every two weeks and a cumulative index at the end of the session. Although the *Record* is supposed to be a verbatim report of activities, it is not. Members of Congress reserve the right to add and delete. Since 1978, a symbol indicates what has been inserted rather than actually spoken in Congress. However, this is hardly meaningful, as the symbol is deleted if the member of Congress delivers only the first sentence of the material. The *Record* remains a sea of confusion.

There are two basic indexes to the *Congressional Record.* (1) *Congressional Record Abstracts—Master Edition* (Washington, D.C.: Capitol Services, 1976 to date, daily). This provides citations and abstracts to the *Record.* It is available on a data base called CRECORD at $80 an hour. (2) *The Federal Index* (Washington, D.C.: Capitol Services, 1976 to date, weekly). This is available online as FEDEX at $90 an hour. Among other items, it indexes, also, the *Federal Register.*[23]

---

[23]*The Federal Register* is used primarily in conjunction with law searches and includes rules and regulations of various departments and agencies and a section on presidential documents. Issued daily, it has its own monthly, quarterly, and annual index.

(2) *Laws.* Passing a law is not necessarily a complicated, matter. It is fully explained in the often revised *How Our Laws Are Made* (Washington: Government Printing Office, 1976). Briefly, the process is this: *(a)* A "bill" either introduces new legislation or amends a previous legislative act. The bill may originate in either the House or the Senate. Various forms of "resolutions" are similar to bills. About 25,000 bills and resolutions are introduced during a congressional session. *(b)* A bill passed by either house goes to the other as a printed "act." If the act is accepted by both houses and passed, it is signed or vetoed by the President. *(c)* Once the bill is signed into law, it becomes a "slip law." These are simply the unbound, first printing of laws passed by Congress, and they may run anywhere from one to several hundred pages. The slip laws are gathered and bound in the *Statutes at Large.* Every six years the *Statutes* is consolidated into the *United States Code,* which affords a subject approach to the laws, as well as various tables which indicate the acts' popular names.

How does the librarian locate this material? The *Statutes at Large* is issued in printed volumes, as is the *United States Code,* and the volumes are usually readily available through the card catalog. The catch is trying to locate the bills, acts, and slip laws. There are numerous, sometimes complicated, approaches, but the various stages of the bill to the act to the slip law may be traced through the *Congressional Record,* the *CIS/Index,* or *CQ Weekly Report.*

When someone wants to know the status of a bill in Congress, if it is a popular, much discussed work, a likely source is almost any newspaper, and certainly *Facts on File* for a capsule account of its standing. However, for the majority of bills, there are two commercial sources which are best and easiest to use: (1) *CIS/Index:* This is useful for a monthly record, but of little value for weekly activities. (2) Commerce Clearing House *Congressional Index* (Chicago: Commerce Clearing House, 1937 to date, weekly) offers the librarian the ability to trace a bill by subject, name, sponsor, bill number, and so on. Larger libraries will want the same firm's *Congressional Legislative Reporting Service,* which offers daily reports on public bills and resolutions.

(3) *Hearings.* The transcripts (as well as the presentation) of testimony before a congressional committee or subcommittee are known as "hearings." Where made public, the printed hearings may be indexed in the *CIS/Index* and similar publications. Occasionally, they are printed as parts of larger reports; when published separately, they are usually offered for sale by the Superintendent of Documents.

(4) *Committee Prints.* Publications issued by the various commit-

tees in addition to transcriptions of the hearings themselves are called committee prints. These are of major importance as they often are independent studies requested by the various committees, e.g., a two-volume study of American foreign policy ordered by the Senate Committee on Foreign Relations. They are indexed in the *CIS/Index* and are usually, though not always, sent to depository libraries, but they may not be listed in the *Monthly Catalog*.

(5) *Serial Set*. This is the term used to describe the Congressional documents and reports which date back to 1789 and continue to be published. The following types of documents are found in the Set: (1) congressional journals, administrative reports, and related internal publications; (2) reports which come from congressional investigations; (3) reports by Congress on public and private legislation considered during the congressional session; (4) annual reports from federal executive agencies and series of survey, research, and statistical publications developed by those agencies. While many of these documents appear in separate form, listed by title or agency in the *Monthly Catalog*, a number are only part of the serial set.

The work is difficult to use, if only because of its size. From 1789 to 1969, it includes about 14,000 separate volumes.

Fortunately, there is now an index: *CIS U.S. Serial Set Index 1789–1969* (Washington: Congressional Information Service, 1978). The index is in parts, each part covering a particular period. There are several ways of finding material, although the most valuable is the index of title-derived subjects, names and keywords. The publisher has the serial set available on microfiche—a form in which almost all libraries have the set.

Current additions to the set may be traced in the *Monthly Catalog* (in part), the *CIS/Index,* and several other sources.

Judicial Publications.   Judicial publications are primarily publications of the courts; the most important consist of the decisions of the Supreme Court. Of all the areas of government documents, the area of judicial publications is the most highly specialized. Work with these materials requires a considerable knowledge of governmental organization and, except for general questions, is probably best left to the special law library or legislative reference service. This is not to say that the reference librarian should not be aware of judicial publications or how to use them, but any use in depth is beyond the scope of the present text. (Of considerable help, even to the non-law-educated librarian, are the basic *Judicial Opinion Reporters* issued by the West Publishing Company. The publisher offers an informative booklet on their use, and they are described in many of the government document guides.)

In terms of subjects, perhaps 15 to 20 percent of all types of documents issued may be of enough general interest to warrant consideration as "popular" sources of information. By far the greatest number are for the expert in government or in a given subject area, thus chiefly for reference work in large libraries. The number of state and local documents which can be termed "popular" are even fewer.

STATE AND LOCAL DOCUMENTS

U.S. Library of Congress. *Monthly Checklist of State Publications,* 1910 to date. $21.90.

The State Publications Index. Denver, Colorado: Information Handling Services, 1977 to date, quarterly. Price on request. (Online; price varies.)

If federal documents are little understood in many libraries, the state and local documents are even more in limbo. The reason is twofold: (1) Proper bibliographical control is lacking, although it is improving; (2) even with such control, the average librarian rarely thinks of state documents as a vital source of information, because most states issue "blue books," manuals which answer recurrent questions: "Who is my representative?" "What is the address of X agency?" "Who is the head of Y agency?" Reference librarians at the Chicago Public Library, for example, rank as sixth in importance and use among 100 reference works: *Legislative Directory* (Chicago: Association of Commerce and Industry, various dates). With the blue books or legislative manuals at hand, most questions involving the state are readily answered. Furthermore, at a local level, the library tends to rely more on its own clipping file and possibly its own local newspaper index.

Considerably more sophisticated and detailed questions about population patterns, forecasts of growth of cities and towns, and other demographic queries relating to marketing and business are usually handled by a separate state agency. For example, in cooperation with the state's universities and research centers, Washington state has a state data center; Georgia has an office of planning and budget with such data; and New York state has a special section of the department of commerce which prepares data on business activities, population projections, and so on.[24]

---

[24]For a description of these and other state and regional centers, see Martha F. Riche, "State and Local Data Sources," *American Demographics,* May 1979, pp. 34–37. See, too: Nancy P. Johnson "Using State Documents," *Reference Services Review,* January/March 1981, pp. 89–91.

Where there is no concerted effort to collect state and local documents, the library should be aware of other libraries in the immediate area that have such collections. Usually, the best single source of information about these collections, as well as of the documents themselves, is the state library. By law, most state agencies must file copies of their various reports with the state library. The state library, in turn, will maintain its own collection and have some arrangement for distributing the excess documents to other libraries in the state, either systematically to state depository libraries (the system varies but is somewhat the same as federal depositories) or informally to the smaller units.

At the state level, there is no entirely satisfactory bibliographical tool that lists the majority of publications. Of considerable help is the *Monthly Checklist of State Publications.* Prepared by the Library of Congress, it represents only those state publications received by the Library. Arrangement is alphabetical by state and then, as in the *Monthly Catalog,* by issuing agency. Entries are usually complete enough for ordering, although prices are not always given. There is an annual, but not a monthly, subject and author index. The indexes are not cumulative. Since 1963, periodicals have been listed in the June and December issues.

The State Publications Index (formerly *Checklist of State Publications,* 1977–1978) offers a systematic control of the majority of state publications. It does *exclude* state laws and statutes and other aspects of state law. Beginning with the 1978/80 state publications issued before 1978 are not indexed. The primary sources for citations are the official state checklists and the *Monthly Checklist of State Publications.* Hence this is a subject, agency, author index to the *Monthly Checklist.* Each document is given a distinctive accession number, and many libraries employ the number as a method of filing.

Beginning in late 1980, the index has been online, and at the terminal the librarian may find material by subject, author, agency and title—much as with the printed version. The search was narrowed with the introduction of a special thesaurus in 1981.

SUGGESTED READING

Cox, Henry B. T., "The Ownership of Public Documents," *AB,* September 4, 1978, pp. 1243–1261. A thorough, well-documented study of the still-argued claim that a bookdealer, private person or institution owns public papers which have come legitimately to the marketplace. Some government officials claim this is not true, i.e., once a public document, always a public document and, as such, can be owned only by the government.

Crowther, Kenneth, "The Ready Reference Collection: Tennessee," *Tennessee Librarian,* Winter 1980, pp. 24–30. This is a review of one state's reference sources, many of them government documents. The type of material listed is a reminder that similar types are available in other states. Also, descriptions of specific titles indicate scope and purpose of similar titles elsewhere.

Hernon, Peter, *Use of Government Publications by Social Scientists.* Norwood, New Jersey: Ablex Publishing Corporation, 1979. A detailed text on the selection and organization of government documents for a specialized readership, it reports on how the documents are used by social science and suggests several methods of preparing such use studies. Summarized in a periodical article by Hernon in *Government Publications Review,* no. 4, 1979, pp. 359–371. See, also, his "Functional Documents Collections," *Microform Review,* Fall 1970, pp. 209–219.

Katz, Marc and Rodd Exelbert, "The Congressional Information Service Study," *The Information Manager,* September/October 1979, pp. 30–34. A brief history of the firm responsible for the basic government indexing services. How two million pages of government information is handled each year is briefly and clearly explained. (Note: In 1979, the firm was acquired by the American Elsevier Publishers, the holding company for the Dutch publisher.)

Moorehead, Joe, "Basic Bibliographic and Current Awareness Sources for Government Documents," *The Serials Librarian,* Fall 1979, pp. 5–13. A fast moving, lucid explanation of the basic reference works used with government documents by the author of the basic text in the field.

RQ, Spring 1980, pp. 231–253. This is a series of three articles on various aspects of government documents: Benjamin Shearer, "An Urban Statistical Abstract: A Guide to Local Government Documents"; Frank Goudy, "American Political Behavior and the Election Process: A Bibliographic Essay"; and Ray Jones and Barbara Wittkopf, "Computerized Census Data: Meeting Demands in an Academic Library." The three articles give a general idea of the wide variety of topics considered in government documents and related works.

Schorr. Alan, *Government Documents in the Library Literature,* Ann Arbor, Michigan: Pierian Press, 1978. The most comprehensive bibliographic guide to articles, books, reports, and so on (published from 1909 to 1974), on all aspects of U.S. federal, state, and municipal documents. Includes a section on the United Nations. About 1200 entries are listed and there are two good indexes.

Steinberg, Charles, *The Information Establishment.* New York: Hastings House, 1980. "Deals with the structure and function of a free press in . . . the government informational bureaucracy, the liaison between the mass media and the . . . federal information apparatus, and the responsibilities and obligations of both." (Preface). For a summary of the current situation see Robert Cuddihy, "Freedom of Information Act," *Special Libraries,* March 1980, pp. 163–168.

White, Peter, "Freedom of Information: A Glance at the U.S. and a Look at Canada," *The Australian Library Journal,* June 1978, pp. 151–157. A clear explanation and overview of the workings of the Act in the United States and its equivalent in Canada.

INDEX